The Brazilian Economy since the Great Financial Crisis of 2007/2008

Philip Arestis · Carolina Troncoso Baltar
Daniela Magalhães Prates
Editors

The Brazilian Economy since the Great Financial Crisis of 2007/2008

palgrave
macmillan

Editors
Philip Arestis
Department of Land Economy
University of Cambridge
Cambridge, UK

Daniela Magalhães Prates
Institute of Economics
University of Campinas
Campinas, São Paulo, Brazil

Carolina Troncoso Baltar
Institute of Economics
University of Campinas
Campinas, São Paulo, Brazil

ISBN 978-3-319-64884-2 ISBN 978-3-319-64885-9 (eBook)
https://doi.org/10.1007/978-3-319-64885-9

Library of Congress Control Number: 2017952832

Printed on acid-free paper

This Palgrave Macmillan imprint is published by Springer Nature
The registered company is Springer International Publishing AG
The registered company address is: Gewerbestrasse 11, 6330 Cham, Switzerland

Contents

List of Figures

New Features of the Brazilian External Sector Since the Great Global Crisis

Brazilian Industry: Recent Performance and Future Challenges

Brazilian Fiscal Policy in Perspective: From Expansion to Austerity

List of Graphs

List of Charts

Financialisation and Investment Behaviour Among Non-Financial Corporations in Brazil Since the Global Crisis

List of Tables

Introduction

Philip Arestis, Carolina Troncoso Baltar and Daniela Magalhães Prates

Brazil has gone through 'ups and downs' since the Great Financial Crisis (GFC) of 2007/2008. At the beginning of 2010, the country became an international reference for withstanding quite successfully the contagion effects of the crisis as well as for improving the level of economic activity along with sustaining the income redistribution and poverty reduction. The economy recovered quickly and recorded a growth rate of 7.5% in 2010. Yet, economic growth began to slow down in late 2011 and turned into the worst recession of the Brazilian history subsequently. The GDP growth rate declined sharply to −3.6% on average over 2015 and 2016 and the per capita GDP was more than 10%

P. Arestis (✉)
University of Cambridge, Cambridge, UK
e-mail: pa267@cam.ac.uk

C.T. Baltar · D.M. Prates
University of Campinas, Campinas, Brazil
e-mail: cbaltar@gmail.com; cbaltar@unicamp.br

D.M. Prates
e-mail: danimagaprates@gmail.com

P. Arestis et al. (eds.), *The Brazilian Economy since the Great Financial Crisis of 2007/2008*, https://doi.org/10.1007/978-3-319-64885-9_1

smaller by the end of 2016 than in 2013. Beyond the political crisis that ended with the impeachment of the President Dilma Roussef in August 2016 amid an extensive corruption scandal, there is a heated debate about the causes of the Brazilian economic crisis.

This book aims at analyzing the performance of the Brazilian economy since the GFC with the focus on both the productive and financial dimensions, along with distributional and social issues. The book comprises a total of twelve chapters that bring to light the causes of both the fast recovery after the contagion effect of the GFC (2009–2010) and the subsequent slowdown and crisis (2011–2016) in Brazil.

In Chap. "Brazil at Crossroads: A Critical Assessment of Developmentalist Policies", Daniela Prates, Luiz Fernando de Paula, and Barbara Fritz evaluate the recent experience of developmentalism in Brazil since the GFC based on a Keynesian-structuralist theoretical approach. They ask if and how a developmentalist approach can be blamed for the recent economic crisis. To address this question, they first deliver a more precise definition of different variants of developmentalism. Second, based on stylized facts of the Brazilian economy in the period of three successive leftist governments between 2003 and 2016, they classify relevant macroeconomic, social, and industrial policies. They find that different types of developmentalist policies came to application to a certain degree, with the dominance of redistributional policies fostering domestic consumption. However, this period could not be labeled as developmentalist inasmuch the macroeconomic policies were, predominantly, orthodox. They conclude that the ambiguity of the economic policies combined with the worsening in the international scenario can explain the downturn in the Brazilian economy.

In Chap. "Monetary Institutions and Macroeconomic Performance in Brazil After the Global Financial Crisis of 2007–2008", Fernando Ferrari Filho, Elisangela Araújo, and Eliane Araújo examine theoretically and empirically the relationship between monetary institutions and macroeconomic performance in Brazil, since the adoption of the Inflation Targeting Regime (ITR) in 1999. They show that the monetary institutions have inhibited economic growth, have affected the public debt, and have not been successful in fulfilling its single objective, that is, to stabilize the inflation rate and to maintain it below its targets. They estimate, for the period 2002–2016, a structural Vector Autoregression (VAR) model, which aims to show that the monetary institutions and restrictive monetary policy have reduced the GDP growth rates, have increased the public debt, and have contributed to appreciate the exchange rate. Given that, first, they present a brief theoretical discussion on the ITR, providing details of the Brazilian experience. Second, they discuss the determinants of inflation in Brazil. Finally, they analyse the main results of the VAR model.

In Chap. "Asymmetric Exchange Rate Pass-Through: Evidence, Inflation Dynamics and Policy Implications for Brazil (1999–2016)", André de Melo Modenesi, Viviane Luporini, and Debora Mesquita Pimentel investigate the existence of an asymmetry in the exchange rate pass-through (ERPT) to the Brazilian consumer price index (CPI). Using a decomposition of the exchange rate series, into appreciations and depreciations of the Brazilian currency during the 1999–2016 period, they estimate Structural Vector Autoregression (SVAR) models with different identifying restrictions. The results are robust and indicate a relevant asymmetric behavior of the ERPT. Estimates indicate a pass-through of 16% in case of depreciation and of 5.8% in the case of appreciation of Brazilian Real (BRL) against the US Dollar. Accordingly, the inflationary effect resulted from a (systematic) depreciation is only partially compensated by a deflationary effect due to an (systematic) appreciation of the same magnitude. The mere existence of an asymmetric ERTPT generates an inflationary bias. These findings might help to explain the observed downward rigidity of the CPI and may cast doubts on inflation control strategies based on inflation targeting (IT) and floating exchange rate (with capital mobility). Therefore, the chapter provides a strong case against excess exchange volatility and capital mobility. Accordingly, a stable exchange rate may favor price stability.

In Chap. "New Features of the Brazilian External Sector Since the Great Global Crisis", André Martins Biancarelli, Renato de Souza Rosa, and Rodrigo Vergnhanini analyse the external vulnerability of the Brazilian Economy since the GFC. They stress that in Brazilian history, like in most peripheral countries, there were various episodes of 'dollar shortage' leading to the domestic crisis. From 2008 to 2014, many of the typical ingredients of such events were present: international crisis, volatile exchange rate, increasing current account deficits and subsequent decline in economic activity. This time, however, there was no lack of foreign currency. From the analysis and periodization of the flows and stocks of the Balance of Payments between 2011 and 2015, they argue that a 'new reality' of Brazilian external liabilities allowed for lasting Current Account deficits at high levels, even in the context of worsening international scenario. They also state that the global economy did play an important role in the deceleration of the Brazilian economy after 2011, but this operated mainly through indirect channels, related to the financial and productive structural linkages to the international cycles.

In Chap. "Brazilian Industry: Recent Performance and Future Challenges", Celio Hiratuka and Fernando Sarti evaluate the recent performance of Brazilian manufacturing industry, emphasizing the difficulties encountered after the GFC. An overview of its evolution is presented in terms of production, investments, international trade, and innovation. They show that the Brazilian industry has shown signs of recovery in terms of generation of employment and added value at the beginning of the XXI century, in sharp contrast with the stagnation observed in the last two decades of the XX century. But after the GFC, it has experienced difficulties in maintaining its momentum, given the fierce competition at the international scenario, which resulted in rapid growth of imports in the internal market and difficulty to expand exports. The chapter also highlights the main challenges ahead for the Brazilian manufacturing industry to recover its dynamism and contribution to the country economic development

In Chap. "Financialisation and Investment Behaviour Among Non-Financial Corporations in Brazil Since the Global Crisis", Ricardo Gottschalk and Edgardo Torija-Zane examine the financialization of corporate strategies and recent investment patterns in Brazil. They stress that Brazil's growing integration in global financial markets, followed by financial shocks and associated macroeconomic instability, has been a critical factor behind financialized practices associated with the so-called shareholder primacy, along with the fragmentation of productive processes in global value chains and a refocusing of activities toward 'core business.' Yet, in Brazil, the shift toward such practices has also included carry-trade activities fostered by specific features of the country macroeconomic context (namely high interest rate and exchange rate volatility). Finally, they show that, against this backdrop, corporate investment as a proportion of total capital stock has declined since the GFC, despite the rapid increase in corporate indebtedness, to which natural resource-based industries have been the largest contributors.

In Chap. "Income Distribution, Productivity and Economic Growth: Empirical Evidence in the Case of Brazil", Philip Arestis and Carolina Troncoso Baltar address the relationship between income distribution, productivity, and economic growth in Brazil over the 2000s by analyzing the changes in the purchasing power of workers in the 2000s. More specifically, it is verified whether it has been a result of changes in productivity or in the real exchange rate in the years before and after the GFC. The theoretical background is the Kaleckian literature on income distribution and economic growth that accounts for the effects of wage share on economic growth, including the effects of productivity. However, in the case of an open developing economy dependent on the international scenario, such as Brazil, the analysis of the changes in the purchasing power of workers and its effect on the economic activity is more complicated than what this literature suggests. The chapter advances the analysis by considering specificities of the Brazilian economy. An equation for wage share is suggested and it is estimated for the country manufacturing sector.

In Chap. "Brazilian Fiscal Policy in Perspective: From Expansion to Austerity", Rodrigo Octávio Orair and Sergio Wulf Gobetti present an overview of the main trends of Brazilian fiscal policy over the last decade, particularly for the period since the GFC. They focus on the changes in composition and orientation of fiscal policy during three sub-periods. The first was a sub-period characterized by fiscal expansion (2005–2010), whose space was channeled mainly toward public investment and redistributive transfers. It had an extraordinary economic performance. During the second sub-period (2011–2014), subsidies and tax cuts played a central role in the fiscal expansion. This new fiscal policy mix proved ineffective in preventing the economy from entering a downturn. The third sub-period (from 2015 onwards) has been characterized by the shift to fiscal austerity, and by the worst recession ever recorded in the country's history. Finally, they discuss some of the challenges and socioeconomic risks resulting from the recent and radical shift toward fiscal austerity.

In Chap. "Economic and Social Policies Inconsistency, Conventions, and Crisis in the Brazilian Economy, 2011–2016", Marco Flávio da Cunha Resende and Fábio Henrique Bittes Terra access the causes of the Brazilian crisis, based on a Post-Keynesian point of view. They focus on two issues: (i) an inconsistency between the social and macroeconomic policies, in particular, the exchange rate policy, adopted over 2003–2014; (ii) some macroeconomic policies mistakes and their inappropriate management by the government. They argue that at the first sight, these policies were intended to boost the agents' confidence by creating an optimistic convention about the future of the Brazilian economic what would trigger the entrepreneurs' animal spirits and foster investments. However, that strategy had gone wrong and reached the opposite effect. Finally, they suggest some macroeconomic policies for the economic recovery of Brazil.

In Chap. "The Impact of the Global Financial Crisis on the Brazilian Stock Market", Michel Ferreira Cardia Haddad and Bruno Pontes de Arruda examine the impact of the GFC on the Brazilian Stock Market. They stress that over the last decades, the vast expansion of international trade and financing has resulted in a global integration of economies as well as stock markets. The deepening of the commercial and financial linkages between countries, in contrast to their expected economic opportunities and benefits, increased the frequency and intensity of propagation of negative financial shocks. The GFC affected a wide range of sectors as well as stock markets in developed and developing countries; the Brazilian stock market did not escape unscathed. The chapter has two main focuses. Firstly, it identifies the most important negative movements seen in the Brazilian stock market over a time span of more than 17 years. Subsequently, financial contagion effects and the transmission of the GFC from financial markets in the USA to the Brazilian stock market are analysed and econometrically tested.

In Chap. "Foreign Exchange Derivatives and Financial Fragility in Brazil", Maryse Farhi accesses the impact of the GFC on the Brazilian foreign exchange (FX) derivatives market. Yet, for the understanding of the crucial role of FX derivatives in Brazil, the chapter provides a brief retrospective analysis on the relationship between the FX derivatives market, banking Competition and Financial Fragility in Brazil since the adoption of the Real Plan in 1994. She stresses that FX rates have always been at the core of emerging countries crisis. FX derivatives, in turn, have a heightened potential to allow hedging risks, mitigating the crisis, but also to exacerbate its depth due to leveraged bets that turn sour. Brazilian FX derivatives stand out among the emerging countries because of the greater liquidity and depth of its organized segment in comparison with both the FX spot market and the FX over-the-counter market. Thus, the first dollar future contract has become the locus of formation of the Brazilian Real/USD exchange rate. This and other specific features of the FX derivatives in Brazil have reinforced their dual role (hedge and speculation) and their macroeconomic impacts in the period analysed.

In Chap. "The Brazilian Credit Market During the Great Recession", André Moreira Cunha, Andrés Ernesto Ferrari Haines, and Pedro Perfeito da Silva analyze the Brazilian credit market after the GFC. They point out that since the late 1990s, conventional wisdom has been challenged by the increasing instability of the financial markets. In this context, the GFC, which began in August 2007, and the 'Great Recession' (GR) that followed, led the governments of advanced and emerging countries to adopt countercyclical fiscal and monetary policies, mainly monetary policies, in an attempt to rescue financial and non-financial corporations. Brazil was not an exception. Using two different econometric approaches, Markov-Switching Vector Autoregressive Models (MS-VAR) and Vector Error Correction (VEC) models, the chapter provides relevant evidence suggesting that the credit originated in State-Owned Banks (SOB) showed countercyclical characteristics, while private banks behaved in a typical pro-cyclical manner in the period under review.

The contributions that follow in this book provide originality on the Brazilian economy dynamics after the GFC, taking into account their multiple and intertwined determinants from the point of view of the relevant theoretical and empirical aspects. The main features of the contributions contain the influence of the international context, the role of economic policies, the macroeconomic performance (with a focus on inflation, the external sector, industry, investment, income distribution, and public finance), and the features of the domestic financial market.

Brazil at Crossroads: A Critical Assessment of Developmentalist Policies

Daniela Magalhães Prates, Barbara Fritz and Luiz Fernando de Paula

1 Introduction

Within few years, Brazil went through extreme ups and downs. At the beginning of the 2010s, the country had become an international reference not only for weathering rather well the effects of the Global Financial Crisis (GFC). The country also gained special attention for being able to recover the path of economic growth with income distribution recorded over 2004–2007. This combination was so remarkable

D.M. Prates (✉)
University of Campinas, Campinas, SP, Brazil
e-mail: danimagaprates@gmail.com

B. Fritz
Freie Universität, Berlin, Germany
e-mail: barbara.fritz@fu-berlin.de

L.F. de Paula
University of the State of Rio de Janeiro, Rio de Janeiro, Brazil
e-mail: luizfpaula@terra.com.br

P. Arestis et al. (eds.), *The Brazilian Economy since the Great Financial Crisis of 2007/2008*, https://doi.org/10.1007/978-3-319-64885-9_2

because it was going against the global trend especially in terms of income concentration. A few years later, the country found itself in its worst economic crisis for decades. Its per capita GDP was more than 10% smaller by the end of 2016 than in 2013 and both the share of industrial production at the national level and its participation in exports fell significantly. Beyond the political upheaval that ended with the impeachment of the president Dilma Roussef in August 2016 amid an extensive corruption scandal, there is a heated debate about the economic reasons of the crisis.

This debate encompasses supporters and opponents of the strategy followed by successive Brazilian governments over more than a decade, which many have labeled, even if with different prefixes, as 'developmentalist' (Ban 2012; Bielschowsky 2015). Following Fonseca (2014), developmentalism is a rather ambiguous term by definition, nurtured both by theoretical concepts and economic policy experiences. Yet, a common denominator, shared by academics as well as explicitly expressed by the Brazilian governments in this period (Ministério de Planejamento 2003), has been the aim to combine sustained economic growth with productive restructuring and income distribution by giving the State an active role.

In this chapter, we evaluate the recent experience of developmentalism in Brazil since the GFC based on a Keynesian-structuralist theoretical approach. According to this approach, the interplay of monetary and financial asymmetries results in a key influence of the dynamics of the international economy on the performance of peripheral emerging economies such as Brazil, mainly through the boom-bust cycles of capital flows. Consequently, these asymmetries also constrain the policy space in these economies, shaping the degree of autonomy of economic and social policies. Yet, the specific mix of policies adopted depends on domestic factors, specifically the institutional framework and political power relations.

As there has been, in political terms, a continuum of four successive governments led by the *Partido dos Trabalhadores* (PT, Workers' Party) since 2003, we also include the years before the outbreak of the GFC. Our analysis covers the period from 2003 to mid-2016, i.e., four terms led by the PT, the first two by the well-known Luis Inácio Lula da Silva and the others by Dilma Rousseff, whose second government lasted only one year and a half due to her impeachment.

We ask *if* and *how* a developmentalist approach can be blamed for the dramatic downturn at the end of this period. Hence, we address a lacuna in the current literature on the Brazilian case, which tries to explain this downturn at analyzing the economic outcome in terms of the complex interdependence among income redistribution, demand, and changes of production patterns. Conversely, we look into the policies applied and ask how they can be classified in terms of their paradigmatic background.

To address our research question, we derive three main hypotheses. First, we assume that a wide range of policies were applied, of which some can be labeled as developmentalist, but it is needed further specification in terms of the type of developmentalist approach applied by policy makers. Our second hypothesis is that not all policies adopted during this period can be labeled as developmentalist. Third, the significant and repeated changes of the policy mix over time were conditioned by the external context, but also shaped by domestic factors.

Then, the main contribution of this chapter is to assess the economic policies during PT governments, analyzing if these policies can be considered developmentalist and, if they can, what type of developmentalist policies were implemented. A second contribution is to introduce a differentiation of developmentalist approaches from a macroeconomic point of view.

The following section presents the different variants of the concept of developmentalism. The third section, firstly, presents stylized facts of the external context and details of our theoretical approach, and secondly, summarizes the macroeconomic outcomes of the Brazilian economy in the period under review. The fourth section sums up the economic and social policies applied from 2003 to mid-2016 while the fifth proposes a periodization for the time span analyzed and a typology of policies during PT governments along the different developmentalist and non-developmentalist variants. Finally, the sixth section concludes. It is worth to mention that we deviate from the standard structure of first introducing empirical evidence and subsequently the theoretical framework, because we present highly selective empirical evidence in terms of policy outcomes, based on the concepts of developmentalism, in order to then come to our main contribution of policy analysis.

2 Concepts of Developmentalism

The concept of developmentalism is a rather ambiguous term per definition. It involves two perspectives, which are intertwined, but are not the same neither from an epistemological viewpoint nor in daily practice: (i) a phenomenon of the 'material world,' i.e., a set of practices of economic policies proposed and/or executed by policy makers and (ii) a phenomenon of the 'world of ideas,' i.e., a set of ideas proposed to express theories, concepts, or visions of the world. The former expresses itself also as political discourse, while the second seeks to form a school of thought (Fonseca 2014, p. 30).

The origin of developmentalism is related both to studies of development in the 1950s and the Latin American structuralist approach, which sought to understand the specificities of underdevelopment and how to overcome it. Classic developmentalism departed from the idea that the typical division of labor between developed and developing economies created a structural balance of payments constraint and impaired domestic growth. As a phenomenon of the 'material world,' developmentalism translated to national-developmentalist strategies supporting that industrial development was the most efficient way to achieve an increase in productivity and in national income; thereby retaining the 'fruits' of technical progress in peripheral economies. Latin American structuralism, also known nowadays as 'classic developmentalism,' used the metaphor 'center-periphery' to translate the productive and technological asymmetries of the international order and saw industrialization as the only way for the peripheral economies to gain access to part of the technical progress from the developed economies, allowing them at the same time to progressively raise the living standard of the population (Prebisch 1950; see also Ocampo 2001).

The current debate is intensively nurtured and intertwined with the economic policy discourse and policy making, especially in Latin American countries where leftist parties dominated governments in many countries until recently. Updated concepts of developmentalism gained space in semi-mature economies of the continent, which are featured by a more diversified productive structure and the risk of premature deindustrialization. This also resulted from profound discontentment with policies based on the economic orthodoxy, also dubbed as 'Washington Consensus.' Indeed, the region that has the highest degree of economic inequality in the world experienced a stagnation or even further worsening of inequality though the period of liberalization. Within the critical assessment of the orthodox agenda of domestic market liberalization, trade and financial openness and reduction of the role of the State, income distribution emerged at the center of public debate.

Within this renewed debate, we identify two major new concepts: social developmentalism (SD) and new developmentalism (ND). These have updated classic developmentalism and added new dimensions. Both clearly reject the neoclassical idea of welfare maximization by specializing on comparative advantages at the global level, similar to classic developmentalism, at seeing structural external constraints caused by integration of peripheral economies in the global market as the cause of lacking economic dynamism at the domestic level. Thus, they support a national strategy of economic development with an active role of the state to achieve structural change toward (re-) industrialization, resulting in social transformation (Fonseca 2014, p. 41; Bielschowsky 2015).

To facilitate the analysis of policy coordination, we analytically disaggregate the concepts into three different layers of policy aims, targets, and tools.[1] When comparing SD and ND, they are rather similar in their policy aims as both seek to achieve productive change with income redistribution. But, they clearly differ regarding the targets and tools to achieve these aims.

SD is closer to the classic developmentalist approach, as it continues focusing on the shortage of domestic demand to push investment into productive diversification. Yet, while the former sees income redistribution more as an outcome of structural change pushed by State action,

[1]For an extended comparative analysis to the two recent developmentalist concepts see Fritz et al. (2017).

SD gives the aim of a more equal income distribution a prominent role[2] for increasing domestic mass consumption, which would push economic growth and productive change (Lavinas and Simões 2015). The structural balance of payments' constraint would be mitigated by export growth induced by scale effects and industrialization as well as fostered by domestic demand, given the complementarity between domestic and foreign markets. It also could be supplemented, at least temporarily, by the expansion of the natural resource-intensive sector and its supply chains (Rosa and Biancarelli 2016).

Differently, ND has a predominantly macroeconomic perspective and is more inspired by the development path of Asian emerging markets with their marked strategy of export surplus. It sees two hindering factors for development: first, the tendency toward currency overvaluation as a result, mainly, of the specialization in commodity exports and[3] second the net flows of foreign capital, stimulated by the policy of growth-cum-foreign savings. Also, the tendency of wages to increase below productivity due to the availability of an unlimited supply of labor. Here, the aim of (re-) industrialization is directly linked to the target of an export surplus of manufactured goods, pushing for further investment in this sector. With this, the country should be enabled to avoid incurring into external debt. In this view, the exchange rate plays the key role to influence both imports and exports. An improvement in the income redistribution basically would result from (formal) job creation in the manufacturing sector and from wages increasing along productivity gains (Bresser-Pereira 2011).

Regarding the policy tools attached to each of these approaches, Carneiro (2012) notes that the reflections regarding SD are rather fragmented. This holds especially for the first generation of papers (Bastos 2012; Bielschowsky 2012; Carneiro 2012), where the focus is exclusively on policies oriented toward redistribution and shifting production patterns, as follows:

---

[2] This should be reflected rather quickly in a significant reduction of the Gini index.

[3] This is also discussed as the phenomenon of Dutch disease.

- Wage policies, being the minimum wage a powerful policy instrument to foster wage increases especially in the lower income range;
- Social transfers targeted toward the poorer part of the population;
- Stimulus to consumer credit;
- Public investment especially in (physical and social) infrastructure, seen as crucial for directly creating demand, but especially for giving incentives for private investment;
- Industrial policies and subsidized financing by public banks, designed to further stimulate private investment.

Macroeconomic considerations are mainly included in a second wave on publications on SD. Rossi (2014) makes an explicit attempt to include monetary, fiscal, and exchange rate policy tools, but this remains rather imprecise.

Within ND, Bresser-Pereira (2011) offers a well-developed theoretical approach and clearly deduces the policy tools necessary for this strategy of export-led growth:

- Priority is given to currency devaluation and subsequent maintenance of the exchange rate at a level where domestic industry becomes internationally competitive. If necessary, this undervalued currency should be supported by capital controls.
- Other macroeconomic instruments, such as monetary and fiscal policies, are thought to support this nominal and exchange rate level, at maintaining price stability.
- Industrial policy is a secondary policy tool and should be targeted exclusively toward exports, as only these are seen as the engine for investment and growth at the domestic level, until catching up with advanced economies.
- Wages, at the short term, might lose in terms of purchasing power as a consequence of the currency devaluation. In the medium term, however, wages should grow along productivity gains to prevent spurring inflation and to maintain the functional distribution between wages and profits. Income redistribution is expected to stem from additional job creation in the manufacturing sector.

- Redistributive policies are included as an addendum in later publications (Bresser-Pereira 2015), reacting to the heated debate around redistributional issues, which, however, are not vital to the ND strategy of export-led growth.

3 Empirical Assessment of Outcomes Based on Stylized Facts

Before analysing the policies adopted in Brazil from 2003 to mid-2016 in Sect. 4, this section summarizes the changes in the external context overtime as well as the economic outcomes of the Brazilian economy during this period through stylized facts regarding the most relevant goals targeted by developmentalist approaches.

External Context

Over the period under consideration, the external context underwent important changes. From 2003 to the threshold of the GFC, the international economy was characterised by a very favorable scenario in terms of trade (high commodity prices and external demand) and capital flows. Yet, after the double speed recovery and the new 'twin boom' of commodity prices and capital flows from mid-2009 to 2010, the international setting deteriorated. The global trade volume increased at a much lower rate in comparison with the pre-crisis setting, commodity prices begun to fall in 2012 and capital flows to emerging economies lost momentum from 2011 (Fig. 1 and Table 2 in Appendix).[4]

Supporters and opponents of developmentalist policies agree on the positive influence of the benign external environment before the GFC on the Brazilian economy. However, they definitely diverge on the role of its deterioration since 2011 on the recent crisis: while orthodox authors put the blame on these policies (Barbosa Filho and Pessoa

[4]On the external context over the analysed period, see also Chap. "New Features of the Brazilian External Sector since the Great Global Crisis" of this book.

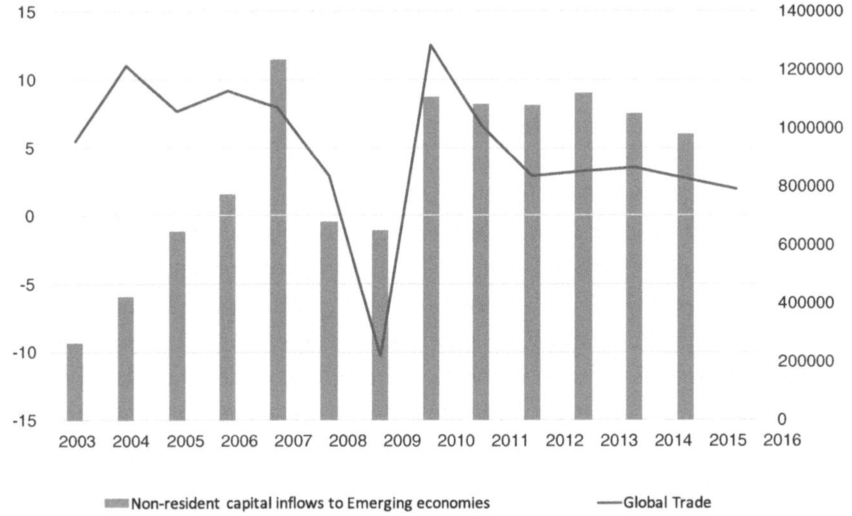

Fig. 1 World Trade (annual change in percent) and capital flows (USD billion). *Source* IMF (2017). Authors' elaboration

2014); social developmentalist authors (Bastos 2015) stress the dominance of external shocks.

We follow herein a Keynesian-structuralist approach,[5] which emphasizes the center-periphery asymmetries of the international economy (Prebisch 1950) and the resulting higher vulnerability of peripheral economies to external shocks. Yet, in the post-Bretton Woods era, although current account (specially, terms of trade) shocks have remained relevant, particularly in commodity dependent economies, financial shocks have assumed the leading influence due to monetary and financial asymmetries.

The monetary asymmetry is a consequence of the so-called currency hierarchy, namely currencies are hierarchically positioned according to their degree of liquidity, which relates to their ability to perform the three functions of money internationally. The key currency (currently, the US dollar) is placed at the top of the hierarchy; the currencies of other center countries or regions (such as the yen and the euro) are in

[5]For more details, see Fritz et al. (2017).

intermediate positions and at the bottom are the currencies issued by peripheral economies that are incapable of fulfilling these functions. Yet, this asymmetry has revealed itself more deleterious due to financial asymmetries, which refer to the patterns and magnitude of capital flows to peripheral countries that joined financial globalization, becoming 'emerging economies.' Firstly, capital flows toward these economies depend mainly on exogenous sources, rendering them permanently vulnerable to their reversal by virtue of changes in the monetary conditions in the center as well as by the rise in the liquidity preference of global investors. Secondly, despite the residual nature of capital flows directed to those economies, their potentially destabilizing effects on local financial markets and exchange rates are significant, since the volume allocated by global investors is not marginal in relation to the size of these markets.

Therefore, according to this approach, the interplay of the monetary and financial asymmetries results in a key influence of the international economy dynamics on the performance of peripheral emerging economies such as Brazil, mainly through the boom-bust cycles of capital flows. Consequently, these asymmetries also constrain the policy space in these economies, shaping the degree of autonomy of economic and social policies (Paula et al. 2017). Yet, the specific mix of policies adopted depends on domestic factors, among which the institutional framework and political power relations.

Stylized Facts of Outcomes

Growth Performance

The Brazilian economy had an unprecedented performance from 2004 to mid-2008 compared to the 1980s and 1990s, with an average growth rate of 4.8% per year. During the pre-crisis boom, the main engine of growth was household consumption (which responds to the biggest share of the Brazilian GDP, around 60%). Another novelty of this period was the continuous credit growth to households and enterprises.

In line with other emerging economies (Canuto and Leipziger 2012), the recession caused by the contagion effect of the GFC was brief. In

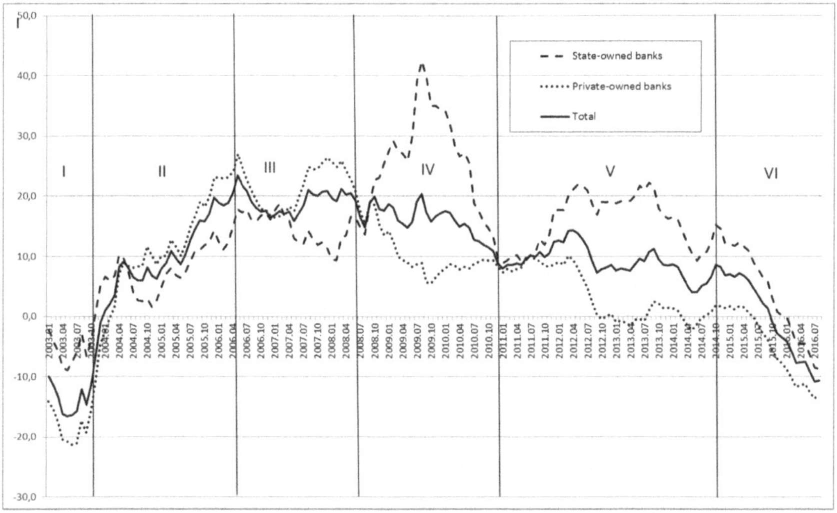

Fig. 2 Credit supply by ownership (%)*. *Source* Central Bank of Brazil (2017). Authors' elaboration. (*) Growth rate compared to 12 months before with data in real values (deflated by IPCA)

contrast, due to its distinct cyclical behavior, investment recorded an abrupt reduction in face of the contagion effect of the GFC, being the main responsible factor along with exports for the recession in the first half of 2009; while household consumption mitigated the decline in aggregate expenditure. The economy recovered quickly and in 2010, the GDP recorded a growth rate of 7.5%; investment and consumption contributed to that healthy economic recovery.

Growth, however, began to slow down in late 2010. The deceleration intensified in 2012, turning into the worst economic recession since at least the Great Recession of the 1930s (Table 2 in Appendix). After the GDP growth of 3.9% in 2011, economic growth dropped to 1.7% p.a. on average in 2012–2014 (2.0% p.a in the case of industrial output) and declined sharply to −3.6% over 2015–2016. A set of shocks that reached the economy over those two last years contributed to the crisis, among which a deterioration in the terms of trade, accelerated inflation due to a de-freezing of monitored service prices and strong currency devaluation, and a hydric crisis. The recession, which was further fueled by a tightening of monetary and fiscal policies, produced declining wages and profits. This also caused a huge slowdown in credit supply that occasionally resulted in a credit crunch, further delaying the recovery of the economy (Fig. 2).

Finally, economic growth in 2003–2013 was followed by a sharp reduction in unemployment rate, from 12.4% in 2003 to 5.1% in 2013 (this rate increased to 8% in 2015 due to the recession). The combination between low employment and increase in real wages contributed to the improvement in social indicators, as we will see in the next subsection.

Income Distribution: Functional and Personal

An important and unique feature of the Brazilian economy performance over the period under consideration was the reduction in inequality, a trend also observed in other Latin America countries (Fritz and Lavinas 2015). In the case of Brazil, the process of income redistribution encompassed both the personal dimension, with a reduction of the Gini index, and the functional one, with an increase of the wage share in total income.[6] On the other hand, poverty rate fell down sharply from 35.8% of the population in 2003 to 13.3% in 2014[7] (Table 2 in Appendix).

However, analysing the dynamic of top incomes based on income tax data between 2007 and 2013, Gobetti and Orair (2015) conclude that the Gini index of household survey data overestimates improvements in the personal income distribution. In other words, the level of inequality and concentration of income in Brazil is significantly higher than what has been estimated by this type of data. Upon their estimation, income concentrated by the 0.1% and the 10% richest households comes to 10.9% and 54.1% of disposable income of households, respectively.

[6] On the Brazilian income distribution, see Chap. "Income Distribution, Productivity and Economic Growth: Empirical Evidence in the case of Brazil" of this book.

[7] Poverty index is the percentage of the population with household income lower than poverty line.

Productive Restructuration and External Vulnerability

The third aim of developmentalism is the so-called structural change or reindustrialization that refers to the reallocation of productive resources from the traditional sector (especially agriculture) to the manufacturing sector (mainly those segments of higher technological sophistication). Yet, over the period of 2008–2015, the fall of this sector's share in the GDP that had started in the 1990s gained momentum.[8]

Moreover, since 2008, this descending trajectory has been accompanied by increasing deficits in manufacturing goods trade balance along with surplus in non-manufacturing goods, certainly fostered by the appreciation of the domestic currency in real terms until 2012 (see Sect. 4). Even with a subsequent reverse in the appreciation trend, however, profitability of exports increased only slightly. In this setting, industrial output firstly stagnated and, from 2013, begun to fall. Meanwhile, retail sales and the import coefficient of industry inputs kept growing, indicating a substitution of domestic production by imports both in final and intermediary manufacturing goods (Paula et al. 2015).

In terms of external vulnerability, results are mixed. Considering external liquidity, the situation improved thanks not only to the policy of foreign exchange (FX) reserves accumulation (see Sect. 4), but also to the reduction in the currency mismatch associated with a change in the composition of the short-term gross external liability. This change stemmed from two simultaneous trends: a decrease in external debt and a rise in foreign portfolio investment in the domestic market. Further, the increasing current account deficit (CAD) between 2009 and 2014 was financed almost fully by foreign direct investment (FDI). In 2015 and 2016, the FDI was higher than the CAD by 0.8 and 3%. Thus, in the short term, Brazil did not face an external constraint, what explains,

[8]On the Brazilan industry performance, see Chaps. "Brazilian Industry: Recent Performance and Future Challenges", "Financialisation and Investment Behaviour Among Non-Financial Corporations in Brazil Since the Global Crisis" and "Income Distribution, Productivity and Economic Growth: Empirical Evidence in the case of Brazil" of this book.

along with the dirty floating regime, why a balance of payment crisis did not break out despite the huge outflow of foreign portfolio investments amid a deep economic crisis[9] (Table 2 in Appendix).

On the other hand, external solvency deteriorated, as the growth rate of the total net external liability was greater than the one of exports. The situation rather worsened when considering only the exports of manufactured products, characterized by lower price volatility and higher income-elasticity than commodities. From this perspective, the country's capacity of generating autonomously foreign currency to serve its external liability decreased during the period covered (Table 2 in Appendix).

4 Public Policies Over 2003–2016

In this section, we analyze public policies implemented during Lula da Silva's and Dilma Roussef's terms. Based on this assessment, we will elaborate in Sect. 5 a typology of these policies along the different developmentalist and non-developmentalist strategies. This typology, in turn, will enable us to answer our research question and confirm (or not) the hypothesis presented in the introduction.

Macroeconomic Policies

The first term of Lula da Silva's government (2003–2006), following a confidence crisis in 2002 with a massive speculative attack against the Brazilian currency, was characterized by the continuity of the combined macroeconomic policy adopted after the 1999 currency crisis, namely inflation targeting, primary surplus targets, and a dirty floating

[9] For more details on Brazil's external sector, see Chap. "New Features of the Brazilian External Sector since the Great Global Crisis" of this book.

Fig. 3 Policy rate (SELIC interest rate—% p.a.) and real effective exchange rate (June 1994 = 100). *Source* Central Bank of Brazil (2017). Authors' elaboration

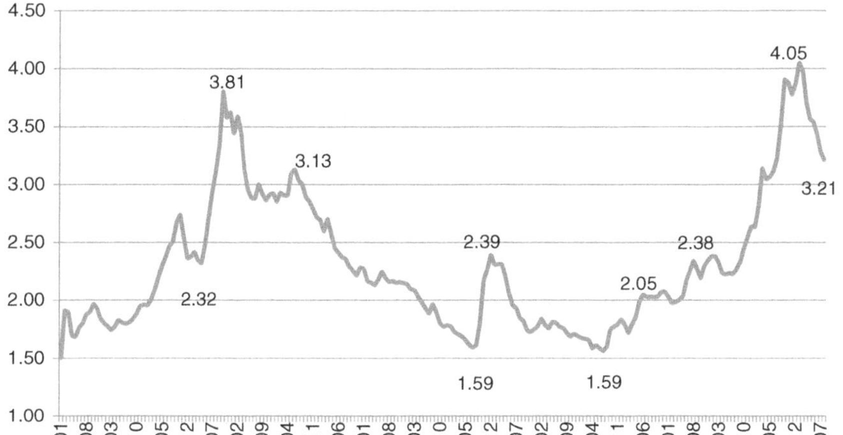

Fig. 4 Exchange rate (BRL/USD)—Jan/1999-Aug/2016. *Source* Central Bank of Brazil (2017)

exchange rate regime. Under this framework, both fiscal and monetary policies were kept mostly orthodox, featured by a wide primary surplus and the maintenance of a high real interest rate (albeit with a decreasing path), while the currency appreciated gradually (Figs. 3 and 4).[10]

Amid a positive external environment in terms of trade and capital flows, the high interest rate stimulated speculative operations through portfolio investment and FX derivatives. These operations along with the current account surplus resulted in a significant currency appreciation. The interventions of the monetary authority in the FX market in 2005 did not curb this appreciation, but came out with the buildup of FX reserves.[11] The so-called precautionary demand for reserves contributed to the decrease of net public external debt (Table 2 in Appendix) and the improvement in the country's external liquidity (see Sect. "Stylized Facts of Outcomes"). Moreover, in this period bank credit to the private sector recorded a significant growth, stimulated, among other factors, by the implementation of payroll-deductible credit operations, which reduced bank risk and, consequently, the cost of loans to households.

Yet, both the currency appreciation trend and the credit boom were reversed in September 2008, when the contagion effect of the global financial crisis resulted in huge capital outflows. This marked the beginning of the second phase under analysis here.

The Brazilian authorities responded to the financial crisis by adopting a number of countercyclical measures (Barbosa 2010; Paula et al. 2015): (i) to avoid the spread of the credit crunch, the Central Bank of Brazil adopted a series of liquidity-enhancing measures; (ii) the BCB intervened in the FX markets; (iii) the state-owned banks were encouraged to expand their credit operations to compensate for the deceleration in the credit supply by private banks (Fig. 2)[12]; and (iv) the Ministry of Finance undertook fiscal measures to stimulate aggregate demand.

[10]For more details on monetary policy, see Chaps. "Monetary Institutions and Macroeconomic Performance in Brazil After the Global Financial Crisis of 2007–2008" and "Asymmetric Exchange Rate Pass-Through: Evidence, Inflation Dynamics and Policy Implications for Brazil (1999–2016)" of this book.

[11]On the role of FX derivatives on the Brazilian exchange rate dynamics, see Chap. "Foreign Exchange Derivatives and Financial Fragility in Brazil" of this book.

[12]For more details on the countercyclical role of public banks after the global financial crisis, see Chap. "The Brazilian Credit Market During The Great Recession" of this book.

Such countercyclical reaction was possible, to a large extent, due to the policy space created by the shift toward a net creditor position in foreign currency of the Brazilian government. Consequently, the currency devaluation favored public finance. In the context of quick recovery of the economy and a new surge of capital flows to emerging economies from the middle of 2009, Brazil faced again huge short-term inflows boosted by a still high differential between the internal and external interest rates. As the BCB resumed the exchange rate policy adopted before the crisis, Brazil's currency recorded a huge appreciation in 2009 (Fig. 4).

In this setting, the Ministry of Finance started imposing regulations on capital flows, starting with a tiny financial transaction tax on foreign portfolio investments in October 2009. One year later, these regulations were strengthened with the first measure targeting FX derivatives operations and administrative controls. Moreover, the Central Bank of Brazil adopted macro-prudential regulations to curb the domestic credit boom, fostered by countercyclical policies.

In mid-2011, during Roussef's first term, a gradual change was introduced for what the government itself called the 'New Macroeconomic Matrix,' to boost growth. The regulatory toolkit on spot and derivatives' FX markets had been further broadened as the previous measures had only mitigated the currency appreciation trend underlying the deterioration in competitiveness of Brazil's manufacturing sector in both external and domestic markets (Prates and Fritz 2016; Paula and Prates 2015). It was completed by a progressive reduction both in the policy rate and the primary fiscal surplus. The interplay of the new FX regulations, the monetary policy loosening, and the increase in the risk aversion of global investors due to the worsening of the euro crisis eventually came out with the intended depreciation of the Brazilian currency (Fig. 4).

Additionally, the government used a wide range of instruments: a nominal freeze of relevant public tariffs (energy and gasoline) for price stabilization purposes, the use of state-owned banks to reduce bank spreads, etc. Furthermore, due to the economy's positive fiscal performance in the first half of 2011, the Ministry of Finance adopted several fiscal stimulus measures, especially tax exemptions that mainly favored the domestic manufacturing sector. These exemptions were gradually extended, aimed at increasing the international competitiveness of this sector, damaged by both currency appreciation, and greater competition in the external markets (see Sect. "Industrial Policies"). It is worth mentioning that in the first year, these measures did not change the overall fiscal policy stance.

Yet, in April 2013, due to an increasing inflation rate, the BCB restarted to rise gradual and continuously the policy rate (Fig. 3), and removed regulations on FX operations due to signaling by the Federal Reserve that its quantitative easing policy would to be withdraw soon ('tapering'). At the same time, the Brazilian government further enlarged tax exemptions, and tried to intensify investment in infrastructure. Moreover, affected by the decline of oil prices and the first effects of 'Lava-jato'[13] operation, Petrobras reduced its investments, with a strong impact on overall investment (Afonso and Fajardo 2015).

Compared with the policies launched to counter the GFC contagion effect, the countercyclical fiscal policies implemented in 2012–2014, with the use of tax exemptions instead of public expenditures, were very limited, with small aggregate impact on production and employment. The same holds for public investment, which was significantly higher over 2006–2010.[14]

In 2015, after the reelection of Dilma Roussef, the government shifted its economic policy somehow radically toward a more orthodox policy stance. The main aim of the economic policy was to implement fiscal adjustment mainly by the side of public expenditures, understood as fundamental for retaking the agents' confidence as a precondition for economic recovery. For this purpose, the Brazilian government committed itself to a primary fiscal surplus of 1.2% of GDP, implementing a set of measures to reduce public expenditures (mainly by the budget contingency), readjusted monitored prices (energy and oil), while the

[13]'Car Wash operation is an investigation being carried out by the Federal Police of Brazil and the Court since March 17, 2014. Initially a money laundering investigation, it has expanded to cover allegations of corruption at the state-controlled oil company Petrobras, see https://nacla.org/news/2017/03/30/corruption-and-controversy-brazil.

[14]for more details on brazilian fiscal policy, see Chap. "Brazilian Fiscal Policy in Perspective: From Expansion to Austerity" of this book.

BCB further increased its policy rate from 10.92% p.a. in October 2014 to 14.14% p.a. in August 2015. Due to strong devaluation in 2015, the BCB had to intervene in the FX market to reduce exchange rate volatility and to offer exchange rate hedging to private agents, with the use of swap operations.

The efforts of fiscal adjustment failed as fiscal revenues dropped dramatically in 2015, so that the Ministry of Finance had to revise its fiscal targets. Due to the recession and increasing interest payments, the public nominal deficit increased even more in 2015. Net public debt over GDP, which had recorded its lowest level during the period under analysis in 2013 with 30.5%, again grew steeply (to 46% of GDP in 2016). Gross debt over GDP increased even more, from 51.5% to 69.6% in the same period. This means that government's assets (mainly, foreign reserves and loans to public banks) shrunk in relative terms, contrary to the period 2010–2014, when they rose significantly (Table 2 in Appendix).

At the beginning of 2016, Nelson Barbosa, the new Finance Minister, announced his agenda of measures for the year: establishing a limit for the growth of government's current and personnel expenses, untying of part of tax revenue, simplification of the tax system, and a pension reform, the proposal of which was not presented to the public. Its great challenge was to establish a strategy of fiscal consolidation, which, among other things, would be able to reverse the upward trend of public spending that contradictorily compromised the capacity of the Brazilian State to implement public policies in the long term. As for 2016, the spread of political crisis virtually paralyzed the government's actions, making impossible the adoption of any economic policy agenda until the impeachment of President Roussef in 2016.

Industrial Policies

After a longtime span of almost complete absence of industrial policies, three programs of industrial policy were launched during the period analyzed here, each of them containing a different focus. Industrial policy in this period oscillated between two types of strategies: to prioritize high-tech sectors and to select national champions in industries with comparative international advantages, such as agribusiness, steel, and mining, as well as to favor sectors damaged by strong foreign competition (Almeida and Novais 2014, p.211).

The first program called PICTE ('*Politica Industrial, Tecnológica e de Comércio Exterior*'—'Industrial, Technology and Foreign Trade Policy') was launched in 2004 aimed to address Brazil's external vulnerability, emphasizing an active policy of adding value to exports based on innovation. To this end, three areas were defined: (i) incentives for strategic sectors (capital goods, software, semiconductors, pharmaceuticals, and medicines), through specific programs; (ii) horizontal actions to stimulate innovation and technological development, international integration via exports and modernization of institutional environment; and (iii) priority to three areas considered relevant for national technological development: biotechnology, nanotechnology, and renewable energy.

With the rapid and intensive improvement of Brazilian terms of trade from 2004, which resulted in substantial surpluses in the trade balance, priorities for industrial policy changed (Kupfer 2013). The 'Productive Development Policy' (PDP) was launched in May 2008, in a context where, according to the underlying diagnosis, Brazil had received the investment grade due to its sound economic fundamentals (low inflation, fiscal surplus, etc.). The main policy objective was then set to foster growth and productive investment in the domestic market. For this purpose, the PDP set ambitious investment goals (from 17.6% of GDP in 2007 to 21.0% of GDP in 2010) and a increased participation of Brazilian exports in world trade.[15] The changing global scenario led to the launch of a third program, called 'Plano Brasil Maior' (PBM—Plan Bigger Brazil), in August 2011, with continuous modifications in the following years in view of worsening global economic conditions. The initial objectives of the PBM were creating capabilities aiming at the productive and technological consolidation of value chains, but the

[15] Almeida and Novais (2014) criticized PDP for its absence of reciprocity mechanisms along the lines adopted in South Korea. According to Kupfer (2013), the PDP had a more countercyclical role and less than the expected function of providing stimulus to the investment pattern of the economy.

intensification of international competition in domestic and foreign markets forced the plan to be directed to the defense of the domestic market and the recovery of systemic competitiveness conditions (Kupfer 2013). Given the speed of the penetration of imported goods in Brazil, the government adopted compensatory measures to minimize the impact on domestic manufacturing output. The measures included the expansion of subsidized credit by BNDES and further tax and social security payment exemptions, causing significant fiscal costs with limited effects on industrial production.

Kupfer (2013), in doing a balance of industrial policies in the period analyzed here, concludes that they remained an auxiliary line of macroeconomic policies, but often in conflict with these. Their effectiveness was reduced by different systemic determinants that were outside their scope, the most important being the strong currency appreciation until 2011 and very high interest rates.

Social Policies

Highly active social policies were one of the major traits of policy orientation during the period examined in this chapter. These policies were crucial for attaining the aim of income redistribution, which would foster domestic consumption. The two main factors that contributed to improve income distribution was the huge increase in the minimum wage (66.9% in real terms from December 2003 to December 2014) and the policy of income transference due to both increase of the pension benefits and 'bolsa familia' program.

The most important instrument certainly was the increase of the minimum wage (Fig. 5). The rule for adjusting such wage adopted over this period was to add the inflation of the previous year and the GDP growth rate of the second year before the relevant one. In this way, high economic growth resulted in high real wage increases as in Brazil wages of low-qualified workers in the public and in the private formal and informal sector, as much as public pension payments, are all linked to the minimum wage. Within this institutional setting, minimum wage policy turned a powerful redistributional instrument.

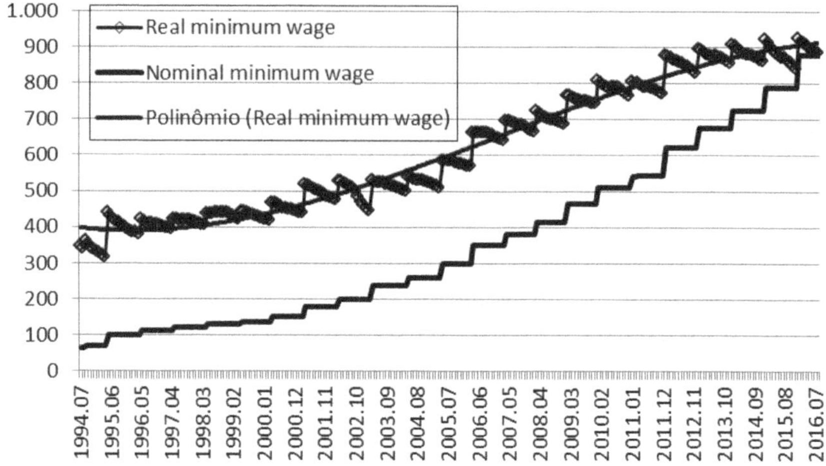

Fig. 5 Minimum wage—nominal and real*. *Source* IPEADATA (2017). Authors' elaboration. (*) Deflated by the National Index of Consumer Prices (INPC)

Another social policy instrument that gained high national and international visibility was the conditional cash transfer program *Bolsa Família.* It was designed to combat extreme poverty, and achieved an almost complete coverage of very poor families with kids in school age in the country. Its costs for public spending together with other anti-poverty programs remained very low.

Finally, fiscal policy was completely absent in the area of redistribution policies. While in OECD countries taxes are responsible for the bulk of public redistribution, in Brazil the tax system even has a slightly regressive effect, as Lustig et al. (2014) show.

5 An Assessment of Public Policies in the PT Governments

When we assess the policies adopted during the four PT governments, we find significant and repeated changes in the policies over time. Even if for some aspects exact and uniform periodization is rather difficult, we also find that these changes were largely associated to the external context. As pointed out in Sect. 3, it is possible to identify three

Table 1 Typology of policies

	2003–Aug. 2008	Sept. 2008–2010	2011–mid 2016	
	Lula before GFC	Lula during GFC and double speed recovery	Dilma I (2011–2014)	Dilma II (2011–2015–8/16)
Macroeconomic policies				
Monetary policy	ORT	ORT; ND; ORT	ND; ORT	ORT
Exchange rate policy	ORT	ORT; ND	ND; ORT	ORT
Fiscal policy	ORT	SD; ORT	ORT; (SD)	ORT
Social policies	SD	SD	SD	SD
Public investment	SD	SD	(SD)	ORT
Financial policies	SD	SD	SD	ORT
Industrial policies	ND	SD	SD	SD

Source Authors' elaboration
Notes Strategy in parenthesis: influenced by a certain strategy. *ORT* orthodoxy policies; *SD* social developmentalist policies; *ND* new-developmentalist policies. Classifications separated by ';': temporal sequence of strategies within one phase

different phases in the relevant period, which defined the limits and possibilities of the domestic economic and social policies: the first one before the GFC, benign in terms of trade and financial flows to emerging economies; the second one, from September 2008 to 2010, featured by the GFC, the double speed recovery and the new 'twin boom'; the third one, from 2011, with the deterioration of external conditions due to the slowdown of both world trade volume and capital inflows and the boost in commodity prices (Fig. 1 and Table 2 in Appendix).

Hence, these same periods are used herein to elaborate a typology of policies along the different developmentalist and non-developmentalist strategies. Yet, the last phase (2011 to mid-2016) is split into two subphases in view of the changes in economic policies in Dilma's second term that were shaped, largely, by domestic factors, especially the political confidence crisis triggered by a mix of economic crisis and corruption scandal, which made President Roussef loose political majority (Table 1).

The first phase from 2003 to September 2008 was marked by an orthodox macroeconomic policy. Moreover, following the path of other emerging economies, from 2005 the favorable external context had enabled Brazil to adopt the precautionary strategy of accumulating FX reserves, which had a key role in reducing external vulnerability. This policy stance was mixed with increasing elements of social developmentalism, namely the formation of a market of mass consumption. That was boosted by increasing the minimum wage in real terms, stimulating private credit, as well as rising households' purchasing power in a setting of lowering prices of imported goods due to the currency appreciation. However, as industrial policy was mostly oriented toward strengthening exports, this policy field can be characterized as new-developmentalist, even if it has a secondary place in this perspective.

A second phase, from October 2008 to 2010, was the time when 'we were all Keynesians.' In the context of the contagion effect of the GFC, Lula's second term launched a more flexible fiscal policy, including an increase in public investment, promoted a countercyclical role of state-owned banks and boosted social policies, further increasing the real minimum wage and anti-poverty programs. These measures, coherent with social developmentalism, were taken with some pragmatism and departed from what we labeled as orthodox policies before the crisis. In a second stage, when the economy recovered, the government adopted price-based capital controls and macro-prudential regulations on the credit market to curb, respectively, the currency appreciation and the credit boom. Although these two types of financial regulation (Ocampo 2012) were included to some degree in the conventional toolkit of macroeconomic recommendations after the 2008 global crisis (Blanchard et al. 2010), they fit within the new-developmentalist approach.

The transition period, from the second to the third phase (2011–2014), is difficult to be set, and classification becomes especially difficult. This phase was characterized by strong oscillation in the macroeconomic policy between orthodoxy and developmentalism. One could interpret the so-called New Macroeconomic Matrix as influenced by new developmentalism prescriptions, due to the currency devaluation and the decreasing policy rate, but other elements of this approach were not present, especially regarding fiscal policy in 2013–2014. This policy was not only increasingly expansive, but also supply side-oriented instead of focusing on the public demand side. Then, they were even criticized by social developmentalists (Bastos 2015). However, from 2013, a more orthodox approach in terms of monetary and exchange rate policies toward inflation stabilization was resumed. At the same time, in the first Roussef's government, the pillars of social developmentalism of the first two phases were maintained, i.e., minimum wage increases, stimulus to private credit, an active role of public banks and of industrial policies. Yet, public investment decreased in 2010–2014, so it is imprecise to define Roussef's macroeconomic policy in this field as social developmentalist.

As we have already pointed out, the second Roussef's government (2015–2016) was marked by a radical shift, with the implementation of orthodoxy mainly in the field of fiscal and monetary policies. As for the exchange rate policy, Central Bank of Brazil implemented a strategy to reduce volatility and provide a hedge against exchange rate risk, but did not intend to be involved with the determination of the exchange rate. In terms of social policies, there were no significant changes. As we have seen in the former section, the rule for minimum wage readjustment remained in place, although high inflation in 2015–2016 and low growth in the years before limited real wage increases.

As we can conclude from Sect. 4, the ambiguity and lack of coordination of economic policies combined with the worsening in the international scenario can explain the downturn in the Brazilian economy, especially since 2014. On the contrary, orthodox economists assign the downturn to the implementation of developmental policies in Brazil (Barbosa Filho and Pessoa 2014).

6 Summary and Conclusions

Recent approaches of developmentalism are characterized in general terms by the aim to combine sustained economic growth with productive restructuring and income distribution by giving the state an active role. Our assessment of the experience of policies during the long period of PT-led governments in Brazil from 2003 to mid-2016 with focus on the years after the GFC, shows that, when using this broad definition, we could not label this period as developmentalist inasmuch the macroeconomic policies were, predominantly, orthodox.

When taking a closer look, we can confirm our first hypothesis. We find more than one recent type of developmentalist strategy available at the conceptual level. The two most relevant concepts we identified, social and new developmentalism, show significant differences. On the one hand, within the new-developmentalist approach, it is given priority to manage macro prices such as the exchange rate in order to prevent the appreciation of the domestic currency and, thus, to achieve an export surplus in manufactured goods. On the other hand, the social developmentalist approach favored redistributional policies to foster domestic demand and domestic diversified investment.

So, when asking if developmentalism could be blamed for the recent economic crisis, the question should also consider what type of developmentalist concept we should account for in this context. We support herein that the use of the same label for varied approaches without clarifying their similarities and differences, and the absence of a broader attempt to bring these views together to a more consistent approach (which might inspire policies in a more coherent manner) is a major weakness of this recent debate.

Regarding the classification of policies applied, it seems that these followed more explicitly the social developmentalist version. Not only social policies, but also subfields of economic policies, such as public investment and financial policies regarding credit access of lower income households and the outstanding role given to public banks, can be attributed to this concept. The core of new-developmentalist policies, the policy of achieving an undervalued currency, were applied only for a rather limited period of time, which started actually in 2010 and ended rather quickly with the worsening of the external context.

Second, when concretely assessing the macroeconomic policies applied during this period, it is clear that they were highly orthodox or conventional during the first phase. Yet, against widespread interpretation, we cannot find a clear pattern of shifting macroeconomic policies toward a more developmentalist stance in uniform terms after the GFC. Rather, the second phase, of reaction to the spillovers of the financial crisis in center economies, is shaped by anti-cyclical policies that were global standard in this context, but applied rather cautiously in Brazil especially with regard to monetary policy. And the third phase is characterized by a mixture of policies, which changed in an astonishingly quick manner and include all kinds of paradigmatic orientation, including orthodox policies. This, for instance, applies to the monetary policy from the second half of 2012 on, and features especially president Roussef's second term. In its struggle against a widening and mutually nurturing economic and political crisis that term was dominated by orthodox policies.

This takes us to conclude that our third hypothesis has higher relevance than expected. To our surprise, we encountered a number of difficulties to find clear criteria both in terms of periodization and classification, as the policy changes especially in the areas of monetary, exchange rate, and fiscal policies were highly frequent and irregular. Policies should not be expected to be a pure result of theoretical considerations or a mechanistic reaction to the changing nature and intensity of external constraints, but they are highly dependent on institutional path dependency and concrete circumstances, in interplay with specific interests. However, it is clear that the external context strongly shaped policy options over the period. Regarding the third phase, the swift shifts in the relevant macroeconomic policy fields certainly had to do with necessary adjustments to a volatile international environment, characterized by unstable international capital flows and decreasing commodity prices on the one hand, and the need to reactivate the domestic economy in a context of sharpened international competition, on the other hand. Beyond this, however, they may also reflect accumulating domestic conflicts among economic actors over the redistributional aims and outcomes of public policies, which grew acute with the enlarging of the political corruption affair involving the governing parties.

Overall, we have to state that the several changes in the policy mix certainly could not increase investors' confidence in public policies in Brazil in this period due to an astonishing lack of clearness regarding its economic strategy. On this, we conclude that it is difficult to interpret developmentalist approaches per se as a fallacy, even if this recent experience in Brazil might not be helpful in further spreading such concepts. We detect the major weaknesses rather the lack of both a conceptual clearness regarding this approach and a coherent policy strategy at the level of policy formulation and execution. As we have pointed out in this chapter, the ambiguity and lack of coordination of the economic policies in the analyzed period combined with the worsening in the international scenario can explain the downturn in the Brazilian economy.

Appendix

See Table 2

Table 2 Brazil: Main economic indicators

Economic Indicator/Year	2003	2004	2005	2006	2007	2008	2009	2010	2011	2012	2013	2014	2015	2016
ECONOMIC ACTIVITY														
Inflation Rate (IPCA[1]), %	9.3	7.6	5.7	3.1	4.4	5.9	4.3	5.9	6.5	5.8	5.9	6.4	10.7	6.3
GDP growth (%)[1]	1.14	5.76	3.2	3.96	6.07	5.09	-0.13	7.53	3.97	1.92	3.0	0.5	-3.77	-3.5
Agricultural	8.31	2.0	1.12	4.64	3.25	5.77	-3.73	6.7	5.64	-3.08	8.36	2.79	3.61	n.a.
Industry	0.1	8.21	1.99	2.01	6.21	4.1	-4.7	10.2	4.11	-0.72	2.17	-1.51	-6.33	n.a.
Services	0.99	5.01	3.66	4.33	5.83	4.82	2.07	5.8	3.46	2.9	2.75	0.99	-2.7	n.a.
Unemployment rate (%)	12.4	11.0	9.7	9.7	8.6	7.9	8.0	6.2	5.5	5.4	5.1	5.0	8.1	n.a.
Investment rate (% GDP)	16.6	17.3	17.1	17.2	18.0	19.4	19.1	20.5	20.6	20.7	20.9	19.9	n.a.	n.a.
Manufacturing sector (% GDP)	26.1	26.8	26.5	26.1	26.2	26,0	24.8	25.6	25.7	25.1	24.9	24.7	23.9	n.a.
MONETARY AND CREDIT INDICATORS														
Interest rate (Selic), average (%)	16.5	17.75	18.0	13.25	11.25	13.75	8.75	10.75	11.0	7.25	10.0	11.75	14.25	13.75
Domestic credit (% GDP)	n.a.	n.a.	n.a.	n.a.	34.7	39.68	42.62	44.08	46.48	49.19	50.85	52.21	53.65	49.39
Household credit (% GDP)	n.a.	n.a.	n.a.	n.a.	15.88	17.18	18.8	19.96	21.06	22.33	23.38	24.44	25.2	24.82
Corporate credit (% GDP)	n.a.	n.a.	n.a.	n.a.	18.82	22.5	23.82	24.11	25.41	26.86	27.47	27.77	28.45	24.57
EXTERNAL SECTOR														
Real effective exchange rate[2]	137.4	135.0	110.3	98.5	91.4	88.9	88.4	77.1	75.0	84.1	89.9	91.2	111.4	105.7
Commodity price index (% growth p.a.)	10.2	4.8	13.7	26.0	8.2	-23.4	33.0	29.0	-12.2	4.2	-3.4	-9.3	19.1	13.6
Brazil's terms of trade (% growth p.a.)	3.1	-2.0	5.1	7.3	-0.9	0.5	7.8	14.9	-3.4	-3.4	-1.8	-6.7	-12.3	16.4
Trade balance (US$ billion)	23,75	32,54	43,43	45,12	38,483	23,802	24,958	18,491	27,625	17,42	389	-6,629	17,67	45,037
Net public external debt (US$ billion)	65,686	57,744	29,021	-13,015	-112,036	-142,299	-168,083	-215,979	-287,168	-303,206	-305,156	-296,129	-295,124	-295,864
Manufacturing import coeficient (%)[3]	15.2	15.5	14.5	14.9	15.3	17.0	15.3	16.3	17.4	18.7	19.4	19.2	21.7	19.1
Current account (% GDP)	0.67	1.70	1.52	1.18	0.03	-1.81	-1.57	-3.43	-2.95	-3.02	-3.04	-4.31	-3.31	-1.30
Foreign Direct Investment (% GDP)	1.83	2.73	1.71	1.76	2.59	2.84	1.25	4.00	3.87	3.52	2.80	3.95	4.16	4.37
Foreign reserves (US$ billion)	46,684	52,411	53,145	84,463	163,526	190,929	228,644	276,148	343,180	362,064	349,029	354,805	348,844	353,851
External solvency indicators[4]														
Net external Liability/Total exports	3.65	2.91	2.52	2.54	3.08	1.23	3.65	4.49	3.20	3.32	3.06	3.44	2.50	3.77
Net external Liability/Manufacturing exports	4.66	3.71	3.25	3.33	4.17	1.77	5.49	7.27	5.54	5.59	5.07	5.81	3.98	5.73
External liquidity indicators														
Standard&Poors indicator[5]	2.71	1.52	0.50	0.32	0.34	0.46	0.33	0.53	0.44	0.40	0.41	0.62	0.47	0.36
Standard&Poors + Portfolio in the country[6]	5.43	4.42	2.92	2.76	2.48	1.37	2.14	2.41	1.75	1.67	1.64	1.76	1.20	1.37
PUBLIC FINANCE														
Primary fiscal result (% GDP)	3.2	3.7	3.7	3.2	3.2	3.3	1.9	2.6	2.9	2.2	1.7	-0.6	-1.94	-2.5
Public debt service (% GDP)	-8.4	-6.6	7.3	-6.7	-6.0	-5.3	-5.1	-5.0	-5.4	-4.4	-4.7	-5.4	-8.4	-6.5
Nominal fiscal result (% GDP)	-5.2	-2.9	-3.5	-3.6	-2.7	-2.0	-3.2	-2.4	-2.5	-2.3	-3.0	-6.0	-10.2	-9.0
Gross public debt (% GDP)[7]	n.a.	n.a.	n.a.	55.5	56.7	56.0	59.2	51.8	51.3	53.8	51.5	56.3	65.3	69.6
Net public debt (% GDP)	54.3	50.2	47.9	46.5	44.5	37.6	40.8	37.9	34.5	32.2	30.5	32.6	35.6	46.0
SOCIAL INDICATORS														
Gini index (%)	0.58	0.57	0.57	0.56	0.56	0.55	0.54	n.a.	0.53	0.53	0.53	0.52	n.a.	n.a.
Poverty index (% of population)	35.75	33.71	30.83	26.75	25.36	22.6	21.41	n.a.	18.42	15.93	15.09	13.29	n.a.	n.a.
Wage share[8]	36.55	35.7	36.68	38.15	38.87	39.81	41.53	41.81	42.68	45.28	45.14	n.a.	n.a.	n.a.

Source Banco Central do Basil (2017), except investment rate, Gini index and poverty index (IPEADATA), manufacturing import coefficient and manufacturing sector as share of GDP (CEMACRO), terms of trade (FUNCEX) and Wage share (authors' calculation based on IBGE)

Notes (1) For 2016, IMF estimates; (2) Yearly average, June 1994 = 100; (3) Ratio "total value of imports industrial sector" over "total value of domestic output of industrial sector" over "total value of domestic output of indutrial sector"; (4) "Net external liability" refers to the "Net international investment position"; (5) Ratio "Gross External Financing Needs (GEFN)" over "External Reserves", where GEFN = current account + short term external debt + long term external debt repayment in the next 12 months; (6) Ratio "GEFN + portfolio investment in the country" over "External Reserves" (7) Data according to new metodology implemented in 2006; (8) Salary mass (deflated by INPC) divided by GDP (deflated by the implicit deflator)

References

Afonso, J. R., & Fajardo, B. (2015, April). Evolução da taxa de investimentos e a indução pelo setor público. *Nota técnica IBRE/FGV*, Rio de Janeiro.

Almeida, J. S., & Novais, L. F. (2014). Indústria e política industrial no contexto pós-crise. In L. F. Novais et al. (Eds.), *A Economia Brasileira no Contexto da Crise Global*. FUNDAP: São Paulo.

Balbim, R. (2105). Para além do Minha Casa Minha Vida: Uma política de habitação de interesse social? IPEA, *Texto para Discussao* 2116.

Ban, C. (2012). Brazil's liberal neo-developmentalism: New paradigm or edited orthodoxy? *Review of International Political Economy, 20*(2), 298–331. http://dx.doi.org/10.1080/09692290.2012.660183.

Barbosa Filho, F. H. F., & Pessoa, S. (2014). Desaceleração recente da economia. In CDPP [Centro de Debate de Políticas Públicas] (Ed.), *Sob a Luz do Sol: uma agenda para o Brasil* (pp. 15–30).

Barbosa, N. (2010). Latin America: Counter-cyclical policy in Brazil: 2008–09. *Journal of Globalization and Development, 1*(1), 1–12.

Bastos, P. P. (2012). A economia política do novo-desenvolvimentismo e do social desenvolvimentismo. *Economia e Sociedade 21*, special issue, 779–810.

Bastos, P. P. (2015). *Austeridade para quem? A crise global do capitalismo neoliberal e as alternativas no Brasil* (p. 257). Texto para Discussao: Instituto de Economia da UNICAMP.

Bielschowsky, R. (2012). Estratégia de desenvolvimento e as três frentes de expansão no Brasil. *Economia e Sociedade 21*, special Issue, 729–748.

Bielschowsky, R. (2015). Structuralist reflections on current Latin American development. In B. Fritz & L. Lavinas (Eds.), *A moment of equality for Latin America? Challenges and limits for redistributive policies* (pp. 129–144). Burlington: Ashgate.

Blanchard, O., Dell' Ariccia, G., & Mauru, P. (2010). Rethinking macroeconomic policy. *IMF Staff Position Note* SPN/10/03.

Bresser-Pereira, L. C. (2011). From old to new developmentalism in Latin America. In J. A. Ocampo & J. Ros (Eds.), *The Oxford handbook of Latin American economics* (pp. 108–130). Oxford: Oxford University Press.

Bresser-Pereira, L. C. (2015). Reflecting on new developmentalism and classical developmentalism. FGV São Paulo, *Working Paper* 395.

Canuto, O., & Leipziger, D. M. (Eds.). (2012). *Ascent after decline: Regrowing global economies after The Great Recession*. Washington, DC: World Bank.

Carneiro, R. M. (2012). Velhos e novos desenvolvimentismos. *Economia e Sociedade 21*, special issue, 749–778.
Central Bank of Brazil (2016). Accessed October 3, 2016, from http://www.bcb.gov.br/pt-br/#!/n/SERIESTEMPORAIS.
Central Bank of Brazil. (2017). Accessed February 21, 2017, from http://www.bcb.gov.br/?serietemp.
Fonseca, P. D. (2014). Desenvolvimentismo: a construção do conceito. In A. Calixtre, A. Biancarelli, & M. A. Cintra (Eds.), *Presente e Futuro do Desenvolvimento Brasileiro* (pp. 29–78). IPEA: Brasilia.
Fritz, B., Paula, L. F., & Prates, D. (2017). Developmentalism at the periphery: Can productive change and income redistribution be compatible with global financial asymmetries? *desiguALdades Working Paper* No. 101.
Fritz, B., & Lavinas, L. (Eds.). (2015). *A moment of equality for Latin America? Challenges and limits for redistributive policies*. Burlington: Ashgate.
Gobetti, S. W., & Orair, R. (2015). Progressividade Tributária: a agenda esquecida. Concurso de Monografia em Finanças Públicas, Tema 3—Tópicos especiais.
IBGE. (2016). Accessed February 2, 2016, from http://www.ibge.gov.br/home/mapa_site/mapa_site.php#indicadores.
IMF. (2017). *World economic outlook database*. Washington, DC: International Monetary Fund.
IPEADATA. (2016). Accessed October 4, 2016, from http://www.ipeadata.gov.br.
Kupfer, D. (2013). Dez anos de política industrial, *Valor,* July 8, 2013.
Lustig, N., C. Pessino, J., & Scott. (2014). The impact of taxes and social spending on inequality and poverty in Argentina, Bolivia, Brazil, Mexico, Peru, and Uruguay. *Introduction to the Special Issue Public Finance Review, 42,* 287–303.
Ocampo, J. A. (2012). The case for and experience with capital account regulations. In K. P. Gallagher, S. Griffith-Jones, & J. A. Ocampo (Eds.), *Regulating global capital flows for long-run development* (pp. 13–22). Boston, MA: Pardee Center Task Force Report.
Ocampo, J. A. (2001). Raúl Prebisch and the development agenda at the dawn of the twenty-first century. *CEPAL Review, 75*(1), 25–40.
Paula, L. F., Fritz, B., & Prates, D. M. (2017). Keynes at the periphery: Currency hierarchy and challenges for economic policy in emerging economies, *Journal of Post Keynesian Economics, 40*(2), 183–202.

Paula, L. F., & Prates, D. M. (2015). Cuenta de capitales y la regulación de derivados del mercado de divisas: la experiencia reciente de Brasil. *Investigación Económica, LXXIV*(291), 79–115.

Paula, L. F., Modenesi, A. M., & Pires, M. C. (2015). The tale of the contagion of two crises and policy responses in Brazil: A case of (Keynesian) policy coordination? *Journal of Post Keynesian Economics, 37*(3), 408–435.

Prates, D. M., & Fritz, B. (2016). Beyond capital controls: Regulation of foreign currency derivatives markets in the Republic of Korea and Brazil after the global financial crisis. *Revista de la CEPAL, 118,* 193–213.

Prebisch, R. (1950). *The economic development of Latin America and its principal problems.* New York: United Nations Department of Economic Affairs/ mimeo.

Rosa, R. S., & Biancarelli, A. M. (2016). Determinantes do processo de "desdolarização"do passivo externo brasileiro. Proccedings of 44° National Meeting of Anpec.

Rossi, P. (2014). Regime macroeconômico e o projeto social-desenvolvimentista. In A. Calixtre, A. Biancarelli & M. A. M. Cintra (Eds.), *Presente e Futuro do Desenvolvimento Brasileiro* (pp. 195–226). Brasilia: IPEA.

Monetary Institutions and Macroeconomic Performance in Brazil after the Global Financial Crisis of 2007–2008

Eliane Araújo, Elisangela Araújo and Fernando Ferrari Filho

1 Introduction

The Global Financial Crisis (GFC) that hit the world economy in the last quarter of 2008 had several economic consequences for the world economy, and in particular for Brazil, where it accounted for the exhaustion of the growth cycle that had begun around 2003. More specifically, from 2003 until the GFC, the country had experienced a unique moment in its recent trajectory of development: the Gross

E. Araújo (✉)
University of Maringá and CNPq, Maringá, Paraná, Brazil
e-mail: elianedearaujo@gmail.com

E. Araújo
University of Maringá, Maringá, Paraná, Brazil
e-mail: elaraujo@uem.br

F. Ferrari Filho
Federal University of Rio Grande Do Sul and CNPq, Porto Alegre, RS, Brazil
e-mail: ferrari@ppge.ufrgs.br; ferrari@ufrgs.br

P. Arestis et al. (eds.), *The Brazilian Economy since the Great Financial Crisis of 2007/2008*, https://doi.org/10.1007/978-3-319-64885-9_3

Domestic Product (GDP) registered an average growth of 4.8% per year between 2004 and 2008, the unemployment rate fell to historically low levels, inflation was low, and several economic and social indicators improved.

For some authors (Baer 2013; Bielschovisky 2012), the country had the conditions to lead a strategy of sustained growth from the opportunities and changes created during that period, and, from there, to consolidate itself as an emerging power in the global scenario. However, the advent of the GFC, demonstrated that such beliefs were based on a largely optimistic, yet mistaken analysis, mainly because the foundations that sustained the growth in the previous period were fragile and that the Brazilian economy had not managed to overcome serious structural obstacles.

It should be noted that, despite relatively favourable developments in the immediate post-crisis period—in 2009 the GDP fell modestly by 0.2% and in 2010 it increased by 7.6%—the performance of the Brazilian economy in subsequent years proved extremely disappointing, passing first through a period of semi-stagnation (1.8 and 2.7% in 2011 and 2012), then into a deep recession (−3.8% in 2015 and −3.6% in 2016). Not only were GDP growth rates negative in this last period, but inflation continued its upward trajectory, unemployment returned to the high levels seen in the 1990s, and the public accounts were becoming extremely unfavourable.

Although the causes of this poor performance are varied and complex, one aspect that draws attention is that the monetary institutions in the country, embodied in the Inflation Targeting Regime (ITR) and its management, have a central role in explaining the recent trajectory, particularly after the GFC. In fact, by using the basic interest rate (Selic) as the main tool to combat inflation, this policy implies large costs for the economy, the most evident being: (i) the discouragement of private investment; (ii) the carry trade operations, which create the tendency to appreciate the domestic currency (*real*), which, in turn, negatively affects the current account balance of payments; and (iii) the increase in the level of public indebtedness, given the increased expenditures on interest payments on domestic debt.

In view of the above discussion, the purpose of this chapter is to study the relationship between monetary institutions and the macroeconomic performance in Brazil. The hypothesis is that these institutions played a central role in explaining the poor economic performance, but they were not efficient to bring the inflation rates below the target, whose causes are predominantly structural and institutional, and not only linked to excess demand as assumed by the ITR. The methodology employed consists of a theoretical analysis and an empirical investigation using an estimated Vector Autoregression (VAR) model. The idea is to understand how monetary institutions impacted important variables, namely inflation, GDP, exchange rate and public debt.

This chapter is structured as follows. Section 2 gives a brief theoretical discussion on the ITR, providing details of the Brazilian experience. Section 3 discusses the determinants of inflation in Brazil, as well as analyses the imbalances arising from the implementation of the ITR. Section 4 presents the results of the estimated VAR model, which shows that the restrictive monetary policy, on the one hand, was not successful in maintaining a low inflation rate and below its targets; and, on the other hand, affected negatively several macroeconomic variables. Finally, the last section summarizes and concludes.

2 The Brazilian Central Bank (BCB) Macroeconomic Model of ITR and the Brazilian Experience with ITR

As is known, monetary stability has long been a major concern in the Brazilian economy, which over the last decades has promoted a series of institutional changes with the objective of achieving stability. To this end, after the high and chronic inflation period, caused by the external debt crisis and the economic stagnation of the 1980s, the economy entered a new standard of development and international insertion, in the 1990s, based on the principles established by the Washington Consensus—trade and financial liberalization, deregulation, privatization of state-owned enterprises, and fiscal discipline, among others—which have decisively influenced the performance of the economy since then (Ferrari Filho and Paula 2003).

Within the scope of institutions for monetary stability, as part of the introduced changes, the Real Plan (RP) was adopted in 1994, which had the exchange rate anchor and high interest rate as its main instruments of stabilization. The high interest rate differential, in addition to contributing to financing the balance of payments, prevented further pressure on domestic demand, actions that ultimately kept inflation under control (Bacha 1995). It is worth noting that the strategy led to a very low average growth rate in that decade of 1.6% per year. Because of this, throughout the 1990s the 'second lost decade', in reference to the 1980s, emerged, which was the first turbulent period.

Then in 1999, a major institutional change took place, the introduction of the ITR, a result of the change in the exchange rate regime, which has been floating ever since. Despite the change in the monetary regime, the rationale for conducting monetary policy did not, in essence, change. Monetary policy remains highly restrictive and the exchange rate continues to be one of the main transmission mechanisms of monetary policy.

According to the New Consensus Macroeconomics (NCM), the ITR is seen as 'state-of-the-art' and posits that the inflation rate should be low and stable for long-term growth. Supported in the theoretical and empirical elements of various stands of thought, notably in the new classical economics, which includes the hypothesis of rational expectations, the temporal inconsistency of monetary policy and the inflation bias, the NCM implicitly brings out old ideas in macroeconomics, such as the existence of a natural rate of unemployment and the neutrality of currency in the long run (but not in the short run, due to the rigidity of prices and wages, as the new-Keynesians suggest).

The NCM model is characterized by three equations, as follows: Eq. (1), representing the demand side; the inertia-augmented Phillips curve (PC), in Eqs. (2) and (3) is the monetary policy rule (MPR), derived from the independent central bank's loss function (Fontana 2009; Arestis and Sawyer 2008). Analytically:

$$Y = C_0 + c_y(1 - t_y)Y + A - ar + g + NX(er), \tag{1}$$

where Y is GDP, C_0 autonomous consumption, c_y is the marginal propensity to consume, t_y is taxation, A is exogenous investment, a is a constant, r is the real interest rate, g is the government spending, NX is net export and er is the nominal exchange rate;

$$\pi = \pi_{-1} + \alpha\left(Y - Y^e\right), \tag{2}$$

where π is the inflation rate, π_{-1} is the previous inflation, α is a constant and Y^e is the potential GDP;

$$i = \alpha\left(\pi_{-1} - \pi^*\right) + \beta\left(Y - Y^e\right) + \mu. \tag{3}$$

where i is the nominal interest rate, π_{-1} is the inflation rate in the previous period, π^* is the inflation target, $Y - Y^e$ is the output gap and μ is a random shock.[1]

Regarding the Brazilian experience, the monetary authorities have adopted the NCM model since 1999, characterized by the ITR, a target for primary fiscal budget as a share of GDP and a floating exchange rate regime. Focusing our attention on monetary policy, the BCB has religiously followed the theoretical framework that underpins the ITR strategy. According to Arestis et al. (2011), the main theoretical features of the BCB macroeconomic model, closely based on the NCM model, can be summarized as follows:

1. Price stability is monetary policy's primary long-term objective. In addition, the price stability goal may be accompanied by output stabilization so long as price stability is not violated;
2. ITR is a monetary policy framework whereby public announcement of official inflation targets is required. In this approach, 'expected inflation' and the transparency of inflation forecasts are important elements of the policy;
3. Monetary policy is the main instrument of macroeconomic policy, and it should be operated by the 'independent' central bank;

[1]These equations are based on Carlin and Soskice (2006).

4. Fiscal policy is no longer viewed as a powerful macroeconomic instrument for stabilizing the economy. Hence, the economic authorities should adopt a fiscal target in terms of primary budget surplus;
5. The level of economic activity fluctuates around a supply-side equilibrium. This means that the level of effective demand does not play an independent role in the long-run level of economic activity;
6. Finally, considering that Brazil is an open economy and has a long history of external imbalances and crises, the exchange rate is of crucial importance because it transmits certain external effects to the inflation rate, among others.

The Brazilian National Monetary Council (CMN) sets the inflation targets. Besides the inflation target, CMN is also responsible for the approval of the main norms regarding monetary and exchange rate policies, as well as the regulation of the financial system. The interest rate is set by the Monetary Policy Committee (COPOM) based on the Selic, an interest rate for overnight interbank loans, collateralized by those public debt bonds. The interest rate is fixed for the period between the COPOM regular meetings.

Another feature of the ITR in Brazil is that the price index considered by the BCB when setting the inflation target is the Broad Consumer Price Index (IPCA).[2] Since 2005, the desired target has been 4.5% per year, with lower and upper limits of 2.5 and 6.5% per year, which must be achieved within the calendar year. Moreover, the Selic interest rate, managed by the monetary authorities, is also the rate, which influences significantly the public debt bond rate, so that these markets are linked.

Table 1, below, shows the point targets, the tolerance intervals, the inflation rate measure by the IPCA, the nominal and real Selic rates and the annual growth rates for 1999–2016.

---

[2]The IPCA is checked by the IBGE (2017a) through a monthly survey covering families with incomes between one and forty minimum salaries, in various metropolitan regions of Brazil. Since 2012, the percentage weight of the groups of items that make up the IPCA is as follows: Food and beverage = 23.12%; Transport = 20.54%; Housing = 14.62%; Health and personal care = 11.09%; Personal expenses = 9.94%; Clothing = 6.67%; Communication = 4.96%; Household items = 4.69%; and Education = 4.37%.

Table 1 Inflation targets and inflation rates (IPCA), selic and growth rates, %: 1999–2016

Year	Point targets	Tolerance intervals	Inflation rate (IPCA)	Annual interest rate (Selic)[1]	Annual real interest rate[2]	Annual growth rate
1999	8	6–10	8.94	19.0	9.2	0.3
2000	6	4–8	5.97	15.75	9.2	4.3
2001	4	2–6	7.67	19.0	8.5	1.3
2002	3.5	1.5–6.5	12.53	25.0	11.1	3.1
2003	4	1.5–6.5	9.3	16.5	6.6	1.3
2004[3]	5.5	3.5–8	7.6	17.75	9.4	5.7
2005	4.5	2.5–7.5	5.69	18.0	11.6	3.1
2006	4.5	2.5–7.5	3.14	13.25	9.8	4.0
2007	4.5	2.5–6.5	4.46	11.25	6.5	6.0
2008	4.5	2.5–6.5	5.9	13.75	7.4	5.0
2009	4.5	2.5–6.5	4.31	8.75	4.3	−0.2
2010	4.5	2.5–6.5	5.91	10.75	4.6	7.6
2011	4.5	2.5–6.5	6.5	11.0	4.2	3.9
2012	4.5	2.5–6.5	5.84	7.25	1.3	1.8
2013	4.5	2.5–6.5	5.91	10.0	3.9	2.7
2014	4.5	2.5–6.5	6.41	11.75	5.0	0.1
2015	4.5	2.5–6.5	10.67	14.25	3.2	−3.8
2016	4.5	2.5–6.5	6.3	13.75	7.0	−3.6[4]

Source Author's elaboration based on BCB (2017a).
Note (1) End of period; (2) Annual Interest Rate (Selic)/IPCA; (3) The original inflation target for 2004 was 3.75%. Subsequently, the BCB changed the inflation target; and (4) Preliminary result

By examining Table 1, the following should be highlighted: (i) over this period, the tolerance intervals were missed for the years 2001, 2002, 2003 and 2015 by a substantial margin, especially in 2002 and 2015, while in 2004 the inflation target was only met after it was raised by mid-2003; (ii) the inflation rates were above the point targets in nine years (1999, 2004–2005, 2008, and 2010–2015); and (iii) from 1999 to 2016, monetary policy (nominal and real) has been characteristically tight, placing Brazil in the ranking of countries with the highest interest rates in the world, with significant effects on domestic performance.

It may thus be concluded that the ITR in Brazil was not completely successful over the seventeen years of its implementation, mainly because it has not been effective in maintaining a low and stable inflation during the entire period. Moreover, it is possible to observe, based on Table 1 that the relationship between monetary policy, mainly the Selic interest rate, and inflation is not direct. That is, despite the fact that price stability has required an excessively rigid monetary policy, this relationship is, at most, weak. There is also some evidence that high interest rates may cause weak economic activity, mainly because from 1999 to 2016 GDP followed a stop-and-go pattern and its average growth rate hovered around 2.7% per year, significantly below the average growth rate of other emerging countries that have adopted an ITR (Arestis et al. 2011; Ferrari Filho and Schifino 2010).

3 The Determinants of Inflation in Brazil and the Macroeconomic Imbalances Under the ITR (1999–2016)

A Brief Analysis on the Determinants of Inflation

Arestis et al. (2011) show that the determinants of inflation in Brazil are, partially, excess demand and, mainly, supply side shocks and institutional factors, such as the indexation system.

In terms of the supply side, as Fig. 1 shows, the exchange rate is one of these determinants. Domestic currency depreciation has a negative impact on tradable goods (and vice versa)[3] changing the cost of raw materials and basic inputs important to the domestic production chain, as well as the price of various final consumer goods.

In turn, indexation is still an important component of the Brazilian inflation. In general, some prices, such as services of public utility (telecommunications and electric energy) and health plans, are controlled

[3]The importance of the exchange rate in determining prices in Brazil has been studied by several authors, such as Belaisch (2003), Minella et al. (2003), Carneiro et al. (2006) and Minella and Correia (2005). When faced with an increase (reduction) in the interest rate, variations in the inflow (outflow) of foreign capital occur, causing a depreciation (appreciation) of the domestic currency. In addition to the direct effects on the price of tradable goods, there is also the indirect effects on domestic prices in the form of variations in the cost of imported raw materials and inputs, as well as the substitution effect of imported products for similar domestic ones, or vice versa.

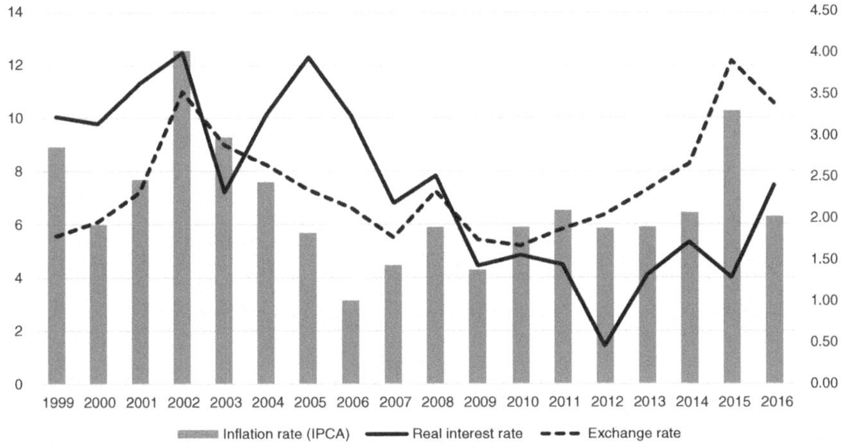

Fig. 1 Exchange rate (R$/US$), inflation (IPCA) and real interest rates, Brazil, 1999–2016. *Source* BCB (2017a) and IBGE (2017b) Authors' own elaboration

and adjusted by the government, according to past inflation, reproducing thus, an inflationary inertia.

An analysis of Fig. 2 shows a better understanding of the prices of the different goods, free (tradable and non-tradable) and monitored goods, which have influenced the behaviour of inflation in Brazil.

Based on Fig. 2, it can be observed that, in the immediate post-crisis period, even with the fall in international commodity prices, the recovery of economic growth pushed up the cost of services, which had already been increasing since 2006, due to domestic policies designed to stimulate aggregate demand. Added to the effects of the currency depreciation that occurred in that period, inflation increased in 2008. In the subsequent two years, given the depressive effects of the IFC, inflation stayed within the target, registering 4.6% in 2009 and 5.7% in 2010. It should be noted that the increase seen in 2010 was due to an unfavourable increase in food prices and to the rise in international prices for the main agricultural and metal commodities (IBGE 2017b).

In 2011 and 2012, the prices of tradable goods presented an upward trajectory, given the continued depreciation of the currency. Likewise, non-tradable goods, such as services, were also sources of inflationary pressure. On the other hand, prices of monitored goods showed a

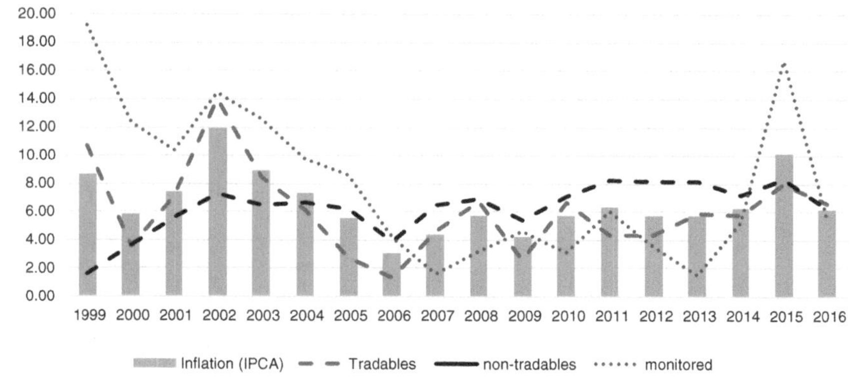

Fig. 2 Variation in inflation (IPCA), and in tradable, non-tradable and monitored goods, Brazil, 1999–2016. *Source* IBGE (2017b) Authors' own elaboration

strong reduction, varying between 6.32 and 5.69%, respectively in those years, a fact that helped inflation stay within its target ceiling.

After 2013 until 2015, the economic situation in Brazil changed, showing a new rise in inflation explained by the trend in prices of tradable and non-tradable goods and especially of monitored goods as part of the government's strategies to adjust the results of the public accounts.

Finally, in 2016, there was a slowdown in inflation, which was once again within the upper limit of the target. The effects of the severe economic crisis, affecting the country since 2014, contributed to the reversal of the increasing trend in prices of tradable and non-tradable goods, which, together with the favourable trend in prices of monitored goods, resulted in the observed fall.

In addition to the influence of the exchange rate and the monitored prices, another source of inflationary pressure comes from the behaviour of agricultural crops. This is because the composition of the IPCA[4] is strongly influenced by the price trend of primary products. Indeed, the rise in food prices was one of the principal sources of pressure on domestic inflation between 2011 and 2015 (IBGE 2017b).

[4]The composition of the Extended National Consumer Price Index (IPCA) is as follows: food and beverages (23.12%), transport (20.54%), housing (14.62%), health and personal care (11.09%), personal expenses (9.94%), clothing (6.67%), communication (4.96%), household goods (4.69%), and education (4.37%).

On the demand side, an important source of pressure was brought on by the behaviour of the prices of non-tradable goods, particularly services. These goods, from 2006 to around 2014, showed an upward trajectory, explained by the increase in domestic income and implied by the increased demand for these goods. The higher demand, together with factors such as low productivity and insufficient investments, both public and private, pushed prices upwards (Ferreira and Azzoni 2011).

In short, the behaviour of inflation has shown to be influenced very little by demand, while being quite dependent on the supply-side conditions and indexation. However, the use of Selic to control inflation brings serious imbalances, including an increase in public debt and the deterioration of the current account balance of payments, as will be discussed next.

The Macroeconomic Imbalances Resulting from the Implementation of the ITR

To understand fiscal imbalances caused by ITR, it is important to mention that in Brazil there is a specific link between the money market and public debt, since the National Treasury (NT) is responsible for issuing public debt bonds that are indexed to the Selic interest rate, the so-called Financial Treasury Bills (LTFs in the Portuguese acronym), and to certain price indexes, such as IPCA.[5]

Thus, every time the Selic rate rises to keep inflation under control, there is a contagious effect on the public debt. This effect not only increases spending on interest payments (see footnote 5), but also has implications on its growth, since a share of the federal security debt is tied to Selic. As a result, since the debt stock has reached sufficiently high levels, further increases in interest are required as a risk premium, increasing the fiscal fragility of the Brazilian economy even more.

[5]According to the NT data, with reference to December 2016, the Brazilian public debt totalled around 70.5% of GDP. The configuration of the public debt bonds was as follows: pre-fixed interest rate, which includes Selic, was around 35.7%, price index was approximately 31.8%, floating interest rates were around 28.2% and 4.2% was indexed at the exchange rate (Tesouro Nacional 2017).

Table 2 Indicators of net public debt in Brazil, 1999–2016

Year	Primary result	Nominal result	Net public debt
1999	3.19	−5.78	35.10
2000	3.46	−3.61	36.50
2001	3.64	−3.57	42.40
2002	3.22	−4.58	44.70
2003	3.39	−5.42	43.30
2004	3.50	−3.61	42.63
2005	3.90	−3.10	43.13
2006	3.29	−3.78	46.30
2007	3.36	−2.84	50.15
2008	3.63	−2.08	49.76
2009	1.89	−3.19	48.95
2010	2.20	−2.82	48.06
2011	3.08	−2.24	47.16
2012	2.52	−2.40	46.18
2013	1.76	−2.70	44.55
2014	0.94	−3.82	44.67
2015	−0.79	−8.23	54,80
2016	−2.48	−8.95	61,30

Source Author's elaboration based on BCB (2017a)

Some indicators of fiscal policy for the period 1999–2016 are presented in Table 2, which shows the primary result (total revenue minus total expenditure), the nominal result (the total government deficit, including interest and the monetary adjustment of the public debt), and the net debt of the public sector, as a percentage of GDP.

As can be seen in Tables 1 and 2, during specific years, there is a close relationship between the public debt and Selic, growing in times when the interest rates remained at high levels, and vice versa. The first column of this Table shows the evolution of the primary result of the public sector. This result shows the amount of saving the government needs to have to meet the debt service and maintain its relatively stable trajectory. It is found that, in moments when interest rates are high, even high primary surpluses cannot stop the growth in debt.

Note also that, in 2015 and 2016, primary surpluses were converted into deficits and the total deficits reached 8.23 and 8.95% of the GDP, impacting the strong expansion of the stock of public debt which reached, respectively, 54.8 and 61.3% of the GDP in 2015 and in 2016.

Among the main explanatory factors of this fiscal deterioration are as follows: (i) the low growth of the Brazilian economy since 2011, which reduced revenues; (ii) the strong increase in interest rates between 2012 and 2016; (iii) the exchange rate depreciation; and (iv) the increase in inflation.

Given the pressure exerted on the public accounts, a strong fiscal adjustment began in 2015,[6] which left the Brazilian economy in an even more dramatic situation, resulting in a drop of 3.8% in the GDP that year and then −3.6% in 2016.

Regarding the imbalances that the ITR implies in the external sector, a key aspect to highlight is the effects of internal-external interest rate differentials on the level of the exchange rate, which maintained a steady appreciation trajectory, notably between 2003 and 2010. As a result of the *real* appreciation, the Brazilian economy showed: (i) a severe deterioration of the current account balance of payments; (ii) a change in the trade balance composition, which became highly dependent on primary products; and (iii) a sharp drop in the relative share of the manufacturing industry in GDP. According to Fig. 3, it can be observed that the currency appreciation in real terms (a fall in the real exchange rate) was accompanied by a worsening of the current account balance of payments, notably between 2003 and 2010.

It is important to mention that, according to the Minister of Industrial Development and External Trade (MDIC 2016), Brazil exports have concentrated on commodities and lower value-added goods in the 2000s. As is known, the dependence of the trade balance on the price trajectory of primary commodities and low-tech products is a problem; this is so because these are products whose prices and export volume are more sensitive to changes in the international environment.

Finally, with regard to the negative effects on the manufacturing industry, it is important to consider the exchange rate appreciation, that

---

[6]Under the command of the then Finance Minister, a strong fiscal adjustment was implemented in order to achieve a primary surplus target of 1.2% of the GDP, equivalent to R$66.3 billion. This would come from reducing spending (a cut in the budget of various ministries, changes in the labour and social security legislation, the end of exemptions in segments, such as the exporter, and late payments) and increasing revenue (a rise in the taxes of various products and services, such as gasoline and electricity). Due to the deterioration in economic performance and after a number of revisions throughout the year, a surplus of around 0.8% of the GDP, around R$51.8 billion was achieved in 2015.

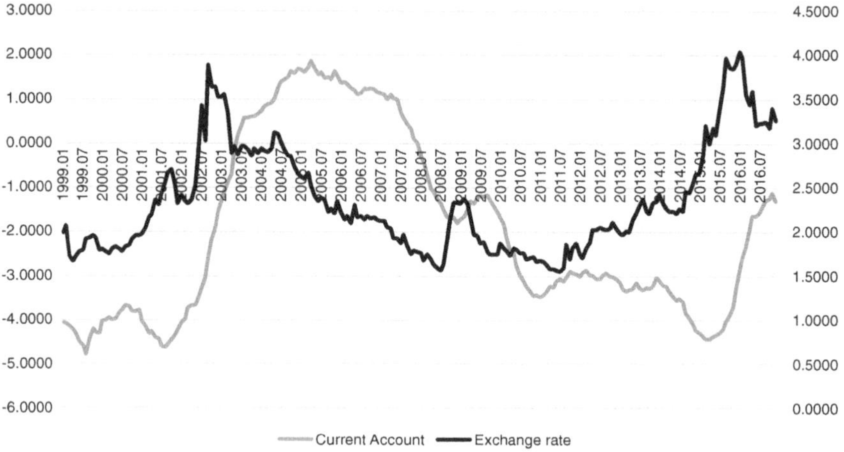

).

Fig. 3 Current account balance of payments (% of GDP) and exchange rate, 1999–2016. *Source* BCB (2017b). Authors' own elaboration. *Note* Current account balance of payments on the right axis

began in 1994, which was associated with a structural change in the composition of national production, resulting in an extreme loss of the industry's share in the total economy.

This significant decrease in the relative share of the industry in GDP indicates the occurrence of a possible process of relative deindustrialization in the period after the liberalization of trade and after the RP. This fact has been a major criticism of the model adopted by the Brazilian economy in the 1990s.[7]

4 Empirical Research on the Effects of Monetary Shocks in Brazil

As discussed in the previous section, the Brazilian economy has shown low and volatile growth rates, inflation above the target, and an imbalance in the external sector, as well as fiscal deterioration.

[7]For evidence on the de-industrialization in Brazil, see Oreiro and Feijó (2010) and Nassif et al. (2015).

With the aim of deepening this discussion, this section tests the hypothesis that monetary institutions played a central role in this process, especially after the adoption of the ITR in 1999. As already stated, after the adoption of the ITR, increasing the Selic rate became the main tool to fight inflation, having, however, considerable negative effects on the economy.

Hence, what we seek to investigate is how monetary shocks, represented by changes in the Selic rate, affected the variables central to the economic performance in Brazil. Specifically, the intention is to measure the effects of a rise in the Selic rate on prices, which is the main objective of monetary policy, and its adverse effects on the GDP growth rate, the appreciation of the domestic currency, and the trajectory of spending on the public debt service.

As discussed in Sect. 2, in the monetary policy of the NCM, following the so-called Taylor's rule, the BCB reacts to inflation and output levels in determining the Selic. Moreover, it is reasonable to consider that the reaction function of the BCB can be amplified by the inclusion of the exchange rate and the debt/GDP ratio. The exchange rate has been included by different authors in the estimations of this type of function, considering the importance of the exchange as a transmission mechanism of the monetary policy. Regarding the inclusion of the debt/GDP variable, authors such as Dornbush (1998) and Bell-Keaton and Ballinger (2005) emphasize that public debt management can jeopardize the effectiveness of monetary policy. Thus the equation here estimated follows:

$$i_t = a_0 + a_1 i_p + a_2 y_p + a_3 \pi_p + a_4 debt_p + a_5 er_p, \quad (4)$$

where i is the interest rate (Effective Selic, annualized), π is inflation (IPCA), y is the physical production index (*quantum*) of general industry (seasonally adjusted), *debt* is the internal federal security debt as a proportion of GDP, *er* is the nominal exchange rate and p is the lag.

The methodology employed is the VAR,[8] which is used to capture the effects of the monetary shocks in the economy. The i (Selic rate) is provided by the BCB (2017a), the *er* is obtained in IPEADATA (2017),

[8]Details for the VAR methodology can be found in Hamilton (1994).

the industrial production index, the GDP and the IPCA are calculated by IBGE, and the stock of internal federal security debt is provided by the Tesouro Nacional (2017). The debt/GDP ratio was calculated by the authors and all the variables are used in logarithmic scale.

It is important to mention that the individual VAR coefficients are very difficult to interpret. One of the problems is the fact that the VAR process analysis generally focuses on the total effect of variation on a given variable. Thus, any individual coefficient captures only a part of the relevant effect; that is, it captures the effect of a single offset value of a specific variable in another variable while keeping the remaining variables constant. The difficulties in interpreting the VAR have meant that few attempts have been made to interpret the coefficients themselves. Instead, response impulse functions have been used which show how endogenous variables react over time to a shock at a single point in time in one of the error terms of the function.

The period under analysis begins in January 2002 and ends in December 2016. The aim is to capture the period from the beginning of the ITR implementation, that is, June 1999. However, due to the fact that the industrial production series used started only in 2002, the period could not be altered.

The estimated VAR model is undertaken with the difference of the logarithm of the series—a concept equivalent to the growth rate—to analyze the dynamic interactions between the variables in which the Selic is the variable representing the monetary policy; the industrial production index represents the economic activity,[9] *er* reveals the changes in the Brazilian exchange rate against its main trading partners, and Debt is the fiscal policy variable.[10]

As is known, the estimation of VAR with only lagged variables does not allow the identification of exogenous shocks in the model's variables

[9]The reason for using this proxy is because there are no data on the monthly GDP in Brazil. Thus, the series that is given is, in fact, an interpolation of the quarterly GDP. Moreover, the choice of the industry's GDP as a proxy for the total GDP of the economy is justified by the fact that the behaviour of these variables is quite similar, even if the industry's GDP represents less than 30.0% of Brazilian GDP.

[10]The choice of the VAR model is justified by the fact that all series used are I(1), but do not have a cointegration relationship.

without making hypotheses about the contemporary relationships between them. Thus, the model uses the Cholesky identification and the structural VAR as a tool to identify the effects of monetary shocks on the model's variables.[11] In the first method, the order was as follows: y, IPCA, Selic, REER and Debt. In the second, only the contemporary relationships of the Selic and the IPCA in public debt were maintained, given the indexing. Regarding the other possible contemporary relationships, it is believed that, with monthly data, they are quite remote.

The results of a monetary policy shock can be seen in Fig. 4 and in Fig. 5, where the accumulated results are presented.

As for the effects of a rise in interest rates on industrial production, used here as a proxy for GDP, there is a clearly negative effect that is felt from the third month on and is reversed only after twelve months. The explanation for this is that an increase in interest rates discourages private investments, cools the economy and implies lower rates of economic growth.

As the series are stationary, the effects of a shock in the Selic on the industrial production start to dissipate after one year (Fig. 4). But when the shocks are accumulated (Fig. 5), the sum of the effects is clearly negative, so that a positive shock in interest rates leads to lower economic performance, represented here by the fall in the growth rates of industrial production.

Concerning the effects of a rise of the Selic on inflation, the actual inflation converges towards the long-term inflation target. Exploring this result, some authors, who have analysed the effect of interest on prices in Brazil, have found the initial impact positive (Modenesi and Araújo 2013; Luporini 2008). Although the mainstream authors (Christiano et al. 1996; Sims 1992) stress the occurrence of this unexpected effect as problems in the functional specification of the BCB's reaction function, especially due to the omission of variables, others (Palley 1996) justify this by the rise in production

[11]The results of these two methodologies and the behavioural patterns are very similar to the relationship between the variables studied. However, we present the results of the structural VAR because the order of the variables in the model is determined according to economic theory and does not follow a strict ordering as in Cholesky's ordering.

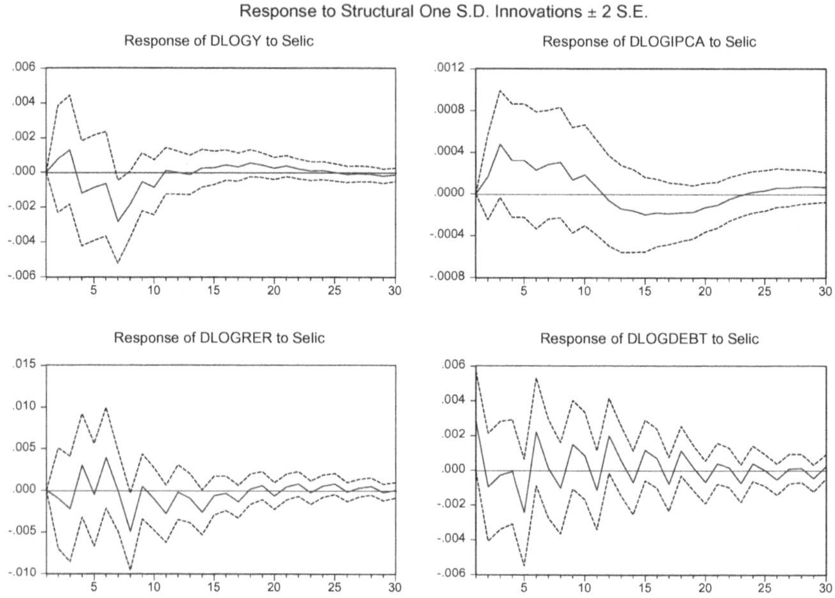

Fig. 4 Effects of monetary shocks. *Source* Author's elaboration based on data from BCB (2017a) and IPEADATA (2017)

costs resulting from an increase in interest rates, which are quickly transmitted to the prices, thus explaining the positive effects of an increase in interest rates on prices. However, after the first months, the increase in interest rates contributes to the reduction in inflation, as assumed by the ITR.

Considering the effects of a Selic rate rise on the exchange rate, in an environment where financial openness implied a renunciation of the management of the capital account and left the country subject to fluctuations in the capital flows, the rise in interest rates promotes capital inflow into the Brazilian economy. It also contributes to the *real* appreciation, making Brazilian products more expensive than external ones.

Figure 4 shows an initially negative response in the exchange rate when faced with an increase in the Selic rate, followed by cyclical movements in the exchange rate. The cumulative effect of a shock in the Selic

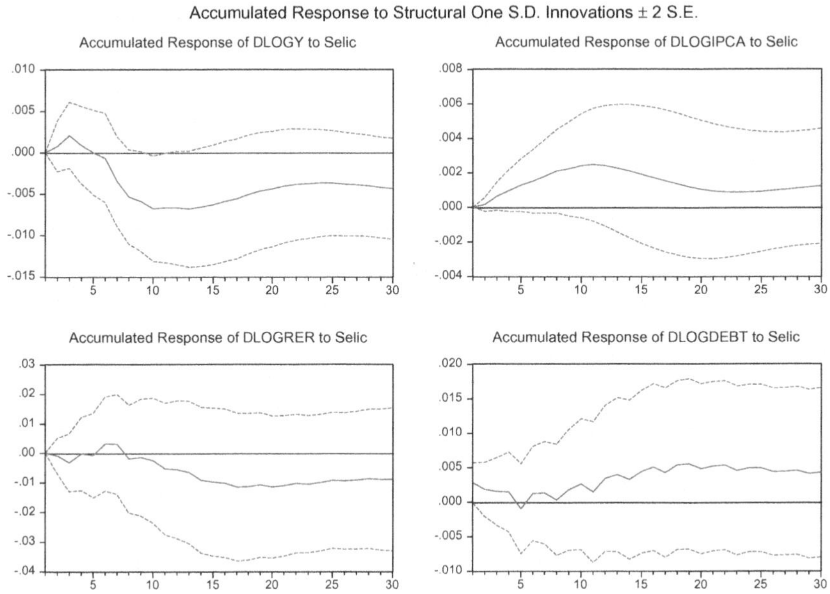

Fig. 5 Effects of cumulative monetary shocks. *Source* Author's elaboration based on data from BCB (2017a) and IPEADATA (2017)

on the exchange rate is negative, as shown in Fig. 5. Thus, increases in the Selic contribute to the *real* appreciation, a fact which can have important effects on the trajectory of growth, especially in emerging and developing economies, as many authors have pointed out.[12]

Finally, in relation to the effects of a monetary shock on the public debt, on the one hand, a rise in the Selic rate increases the payment of the debt interest indexed to it, implying the need to increase the primary surplus to keep the debt/GDP ratio. On the other hand, a rise in the Selic rate may imply a wealth effect in reverse. This is because, as public debt bonds are indexed to the Selic rate, a rise in interest rates

[12]In recent years, a number of authors have defended the importance of the exchange rate as a key variable in a long-term economic growth strategy. According to them, to make a range of products with higher value added and technological intensity, a competitive exchange rate can result in higher economic growth in the long run. See, for example, Rodrik (2008), Williamson (2003) and Bresser-Pereira et al. (2015).

increases the financial wealth of the agents holding these bonds, which may end up stimulating the consumption of this population.[13]

By analysing Figs. 4 and 5, the negative effects on the economy of a rise in interest rates on the debt ratio securities/GDP are observed: given an increase in the Selic rate, the public debt rises (Fig. 5), despite the cyclical results arising from a non-cumulative shock in the Selic rate (Fig. 4).

These results provide important insights for the analysis of the effects of monetary shocks in Brazil. For this reason, it is possible to highlight two central points: one concerns the functional problem of the transmission mechanisms of monetary policy and the other concerns the causes of inflation in Brazil; they together contribute to a reduced effectiveness of monetary policy.

Considering the first point, that is, the existence of failures in the functioning of the monetary policy transmission mechanism, several authors have pointed out that the existence of problems in these mechanisms, which implies the need for higher interest rates to contain rising prices.

The first problem, as already stated, is the significant share of public debt bonds indexed to the Selic rate in the federal security debt. Contrary to what advocates support in terms of the transmission mechanism of monetary policy via asset prices—according to which the increase in interest rates reduces the market price of securities and makes the holders of such assets poorer—in the case of the public debt bonds indexed to the Selic such mechanism is ineffective.[14]

Another problem that leads to the poor functioning of the transmission mechanisms of monetary policy arises from the structure and functioning of the Brazilian banking system. This is due to the obstruction of the interest rate channel and the credit channel. Regarding the obstruction of the interest rate channel, Carvalho (2005) stresses that the absence of longer segments of financing in the Brazilian credit

[13]Several authors such as Barbosa (2006), Carneiro et al. (2006) and Pires (2008) have analysed how the management of public debt in Brazil can undermine the effectiveness of monetary policy.

[14]Theoretical and empirical analyses on this subject concerning the Brazilian economy can be found in Pastore (2006) and Andrade and Pires (2009).

market, whose main focus is on short-term credit, implies that the stimuli generated by monetary policy are not transmitted to these segments, segments such as investment financing.

In relation to the transmission channel of monetary policy via credit, the empirical evidence demonstrates (Souza-Sobrinho 2003; Carneiro et al. 2006) that its effectiveness is questionable in Brazil.

Another aspect that limits the functioning of the transmission mechanism of monetary policy is the existence of regulated prices, which make changes in interest rates have limited effect on the drop in prices. Sicsú and Oliveira (2003), for example, suggest that regulated prices are rather insensitive to the conditions of supply and demand because they are established by contract or government agency and do not react to monetary policies. In Brazil, since approximately 28.0% of the IPCA consists of regulated prices, monetary policy needs to be even more contractionary to induce inflation to the stipulated target, considering that this portion of prices does not respond to changes in interest rates.

Finally, as to the monetary policy transmission mechanism, it is worth highlighting the importance of the exchange rate to affect the price levels in Brazil. Several authors, including Belaisch (2003), Carneiro et al. (2006) and Minella and Correia (2005), have, in fact, presented estimates of the exchange rate pass-through coefficient for the Brazilian economy. An increase or decrease in interest rates results in variations in foreign capital movements, causing currency depreciation when the capital inflow is reduced and an appreciation when the capital inflow is higher. This, in turn, significantly impacts the behaviour of inflation (Fig. 5).

From these direct and indirect ways, the end result of a variation in the exchange rate is expressed in the rate of inflation. In Brazil, between 2004 and 2008, for example, there was a tendency towards the domestic currency appreciation due to the carry trade operations and rising commodity exports, among other reasons. Although contributing to price control by means of an increase in competition with domestic products given the cheap imports, this appreciation proved harmful to some sectors of the economy as it increased external vulnerability, discouraged exports (mainly of manufacturing goods) and generated deficits in the trade balance and the current account balance of payments. The result was an increase in the fragility of the economy, which left the country susceptible to exchange rate crises.

From 2008 on, although reversing in some cases, the exchange rate followed a trajectory of depreciation, accompanied by a rise in the inflation rate. The evidence shows that the domestic currency appreciation contributes to a reduction in inflation, whereas the *real* depreciation has been accompanied by rises in the rate of inflation. This indicates that the exchange rate has been a central mechanism in the transmission of monetary policy in Brazil.

The conclusion regarding the transmission of monetary policy in Brazil is, therefore, that changes in monetary policy are not fully transmitted because of problems in the transmission mechanism of asset prices, interest rates and credit. This ends up making the monetary policy effects highly dependent on the exchange rate level.

Regarding the second point, that is, on the relevant causes of domestic inflation under the ITR, the basic assumption is that inflation is a phenomenon essentially monetary in nature. This considers only demand inflation, which should be cured by raising interest rates, the main instrument of monetary policy. In this light, the strictly non-monetary causes of inflation, such as changing expectations, an inertia phenomenon and a shock in costs, are neglected. This clearly seems to be the case of the Brazilian economy.

An alternative analysis of the causes of inflation, however, can be found in Lavoie (1992) and Davidson (1994). They offer a more comprehensive explanation of the causes of rising prices, such as the decision-making process of the leading price setters, the market structure, interest rates, exchange rate, and wages. In these cases, the inflationary process usually originates on the supply side, regardless of the conditions of demand and the level of employment.

That being so, although contractionary monetary policy, via increases in interest rates, may be effective in reducing inflation that originates from supply shocks, it ends up attacking the effects of inflation and not its causes. To attack its causes would require the adoption of active economic policies such as industrial policy, tax policy, directed monetary policy and exchange rate policy, among others.

A suitable procedure, according to this alternative approach to the causes of inflation, would be to identify what the real cause of inflation is in each case and to act with anti-inflationary measures commensurate with their different causes. This is because the use of contractionary monetary policy to contain an inflationary process originating on the supply side does not contribute to eliminating the cause of the problem. However, by reducing the activity and employment levels, the monetary authority can prevent a rise in costs from being fully passed on to prices. By reducing the inflationary phenomenon to purely demand inflation, the ITR may, therefore, compromise the economic performance, generating an excessive rise in interest rates, which greatly affects output and employment.

In line with this analysis, the conclusion that can be drawn on the effects of monetary shocks in Brazil is that the problems related to the transmission of monetary policy, as well as the inflation diagnosis that is restricted to demand shocks, lead to a loss in the effectiveness of the ITR policy. This is either because the monetary policy decisions are not fully transmitted to the prices, or because the constant attack of demand inflation ends up softening the effects of inflation without, however, eliminating one of its main causes, that is, the exchange rate pass-through.

5 Concluding Remarks

This chapter analysed the relationship between monetary policy, that is, ITR, and macroeconomic performance in Brazil. It was shown that monetary policy has been inefficient to ensure low inflation: from 1999 to 2016, the average annual inflation rate was around 6.9% (it is relatively high compared to international levels),[15] and at the same time has brought high costs for the Brazilian economy, such as the economic growth has been low and unstable and the economy has presented internal and external imbalances, due to, respectively, high interest rates and exchange rate appreciation.

[15]See, for instance, Ferrari Filho and Schifino (2010).

With regard to the international debate on the institutional framework of the ITR, the GFC, which erupted in 2007, severely affected both developed and developing economies, exposing the limits of some macroeconomic policies that had mainstream consensus and were considered fundamental in promoting economic growth and stability.

In this regard Blanchard et al. (2014) and Yellen (2014) mention that many countries have adopted the monetary regime of inflation targets in recent decades, using short-term interest rates to keep inflation under control. However, with the crisis, the previous consensus regarding this regime and its fundamental hypothesis were put to the test, and the knowledge gained on monetary policy management has given important insights in order to rethink the targets and instruments of this policy.

Despite the international critique on the use of monetary policy with only one target and one instrument, the Brazilian orthodox debate on monetary policy cannot advance beyond the more rigid version of the inflation targeting regime. This is because among the countries that either adopted this regime or close versions of it, Brazil is the only country where the only objective of monetary policy is to maintain price stability for a period of one year to reach the inflation target. It is also the only country where the full inflation index is utilized as a reference to the inflation target. In other words, Brazil lacks a core inflation measure to guide monetary policy decisions.

This situation becomes even more serious in a scenario of fiscal contraction, with an imposed ceiling on public spending and various reforms to reduce the size of the state in the economy, not to mention the external difficulties that impede growth through lack of exports and the inability to attract foreign direct investment. This is because monetary policy emerges as an alternative to policies that would help the recovery of economic growth in Brazil. But given the rigidity with which it has been managed, the high real and nominal interest rates reinforce the stagnation of the Brazilian economy.

In view of the foregoing, the main observation that can be made is that, the Brazilian monetary policy has harmed macroeconomic performance, and at the same time has been ineffective in controlling inflation. Are design of this policy is essential for the resumption of economic growth in Brazil.

Among the redesign suggestions for monetary policy, which in our view would help improve the results of effective inflation and economic performance, is the adoption of a discretionary monetary policy, in which the objective of price stability is accompanied by a commitment to maintain the stability of output.

In addition to economic growth, some authors, like Yellen (2014), suggest that monetary policy can have exchange rate stability as one of its goals. In this sense, the adoption of measures that allow the management of the exchange rate and lead this variable to more appropriate levels of economic growth would be essential and would encompass the reduction of the interest rate, the purchase of international reserves and the adoption of measures of capital controls and foreign exchange derivatives regulation.

One last suggestion would be to work on the problems that involve failures in the transmission mechanism of monetary policy in Brazil, highlighting here the question of price indexation. As mentioned earlier, the index is still an important component of Brazilian prices, either because a large part of the administered prices is corrected according to an indexation rule, or because a significant portion of the public debt bonds are indexed to the interest rate, which is the instrument of monetary policy.

References

Andrade, J. P., & Pires, M. C. C. (2009). A transmissão da política monetária pelo canal do efeito riqueza no Brasil. In J. L. Oreiro, L. F. Paula, & R. Sobreira (Eds.), *Política Monetária, Bancos Centrais e Metas de Inflação* (pp. 209–235). Rio de Janeiro, Brazil: FGV Editora.

Arestis, P., & Sawyer, M. (2008). New consensus macroeconomics and inflation targeting: A Keynesian critique. *Economia e Sociedade, 17*(número especial), 631–655.

Arestis, P., Ferrari-Filho, F., & Paula, L. F. (2011). Inflation targeting in Brazil. *International Review of Applied Economics, 25*(2), 127–148.

Bacha, E. L. (1995). Plano real: Uma avaliação preliminar. *Revista do BNDES, 2*(3), 3–26.

Baer, W. (2013). *The Brazilian economy: Growth and development*. Colorado, USA: Lynne Rienner.

Barbosa, F. H. (2006). The contagion effect of public debt on monetary policy: The Brazilian experience. *Revista de EconomiaPolítica, 26*(2), 231–238.
Blanchard, O., Dell'Ariccia, G., & Mauro, P. (2014). Introduction: Rethinking macroeconomic policy II—getting granular. In G. Akerlof, O. Blanchard, D. Romer, & J. Stiglitz (Eds.), *What have we learned? Macroeconomic policy after the crisis*. Cambridge, USA: The MIT Press.
Bell-keaton, S., & Ballinger, R. (2005). The monetary policy outcomes curve: Can the size and structure of public debt undermine policy objectives? In P. Arestis, M. Baddeley, & J. McCombie (Eds.), *The new monetary policy: Implications and relevance*. Cheltenham, UK: Edward Elgar.
Belaisch, A. (2003). Exchange rate pass-through in Brazil, *IMF Working Papers n. 141*.
Bielschowsky, R. (2012). Estratégia de desenvolvimento e as três frentes de expansão no Brasil: um desenho conceitual. *Economia e Sociedade, 21*(número especial), 729–747.
Brazilian Central Bank (BCB). (2017a). *Séries Temporais*. Available at http://www.bcb.gov.br. Accessed 16 March 2017.
Brazilian Central Bank (BCB). (2017b). *Notas Econômico-Financeiras. Setor Externo*. Available at http://www.bcvb.gov.br. Accessed 16 March 2017.
Bresser-Pereira, L. C., Oreiro, J. L., & Marconi, N. (2015). *Developmental macroeconomics*. London, UK: Routledge.
Carlin, W., & Soskice, D. (2006). *Macroeconomics: Imperfection, institutions and policies*. Oxford, UK: University Press.
Carneiro, D. D., Salles, F. M., & WU, T. Y. H. (2006). Juros, câmbio e as imperfeições do canal de crédito. *Economia Aplicada, 10*(1), 7–23.
Carvalho, F. J. C. (2005). Uma contribuição ao debate em torno da eficácia da política monetária e algumas implicações para o caso do Brasil. *Revista de Economia Política, 25*(4), 323–336.
Christiano, L., Eichenbaum, M., & Evans, C. L. (1996). The effects of monetary policy shocks: Evidence from the flow of funds. *Reviewof Economics and Statistics, 78*(1), 16–34.
Davidson, P. (1994). *Post Keynesian macroeconomic theory*. Cheltenhan, UK: Edward Elgar.
Dornbush, R. (1998). Debt and monetary policy: The policy issues. In G. Calvo & M. King (Eds.), *The debt burden and its consequences for monetary policy*. Macmillan and International Economic Association: London, UK.
Ferrari-Filho, F., & Paula, L. F. R. (2003). The legacy of the *real* plan and an alternative agenda for the Brazilian economy. *Investigación Económica, LXII* (244), 57–92.

Ferrari Filho, F., & Schifino, L. A. (2010). *Performance* macroeconômica sob o regime de metas de inflação: uma análise para alguns países emergentes selecionados. *Análise Econômica, 28*(54), 117–140.

Ferreira, T. T., & Azzoni, C. R. (2011). Arranjos institucionais e investimento em infraestrutura no Brasil. *Revista do BNDES, 35,* 37–86.

Fontana, G. (2009). Whither new consensus macroeconomics? The role of government and fiscal policy in modern macroeconomics. *The Levy Economics Institute Working Paper n. 563.*

Hamilton, J. D. (1994). *Time series analysis.* Princenton, USA: Princeton University Press.

Instituto Brasileiro de Geografia e Estatística (IBGE). (2017a). *Sistema Nacional de Índices de Preços ao Consumidor.* Available at https://sidra.ibge.gov.br/pesquisa/snipc/ipca/quadros/brasil/dezembro-2016. Accessed 16 March 2017.

Instituto Brasileiro de Geografia e Estatística (IBGE). (2017b). *Sistema de Contas Nacionais.* Available at http://www.ibge.gov.br. Accessed 16 March 2017.

IPEADATA. (2017). *Séries Históricas.* Available at: http://www.ipeadata.gov.br. Accessed 16 March 2017.

Lavoie, M. (1992). *Foundations of post-Keynesian economic analysis.* Cheltenhan, UK: Edward Elgar.

Luporini, V. (2008). The monetary transmission mechanism in Brazil: Evidence from a VARanalysis. *Estudos Econômicos, 38,* 7–30.

Minella, A., & Correia, A. S. (2005). Mecanismos não-lineares de repasse cambial: um modelo de Curva de Phillips com threshold para o Brasil. *Anais do XXXIII Encontro Nacional de Economia*, Brazil.

Minella, A., Freitas, P. S., Goldfajn, I., & Muinhos, M. K. (2003). Inflation targeting in Brazil: Constructing credibility under exchange rate volatility. *Banco Central do Brasil Working Paper Series n. 77.*

Ministério do Desenvolvimento, Indústria e Comércio Exterior (MDIC). (2016). *Estatísticas do Comércio Exterior.* Available at http://www.midc.gov.br. Accessed 16 Dec 2016.

Modenesi, A., & Araújo, E. (2013). Price stability under inflation targeting in Brazil: An empirical analysis of the monetary policy transmission mechanism based on a VAR model (2000–2008). *Investigación Económica, LXXII*(283), 99–133.

Nassif, A., Feijó, C. A., & Araújo, E. (2015). Structural change and economic development: Is Brazil catching-up or falling-behind? *Cambridge Journal of Economics, 39,* 1307–1332.

Oreiro, J. L., & Feijó, C. A. (2010). Desindustrialização: conceituação, causas, efeitos e o caso brasileiro. *Revista de Economia Política, 30*(2), 219–232.

Palley, T. (1996). *Post Keynesian economics*. Nova York, USA: St. Martin's.

Pastore, A. C. (2006). As Letras Financeiras do Tesouro e a eficácia da política monetária. In E. L. Bacha & L. C. Oliveira Filho (orgs.), *Mercado de Capitais e Dívida Pública* (pp. 261–272). Rio de Janeiro, Brazil: Contra Capa Livraria.

Pires, M. C. C. (2008). *Interação entre política monetária e fiscal no Brasil em modelos robustos a pequenas amostras*, Tese de Doutorado, Programa de Pós-Graduação em Economia. Brasília, Brazil: Universidade de Brasília.

Rodrik, D. (2008). The real exchange and economic growth: Theory and evidence. *Brookings Papers on Economic Activity*, pp. 365–412.

Sicsú, J., & Oliveira, S. C. (2003). Taxa de juros e controle da Inflação no Brasil. In J. Sicsú, J. L. Oreiro & L. F. Paula (orgs.), *Agenda Brasil: políticas econômicas para o crescimento com estabilidade de preços* (pp. 29–64). Barueri, Brazil: EditoraManole.

Sims, C. (1992). Interpreting the macroeconomic time series facts: The effects of monetary policy. *European Economic Review, 36*(5), 975–1000.

Souza-Sobrinho, N. F. (2003). *Uma Avaliação do Canal de Crédito no Brasil.* Rio de Janeiro, Brazil: BNDES, 25º Prêmio BNDES de Economia.

Tesouro Nacional (NT). (2017). *Relatório Anual Dívida Pública Federal 2016.* Available at http://www.tesouro.fazenda.gov.br/documents/10180/RAD_Relat%C3%B3rio_Anual_2015_pdf/b95e87d0-1546e3-b01c-a10d48ec97d8. Accessed 9 April 2016.

Williamson, J. (2003). Exchange rate policy and development, *PaperPresented at Initiative for Policy Dialogue Task Force on Macroeconomics*, New York, USA: Columbia University.

Yellen, J. (2014). Many targets, many instruments: Where do we stand? In G. Akerlof, O. Blanchard, D. Romer, & J. Stiglitz (Eds.), *What Have We Learned? Macroeconomic Policy after the Crisis*. Cambridge, USA: The MIT Press.

Asymmetric Exchange Rate Pass-Through: Evidence, Inflation Dynamics and Policy Implications for Brazil (1999–2016)

Andre de Melo Modenesi, Viviane Luporini and Débora Pimentel

1 Introduction

Brazil's long experience with high inflation and external shocks to its currency makes Brazilian policymakers, and the public alike, worry about the inflation rate every time one observes excessive movement in the exchange rate markets. In the past, in an inflationary environment, shocks to the exchange rate and depreciations of the Brazilian currency in particular, ended up being passed through to consumer prices. Even though inflation rates have stabilized and the exchange rate pass-through have allegedly declined during the last decade, the transmission of exchange rates shocks to domestic prices remains a concern to the

A. de Melo Modenesi (✉) · V. Luporini · D. Pimentel
Universidade Federal do Rio de Janeiro, Rio de Janeiro, Brazil
e-mail: amodenesi@gmail.com

V. Luporini
e-mail: viviane.luporini@gmail.com

D. Pimentel
e-mail: pimentel.deboram@gmail.com

P. Arestis et al. (eds.), *The Brazilian Economy since the Great Financial Crisis of 2007/2008*, https://doi.org/10.1007/978-3-319-64885-9_4

monetary authorities. The exchange rate pass-through is defined as the domestic prices percentage change after a 1% exchange rate variation. Exchange rate fluctuations can affect domestic prices directly or indirectly. Directly, it affects prices of inputs used in domestic production and prices of imported final goods. Thus, the magnitude of direct effects depends on the share of imported goods on domestic consumption and production.

Indirectly, exchange rate fluctuations affect the demand for domestically produced goods that compete with imported goods. Indirect effect depends on the elasticity of substitution between domestic and imported goods. A depreciation of the local currency, for example, raises the internal demand for domestic goods *vis-à-vis* imported goods, while increases the competitiveness of local exports. At a given supply level, a raise in exports may result in inflationary pressures (over domestic inputs and wages). Additionally, administered (or government controlled) prices formally or informally indexed to the exchange rate may also affect domestic inflation.

The literature usually assumes a long-term relationship between price level and exchange rate. Accordingly, it is usually assumed that the exchange rate pass-through is ***symmetric***—or that the effect of appreciations and depreciations of the local currency (on CPI) have the same magnitude (McCarty 2007; Gagnon and Ihrig 2004; Campa and Goldberg 2005; Choudhri and Hakura 2006; Kohlscheen 2010; and for Brazil Belaisch 2003; Minella et al. 2003; Nogueira 2007; Araújo and Modenesi 2010). However, there are several micro and macroeconomic theoretical reasons that justify the possible existence of an ***asymmetric*** exchange rate pass-through—that is, the effect of currency appreciations and depreciations (on CPI) may not have the same magnitude.

This chapter aims at investigating the existence of an *asymmetric* exchange rate pass-through to consumer prices in Brazil. The Brazilian Central Bank (BCB)[1] has adopted the inflation targeting regime in

[1]In Portuguese, *Banco Central do Brasil*.

1999 and uses the Brazilian Consumer Price Index (IPCA).[2] There are many studies estimating the *symmetric* exchange rate pass-through to IPCA. In the international literature, almost all studies that focus on the asymmetry of the pass-through analyzes the pass-through to imported prices.

Our contribution to the current literature is mostly empirical, and the results help highlighting two important and intertwined theoretical points. Firstly, an asymmetric pass-through may be an additional explanation for downward price rigidity. Secondly, our results provide a strong case against excess exchange rate volatility and capital mobility as supported by the Post Keynesian literature. Empirically, we provide evidence on the existence of an ***asymmetric*** exchange rate pass-through to the Brazilian Consumer Price Index. In a departure from the previous literature, we focus specifically on the *asymmetric* exchange rate pass-through to IPCA. We believe that by analyzing the pass-through to a more general price index (the IPCA), we do not restrict ourselves to the possible cost effects of imported prices. Using a decomposition of the exchange rate series into appreciations and depreciations of the Brazilian currency, we estimate Structural Vector Auto-regression (SVAR) models and provide estimates of the magnitude of the pass-through in case of appreciations and depreciations of the local currency. Our results support the hypothesis of a strong asymmetry in the exchange rate pass-through for the IPCA.

Our chapter contains three sections besides this introduction and the concluding remarks. Section 2 presents a very brief overview of the recent macroeconomic performance and macroeconomic policy in Brazil. We highlight three stylized facts: (1) the low inflation's sensitivity to the interest rate; (2) the key role of the exchange rate in the monetary policy transmission mechanism; and (3) the existence of a downward rigidity in the IPCA. Section 3 reviews the literature on the exchange rate pass-through. Finally, we present some implications of the asymmetric pass-through to inflation dynamics and macroeconomic policy.

---

[2]Calculated by the Brazilian Institute of Geography and Statistics (IBGE) and considered the official inflation index of the country.

2 Inflation and Macroeconomic Policy in Brazil: A Brief Overview

During the 1980s and early 1990s, the Brazilian economy presented a process of chronic high inflation. Most economists agreed that inflation had become inertial, as far as the population had incorporated the inflationary memory: (Current) prices were indexed to past inflation (Modenesi 2005, Chaps. 4–5).

With the adoption of the Real Plan in mid-1994, inflation was put under control. The Real Plan was a price stabilization strategy based on the adoption of a new monetary standard and the implementation of an exchange rate anchor. The plan was successful in controlling inflation. Inflation fell sharply after the launch of the Real Plan, reaching levels that had not been observed for decades in the Brazilian economy (Reis et al. 2016, 169–70).

In 1999, a set of policies was adopted, so called *macroeconomic tripod*, based on: inflation targeting regime; floating exchange rate, with high capital mobility; and primary surplus targets. Price stability was pursued by fixing the basic interest rate (*Selic* rate)[3] in line with a Taylor rule. Accordingly, *Selic* rate was set aiming at controlling simultaneously aggregate demand and, though not directly, the exchange rate, which has been the most relevant monetary policy transmission channel. Fiscal policy, in turn, assumed a supporting role, limited to avoiding inflationary pressures and keeping a stable debt/GDP relation (Reis et al. 2016, 170–2). This policy was in line with the *New Consensus in Macroeconomics*.[4]

[3]In Brazil, the basic interest rate goes by the acronym (Selic) for *Sistema Especial de Liquidação e de Custódia* (Special System for Settlement and Custody), which is the settlement system for most domestic securities of the Brazilian government.

[4]The New Consensus on Macroeconomics (Blinder 1981, 1998; Taylor 1993, 2000; Allsopp e Vines 2000; Romer 2000) is associated with the growing popularity of inflation targeting and the resulting acceptance that, even where the regime is not adopted, the main instrument of monetary policy is the (basic) interest rate, and no longer the monetary aggregates of some decades ago, influenced by monetarism. The new consensus theoretical core is given by the confluence of monetarism, new classical, and real business cycle theories. The natural rate of unemployment (Friedman 1968) and rational expectations hypothesis are among the two most relevant assumptions shared by this large group of economists. Another fundamental part is the Taylor

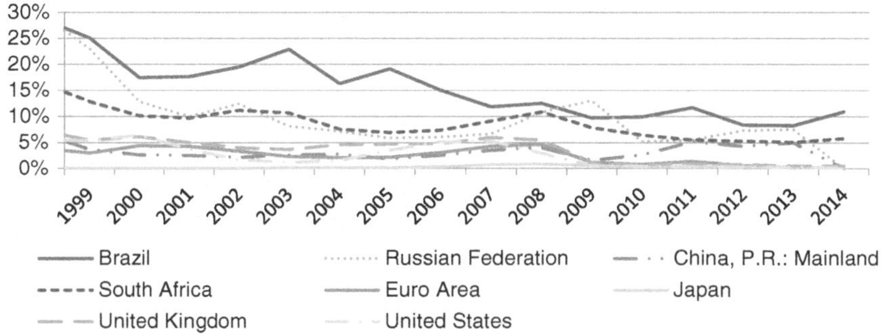

Graph 1 Short-term interest rates—Brazil and selected countries: 1999–2014. *Source* IMF (2016a)

One should note that since the Real Plan, Brazil set a world record in terms of (real) interest rates, and the BRL was one of the most overvalued currencies during the last two decades (Graph 1). The high interest rates attracted carry trade operations and contributed to an overvaluation of the BRL.[5] In turn, the overvaluation of the BRL facilitated inflation control.

Although Brazil has one of the world's higher interest rates, the BCB has had difficulties meeting its inflation targets (see Graph 2). During 18 years of inflation targeting adoption, upper limit was exceeded in four years (2001, 2002, 2003, and 2015); the center of the target was reached in only three years (2000, 2007, and 2009); and IPCA was below the center of the target only in 2006. During this period, annual inflation averaged around 7%, well above the 4.5% target rate.

In fact, Brazilian inflation has proven rather resilient despite high interest levels set by the BCB (annual inflation rates have been below

rule—which holds that the central banks should determine its interest rate aiming at an explicit or implicit inflation target, and at keeping GDP growth near to its potential. We agree with Lavoie that "the only truly new element in the new consensus [...] is the rejection of the exogenous supply of money, and the replacement of money growth rule for a real interest rate targeting rule [...]" (Lavoie 2004, p. 23).

[5]For details on the role of foreign exchange derivative market in Brazil, see Chap. "Foreign Exchange Derivatives and Financial Fragility in Brazil" of this book by Maryse Farhi.

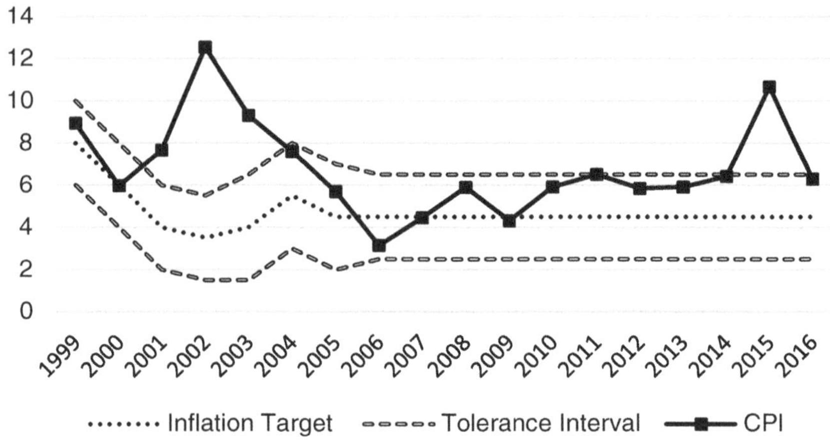

Graph 2 Inflation (IPCA accumulated in 12 months, %) and targets: 1999–2016. *Source* IBGE (2016), BCB (2016)

5% only in three out of eighteen years period). This suggests there is something *sui generis* in inflation dynamics and in the transmission mechanism of monetary policy which causes Brazilian inflation to not respond—or to remain less sensitive—to contractionary monetary policy.[6] Indeed, an ample set of empirical evidence indicates that the monetary policy transmission mechanism may not be properly functioning. For instance, Modenesi and Araújo (2013) found that the sensibility of the IPCA to the Selic rate is low.

The low sensitivity of the Brazilian inflation to the interest rate level is remarkable and has been widely documented (Modenesi et al. 2017, 206–207). This means that an increase in the Selic rate seems to have limited deflationary impact through the demand channel. For this reason, the BCB—according to the inflation targeting regime—would

[6]According to existing literature (Modenesi and Modenesi 2012): among the main empirical-institutional features of Brazilian economy that compromises the monetary policy transmission, these are noteworthy: (i) nonexistence of a *yield curve* for sufficiently long maturity periods; (ii) the high share of *administered prices* in the IPCA; (iii) existence of a perverse *cost channel*; and (iv) the so-called *LFT problem* (Modenesi and Modenesi 2012). LFT (*Letras Financeiras do Tesouro*, in Portuguese) is a special kind of government bonds that are indexed to Selic.

need to maintain the basic interest rate in excessively high levels in order to meet its inflation targets.

The costs of practicing high levels of interest rate are not negligible. The effect of an increase in the Selic rate on the economic activity level is negative. In response to a rise in interest rate, economy decelerates, and employment increases. Monetary rigidity is one of the reasons—although not the sole—for the poor performance of Brazilian economy during analyzed period.[7] The GDP growth rate remained below 6% in the 1999–2016 period (except in 2010, when it exceeded 7.5%) and above 5% in only four years (2004, 2007, 2008, and 2010). Such results have proved to be worse than for other emergent countries that have considerably higher growth rates (Graph 3).

The BRL also appreciates in response to an increase in Selic rate. The high differential between domestic interest rate and foreign rates contributed to the expressive appreciation of the BRL that occurred after 2003, reducing export competitiveness. The BRL is one of the currencies that have appreciated more recently: For instance, in 2011, the average exchange rate was inferior to its value in 1999.

It is worth noting that overvaluation of the BRL is not an undesirable byproduct of the high-interest rate policy. On the contrary, the BRL appreciation has been the core of price stabilization strategy, since the Real Plan. Araújo and Modenesi (2010) suggested that exchange rate was more relevant than the economic activity level to explain Brazilian inflation dynamics. In fact, exchange rate has been the most relevant transmission channel of monetary policy (Arestis et al. 2011; Modenesi and Araújo 2013). This is a second (and well known) stylized fact of Brazilian economy.

Summing up, despite of the extremely high interest rates and strong overvaluation of the BRL, BCB was not able to maintain inflation at expected reasonable levels. In other words, although in relative control, inflation presented downward rigidity. This can be seen as another stylized fact of Brazilian economy after the Real Plan. A common

[7]Even recognizing that Brazil's rates of growth in the 1980s were low, one cannot deny that monetary policy has, at least, constituted a relevant hindrance to the reversal of this situation.

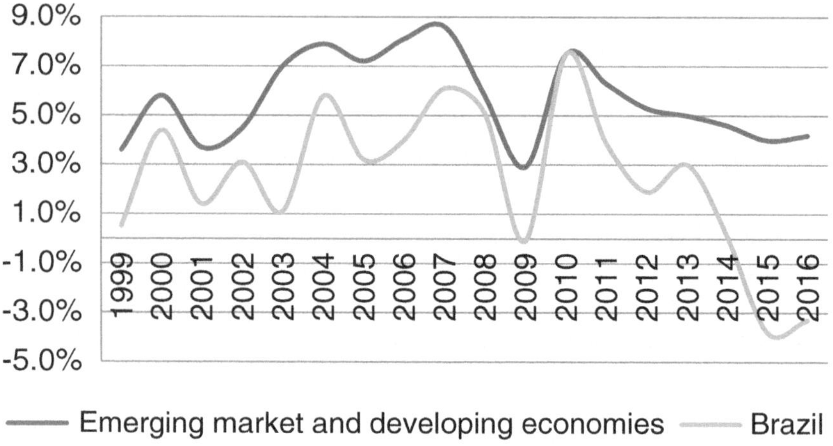

Graph 3 Real GDP growth rate (%)—Brazil and emergent countries: 1999–2016. *Source* IMF (2016b)

explanation is that the practice of price indexation was not fully eliminated. Some key prices—for instance, some public tariffs, such as public transportation and energy, and also petroleum products and rents—are indexed to past inflation by law. Indeed, administrated inflation (one-third of IPCA) drove inflation rates above the target until the early 2007 and after 2015. As a rule, prices in general (and also wages) are also indexed to inflation (in a 12 months basis).[8] Inflation presents a highly inertial component and thus, controlling aggregate demand—via monetary or fiscal policy—has proven to have limited efficacy in curbing inflationary pressures. For instance, in 2017, only after two consecutive years of economic recession and an unemployment rate of 12%, inflation rates finally declined. Note that, in 2015–2016, Brazil experienced the most drastic recession of history (Graph 3).

[8]Administered prices represent around 30% of CPI in Brazil. Many of them are (directly or indirectly) indexed to exchange rate. One should note that not all administrated prices are indexed to past inflation.

We provide evidence for yet another reason for IPCA's downward rigidity or inflation resilience: the existence of an *asymmetric* exchange rate pass-through.

3 Review of Literature

Exchange Rate Pass-Through in Brazil

There is a vast literature that estimates the ***symmetric*** exchange rate pass-through in Brazil. Belaisch (2003) estimates VAR models, from July 1999 to December 2002. Model specification follows McCarthy (2007) and uses the exchange rate, IMF oil index price, and industrial output index (IBGE).[9] The exchange rate pass-through for consumer prices was estimated at 17% after 12 months.

A group of authors also estimated *symmetric* models with specifications based on Belaisch (2003), McCarthy (2007), Squeff (2009), Araújo and Modenesi (2010), Souza and Alves (2011) and Nogueira et al. (2012). Other studies also used VAR models with different specifications: Minella et al. (2003), Nogueira (2006), Menezes and Fernandes (2012) and Fraga and Couto (2013). In all these studies, the econometric model is linear and symmetric.

According to literature, exchange rate pass-through has been reduced over time in several countries. Squeff (2009) and Souza and Alvez (2011) divided the analyzed period into two subsamples. In both studies, it was found that the first period (1999–2003) presented a higher exchange rate pass-through than in the second one (2003–2007 and 2003–2009, respectively).

It is important to highlight, however, that in both studies the second subsample is a period of continuous appreciation of the BRL.

[9]In the McCarthy (2007) model, inflation is determined by "supply" shocks, "demand" shocks, and the exchange rate.

Souza et al. (2013) and Almendra et al. (2015) estimated exchange rate pass-through using State Space models that allowed for time-varying parameters.[10] Marodin and Portugal (2015) estimated a Markov Switching Phillips Curve for Brazil from 2000 to 2015. Their results showed evidence of two distinct regimes for the exchange rate pass-through.[11]

Correa and Minella (2010) analyzed the existence of nonlinearities in the Phillips Curve through estimation of a threshold autoregressive model (TAR) with consumer prices, exchange rate, and the output gap. The results indicate the existence of a nonlinear relationship between the exchange rate pass-through and the economic cycle. When the output gap is below the estimated 1.89% threshold, the exchange rate pass-through is not statistically different from zero. However, when the output gap is above the threshold, the estimated pass-through is 9%. Devaluations of the local currency larger than the 2.1% threshold lead to an estimated pass-through of 11% (after three months). Pass-throughs of appreciations (small or large), on the other hand, were not statistically significant.

Carneiro et al. (2004) estimated a backward-looking Phillips curve with a nonlinear specification to the pass-through coefficient for the period from 1994 to 2001. The model considers different components of consumer price index (industrialized, services, and food) and the exchange rate and unemployment rate as determinants of inflation. The nonlinear specification presented a pass-through of 5.6% for 1999, 6% for 2000, and 7.7% for 2001. The empirical evidence obtained by the authors also suggested the existence of different nonlinear pass-through mechanism among different price groups.

Most international econometric studies estimate exchange rate pass-through to import prices and to producer prices. Only a few

---

[10]One should conclude, that in both studies, the results showed that exchange rate pass-through was higher during periods of depreciation of the local currency than in periods of appreciation.

[11]Under the so-called normal regime, the pass-through to consumer prices was not statistically significant. Comparatively, the expected pass-through under a "crisis" regime is of 10%. "Crisis" periods occurred from 2000 to 2003 and in 2015, years in which the BRL depreciated. The "normal" cycle extends from 2003 to 2014, years of continuous appreciation of the local currency (except for July to November 2008).

studies focus consumer prices.[12] Results, in general, present evidences of asymmetric exchange rate pass-through, although the direction and magnitude vary from country to country and with the industry analyzed.

Although it is possible to use nonlinear estimation methods, most studies estimate autoregressive distributed lag (ARDL) and vector autoregressive (VAR) models and decompose the exchange rate series in two new variables, one for appreciation observations and another for depreciations.

Summing up, there are many studies estimating the *symmetric* exchange rate pass-through to consumer price in Brazil. In the international literature, studies that focus on the asymmetry of the pass-through usually use imported prices. Our main contribution is to provide evidence on the existence of an *asymmetric* exchange pass-through to consumer price in Brazil. We innovate by using a decomposition of the exchange rate series into appreciations and depreciations of the BRL.

Asymmetric Exchange Rate Pass-Through: Theory

According to existing theoretical literature, asymmetric exchange rate pass-through is usually understood to mean that domestic currency appreciations and depreciations have different magnitude impact over prices.[13]

As Webber (1999) notes, the theoretical literature offers three groups of explanations for asymmetry: (i) Marketing constraints, formulated by Foster and Baldwin (1986) and Knetter (1994), refer to the case where exporters are unable to raise their sales in face of an increased demand for imports as a result of a fall in price caused by an appreciation of the local currency (this situation results in exchange rate pass-through after

[12]For instance, Brun-Aguerre et al. (2017), Pollard and Coughlin (2003), Herzberg et al. (2003), Bussiere (2013), Webber (1999), Wickremasinghe and Silvapulle (2004), Campa et al. (2008), Alvarez et al. (2008), Gil-Pareja (2000) and Karoro et al. (2009), estimate asymmetric exchange rate pass-through to import prices. Khundrakpam (2007) employ producer prices. Mihaljek and Klau (2008), Przystupa and Wróbel (2011) and Delatte and Villavicencio (2012) utilize asymmetric exchange rate pass-through to consumer prices. All these papers decompose the exchange rate in appreciations and depreciations.

[13]Sometimes it also refers to the speed that exchange rate fluctuations affect prices.

devaluations greater than after appreciations); (ii) production technology switching, if the producing firm has the possibility to buy its inputs not only domestically but also to import, appreciations may result in a higher exchange rate pass-through than depreciations (Ware and Winter 1988); and (iii) market share objectives, this possibility is usually alluded by Pricing to Market literature, notably by Froot and Klemperer (1989), Marston (1990) and Krugman (1987). It happens when the exporting firms are trying to set the lowest possible price in the importer currency, in order to increase sales and market share. In this case, exchange rate pass-through after appreciations is higher than after depreciations.

Thus, two of the three theoretical reasons found in literature lead to a higher pass-through after a currency appreciation rather than after a depreciation. It is, however, generally believed that prices are rigid downward due to firms being more likely to increase their markup than to reduce it. In this case, the effects over prices after a depreciation of the currency would be greater than after an appreciation. Therefore, literature on downward rigidity of prices and asymmetric price transmission also applies to asymmetric exchange rate pass-through.

From a macroeconomic perspective, the exchange rate pass-through may be asymmetric if the Monetary Authority is concerned with inflationary pressures arising from exchange rate movements and reacts more strongly after a currency devaluation than after an appreciation (Delatte and Villavicencio 2012). Furthermore, the exchange rate pass-through may depend on the level of economic activity. In periods of economic recessions, for example, the effects of a depreciation in raising prices may be smaller than the effects of an appreciation in reducing domestic prices (Goldfajn and Werlang 2000).

In general, literature suggests that price adjustments to exchange rate fluctuations depend on market structures and firm pricing strategies, which will differ from industry to industry and from country to country.[14] The existence and direction of asymmetric exchange rate pass-through to prices may not be asserted a priori. Generally, industries

---

[14]According to Goldfajn and Werlang (2000) and Calvo and Reinhart (2000) ERTP is higher for the emerging countries than for developed countries. Additionally, in emerging countries, with currencies placed at the lower end of the currency hierarchy, exchange rate is prone to be more volatile (Paula et al. 2017).

producing homogeneous and globally marketable products should present a higher pass-through and less possibility of asymmetry, whereas industries whose products are more differentiated and where market structure is less competitive have greater possibility of presenting asymmetries and nonlinearities.

4 Asymmetric Exchange Rate Pass-Through: Empirical Evidence from Brazil (1999–2016)

Data Base

The econometric model estimated is based on Belaisch (2003) and Araújo and Modenesi (2010), and own elaboration as above, and is extensively used in the Brazilian exchange rate pass-through literature. Inflation is determined by its lags and three other factors: (i) aggregate demand (or level of economic activity) as measured by industrial output; (ii) aggregate supply conditions, a commodity price index is used as proxy; and (iii) the nominal exchange rate.

Intuition behind this equation is simple. Inflation dynamics depends on three components: (i) aggregate demand; (ii) supply (or cost) conditions; and (iii) the exchange rate. In line with Vernengo (2006), this equation comprises both orthodox and heterodox theories of inflation. Friedman (1956; 1968), an exponent of orthodox theory, emphasizes demand pressures (resulting from excessive money supply). Davidson (2003), a prominent Post Keynesian author, advocates cost-push inflation pressure. Finally, there is a lot empirical evidence showing that exchange rate plays a significant role in inflation dynamics (Taylor 2001), particularly in emerging economies (see for instance, Silva and Vernengo 2008–2009).

All variables are monthly observations for the period from August 1999 to June 2016 and are used in first difference of logarithms. August 1999 was chosen as the starting period for two reasons. Firstly, inflation targeting regime was officially established in Brazil in June 1999. Secondly, there is a major methodological break in the IPCA in August

1999 when components weights were updated. The variables used are described below (and plotted in the Appendix):

i. CPI: Consumer price index measured by IBGE and used in Brazilian IT Regime
ii. Y: industrial output (*quantum*) measured by IBGE as proxy for aggregate demand.
iii. COMM: a commodities price index constructed with IMF commodities prices data using method proposed by the Brazilian Institute for Applied Economic Research (IPEA) (Nonnenberg and Lameiras 2005) as proxy for aggregate supply conditions.
iv. ER: Exchange rate BRL/USD monthly average provided by BCB.

The industrial output index was chosen as a proxy due to nonavailability of a monthly series suitable for economic activity at the aggregate level. Although industrial output is frequently used in the Brazilian econometric literature, it should be noted that this indicator has limitations because it represents only about 30% of the Gross Domestic Product (GDP).

A commodities price index was calculated using a method proposed by IPEA (Nonnenberg and Lameiras 2005). Commodity prices from IMF database were weighted according to the Brazilian production structure measured by the producer price index (PPI) provided by Fundação Getulio Vargas (FGV).

Usually, the Brazilian exchange rate pass-through econometric literature uses IMF's commodities index. It is an important remark, however, that in IMF's index the oil prices share is higher (53.6%) than in COMM index (18%). Also, food and beverage share in IMF's index is lower (13.8%) than in COMM index (48%).

The commodity price index can be a proxy for international cost conditions. An increase in commodities prices can be interpreted as a supply shock leading to inflationary pressures (Araújo and Modenesi 2010). Furthermore, given the high share of commodities in Brazil's exports, an increase in commodities prices may imply higher profit for exporters and a positive demand shock. In other words, external variables (exchange rate and commodities prices) may represent supply shocks (via costs) and demand shocks (via exports). In both cases, an increase in commodities prices is expected to have a positive effect on consumer prices leading to inflationary pressures.

The exchange rate series was decomposed into two series based on period-to-period price variations, as presented in the appendix. The currency devaluation series presents only **positive** exchange rate variations whereas the currency appreciation series presents only **negative** exchange rate variations. One should note that a decrease in exchange rate (BRL/USD) is equivalent to an appreciation of BRL.

Econometric Estimation and Results

As most macroeconomic variables are interrelated, an autoregressive system (VAR) is the benchmark model widely used by macroeconomists. In VAR models, macroeconomic variables may be all treated as endogenously determine.[15]

Two SVAR models were estimated: a symmetric and an asymmetric model.[16]

(i) Symmetric: $Y_t = (\Delta \text{CPI}_t, \ \Delta \text{ER}_t, \ \Delta \text{COMM}_t, \ \Delta Y_t)'$
(ii) Asymmetric: $Y_t = (\Delta \text{CPI}_t, \ \Delta \text{ER}_t^+, \Delta \text{ER}_t^-, \ \Delta \text{COMM}_t, \ \Delta Y_t)'$

Where CPI is the consumer price index; ER is the exchange rate; ER_t^+, increases in exchange rate (BRL/USD), equivalent to depreciations of Brazilian currency; ER_t^-, decreases in exchange rate (BRL/USD), equivalent to appreciations of Brazilian currency; COMM is the commodities price index; and Y is industrial output, as described previously.

Model specification in SVAR context involves selecting lag order and imposing restrictions on SVAR parameters in order to estimate impulse response functions and variance decomposition. Details about SVAR identification are presented in appendix.

---

[15]"Most recent empirical studies of monetary policy and real economic activity have adopted a vector autoregression (VAR)" (Walsh 2003, 24).

[16]For details on the SVAR models used, and the decomposition of the exchange rate series (*ER*) into ER^+ and ER^- see appendix.

The criterion to impose restrictions was the analysis of the error correlation matrix and the selection of the pairs of variables with high correlation errors. Then, restrictions were imposed only for the selected pairs: (i) Commodities prices contemporaneously affect all other variables; (ii) exchange rate contemporaneously affects industrial output and consumer prices; and (iii) industrial output contemporaneously affects consumer prices.

The selection of the lag order was used to find the most parsimonious model with well-behaved residues that satisfied the stability condition, i.e., that the characteristic polynomial inverse roots lie inside the unit circle.[17] The symmetric and asymmetric models were estimated with the same number of lags so that results could be directly compared.

Wald coefficient restriction tests were performed for the asymmetric model to test the hypothesis that local currency depreciations coefficients are statistically different from currency appreciations coefficients. Two different specifications of the Wald test were implemented, as presented in the appendix, and for both of them test statistics reject the null hypothesis that coefficients are equal at conventional significance levels. Therefore, results indicate the existence of asymmetry, i.e., that exchange rate devaluations have different effects on inflation than exchange rate appreciations.

Variance decomposition analysis can be used for interpreting the interrelated dynamic in SVAR models. This method estimates the amount of variation in each of the endogenous variables in the system of equations due to exogenous shocks in each of the other endogenous variables over some period. Thus, the variance decomposition provides information about the relative importance of shocks in affecting the variables in the SVAR.[18]

[17]Residuals that are not autocorrelated, nor heteroscedastic, and are normally distributed. For residual autocorrelation Portmanteau and Lagrange Multiplier tests were performed. For residual normality, the multivariate Jarque-Bera and White's test for heteroscedasticity of residuals.

[18]The same structural factorization used to calculate impulse response functions was used in variance decomposition.

Table 1 Variance decomposition—Symmetric and Asymmetric models

Symmetric model					
Period	s.e.	ER	COMM	Y	CPI
1	0.27	0.00	0.00	0.00	100.00
2	0.33	4.58	0.90	0.45	94.08
3	0.35	10.35	1.82	0.59	87.25
4	0.36	15.83	2.04	0.54	81.58
5	0.39	21.79	1.90	0.83	75.47
6	0.40	25.03	1.98	1.04	71.95
12	0.40	26.53	2.13	1.10	70.24

Asymmetric model						
Period	s.e.	ER +	ER −	COMM	Y	CPI
1	0.27	0.00	0.00	0.00	0.00	100.00
2	0.32	3.80	0.46	0.76	0.63	94.36
3	0.34	6.50	2.71	1.73	1.10	87.96
4	0.36	10.20	3.98	2.17	1.05	82.61
5	0.38	17.75	3.68	1.93	1.50	75.14
6	0.39	22.25	3.45	1.94	1.67	70.69
12	0.40	24.00	3.57	2.17	1.81	68.45

Source Author's estimation. *Note* ER (−) means a decrease in exchange rate (BRL/USD) and it is equivalent to an appreciation of Brazilian currency

In Table 1, the second column contains the forecast error of the variable at the given forecast horizon. The remaining columns give the percentage of the forecast variance due to each shock with each row adding up to 100.

Table 1 shows variance decomposition of the symmetric and asymmetric models. For the symmetric model, the results show that exchange rate shocks are the major factor affecting consumer price variations. Commodity prices are the second most relevant factor, although its share after 12 periods in consumer price variations (2.1%) is much lower than the exchange rate (26.6%). Industrial output is the least relevant factor with only 1% of the consumer price variance being explained by its shocks.

For the asymmetric model (lower part of Table 1), results indicate that shocks to commodity prices and industrial output result in forecast error percentages in consumer price variations (after 12 months) similar to those obtained for the symmetric model. In the asymmetric

Table 2 Exchange rate pass-through

Period	Symmetric	Asymmetric	
		(+)	(−)
1	0.00	0.00	0.00
2	1.46	1.82	0.93
3	3.10	3.43	2.84
4	4.72	5.36	4.22
5	6.36	7.75	4.69
6	7.77	10.02	4.81
7	8.82	11.82	5.17
8	9.59	12.90	5.70
9	10.37	14.19	5.91
10	11.00	15.61	5.83
11	11.23	16.40	5.80
12	11.21	16.71	5.80

Source Author's estimation. *Note* (−) means a decrease in exchange rate (BRL/USD) and it is equivalent to an appreciation of Brazilian currency

model, the exchange rate series was decomposed into positive (currency devaluations) and negative (currency appreciations) variations. Together, they represent 27.6% of consumer price variance after 12 periods, a result also similar to the symmetric model. However, when analyzed separately, currency devaluations shocks have a greater share in price variance (24%) than currency appreciations (3.6%). This result gives further evidence for asymmetric exchange rate pass-through.

As the exchange rate pass-through can be defined as the percentage response of prices to a one percent shock in the exchange rate (McCarthy 2007; Campa and Goldberg 2005), it can be also calculated from the impulse response functions estimated from SVAR models.

Table 2 shows the symmetric and asymmetric estimated exchange rate pass-through for Brazil from 1999 to 2016. As expected, results show that pass-through after a currency devaluation is higher (16%) than after an appreciation (5.8%).

In summary, the results of the three analyses (Wald tests, variance decomposition, and exchange rate estimation) offer compelling evidence of asymmetric exchange rate pass-through with pass-through after a devaluation being higher than after an appreciation.

5 Concluding Remarks: Inflation Dynamics and Policy Implications

The present chapter analyzes exchange rate pass-through to consumer prices in Brazil. The main objective is to search for evidence of asymmetric pass-through to consumer prices, i.e., that devaluations of the domestic currency affect domestic prices differently from appreciations. The analysis covers the period from August 1999 to June 2016, beginning after the adoption of the IT regime and de facto dirty floating exchange rate.

In this chapter, asymmetric exchange rate pass-through is investigated through the estimation of SVAR models with exchange rate decomposed, period by period, into currency devaluations and appreciations.

Wald coefficient restrictions tests and variance decomposition analysis are performed, and symmetric and asymmetric pass-through is estimated through impulse response functions. Taken together, the results offer compelling evidence of asymmetric exchange rate pass-through in Brazil. Estimated pass-through after a currency devaluation is 16% while after an appreciation 5.8%.

It is important to highlight a relevant implication of our results for inflation dynamics. The asymmetric exchange rate pass-through implies that the inflationary effect of (systematic) currency devaluation is not fully offset by the deflationary effect of (systematic) appreciation of the same magnitude.

For instance, consider a currency devaluation followed by an appreciation of the same magnitude so that the exchange rate returns to its initial level. Given a symmetric exchange rate pass-through, the final effect on inflation would be zero. After the currency appreciation, the price level would eventually return to the level observed before the initial devaluation. In other words, the inflationary impact on prices of the devaluation would be completely offset by the deflationary effect of the currency appreciation. In the presence of asymmetry, the net result will be an increase in price level.

To illustrate this result, we simulated the impact of exchange rate variations on IPCA from 1999 through 2016, based on our estimations

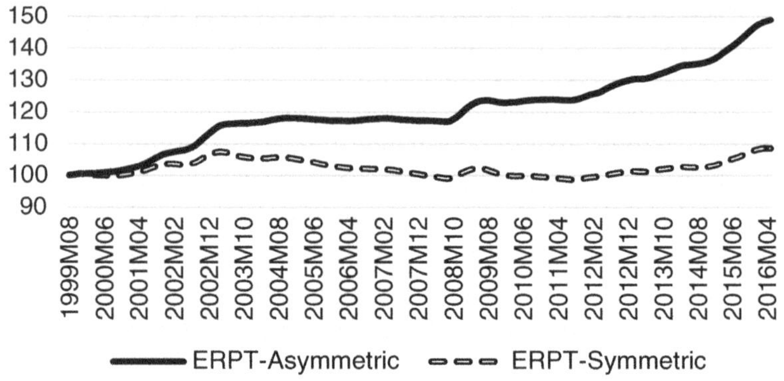

Graph 4 Simulation: Exchange rate pass-through (Asymmetric and Symmetric) (1999.08 = 100). *Source* Author's elaboration

(Table 2). The bold line in Graph 4 shows the trajectory of the IPCA under asymmetric pass-through, while the dotted line shows the simulated index under the hypothesis of a symmetric pass-through. The asymmetric pass-through simulation results in a strong upward trend: Accumulated inflation is around 50%. For the symmetric pass-through (dotted line), the simulated IPCA fluctuates around its initial level: Eventually, accumulated inflation would converge to zero.[19]

In a few words, if pass-through were symmetric, exchange rate fluctuations would have a neutral inflationary impact. The asymmetric exchange rate pass-through implies that the inflationary effect of a (systematic) currency devaluation is not fully offset by the deflationary effect of a (systematic) appreciation of the same magnitude. In a few words, exchange rate fluctuations may result in an (upward) inflationary bias.

This empirical result helps to explain a stylized fact of Brazilian economy, the downward rigidity of the IPCA. This result also cast doubts on the current inflation control strategy, based on IT and de facto dirty floating exchange rate (with capital mobility).

[19]The simulated indexes are a partial analysis that only considers the impact of exchange rate variations on the IPCA for comparative purposes, not considering other factors also important for the dynamics of the Brazilian inflation rate. The upward trend shown by the simulated asymmetric index resembles much more the observed trajectory of actual IPCA.

Our results provide a strong case against excess exchange rate volatility and capital mobility. Accordingly, a stable exchange rate may favor price stability. Indeed, many authors favor a stable exchange rate. For instance, Keynes (1943, 1980, p. 8), Davidson (2003), Kregel (2015), Carvalho (2000–2001) and Paula et al. (2017), amongst others Post Keynesians authors, advocate exchange rate interventions and capital controls to stabilize the exchange rate. For Krugman and Obstfeld (1997), an unstable exchange rate raises uncertainty regarding export/import revenues. Accordingly, excessive exchange rate volatility would jeopardize trade. Although we do not aim at addressing this debate explicitly, the existence of an asymmetric pass-through may be another item in the list in favor of stable exchange rates.

Appendix

SVAR Model

Consider a K-dimensional time series $Y_t = (y_1, y_2, y_3, y_4)'$ where Y_t is a SVAR of finite order p of the structural form

$$AY_t = v_0 + B_1 Y_{t-1} + \cdots + B_p Y_{t-p} + Bu_t \tag{1}$$

where A is a $K \times K$ matrix that defines the causal interrelationships among the contemporaneous variables, and u_t denotes a mean zero uncorrelated error term (also referred to as structural innovation or structural shock) with a variance-covariance matrix $E(u_t, u_t') = \Sigma_u$. Because structural shocks are by definition uncorrelated, Σ_u is a diagonal matrix (Kilian 2011).

Equation (1) cannot be estimated by ordinary least squares (OLS) since the variables have contemporaneous effects on each other. OLS estimates would suffer from simultaneous equation bias since the regressors and error terms would be correlated (Enders 2014).

In order to allow estimation, it is necessary to derive its reduced form representation. Premultiplication on both sides of Eq. (1) by A^{-1} allows the reduced form (2) to be obtained.

$$Y_t = c_0 + \Phi_1 Y_{t-1} + \Phi_2 Y_{t-2} + \cdots + \Phi_p Y_{t-p} + e_t \quad (2)$$

Where $c_0 = A^{-1}v_0$; $\Phi_i = A^{-1}B_i$; $Ae_t = Bu_t$.

Standard OLS method obtains consistent estimates of the reduced form (2) parameters Φ_i, the reduced form errors e_t and their covariance matrix $E(e_t e_t') = \Sigma_e$ (Lütkepohl 2005).

However, the reduced form errors are correlated. Only in the special case where there are no contemporaneous effects among variables (i.e., matrix A elements, $a_{ij}(i \neq j)$, equals zero) the shocks will be uncorrelated.

It is possible, however, to recover the structural VAR coefficients and analyze how Y_t respond to structural shocks in u_t, from the estimates of the model in reduced form since, by construction, $Ae_t = Bu_t$. Hence, the variance of e_t is

$$\Sigma_e = A^{-1}B\Sigma_u B' A^{-1'} \quad (3)$$

Σ_e can be consistently estimated from the reduced form by OLS, and the system can be solved for the unknown parameters provided that the number of unknown parameters do not exceed the number of equations. This involves imposing restrictions on matrix A. Usually, the most common approach is to impose $a_{ij} = 0$ restrictions (Kilian 2011).[20]

The assumption $a_{ij} = 0$ means that *yj* does not have a contemporaneous effect on *yi*. The imposition of different restrictions will result in different impulse response functions depending on the correlation between errors in the reduced form. Only if all reduced form errors are uncorrelated impulse response functions will be the same regardless of the restrictions imposed.

[20]It is necessary to impose $K(K+1)/2$ restrictions on both matrices A and B to satisfy order condition. The order condition is necessary for identification but may not suffice if rank condition fail. Rubio-Ramirez et al. (2010) discuss rank conditions for identification in SVAR models.

Asymmetry

One possible approach to investigate the existence of asymmetric effects of x_t on y_t is to decompose the variable x_t into two new series: x_t^+ of its positive variations and x_t^- of the negative variations.

Based on Schorderet (2004) and Granger and Yoon (2002) method, a time series can be decomposed as follows:

$$x_t = x_0 + x_t^+ + x_t^- \tag{4}$$

Where

$$x_t^+ = \sum_{i=1}^{t} \theta_i(\Delta x_i); \quad \begin{cases} \theta_i = 1 \text{ se } \Delta x_i > 0, \\ 0, \text{ otherwise.} \end{cases} \tag{5}$$

$$x_t^- = \sum_{i=1}^{t} \theta_i^*(\Delta x_i); \quad \begin{cases} \theta_i^* = 1 \text{ se } \Delta x_i < 0, \\ 0, \text{ otherwise.} \end{cases} \tag{6}$$

Such as that, x_t value, for all t, is equal to its initial value (x_0) plus the sum of all its positive and negative variations up to t.

In this way, we have first difference of x_t^+ and x_t^- series:

$$dx_t^+ = \theta_i(\Delta x_i); \quad \begin{cases} \theta_i = 1 \text{ se } \Delta x_i > 0, \\ 0, \text{ otherwise.} \end{cases} \tag{7}$$

$$dx_t^- = \theta_i^*(\Delta x_i); \quad \begin{cases} \theta_i^* = 1 \text{ se } \Delta x_i < 0, \\ 0, \text{ otherwise.} \end{cases} \tag{8}$$

The decomposition in form (5) and (6) is known in literature as decomposition by cumulative variations whereas the form in (7) and (8) is known as period-to-period variations.

Series decomposed by cumulative variations have unit root and cointegrate and are used in the estimation of error correction models (ECM) and its multivariate form vector error correction (VEC).

For purpose of this chapter, that estimates a model with the stationary variables in first difference, the most adequate decomposition, that was used, is the period-to-period decomposition.

Exchange Rate Pass-Through

The exchange rate pass-through can be calculated from impulse response functions estimated by the SVAR model. This method was used by McCarthy (2007) to calculate the exchange rate pass-through for several industrialized countries and by Belaisch (2003) and Araújo and Modenesi (2010) for Brazil.

$$R_{t,t+j} = \left(\frac{\Sigma\,\Delta \mathrm{CPI}_{t,t+j}}{\Sigma\,\Delta \mathrm{ER}_{t,t+j}} \right) \cdot 100 \tag{9}$$

Where ΔCPI is consumer price index variations and ΔER exchange rate variations.

Wald Coefficient Restriction Test

Wald coefficient restriction tests were performed in asymmetric models to test the hypothesis that the coefficients relative to exchange rate positive variations are statistically different from the negative variations.

The test was performed under two different null hypothesis specifications:

H_0 (A) Null hypothesis that the sum of the coefficients of x^+ lags is equal to the sum of the coefficients of x^- lags.

H_0 (B) Null hypothesis that the lag coefficient i of y^+ is equal to the lag coefficient i of y^- for all lags.

To illustrate, generically, a two lags model, SVAR (2), and three variables, $Y_t = \left(y_1^+, y_1^-, y_2\right)$, where y_1^+ and y_1^- are period-to-period decompositions of y_1

In reduced form:

$$Y_t = c_0 + \Phi_1 Y_{t-1} + \Phi_2 Y_{t-2} + e_t \tag{10}$$

Can be written in the form

$$\begin{cases} y^+_{1_t} = c_1 y^+_{1_{t-1}} + c_2 y^+_{1_{t-2}} + c_3 y^-_{1_{t-1}} + c_4 y^-_{1_{t-2}} + c_5 y_{2_{t-1}} + c_6 \Delta y_{2_{t-2}} + c_7 \\ y^-_{1_t} = c_8 y^+_{1_{t-1}} + c_9 y^+_{1_{t-2}} + c_{10} y^-_{1_{t-1}} + c_{11} y^-_{1_{t-2}} + c_{12} y_{2_{t-1}} + c_{13} \Delta y_{2_{t-2}} + c_{14} \\ y_{2_t} = c_{15} y^+_{1_{t-1}} + c_{16} y^+_{1_{t-2}} + c_{17} y^-_{1_{t-1}} + c_{18} y^-_{1_{t-2}} + c_{19} y_{2_{t-1}} + c_{20} \Delta y_{2_{t-2}} + c_{21} \end{cases}$$

The Wald test was then calculated under H_0 with two different specifications

H_0 (A):

$$H_0 : c_1 + c_2 = c_3 + c_4 \text{ and } c_8 + c_9 = c_{10} + c_{11} \text{ and } c_{15} + c_{16} = c_{17} + c_{18}$$

H_0 (B):

$$H_0 : c_1 = c_3 \text{ and } c_2 = c_4 \; e \; c_8 = c_{10} \text{ and } c_9 = c_{11} \text{ and } c_{15} = c_{17} \; e \; c_{16} = c_{18}$$

Under H_0, the Wald statistic is asymptotically distributed as a $\chi^2(q)$, where q is the number of linear restrictions.

Wald test statistics reject the null hypothesis that coefficients are equal at conventional significance levels. Under the null hypothesis A, the test statistic was 8.38 (0.08 p-value). Under the null hypothesis B, test statistic was 16.57 (0.03 p-value). Therefore, results indicate the existence of asymmetry, that is, that exchange rate devaluations have different effects on inflation than exchange rate appreciations.

References

Allsopp, C., & Vivens, D. (2000). The assessment: Macroeconomic policy. *Oxford Review of Economic Policy, 16*(4), 1–32.

Almendra, P., Portugal, M., & Macêdo, G. (2015). Pass-through da taxa de câmbio para a inflação no Brasil: Um estudo econométrico utilizando o filtro de Kalman. *43º Encontro Nacional de Economia (ANPEC)*. Florianopolis.

Álvarez, E., Jaramillo, P., & Selaive, J. (2008). *Exchange rate pass-through into import prices: The case of Chile* (Working Paper No. 465). Santiago: Banco Central de Chile.

Araújo, E., & Modenesi, A. (2010). A Importância do Setor Externo na Evolução do IPCA (1999–2010): uma análise com base em um modelo SVAR. *XXXVIII Encontro Nacional de Economia*—ANPEC, Salvador.

Arestis, P., Ferrari, Filho F., & Paula, L. F. (2011). Inflation targeting in Brazil. *International Review of Applied Economics, 25*(2), 127–148.

Belaisch, A. (2003). *Exchange rate pass-through in Brazil* (IMF Working Paper 03/141). Washington: International Monetary Fund.

Blinder, A. (1981). Monetarism is obsolete. *Challenge*, September/October, pp. 35–43.

Blinder A. (1998). A core of macroeconomic beliefs. *Challenge*, July/August, pp. 36–44.

BCB. (2016). *Inflation targeting in Brazil.* Brazilian Central Bank, Brasília. Available at http://www.bcb.gov.br/pec/metas/InflationTargetingTable.pdf.

Brun-Aguerre, R., Fuertes, A., & Greenwood-Nimmo, M. (2017). Heads I win; tails you lose: Asymmetry in exchange rate pass-through into import prices. *Journal of the Royal Statistical Society: Series A (Statistics in Society), 180*(2), February, 587–612.

Bussiere, M. (2013). Exchange rate pass-through in the G7 economies: The role of nonlinearities and asymmetries. *Oxford Bulletin of Economics and Statistics, 75*(5), 731–758.

Calvo, G., & Reinhart, C. (2000). *Fixing for your life* (NBER Working Papers 8006). Cambridge, MA: National Bureau of Economic Research, Inc.

Campa, J., & Goldberg, L. (2005). Exchange rate pass-through into imports prices. *The Review of Economics and Statistics, 87,* 679–690.

Campa, J., Mínguez, J., & Barriel, M. (2008). *Non-linear adjustment of import prices in the European Union* (Bank of England Working Paper No. 347).

Carneiro, D., Monteiro, A., & Wu, T. (2004). Mecanismos não-lineares de repasse cambial para o IPCA. *Revista de Economia e Administração, 3*(1), 1–14.

Carvalho, F. (2000–2001). The IMF as crisis manager: An assessment of the strategy in Asia and of its criticisms. *Journal of Post Keynesian Economics*, Winter *23*(2), 235–266.

Choudhri, E., & Hakura, D. (2006). Exchange rate pass-through to domestic prices: Does the inflationary environment matter? *Journal of International Money and Finance, 25*(4), 614–639.

Correa, A. S., & Minella, A. (2010). Nonlinear mechanisms of the exchange rate pass-through: A Phillips curve model with threshold for Brazil. *Revista Brasileira de Economia, 64*(3), 231–243.

Davidson, P. (2003). *Post Keynesian macroeconomic theory.* Cheltenham: Edward Elgar.

Delatte, A., & Villavicencio, A. (2012). Asymmetric exchange rate pass-through: Evidence from major countries. *Journal of Macroeconomics, 34*(3), 833–844.

Enders, W. (2014). *Applied Econometric Time Series.* Wiley Series in Probability and Mathematical Statistics. London: Wiley.

Foster, H., & Baldwin, R. (1986). *Marketing bottlenecks and the relationship between exchange rates and prices* (Working Paper). Cambridge, MA: Department of Economics, Massachusetts Institute of Technology.

Fraga, G., & Couto, S. (2013). O pass-through da taxa de câmbio para índices de preços: uma análise empírica para o Brasil. *XVI Encontro de Economia da Região Sul*—ANPEC/SUL, Curitiba.

Friedman, M. (1956). The quantity theory of money—a restatement. In M. Friedman (Ed.), *Studies in the quantity theory of money.* Chicago: Chicago University Press.

Friedman, M. (1968). The role of monetary policy. *The American Economic Review, LVIII*(1), 1–17.

Froot, K., & Klemperer, P. (1989). Exchange rate pass-through when market share matters. *American Economic Review, 79*(4), 637–654.

Gagnon, J., & Ihrig, J. (2004). Monetary policy and exchange rate pass-through. *International Journal of Finance & Economics, 9*(4), 315–338.

Gil-Pareja, S. (2000). Exchange rates and European countries' export prices: An empirical test for asymmetries in pricing to market behavior. *Weltwirtschaftliches Archiv, 136*(1), 1–23.

Goldfajn, I., & Werlang, S. (2000). *The pass-through from depreciation to inflation: A panel study* (Banco Central Do Brasil Working Paper 5). Brasília: Banco Central do Brasil.

Granger, C., & Yoon, G. (2002). *Hidden cointegration* (Department of Economics Working Paper No. 02). San Diego: University of California.

Herzberg, V., Kapetanios, G., & Price G. (2003). *Import prices and exchange rate pass through: Theory and evidence from the United Kingdom* (Bank of England Working Paper No. 182).

IBGE (2016). *National system of consumer price indexes.* Brazilian Institute of Geography and Statistics, Brasília. Available at http://www.ibge.gov.br/english/estatistica/indicadores/precos/inpc_ipca/defaultinpc.shtm.

IMF (2016a). *International financial statistics.* International Monetary Fund, Washington, D.C., US. Available at http://data.imf.org.

IMF (2016b). *World economic outlook*. International Monetary Fund, Washington, DC, US. Available at http://data.imf.org.

Karoro, T., Meshach, A., & Cattaneo, N. (2009). Exchange rate pass-through to import prices in South Africa: Is there asymmetry? *South African Journal of Economics, 77*(3), 380–398.

Khundrakpam, J. (2007). *Economic reforms and exchange rate pass-through to domestic prices in India* (Bank for International Settlements Working Paper No. 225). Basel, Switzerland.

Keynes, J. M. (1943). *International clearing union*, 28 Parl. Deb., H. L. (5th ser.), 527–537.

Keynes, J. M. (1980). *The collected writings of John Maynard Keynes*. In D. E. Moggridge (Ed.), *Activities 1940–1944. Shaping the Post-war World: The Clearing Union*, Vol. 25. London: Macmillan Publishers.

Kilian, L. (2011). Structural vector autoregressions, *CEPR Discussion Papers* No. 8515, London, UK.

Knetter, M. (1994). Is export price adjustment asymmetric? Evaluating the market share and marketing bottlenecks hypotheses. *Journal of International Money and Finance, 13*(1), 55–70.

Kohlscheen, E. (2010). Emerging floaters: Pass-throughs and (some) new commodity currencies. *Journal of International Money and Finance, 29*(8), 1580–1595.

Kregel, J. (2015) Emerging markets and the international financial architecture: a blueprint for reform. *Revista de Economia Política 35*(2), 285–305.

Krugman, P. (1987). Pricing to market when the exchange rate changes. In S. Arndt & J. Richardson (Eds.), *Real-financial linkages among open economies*. Cambridge, MA: MIT Press.

Krugman, P., & Obstfeld, M. (1997). *International economics: Theory and policy* (4th ed.). Massachusetts: Addison Wesley.

Lavoie, M. (2004). The new consensus on monetary policy seen from a Post Keynesian perspective. In M. Lavoie & M. Seccareccia (Eds.), *Central banking in the modern world: Alternative perspectives*. Cheltenham: Edward-Elgar.

Lütkepohl, H. (2005). *New introduction to multiple time series analysis*. Cambridge: Cambridge University Press.

Marodin, F., & Portugal, M. (2015). *Exchange rate pass-through in Brazil: A Markov switching DSGE estimation for the inflation targeting period (2000–2015)* (Working Paper PPGE/UFRGS).

Marston, R. (1990). Pricing to market in Japanese manufacturing. *Journal of International Economics, 29*, 217–236.

McCarthy, J. (2007). Pass-through of exchange rates and import prices to domestic inflation in some industrialized economies. *Eastern Economic Journal, 33*(4), 511–537.

Menezes, G., & Fernandez, R. (2012). Análise do efeito pass-through cambial para a formação dos índices de preços no Brasil (1999–2011*). XV Encontro de Economia da Região Sul—ANPEC/ SUL*, Porto Alegre, Brazil.

Mihaljek, D., & Klau, M. (2008). *Exchange rate pass-through in emerging market economies: What has changed and why?* (Bank for International Settlements Working Paper No. 35). Basel, Switzerland.

Minella, A., Freitas, P., Goldfajn, I., & Muinhos, M. (2003). Inflation targeting in Brazil: Constructing credibility under exchange rate volatility. *Journal of International Money and Finance, 22,* 1015–1040.

Modenesi, A. (2005). *Regimes Monetários: teoria e a experiência do real.* 1. ed. Barueri (SP). Ed. Manole.

Modenesi, A. M., & Araújo, E. (2013). Price stability under inflation targeting in Brazil: An empirical analysis of the monetary policy transmission mechanism based on a VAR model (2000–2008). *Investigación Económica, LXXII,* 99–133.

Modenesi, A., & Modenesi, R. (2012). Quinze Anos de Rigidez Monetária no Brasil: uma agenda de pesquisa. *Revista de Economia Política, 32*(3), 389–411.

Modenesi, A., Modenesi, R., & Silva, T. (2017). Brazil's Macroprudential framework to tackle the great financial crisis: Monetary policy, financial regulation and the banking system. In E. Grivoyannis (Ed.), *The new Brazilian economy: Dynamic transitions into the future.* New York: Palgrave Macmillan.

Nogueira, R. (2006). Inflation targeting, exchange rate pass-through and 'fear of floating'. *Studies in Economics 0605,* Department of Economics, University of Kent.

Nogueira, P. (2007). Inflation targeting and exchange rate pass-through. *Economia Aplicada, São Paulo, 11*(2), 189–208.

Nogueira, V., Mori, R., & Marcal, E. (2012). Transmissão da variação cambial para as taxas de inflação no Brasil: estimação do pass-through através de modelos de vetores autorregressivos estruturais com correção de erros. *XL Encontro Nacional de Economia*—ANPEC, Porto de Galinhas, Brazil.

Nonnenberg, M., & Lameiras, M. (2005). Preços das commodities e o IPA. *Boletim de Conjuntura,* IPEA, No. 69.

Paula, L., Fritz, B., & Prates, D. (2017). Keynes at the periphery: Currency hierarchy and challenges for economic policy in emerging economies. *Journal of Post Keynesian Economics,* Forthcoming.

Pollard, P., & Coughlin, C. (2003). *Size matters: Asymmetric exchange rate pass-through at the industry level* (Bank of St. Louis Working Paper Series No. 2003–2029).
Przystupa, J., & Wróbel, E. (2011). Asymmetry of the exchange rate pass-through: An exercise on the Polish data. *Eastern European Economics, 49*(1), 30–51.
Reis, M., Modenesi, A., & Modenesi, R. (2016). The Brazilian economy after the 2008 Global financial crisis: The end of the macroeconomic tripod's golden age. In H. Cömert & A. McKenzie (Eds.), *The global south after the crisis growth, inequality and development in the aftermath of the great recession* (pp. 95–118). Cheltenham: Edward Elgar.
Romer, D. (2000). Keynesian macroeconomics without the LM curve. *Journal of Economic Perspectives, 14*(2), 149–169.
Rubio-Ramirez, J., Waggoner, D., & Zha, T. (2010). Structural vector autoregressions: Theory of Identification and algorithms for Inference. *Review of Economic Studies, 77,* 665–696.
Schorderet, Y. (2004). *Asymmetric cointegration* (Working Paper). Department of Econometrics, University of Geneva, Switzerland.
Silva, C. & Vernengo, M. (2008). The decline of the exchange rate pass-through in Brazil: Explaining the 'Fear of Floating'. *International Journal of Political Economy, 37*(4), 64–79.
Squeff, G. (2009). Repasse cambial reverso: uma avaliação sobre a relação entre taxa de câmbio e IPCA no Brasil (1999–2007). *II Encontro Internacional da Associação Keynesiana Brasileira*, Porto Alegre, Brazil.
Souza, R., & Alves, A. (2011). Relação entre câmbio e preços no Brasil: aspectos teóricos e evidências empíricas. *XXXVIII Encontro Nacional de Economia*, ANPEC.
Souza, R., Maciel, L., & Pizzinga, A. (2013). State space models for the exchange rate pass-through: Determinants and null/full pass-through hypotheses. *Applied Economics, 45*(36), 5062–5075.
Taylor, J. (1993). Discretion versus policy rules in practice. *Carnegie-Rochester Conference Series on Public Policy, 39,* 195–214.
Taylor, J. (2000). Teaching modern macroeconomics at the principles level. *American Economic Review, 90*(2), 90–94.
Taylor, J. (2001). The role of the exchange rate in monetary-policy rules. *The American Economic Review, 91*(2), 263–267.
Vernengo, M. (2006). Money and inflation. In P. Arestis & M. Sawyer (Eds.), *Handbook of alternative monetary economics.* Northampton, MA: Edward Elgar.

Walsh, C. (2003). *Monetary theory and policy* (2nd ed.). Cambridge, MA: The MIT Press.

Ware, R., & Winter, R. (1988). Forward markets, currency options and the hedging of foreign exchange risk. *Journal of International Economics, 25*(3), 291–302.

Webber, A. (1999). Newton's gravity law and import prices in the Asia Pacific. *Japan and the World Economy, 12*(1), 71–87.

Wickremasinghe, G., & Silvapulle, P. (2004). Exchange rate pass-through to manufactured import prices: The case of Japan. *International Trade*, 406006.

New Features of the Brazilian External Sector Since the Great Global Crisis

André Biancarelli, Renato Rosa and Rodrigo Vergnhanini

1 Introduction

When the first official numbers about Brazilian economic performance in 2016 came into light—a drop of −3.6% in GDP, after −3.8% in 2015—the impression about 'the worst crisis in history' became a consensus, at least in quantitative terms. In fact, the intensity and duration of the crises at the beginning of 1930s, 1980s and 1990s were left behind by the current slump. With the exception of the latter (in which the immediate cause was the blockage of financial assets liquidity

A. Biancarelli (✉) · R. Rosa · R. Vergnhanini
Universidade Estadual de Campinas, Campinas, SP, Brazil
e-mail: ambiancareli@gmail.com; andremb@unicamp.br

R. Rosa
e-mail: renatodsrosa@yahoo.com.br

R. Vergnhanini
e-mail: verg.rodrigo@gmail.com

P. Arestis et al. (eds.), *The Brazilian Economy since the Great Financial Crisis of 2007/2008*, https://doi.org/10.1007/978-3-319-64885-9_5

by the 'Collor Plan'), the biggest recessions in Brazil always had close links with the external sector. The recent trends, at first sight, seem to be typical on this ground: a growing current account deficit amid a global *bonanza*, suddenly reverted with a maxi devaluation of domestic currency and a sharp decline in economic activity.

However, this time the main aspect of these stories was absent namely, the well-known 'foreign exchange shortage'. Neither before nor during the collapse of the Brazilian economy during Dilma Rousseff's presidential term (2011–2015) was there a 'lack of dollars'. This is the biggest novelty of Brazilian external sector since 2008 international financial crisis, and one of the central arguments of the present chapter.

This chapter aims at discussing the relations between the international relations of Brazilian economy and its current crisis. These links are present in the recent macroeconomic debate, but in an insufficient and inadequate way. The main contribution of this chapter, and to this debate, is twofold. On the one hand, we argue that the negative influence of global economy on Brazil is not visible in the traditional channels (i.e. balance-of-payments flows and foreign assets/liabilities analyses), which are marked by important novelties during the last years. On the other hand, we identify indirect (and structural) relations between the external sector and domestic activity, namely the coupling of domestic productive and financial dynamics to international cycles, which seem to play an important role. If acceptable, this situation poses even greater difficulties to the Brazilian development, which are not evaded only by recessions or competitive gains through domestic currency devaluation.

The chapter is divided into five sections besides this introduction. The first one is a brief summary of recent Brazilian economic debate, based on the relations between the downturn and the external sector. In the second, a short outlook of the international economy since the great financial crisis is presented, and a periodization of the main influences is proposed. The third section describes the 'new reality' of the Brazilian external accounts, by means of balance-of-payments flows and external assets and liabilities. In the fourth, some ideas and evidence about the indirect (and structural) channels of influence are outlined. A final section summarizes and concludes.

2 External Sector in the Brazilian Macroeconomic Debate

All the discussions about the recent Brazilian economic crisis have been very intense. The role given to the external sector in the progressive deterioration, however, is discrete in most of the cases. An important part of the arguments was devoted to refuting the thesis widely used by the official rhetoric: that the downturn until 2014 was caused essentially by the worsening global economy.

Hegemonic in this debate, the liberal/orthodox narrative, of which the CDPP (2014) chapters are good examples, concentrates its explanations for the crisis on the misguided economic policy measures, the low productivity of the economy and, particularly, the fiscal imbalance. Marginal considerations about the external sector are made. Barbosa Filho and Pessoa (2014) emphatically refute, with regional and global comparisons, the 'blame' of the bad international scenario in the loss of dynamism. This would be better explained by the combination of a political choice, which limits growth potential and an ideological shift in economic policy since 2006. This latter option, by means of the various state intervention mechanisms, had hit capital productivity. An example of this was the growth rate of real wages, above labour productivity by compressing profits, which led to a reduction in the saving rate and, therefore, a worsening of the external deficit.

The understanding of the current account balance, as the product of domestic absorption (i.e. the external financing, which is just a result of low domestic savings), is also the foundation for the reasoning of Pastore and Pinotti (2014). Nevertheless, there is no rejection of external influence on the downturn. Countries such as Brazil, with insufficient domestic savings, would need to finance the excess of investments with current account deficits, depending on the availability of capital flows (external savings). Phases in which this occurs constitute a bonanza, which sometimes (as it was in the recent cycle) can be strengthened by gains also in terms of trade resulting from the rise in basic commodity prices. The two sources of bonanza would have weakened during the first half of this decade, forcing a costly but necessary recessive adjustment and currency devaluation.

Elsewhere in the Brazilian ideological spectrum, the most important authors of the 'new-developmentalism' (especially L.C. Bresser-Pereira and J.L. Oreiro)[1] have been warning for years about the dangers of 'growth *cum* external savings strategy'. They were, until the worsening of macroeconomic conditions in 2015, emphatic advocates of a strong fiscal and exchange rate adjustment in order to prevent the current account deficit. The background inspiration of this literature lies in balance-of-payments constrained growth models, and the structural proposal is to emulate in Brazil an Asian-style export-led growth.

Also focused on macroeconomics, but with opposite assumptions and conclusions, papers like Serrano and Summa (2015) and Lara (2015) not only do they reject the projected pessimism about the external sector, but also the official explanation for the slowdown. They point out that there was no difficulty in financing the current account deficits. The deceleration, therefore, had domestic causes, essentially the reversal of the expansive macroeconomic policy that was implemented until 2010 and was not required by the external conditions of the economy. Biancarelli (2012, 2016), as well as Biancarelli & Rosa (2015), develops similar reasoning, arguing that the external vulnerability of the Brazilian economy has reduced and changed its nature.

With the benefit of some time that has passed, and in view of the current processes in the Brazilian economy, this last approach, in fact, seems the most adequate—as argued in the next sections. However, it must be complemented now with another dimension. Even without causing the traditional problems of restraining foreign exchange, the idea is that the close links of Brazil with the financial and productive gears of the global economy indirectly transmit its negative impulses and contribute to the downturn and the crisis. This is the perspective that seems to be lacking in the debate, and that is raised in the last section of this chapter, as a suggestion for further research.

[1]See, for example, Bresser-Pereira and Gala (2008); Bresser-Pereira et al. (2014).

3 A Changing World Since 2008

This section summarizes the evolution of global conditions for the 'emerging economies', in the aftermath of the great financial crisis, focusing on the financial (international liquidity) and productive/commercial aspects (prices and quantities in international trade).

From the data related to the international liquidity (Fig. 1), and the global trade (Fig. 2), three major phases can be identified in the post-crisis: i) a 'sudden resumption' immediately after the collapse that lasted until the end of 2010; ii) a 'post-bonanza' from 2011 to 2014; and, finally iii) a third phase since mid-2014 better described as a 'double storm'.

The context and determinants of the 'sudden resumption' are well known: the anti-cyclical fiscal and monetary measures applied by major economic powers prevented the full transmission of the financial meltdown to economic activity and, as a side effect, reassembled the international liquidity. Gross capital inflows to emerging markets in this context reached in 2010 levels slightly below the pre-crisis levels

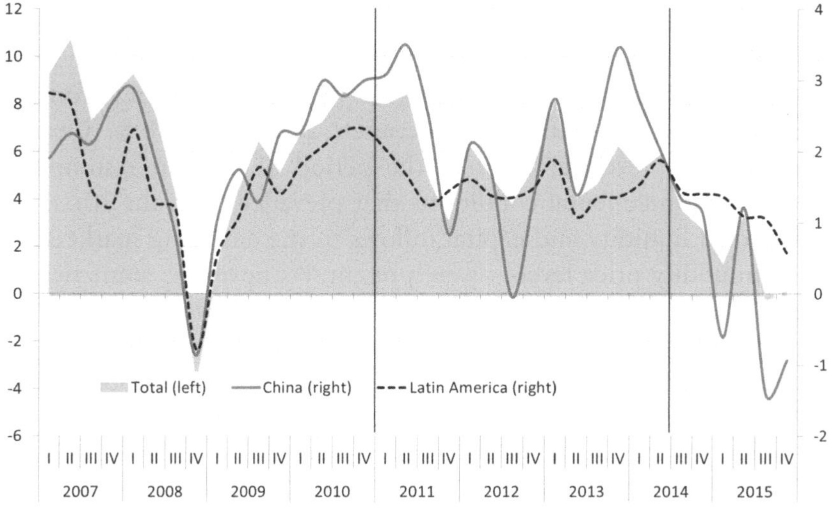

Fig. 1 Capital inflows to emerging markets, GDP share, 2007–2015. *Source* IMF (2016). Authors' elaboration

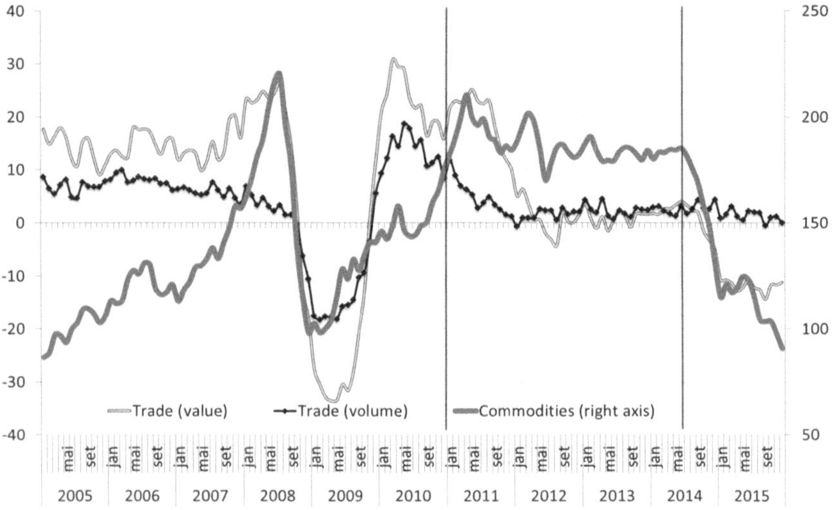

Fig. 2 World trade annual growth (%) and basic commodity prices (2005 = 100), 2005–2015. *Source* IMF (2016). Authors' elaboration

(Fig. 1), and the movement of global trade in values and in basic commodity prices (Fig. 2) was also marked by fast recovery.

Here, the period that started in 2011 is qualified as 'post-bonanza'. The goal is to emphasize both the differences and the similarities with the extraordinary period of favourable impulses, resulting from the global arrangement that existed between 2003 and 2008 (Ocampo 2007). Even at levels lower than the period of 'sudden resumption', some of the fundamental conditions that prevailed until the crisis—i.e. ample global liquidity and capital inflows to the emerging markets, still high commodity price levels—were present. As novelties, some destabilizing elements exist: much greater financial instability and crisis threats, lower dynamism and tougher competition in international trade.

The main determinant of the rapid reassembly of global liquidity during the 'sudden resumption' and also in the 'post-bonanza' is undoubtedly the unusually expansionist nature of central monetary policies. Policy rates held close to zero for several years, and securities purchase programs along the yield curve, in an attempt to further expand liquidity (*Quantitative Easing* in subsequent rounds and some national qualitative variations). In this regard, attention should be paid not only to the US Federal Reserve, but also to the monetary authorities of the UK, Japan and, with an additional grain of conservatism, Europe. In this context, it emerged, and in the international arena, the Brazilian claims about a 'currency war' or a'monetary tsunami' that would be harming the country until 2012 or 2013. Crisis episodes (or threats) that increased risk aversion and volatility, as well as the somewhat lower levels of capital inflows over this period (in relation to the peak reached before and immediately after the crisis), do not invalidate the characterization of them as also a phase of excess, and not lack, of external financing.

On the commercial side, the lower dynamism during the 'post-bonanza' is explained mainly by the weakening of US demand, of which China had been the biggest beneficiary and transmitter around the world. The Asian power, after the crisis, began to compensate the lesser dynamism of exports to the USA with a greater force in other markets, making international competition much more intense. In this context, the enormous idle capacity in that country functioned as a powerful element of influence on the decisions of investment and production worldwide, as commented in Sect. "The Current Account".

At the same time, the other favourable element of the previous bonanza phase—the high prices of basic commodities—was rebuilt, motivated not only by the support of Chinese growth, but also by the abundant liquidity and low interest rates, which reinforced the speculation and financialization of the markets of these products (UNCTAD 2011). As a result, the terms of trade for primary commodity exporters were, by mid-2014, still very favourable in historical terms, even though they were already below the peaks of before 2008.

However, these two benign ingredients of the 'sudden resumption' and 'post-bonanza' (upturns in liquidity cycles and commodity prices) reverted sharply in the middle of 2014, and the 'double storm' phase started. The relationship between them decreases, and the mitigation of global monetary expansionism obviously exists, but it is complex: signs for the normalization of monetary policy in the USA date back to the first half of 2013, and the first increase of the basic interest rate only came to materialize at the end of 2015. Meanwhile, the central banks of the other economies issuing 'funding currencies' for capital flows have maintained or even extended their monetary easing. More directly and decisively, the slowdown in the Chinese economy, which influences commodity prices and concentrates the bulk of the decline in capital inflows over 2014 and 2015 (Fig. 1), seems to have been decisive.

4 The 'New Reality' of the External Sector

As stated in Sect. 1, our contribution defends the existence of a 'new reality' of the Brazilian external sector, even before the current domestic crisis. In essence, it means a greater capacity to maintain deficits in current account, already identified in previous works (Biancarelli 2012, 2016; Biancarelli and Rosa 2015). In the present chapter, written in a very different environment (both domestic and external), the focus is to reassess this diagnosis, in two steps.

On the one hand, the periodization proposed in the preceding section will be used to analyse Brazilian external accounts since 2008. This is developed throughout the present section by examining the flows in the balance-of-payments and stocks of external assets and liabilities. On the other hand, some preliminary ideas and evidence will be presented in Sect. 5 in order to sustain the argument that global economy did contribute to the development of recent economic crises, albeit not through the traditional mechanism of dollar shortages.

The Current Account

From 2008 to 2016, Brazilian current account went through different phases, which closely corresponded to the international periodization developed in the previous section. The configuration of these phases depended more on some structural trends (i.e. domestic and international growth conditions) than on the evolution of the exchange rate. Figure 3 shows the general trajectory of current account, whose value, just as for every other time series in this section, was accumulated over 12 months and based on the most recent methodological revision of the Brazilian Central Bank (IMF BPM6, as in April of 2015).

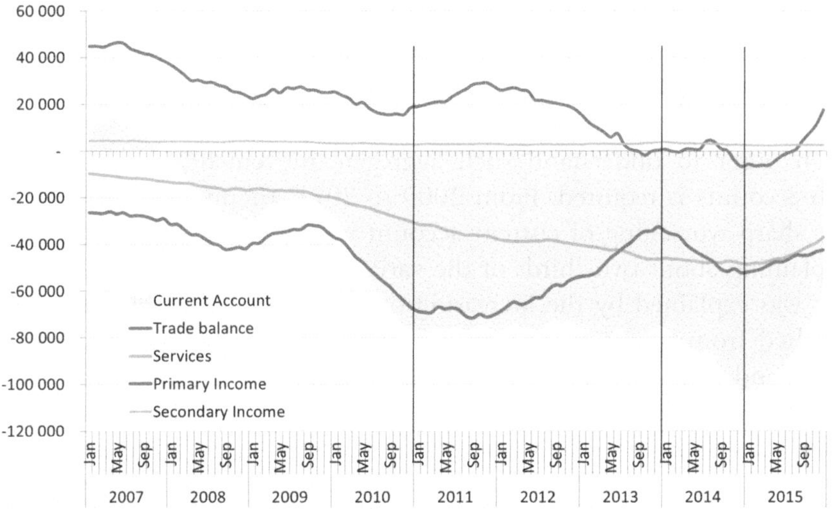

Fig. 3 Current Account and components, 12-months accumulated (US$ million), 2007–2015. *Source* Brazilian Central Bank (various issues). Authors' elaboration

In the first phase (2009–2011), which corresponds to the immediate post-crisis period, there was a 'sudden resumption' of main flows, such as exports, imports and primary income flows. As a result, current account deficit experienced a sharp deterioration, departing from US$20 billion (−1.2% of GDP) and reaching almost US$80 billion (more than 3% of GDP) in only 16 months.

In the second phase, the current account global balance was kept stable around the negative value of almost US$80 billion, (around 3% of GDP) for as long as three years (from 2011 to 2013).

The third phase, which corresponds to the year of 2014, was marked by rapid worsening of current deficit until reaching US$104 billion by the end of that year (or 4.5% of GDP).

Until then, the evolution of current account was in line with international cycle, moving from a 'post bonanza' (2011–2014) to a'double storm' (2014) type of performance. However, from the beginning of 2015, Brazilian current account detached from the international trend, and responded to the severe adjustment policies that started to be pursued by domestic authorities. Until December of that year, the deficit was downsized to less than US$60 billion (2.9% PIB). After having kept the same intensity throughout 2016, the adjustment in external accounts generated the impressing low deficit of US$23.5 billion (1.3% of GDP) in December of 2016.

In order to understand such aggregate movement, analysis of the sub-accounts is required. From 2009 to 2011, the main contributor to the sharp worsening of current account was direct investment income, explaining about two-thirds of the variation. The one-third of variation left was explained by the increasing deficit in the trade balance, which resulted from imports growing at a faster pace than exports. Between 2011 and 2013, when there was relative stability in the aggregate balance (around 4.4% of variation), reinvested earnings and exports contributed positively to the global result, whereas imports, and to a lesser extent, the services of travel and operational leasing, had a negative contribution. In 2014, the reduction in imports was not enough to compensate the deterioration in exports and reinvested earnings, so that the global result was reduced by −36.7%. Lastly, the adjustment of external accounts during 2015 and 2016 was based mainly on a sharp fall of imports, enough to compensate the worsening in exports. The combination of these moves resulted in the impressive reduction by 77.4% of current account deficits within only two years.

Some special attention should be given to movements in the trade balance, always using data from Brazilian Ministry of Development, Industry and Trade (MDIC). Until 2006, exports grew at a faster rate than imports, creating increasing commercial surpluses. Between 2007 and 2010, with the exception of the first semester of 2009 (which suffered the effects of the international financial crisis), there was a clear reversal of this tendency: imports grew faster than exports, reducing the trade balance from US$45.5 (April/2007) to US$15.4 billion (September/2010).

After almost one year of recovery, the deterioration in the trade balance was resumed in October 2011. From this date until October 2013, the surplus was progressively reduced to zero. This striking outcome has yielded different interpretations regarding its determinants, whether external or domestic, and its structural or conjectural nature.

The analysis of the quantum of exports by aggregate factor reveals an important trend: the volume of basic products grew continuously throughout the period; the volume of semi-manufactured goods remained virtually stagnant; and the volume of manufactured goods suffered a 20% reduction in the immediate post-crisis, remaining stagnant at the same level thereafter.

This indicates a regressive specialization trend of exports over the period. The stagnation of exported manufactured goods must be understood in the context of weak dynamism of developed economies, accumulation of global idle capacity and intensified competitiveness in international trade after the great financial crisis, as stated above. Export prices, in turn, presented important oscillations for all aggregate factors, and the variance was significantly higher for basic goods.

Attention must be paid to oscillations in the imported volume. From mid-2010, it quickly resumed the pre-crisis dynamism. Between October 2012 and July 2013, it remained stagnant. Then, between August 2013 and March 2014, the monthly average growth (in annual terms) was 6%. As to the other months of 2014, there was modest decrease (−3%) in this indicator. Finally, 2015 was marked by a progressive accentuation in the fall of imports, until it reached the monthly contraction by −25% over the last quarter of the year.

Overall, there is significant stability in the composition of imported value. Durable consumer goods have increased their share from 4% in 2007 to 8% in December 2012. Since then, possibly because of the already high level of household indebtedness and of exchange devaluation, these imports shrank more than the average and in 2013, they returned to the initial share of 4%. Fuels maintained their share in total imported value (until 2014), although their prices have fallen about 20% over the same period. That indicates a greater dependence on fuel imports. Delays in refinery construction and maintenance shutdowns on extraction platforms are some of the isolated causes of this significant loss in the 'oil account'. The bad results were obtained shortly after the country had celebrated its self-sufficiency in this commodity and had been expecting a boom in production with the exploration of the pre-salt layer.

In short, the reduction in the trade balance throughout the post-crisis period can be understood by the unfavourable reversal of the terms of trade as of the end of 2011, by the stagnation of the exported volume, and by the rigidity of the import structure, not to mention the significant losses in fuel trade. Despite the currency devaluation, the current account balance only began to improve after 2015, with a further strong depreciation and the adoption of economic policies to contain domestic demand. In this sense, the external adjustment promoted after 2015 was not virtuous, since it was not based on the expansion of exports or the substitution of imports, but on the contraction of the latter as an indirect result of the restrictive economic measures imposed domestically.

From a structural point of view, the deepening of some regressive and long-term tendencies marked the external sector in the post-crisis. The deficit in the primary income account and its pro-cyclicality is a structural feature of the Brazilian economy, reflecting the high degree of internationalization of productive and financial.

Another relevant aspect is the persistent increase in 'equipment rental' expenses which, although largely derived from Petrobras' strategy to import oil platforms, has actually made the services account deficit more rigid and substantial in relation to GDP (in 2007, it was −0.9%, going to −1.4% in 2011 and −2.1% in 2015).

To sum up, the performance of the Brazilian current account in the post-crisis was to a greater extent the result of aggravating structural problems than of short-term macroeconomic imbalances. It followed the evolution of the post-crisis global scenario: sharp decline during the 'sudden resumption'; relative stability in the 'post-bonanza' and worsening in the 'double storm' phase. Finally, for little virtuous reasons, brought about by the shift in economic policy, this trajectory is reversed in 2015.

Overall, as we argue here, the most important novelties regarding the 'new reality' of the Brazilian external sector do not refer to the current account aspects. In order to understand this alleged change in the nature of the external sector, it is necessary to understand how the persistent current deficits were financed throughout the post-crisis period.

Financial Flows

The conventional view understands the financial flows recorded in the balance of payments as an automatic replication of current account deficits: it is taken as 'import of savings', and therefore it would suffice to look at net capital flows. In the new methodology of the organization of external accounts (BPM6), this impression of 'automatism' is reinforced, since the variation of international reserves, before a 'closing' balance sheet item, is now included in the financial account.

Cross-border capital flows are understood here as portfolio allocation (and assets/liabilities creation) linked to decisions that are unrelated to 'savings needs', generally driven more by financial than real determinants, with a cyclical behaviour. This oscillating availability, influenced much more by external factors than domestic ones, is usually the main (and much faster) determinant of the phases of tranquillity or distress in the balance of payments (see, e.g. Akyuz 2014). However, in order to assess this phenomenon, it is not enough to observe the net register of capital flows like those depicted in Fig. 4. Gross data about the

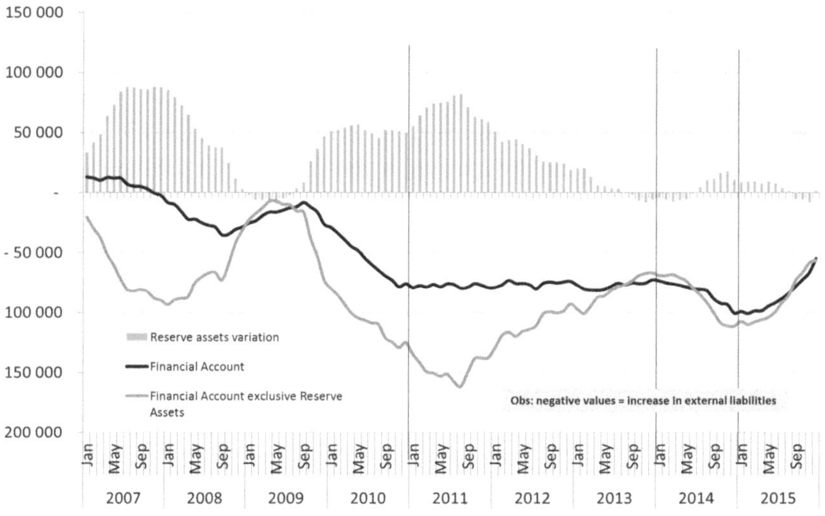

Fig. 4 Financial Account (BPM6), 12-month accumulated (US$ million), 2007–2015. *Source* Brazilian Central Bank (various issues). Authors' elaboration

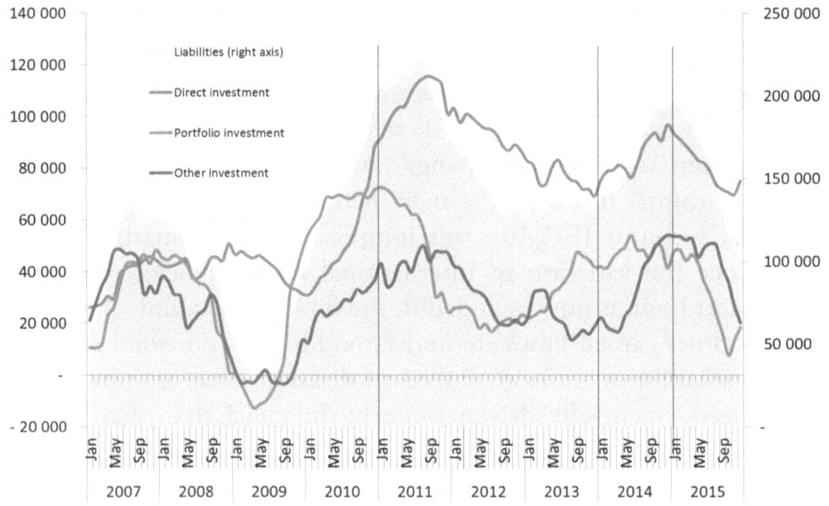

Fig. 5 Non-residents capital inflows, 12-month accumulated (US$ million), 2007–2015. *Source* Brazilian Central Bank (various issues). Authors' elaboration

non-residents movements (inflows, Fig. 5) is also a necessary measure, showing the real conditions of external financing, its phases and components.

The periodization that emerges from this examination is the same as that obtained for current account, in four phases: i) 2009 and 2010, with an evident 'sudden resumption'; ii) from 2011 to 2013, with moderation in inflows and improvement in its profile; iii) 2014, marked by the increase in inflows and worsening in its composition; and finally, iv) 2015, with a fast drop.

The first phase corresponds to the initial 'tsunami' of liquidity in 2009 and 2010, bulky streams of money chasing yields triggered by the unusual expansionary monetary policy in the financial centres. Brazil was one of the main destines of this wave, thanks to its extraordinary high level of interest rates that attracted especially portfolio flows and bank loans (Fig. 5). The total amounts received were higher than the pre-crisis records, both in net and gross accountings.

The second period (2011–2013) can be understood as a controlled (and desired) moderation in the absorption of external resources. In view of the stability of the current account deficit, net funding (Fig. 4) contracted at US$90 billion (or 60% of the previous total) and the reduction in inflows was of 40%. The weakening in the global liquidity cycle (see Fig. 1) at this stage influences this reduction, but it is not the main factor—even because for the emerging economies as a whole, the figure was of stability at high levels, not this sharp drop.

Brazil sought to discourage the capture of these resources. After all, they far outweighed the 'needs' dictated by the current account and resulted in an important but costly accumulation of international reserves—at its peak in the 12 months ending in August 2011, the country accumulated $82 billion. Two major instruments were used on that occasion: the significant fall in the interest differential until the first quarter of 2013 and the gradual imposition of controls on capital inflows.[2]

These measures had a positive effect on the composition of external financing. As noted in Fig. 5, the attractiveness of 'other investments' and 'portfolio investment' had decreased quickly and intensely. Regarding direct investment in the country, there was also a significant reduction in values (from US$115 billion accumulated in September 2011 to US$70 billion in December 2013), but it must be taken into account that more than 80% of that drop was the counterpart of the fall in 'reinvested earnings', already discussed in Sect. "The Current Account". Even with this accounting effect, inflows of FDI gained importance in the total absorbed at this stage and were for almost the entire period more than sufficient to cover the current account deficit.

In the second quarter of 2013, despite the fact that the total inflows remained stable, its composition started to change again, and the improvement previously verified simply reversed. Domestic securities gained importance, attracted by the widening of the interest rate differential in April of 2013, by the withdrawal of capital controls and the maintenance of ample global liquidity, despite fears of tightening Federal Reserve policy.

However, it is only in 2014 that we can talk about a third phase, marked not only by this qualitative deterioration in the composition of external financing—now with a growth in loans and bonds abroad,

[2]On capital control measures adopted at that time, see Prates and De Paula (2017).

other liabilities and even shares of domestic companies—but by a surge in total amount attracted. There was a strong increase in net funding (US$40 billion or 60%) and inflows (US$54 billion or 40%) amid the 'dip' in the current account deficit and the 'double storm' of the global liquidity and trade cycles. As Fig. 2 depicts, the share of Latin America in total inflows to emerging countries rose, thanks to Brazil, with the contraction led by China. More than that, the year 2014 ends with net gain in international reserves ($10 billion, Fig. 5), contrary to the loss of 2013 and the equilibrium in 2015.

The third phase is best described as a necessary increase in external funding, suggesting that the greater capacity for coexistence with high current account deficits, even in bad international conjunctures, is in fact a good novelty. The instruments for such attraction, and consequently the composition of the flows, are hardly virtuous. However, the point to emphasize again is the absence of external constraint, the lack of dollars to 'close' the balance of payments, on the eve of the greatest recession in Brazilian history. It is here that we can see the 'new reality' and the lack of direct connection with the crisis.

In 2015, once the strong macroeconomic policy shift was implemented, and in line with the rapid reversal of the current account deficit, the Brazilian financial account also shrank, dropping by $50 billion (45%) in net terms and $80 billion (40%) in inflows. This occurred even with the sharp rise in the interest rate differential, and the lowering value of domestic assets, with the drop in market prices and the strong devaluation of the national currency. Brazil was again in line with of the global liquidity cycle after a period of decoupling. Nevertheless, internal factors also contributed to the fall in capital flows, especially the collapse of several important domestic productive sectors and the political crisis that marked that year in the country.

Stocks, 'De-Dollarization' and External Debt

If a country registers successive current account deficits but faces no problem to finance them, the discussion about external sustainability moves from the flows to the stocks dimension. Some of the most important changes in Brazilian economy over the past few years took place in this dimension, justifying our hypothesis of a ‘new reality’ of the external sector.

Brazilian foreign assets increased from approximately $100 billion in the first quarter of 2002 to $600 billion in 2011 and $750 billion at the end of 2015—most of which are composed of direct investments and reserves (86% in 2015). Those amounts are significantly lower than the liabilities—as a consequence, the Net International Investment Position (NIIP) remained negative. Moreover, portfolio investment liabilities alone were kept at higher levels than that of international reserves, justifying the worries of some economists about an increased source of external vulnerability (e.g. Gonçalves 2012).

It should be noted that NIIP increased considerably until 2011 (when it reached the record value of $1 trillion at the end of the second quarter), and then fell as the result of increasing assets and stable (and later decreasing) liabilities. By the end of 2015, this indicator was at $460 billion, the lowest value since the second quarter of 2009.

Here is a great novelty: from 2011 to 2015, Brazil’s accumulated current account deficit was approximately $390 billion, and yet the amount of foreign commitments of the country was reduced by exactly $255 billion. Regarding NIIP, the improvement was even more expressive: $430 billion. A closer analysis of the composition of these liabilities (Fig. 6) helps to illuminate this paradoxical result.

That movement should be understood through the consideration of an important composition change: a significant increase in bonds and

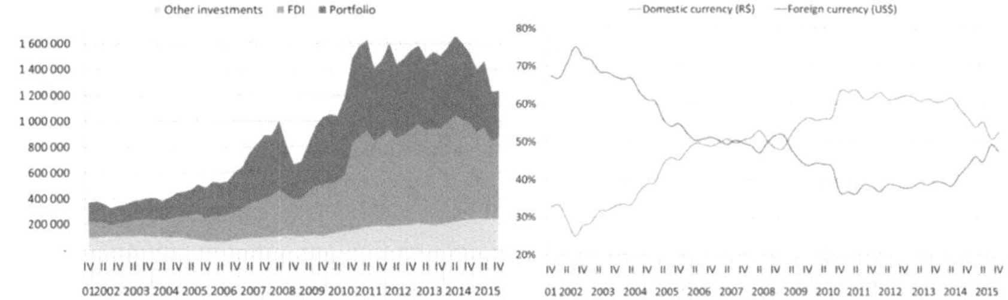

Fig. 6 Foreign liabilities, by type (US$ million) and currency denomination (%), 2001–2015. *Source* Brazilian Central Bank (various issues). Authors’ elaboration

shares that were traded in the domestic market. Adding these liabilities to the share of the FDI relative to equity participation, we have the total of commitments denominated in national currency. Figure 6 also illustrates the share of liabilities according to currency denomination.[3]

Because of the expressive 'de-dollarization' of foreign liabilities, the devaluation of Brazilian currency starting in mid-2014 contributed to improving the country's external position, contrary to what happened at other times in history. Since an important part of these commitments is set at market values, an eventual fall in the prices of bonds and shares also contributes to the devaluation of total liabilities. As a result, the movement of Brazilian total foreign liability, as well as of its NIIP, became completely detached from the flows registered in the balance of payments.[4]

Considering the traditional measures of solvency and illiquidity, it is evident that the relative worsening of some indicators was a movement concentrated in 2015. In this year, which was marked by economic recession and currency devaluation, there was an increase in the debt service in relation to exports and to GDP, as well as in the interest rate in relation to exports. For most of indicators, however, the situation is still much more comfortable than in 2002 (see Cintra 2015).

Against this background, the upward trend in Brazilian external debt (which has generated concern in domestic and international analysts in recent times) can be more accurately evaluated. According to Brazilian Central Bank (BCB 2015), the concept of external debt may be subdivided into three levels: i) 'traditional' external debt; ii)'traditional' external debt plus intercompany operations; and iii) 'traditional' external debt plus intercompany transactions and securities (at market values) issued by public and private sectors, including those settled in BRL, held by non-residents. The evolution of the debt, following this division, is depicted in Fig. 7.

[3]The whole value of 'other investments' and 'intercompany loans' are denominated in foreign currency.

[4]See Biancarelli and Rosa (2015) for an empirical assessment of this aspect.

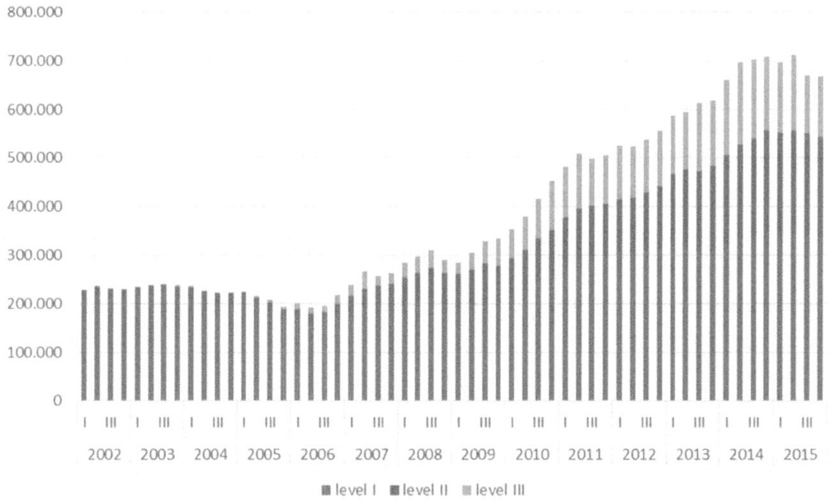

Fig. 7 External debt, by level (US$ million), 2002–2015. *Source* Brazilian Central Bank (various issues). Authors' elaboration

External debt (level 1) lost the relative share in the composition of total liabilities over the last decade, but has recently increased again: from about 30% in 2002 to 10% in 2011 and 20% in 2015. In terms of maturity, the share of short-term commitments is less than 20%. Private external debt was US$84 billion (48% of total) in 2006, moving up to $194 billion (65% of total) at the end of 2010 and reaching $205 billion (61% of total) by 2015. The growth of private indebtedness is even more pronounced considering level 2, incorporating the intercompany loans. These operations went from $20 billion in 2006 to more than $100 billion in 2010, and doubled five years later.

As for the third level, the same pattern is repeated: strong growth, but with a much less risky nature. Thus, it is necessary to consider the new profile of the indebtedness: half of these commitments are intercompany and/or denominated in merchandises, or in the national currency. The actual threats to the sovereign solvency are much smaller than in past experiences with external debt.

5 Indirect Channels

Although there is no dollar shortage to the country as a whole, important external disincentives to domestic growth played a role in Brazilian downturn, which had already been manifested during the 'post-bonanza' of the first three years of President Rousseff's rule. Moreover, they were intensified by the 'double storm' since 2014. The linkage of the Brazilian economy to international cycles, which is a long-standing structural process, seems fundamental to understanding such effects. These are presented in a preliminary manner in the following two sections.

Global Productive Cycle, Markets and Domestic Production

Assessments of the relations between the Brazilian productive structure and external impulses are usually based on two different assumptions, with important consequences for the conclusions drawn. On the one hand, there is a 'mantra' in the liberal reasoning about the commercial closure of the Brazilian economy, measured by the relation between foreign trade and GDP; this would weaken the influence of the international economy on the domestic activity. On the other hand, there is sometimes an approximation of the Brazilian productive structures to that of its South American neighbours, which are much more dependent—in terms of employment, level of activity and fiscal revenues—on the production of few commodities.

Both the relatively low weight of foreign trade in GDP and the trends of re-privatization or deindustrialization are indisputable facts, but by different paths. These two perspectives minimize three fundamental aspects to understand the processes analysed here: (i) the still relevant diversification of the economy, which gives industry a key role in determining the pace of activity; (ii) the changes occurred in the dynamics of industrial production and consumption, especially since the post-crisis recovery of 2008, marked by an 'asymmetric internationalization'; and (iii) the importance of multinational companies in controlling production and investment decisions, in the context of integrated and hierarchical global production.

Analysing the influence of the external sector on the productive side in the recent period must start from the relations between foreign trade and domestic aggregate demand. The contractionary impact was definitely not caused by the reduction in exports, as they were not the dynamic element in the previous growth phase (except, perhaps, in the recovery in 2003 and 2004). External sales represent a small part of the Brazilian GDP, and in this period, they are in fact reduced in line with the rest of the world.

On the imports side, the picture is more complex, and there is controversy whether its rise in the post-crisis period 'steals demand' from the country. For Serrano & Summa (2015), the thesis of the leakage of demand does not hold, since there would have been only a small increase in imports in terms of the total supply of the economy. Squeff (2015), in a similar sense, shows that the relationship between GDP growth rates and imports is stable between 1996 and 2013.

However, the arguments and data provided by Sarti and Hiratuka (2016) seem more important for the effects that we wish to emphasize here. A divergence between the behaviour of imports, particularly industrial ones, and other categories of demand, especially after the crisis of 2008/09, is indisputable. More than that, there is a more permanent detachment between apparent consumption and domestic production, especially in intermediate goods, suggesting a process of disentangling productive chains. In other words, not only is there a structural increase in the coefficient imported from Brazilian industry, but also an increase in the external constraint of a structural nature, as a result of the reliance on the exports profile and the non-substitution of imports.

For these authors, more than a commercial closure, there is in fact a deepening of the asymmetric integration of the Brazilian economy. In other words, a strong expansion of imports disputing the domestic market—which was still relatively heated until 2013—but decreasing access and increasingly difficulties for Brazilian industrial exports. The domestic market, therefore, has been further outsourced, and the country is predominantly a buyer in the global value chains.

Brazilian industry, dealing with the adverse international environment described in Sect. "Introduction" (fierce competition and less dynamic trade), loses dynamism and did not recover, even after the fiscal benefits of a large and costly support policy, implemented mainly after 2013. With the core of the industrial structure commanded by multinationals—a process accentuated by the strong entry and sector diversification of FDI in recent years—production and investment decisions gained autonomy relative to domestic cost and demand conditions, and responded more to their global strategies.

Since the 'post-bonanza' period, at least, these strategies have been heavily influenced by the installed and unused production capacity, notably in the country that commands the global production of manufactured goods (China). In other words, the idea here is that an 'arbitrage of idle capacities' was the main determinant of a global production cycle that, more intensely than in the period prior to the 2008 crisis, concentrated industrial production at the Asian factories.

These effects on the Brazilian economy are not measured only by trade balance data; they are not related to the weight of the export sector in domestic activity and are relatively independent from the prevailing exchange rates. The nature of this relation is structural and seems to be fundamental to the understanding of one of the great paradoxes of the recent period namely, the weak response of domestic production and investment to 'supply' policies (interest rates, exchange rates, energy prices and tax exemptions).

Global Financial Cycle, Credit, Wealth

In previous sections of this chapter, one of the most emphasized aspects was the cyclical behaviour of international liquidity, especially for emerging economies. This perspective, the starting point for critical approaches of global finances, has been consolidating in recent years also in the international academic and financial mainstream. One of the most interesting derivations in this plan is the work of Rey (2013), a fundamental reference. This author postulates the existence of a 'global financial cycle', governed by the monetary policy of developed countries and the degree of risk aversion of global investors. Beyond this, her econometric results show simultaneous movements not only in international capital flows but also in domestic credit markets, especially in emerging economies. The processes underway in the global economy, particularly since the implementation of Quantitative Easing in the USA and other financial centres, are the novelty that draws the attention of this contributor.[5]

The relationship between the two-dimensions (external and internal) of the liquidity cycle has been discussed in the literature in two channels of influence. The first one would be direct, and economists from BIS (Borio et al. 2011) are warning of their risks. This is the simple extension of international bank loans and issues of securities in foreign currency in the post-crisis period. The novelty would be the increasing use of offshore subsidiaries (often-mere representative offices) of domestic corporations to raise funds in the international market, and a subsequent transfer in the form of intercompany loans to the local unit (McCauley et al. 2015; Avdjiev et al. 2014).

A second channel would be indirect and is formally argued by Bruno and Shin (2014a). Global banks, taking advantage of the very favourable conditions for accessing wholesale dollar funding sources, lend to domestic banks that, in turn, provide dollar credit to local companies. It is a local relending of external credit, in a scheme similar to that used in Brazil in the 1970s, where the exchange rate risk is transferred to the borrower.

In previous section of this chapter, there is evidence that these two channels have operated significantly in Brazil over the recent years. Regarding the direct external credit, in addition to the growth of bank loans, the level 2 of external indebtedness (related to intercompany operations) has also increased significantly since 2010. In addition, and from the flows perspective, there is a strong growth of what is called 'reverse investment'—intercompany loans from overseas branches to headquarters in Brazil—as warned by BIS economists (Borio et al. 2011, e.g.).

[5]For an argument with similar conclusions, departing from different theoretical assumptions and evidence, see Biancareli (2007).

Regarding the indirect channel, the main evidence is that the banks are the largest foreign debt holders and, at the other end, the largest creditors.

This trend, despite all the necessary qualifications (made in Sect. "Stocks, 'De-Dollarization' and External Debt") about the lower potential for sovereign exchange risk, has had a negative effect on private borrowers' balance sheets. In this sense, the findings of Rezende (2016), Almeida et al. (2016) and CEMEC (2016) leave no room for doubt. With a high stock of debt denominated in foreign currency, the exchange devaluation (in 2014, and even more in 2015) was one of the factors responsible for the increase in financial expenses of non-financial corporations in the period, with negative impacts on profitability and the overall rate of investments.

However, as emphasized in CEMEC (2016), private external debt is concentrated in some sectors (particularly mineral, oil and gas, that have natural hedge) and especially in large publicly traded companies, which is more a 'microeconomic' or sectoral problem.

Thus, even if there is no 'dollar shortage'—for the country as a whole, as seen, there is no problem of external solvency, liquidity or aggregate mismatch—the size and service of debt in dollars negatively influence investment and production decisions. Contrary to the effects suggested in the previous subsection (relative to the influence of the global productive cycle), this factor must have had more weight on the collapse in 2015 than in the deceleration until 2014. Moreover, these factors seem fundamental to understand the serious difficulties of growth resumption in 2016 and 2017. Yet, this is one of the hypotheses presented here for future investigations.

Another channel, also related to the global financial cycle, refers to the probable existence of a third channel of influence on domestic credit even more indirect. It would be the 'collaterals channel', similar to what Bruno and Shin (2014b) called the 'risk-taking channel'. In times of high-risk appetite and high global liquidity, emerging from the ultra-expansionary central monetary policy, the leverage of financial agents worldwide is increasing, even those not directly involved in cross-border operations.

This is because—as also commented by Rey (2013) and empirically verified by Miranda-Agripino and Rey (2015)—a wide range of risk asset prices is also related to the global financial cycle. Currencies, stocks, commodity prices, real estate fluctuate in large part along with the two key variables: the VIX and the Fed Funds Rate. Thus, the total value of wealth stocks, which serve as collateral for credit operations but also for new issues of securities, shares, etc., is also cyclical.

For a country like Brazil, two aspects seem to reinforce this third channel. Firstly, the importance of commodity production, which is moderate for employment and activity but critical to stock market prices and investment rates. Secondly, the fact that the Brazilian currency is one of the most sensitive, among emerging-countries ones, to the international liquidity cycle.[6] In general, the flexibility of the exchange rate regime reinforces (and do not inhibit, as one might think) the effects of the liquidity cycle on domestic finances.

When one observes the behaviour of stock prices in Brazil, and the evolution of domestic credit—which was 'stretched' by anti-cyclical role played by public banks but was already losing dynamism even before the crisis—there is evidence of this indirect mechanism acting in a decisive way.[7]

6 Summary and Conclusions

This chapter departs from the impression that the current debate about Brazilian economic crisis does not consider the role of external sector in a proper way, thanks to an inadequate approach to the macroeconomics of external sector, or to a narrow approach about the influences of the global environment. In order to contribute to this discussion, this chapter presents two sets of results, which lead to different conclusions about the external sector in Brazil and its role in the current crisis. At a

[6] See Rossi (2016, Chap. "Financialisation and Investment Behaviour Among Non-Financial Corporations in Brazil Since the Global Crisis").

[7] For preliminary quantitative evidence of these relations between the global liquiditycycle and domestic credit, with emphasis on the role of public banks, see Cunha et al. (2016) and Biancarelli et al. (2017).

first glance, emerges the new reality, which can be summarized in four conclusions.

Firstly, it should be considered that the international scenario, faced by the Brazilian economy after the international crisis in 2008, was in most of the time relatively favourable, in terms of commodity prices and the cycle of liquidity. This is true for the 'sudden resumption' immediately after turmoil but also for the 'post bonanza' of the following years. Only after mid-2014 is it fair to talk about a real adverse world—that in fact deteriorates in a fast and intense way.

Secondly, the behaviour of the Brazilian current account suffers the consequences of this changing international scenario and the domestic macroeconomic situation, but also of older structural depression trends. From the accounting point of view, after the drop in the wake of the crisis, until 2013, the record is the stability of the deficit (at historically risky levels and influenced by the exceptional accounting of 'reinvested earnings'). This deepened sharply in 2014 and was reverted by domestic adjustments in 2015 and 2016.

Thirdly, and reflecting the 'new reality', it was possible for the country to finance its deficits in the different external conjunctures. Firstly, after the crisis, it suffered a 'monetary tsunami' and until 2013 intentionally reduced and selected the attracted flows. In 2014, Brazil was able to strongly raise this absorption in the face of greater needs (despite the reversal of the global liquidity cycle). Finally, in 2015 and 2016, the external accounts suffered more intensely the effects of this global scenario, but already faced with a lesser need of external financing.

Lastly, the fourth conclusion refers to stocks, particularly of external liabilities, and reveals positive news for Brazil's historical vulnerability: most of the commitments are denominated in national currency and/or refer to intra-corporate debt, with a minor risk of sovereign insolvency.[8] In addition, to put it another way, the sharp rise in recent external indebtedness seems to be a problem much more of the companies involved than of the country as a whole.

[8]This obviously does not revoke other sources of vulnerability, like the growing share of public debt held by foreign investors, as highlighted for example by Akyuz (2014).

On the other hand, the new approach that seems to be missing in this debate is presented in Sect. 4 above, even in a preliminary way. Some structural linkages of production and local finances to the international cycles are identified, and its role in the deceleration and crisis is discussed. If this hypothesis, to be developed in further research, makes sense, its importance is much bigger than one more explanation for the recent collapse of the Brazilian economy. Certainly, coping with its effects on the level of activity and the development possibilities would require much more than corrections in key macroeconomic prices.

This last agenda is probably the most difficult and important one for research and debate about the Brazilian external sector, along with the monitoring of the 'new reality', as identified in this contribution.

References

Akyuz, Y. (2014). Internationalization of finance and changing vulnerabilities in emerging and developing economies. *UNCTAD Discussion Papers, No. 217.*

Almeida, J. S. G., Novais, L. F., & Rocha, M. A. A. (2016). Fragilização Financeira das Empresas Não Financeiras no Brasil Pós-Crise. *Texto para a Discussão No 81*, IE-UNICAMP.

Avdjiev, S., Chui, M. E., & Shin, H. S. (2014, December). Non-financial corporations from emerging market economies and capital flows. *BIS Quarterly Review*, 67–77.

Banco Central do Brasil. (2015). *Nota Metodológica* nº 4. Available at www.bcb.gov.br.

Barbosa Filho, F. H., & Pessôa, S. (2014). Desaceleração recente da economia. In *CDPP, Sob a Luz do Sol, uma agenda para o Brasil.* São Paulo: Insper.

Biancareli, A. (2007). *Integração, ciclos e finanças domésticas: o Brasil na globalização financeira.* Campinas: IE/Unicamp, tese de doutoramento.

Biancarelli, A. (2012). Uma Nova realidade do setor externo brasileiro, em meio à crise internacional. *Texto para Discussão*, No. 13, RedeD.

Biancarelli, A. M. (2016). Constrangimentos externos, de natureza financeira, ao desenvolvimento: um olhar dissidente sobre o Brasil no cenário pós-bonança, in CGEE, *Dimensões estratégicas do desenvolvimento brasileiro. Vol. 5—Continuidade e mudança no cenário global: desafios à inserção do.* Brasília: CGEE.

Biancarelli, A. M., & Rosa, R. S. (2015). Currency denomination and external vulnerability in developing economies: A new picture from Brazil. In 19th Conference of the Research Network Macroeconomics and Macroeconomic Policies (FMM), *The Spectre of Stagnation?* Berlin, Germany.

Biancarelli, A. M., Rosa, R. S., & Verghanini, R. (2017). Ciclos de liquidez global e crédito doméstico: canais de transmissão e a experiência brasileira recente. *Mimeo.* Campinas: IE/Unicamp.

Borio, C., McCauley, R., & McGuire, P. (2011). Global credit and domestic credit booms. *BIS Quarterly Review*, 43–57.

Brazilian Central Bank (various issues). Balance of Payments time series. Available at http://www.bcb.gov.br/en/#!/n/BALANCESPECIAL.

Bresser-Pereira, L. C., & Gala, P. (2008). Foreign savings, insufficiency of demand and low growth. *Journal of Post Keynesian Economics, 30*(3), 315–334.

Bresser-Pereira, L. C., Oreiro, J. L., & Marconi, N. (2014). A theoretical framework for a structuralist development macroeconomics. In L. C. Bresser-Pereira, J. Kregel, & L. Burlamaqui (Eds.), *Financial stability and growth: Perspectives on financial regulation and new developmentalism.* London: Routledge.

Bruno, V., & Shin, H. S. (2014a). Cross-border banking and global liquidity. *BIS Working Papers, No.* 458.

Bruno, V., & Shin, H. S. (2014b). Capital flows and the risk-taking channel of monetary policy. *Journal of Monetary Economics, 71,* 119–132.

CDPP. (2014). *Coletânea de capítulos da agenda 'Sob a luz do sol.* São Paulo, Brazil: Insper.

CEMEC. (2016). Endividamento das Empresas Brasileiras: Metade das Empresas não gera caixa para cobrir despesas financeiras em 2015/2016. *Nota CEMEC* 06.

Cintra, M. A. M. (2015). O financiamento das contas externas brasileiras: 1995–2014. In Squeff, G (org., 2015), *Dinâmica macrossetorial brasileira.* Brasília: IPEA.

Cunha, A. M., Silva, P. P., Lélis, M. T. C., & Lopes, L. U. (2016). Ciclos Financeiros e o Comportamento do Crédito no Brasil entre 2004 e 2015. *44° Encontro Nacional de Economia*, Foz do Iguaçu.

Gonçalves, R. (2012). Ciclo econômico global e vulnerabilidade externa estrutural do Brasil. *Mimeo*. Rio de Janeiro: UFRJ.

IMF. (2016). World Economic Outlook: Subdued Demand: Symptoms and Remedies. Washington: IMF.

Lara, F. M. (2015). As contribuições à desaceleração do crescimento no Brasil (2011–14). *Indic. Econ. FEE, 43*(2), 23–40.

McCauley, R., McGuire, P., & Sushko, V. (2015, December). Dollar credit to emerging market economies. *BIS Quarterly Review,* 27–41.

Miranda-Agripino S., & Rey, H. (2015). World asset markets and the global financial cycle. *NBER Working Paper Series,* No. 21722, Cambridge, MA: National Bureau of Economic Research.

Ocampo, J. A. (2007). La macroeconomia de la bonanza econômica latino-americana. *Revista de la Cepal, 93,* 7–29.

Pastore, A. C., & Pinotti, M. C. (2014). Demografia, reformas e bonança externa. In CDPP, *Sob a Luz do Sol, uma agenda para o Brasil.* São Paulo: Insper.

Prates, D. M., & De Paula, L. F. (2017). Capital account regulation in Brazil: An assessment of the 2009–2013 period. *Brazilian Journal of Political Economy, 37*(1), 108–129.

Rey, H. (2013). Dilemma not trilemma: The global financial cycle and monetary policy independence. *NBER Working Paper Series,* No. 21162. Cambridge, MA: National Bureau of Economic Research.

Rezende, F. (2016). Financial fragility, instability and the Brazilian crisis: A Keynes-Minsky-Godley approach. *MINDS Discussion Paper,* No. 1.

Rosa, R. S. (2016). *Passivo externo e 'desdolarização': a vulnerabilidade externa brasileira em mutação.* Campinas: IE/Unicamp, dissertação de mestrado.

Rossi, P. (2016). *Taxa de câmbio e política cambial no Brasil: teoria, institucionalidade, papel da arbitragem e da especulação.* Rio de Janeiro: FGV Editora.

Sarti, F., & Hiratuka, C. (2016). Assimetrias no processo de internacionalização da economia brasileira no século XXI. In H.M.M. Lastres, J.E. Cassiolato, J. E., G. Laplane and F. Sarti (Eds.), *O futuro do desenvolvimento: ensaios em homenagem a Luciano Coutinho.* Campinas: IE/Unicamp.

Serrano, F., & Summa, R. (2015). Aggregate demand and the slowdown of Brazilian economic growth in 2011–2014. *Nova Economia, 25,* 803–833.

Squeff, G. (2015). Rigidez produtiva e importações no Brasil: 1995–2009. In G. Squeff (Ed.), *Dinâmica Macrosetorial Brasileira* (pp. 15–46). Brasília: Ipea.

UNCTAD. (2011). *Price formation in financialized commodity markets: The role of information.* New York and Geneva: United Nations.

Brazilian Industry: Recent Performance and Future Challenges

Celio Hiratuka and Fernando Sarti

1 Introduction

The Brazilian productive structure is facing great challenges that are related both to changes in the global scenario and in the internal dynamics itself. In the international scene, there is an intensification of the competition, exacerbated by the stagnation in the world economy after the global financial crisis (GFC). In the internal scenario, despite the higher growth and the positive results of the industry between 2003 and 2008, the unfolding of post-crisis impacts revealed the weaknesses accumulated by the Brazilian productive structure since the end of the twentieth century, and that the short investment cycle during the growth period was not able to reverse.

C. Hiratuka (✉) · F. Sarti
Universidade Estadual de Campinas, Campinas, Brazil
e-mail: celiohiratuka@gmail.com

P. Arestis et al. (eds.), *The Brazilian Economy since the Great Financial Crisis of 2007/2008*, https://doi.org/10.1007/978-3-319-64885-9_6

This chapter seeks to analyze these transformations, making a brief analysis of the Brazilian industrial performance in the post-crisis period. This chapter is structured in 4 sections, besides this introduction. Section 2 presents a brief rescue of the main transformations in the global industry and summarizes some aspects of the process of productive, commercial, and technological internationalization in recent years that placed important challenges to the Brazilian manufacturing industry. Section 3 presents the theoretical framework that guides the analysis of the evolution of the productive structure to be carried out in the next section. Section 4 presents a retrospective on the recent development of the Brazilian industrial production, emphasizing the effects of the global crisis on domestic production. This chapter, briefly points out the prospects for the Brazilian industrial development in the post-crisis scenario.

The main contribution of this chapter is to underline, based on the theoretical literature analyzed, that the Brazilian economic development cannot be achieved without a more robust industrial structure and without structural changes that progress toward a more effectively incorporation and development of sectors with a greater degree of technological knowledge and innovative capacity. At the same time, it highlights how, in the post-crisis period, these challenges have become greater, given the context of fierce competition in the global market and the fast occupation of the domestic market by imports.

2 Changes in the Global Productive Structure

The range of competitive, productive, and patrimonial transformations in the global economy in the last years has been very prominent, making it difficult to analyze the challenges posed to the Brazilian productive structure without an understanding of these transformations. This section seeks to synthesize some of these changes, emphasizing the post-crisis scenario.

Four trends are highlighted in the following paragraphs, which we consider fundamental to organizing the analysis of the transformations that have been taking place in the global productive structure in recent years.

The first one concerns the reorganization of the global strategies of TNCs and how this affected the possibilities of industrial development.

The second is associated with the emergence of China as the world's largest supplier of manufacturing goods. The third concerns the continuity of concentration in the field of technological knowledge by large TNCs. Finally, the fourth refers to the launch of active policies by several countries to recover their industrial activity and foster innovation in new areas and economic sectors after the GFC.

Regarding the changes in the strategies of TNCs, it was a result of the strong competition among companies from developed countries after the Second World War. It is worth remembering that in that period, from a renovated industrial park and active industrial policies, mainly companies from Germany and Japan, quickly came about to challenge the superiority of large American corporations (Imai 1990).

American companies were also pressured by the growing questioning about the efficiency of the management model of the large diversified multidivisional corporation. For critics of this model, managers' autonomy to allocate retained earnings had created overly diversified corporations with the implementation of investment projects that did not necessarily generate returns to shareholders, resulting in losses of efficiency and international competitiveness. More active shareholders, compensation linked to the shares values, and the movement of hostile takeovers would be the ways to discipline and implement a new management model, more aligned with the interest of the shareholders, in these large corporations[1] (Jensen 1990).

This process resulted in a profound restructuring in the TNCs strategies since the 1980s. It aimed to combine the accumulation of intangible assets with rationalization and search for flexibility; this was in order to respond to competitive pressure, greater instability of macroeconomic variables, growing concern from the financial market with higher and faster return, and demands for changes in corporate governance.

From the point of view of the organization of economic activities, there was an intense de-verticalization, with the fragmentation of activities accompanied by a strong international outsourcing; this

[1]See Jensen (1990) for the foundations of this new shareholder value management model and Aglietta and Riberieux (2005) and Lazzonick and O'Sullivan (2000) for a critical view.

was so to take advantage of the possibilities of reducing costs, accompanied by the gains of economies of scale and scope made possible by the management of geographically dispersed activities. The production process began to occur therefore increasingly in the form of an international network, integrating different countries and different companies, performing steps in the value chain under the coordination of large corporations.[2]

As a result, the articulation between manufacturing production and economic development has changed significantly. As Baldwin (2011) highlighted, the incorporation of industrial activities by developing countries has become much easier, since it has become possible to carry out specific manufacturing stages, even those for which practically the only requisite is the low cost of labor. Prior to the advent of global production networks, this incorporation required the internalization of entire productive chains and often a set of complementary productive chains, which meant a great need to mobilize and coordinate financial, human, technical, managerial, and technological resources. Industrialization and structural change were, then, synonymous with the creation and assembly of this structure.

In the new context, it became possible to attract specific steps in the value chain, given the reduction of barriers to the start of manufacturing activity as well as for exporting manufacturing goods. That is, in Baldwin's (2011) terms, it became possible to internalize manufacturing activities through the insertion in stages of the value chain, whereas in the past, it was necessary to create the whole value chains internally. But while the incorporation of manufacturing activities has become easier, its impacts and their significance from the point of view of economic development can be much smaller, since depending on the type of internalized activity, the magnitude of the spillovers effects can be very small.

Within this background, it is possible to better understand the intense shift of industrial activity toward the developing countries and

---

[2]This movement was captured by the literature of industrial organization and international economy in different ways and with different denominations. See, among others, Gereffi and Korzeniewicz (1994), Sturgeon (2002), Gereffi et al. (2005), UNCTAD (2013) and OECD, WTO and UNCTAD (2013).

the emergence of the Asian region, especially China, as a major global manufacturing producer center. East Asian developing countries' industrial dynamism, in turn, was largely leveraged by the emergence of China as an industrial power.

According to UNIDO (2011), China accounted for about 1.4% of manufacturing value added and 1% of global exports in 1980. In 2010, these indicators increased to 15.4% and 10.3%, respectively. The Chinese economy was able to take advantage of the movement of outsourcing manufacturing activities to leverage its industrial development process, initially with the simpler steps of the assembly process within TNC value chains, but moving rapidly to more complex tasks and with increasing participation of national and State Owned Enterprises (Haley and Haley 2013). China's level of economic development, also reflected in its high production and consumption scales, has positioned the country not only as a major producer of industrial manufactures but also as a major importer of inputs and raw materials.

Regarding the impact of Chinese growth in developing countries, although the effect on rising commodity prices is the most emphasized fact, there are two other aspects, more directly linked to manufacturing production that should be highlighted (Haley and Haley 2013). The first one is related to the incorporation of a large contingent of low-cost labor to the production processes, within the international value chains, and at the same time increasing the scale of production and the number of producers in the less complex stages of the chain. This process had strong impacts on the world price of some manufactured products, mainly computers and semiconductors, but also in other sectors.

The second aspect concerns the extraordinary increase in manufacturing capacity in various industries still focused on the Chinese domestic market, but which might further increase the impacts on the global industry if they were more directed to the international market. One example is the steel industry, where Chinese production accounted for 47% of world output in 2012 according to the World Steel Association. Only China's capacity increase in 2012 was 119 million tons, which accounted for more than all of Japan's production (the world's second largest producer, with 107 million tons) in the same year and about 3.5 times the total production in Brazil (9th largest producer).

Another example is the automotive industry, where, according to the OICA (International Organization of Motor Vehicle Manufacturers), the production of 18 million passenger cars in China accounted for 27% of world production in 2013 and was larger than the production of the sum of the three largest producers in the ranking (Japan, Germany, and the USA).

Therefore, the establishment of a group of Asian producers, led by China, while raising the demand for different commodities and basic inputs, has created an extremely fierce competition in the markets for manufacturing products. It is noteworthy that the high and synchronized growth of the global economy between 2003 and 2008 heightened the first aspect and attenuated the second. The period after the crisis, on the other hand, lessened the first phenomenon and accentuated the second (Hiratuka 2015).

The third trend is related to a rather important and often neglected aspect in the literature on global value chains. In spite of the opening of spaces at specific stages of manufacturing activity in several productive chains for companies from developing countries, the process of productive decentralization does not necessarily mean the possibility of reducing competitive asymmetries. On the contrary, large firms, while outsourcing non-core business activities, even in manufacturing, sought to strengthen their intangible assets, increase control over technology standards, and acquire assets from strategic competitors through a process of mergers and acquisitions. The result was an increase in the power of the large TNCs, mainly from developed countries to capture the value created along the global value chains (Chesnais 1996; Dedrick et al. 2009; Serfati 2008).

Thus, on the one hand, increasing internationalization, measured by data on trade, investment, and manufacturing, shows signs of increasing participation of developing countries, albeit from a relatively limited set of countries. On the other hand, when one observes the internationalization data of the technological activities of TNCs, which give to these companies the capacity to absorb much of the value created along these global chains, a situation of great concentration is still observed.

Dernis et al. (2015) analyzed the ranking of the 2,000 top companies that invest most in R&D in global terms and crossed them with patent information. The total volume invested in R&D by these 2,000 companies and their 500,000 subsidiaries accounted for about 90% of total R&D business spending worldwide in 2012 and about 66% of patent deposits in the top five global patent offices.

The data show a great concentration either by the company or by the country. In terms of enterprises, the 100 largest companies accounted for 54.6% of total R&D expenses and 52.6% of the patents. The 250 largest companies accounted for 72.5% and 71.2%, respectively. Regarding the home country of the companies in the ranking, TNCs from the USA, Japan, and Germany was responsible for 64.6% of R&D expenses and 67.6% of patents.

We also note that the last trend is the reinforcement of national policies to encourage technological change and industrial restructuring as a way to recover economic dynamism, especially in the central countries after the crisis.

The most notorious case is the USA, a country where traditional support policies for sectors considered strategic, although strongly present, are less explicit. As a reaction to the crisis, the American Recovery and Reinvestment Act has announced $800 billion in resources to be spent in 2009–2019 not only to combat the immediate effects of the crisis, but also to fund long-term industrial and technological restructuring to foster the competitiveness of US companies. Pisano and Shih (2012), Sperling (2013), and Berger (2013) emphasize that innovation can often only progress effectively when it is colocated with a set of activities that includes manufacturing activity. They recognize that the outsourcing movement of manufacturing may have gone too far and underscore the need to strengthen the ecosystem of producers, suppliers, research institutions, and labor training institutions, with the aim of accelerating the generation of innovative products and processes.

Thus, while US policy seeks to strengthen ties between manufacturing and innovation, it also points to more robust support for scientific research on new technology platforms. In an official document of the USA Government (National Economic Council and the Office of Science and Technology Policy, 2011), the need to accelerate innovation is highlighted and in the following areas: clean energy, biotechnology, nanotechnology and advanced manufacturing, educational technologies, and technologies for health and aerospace.

Also in the case of the European Union, there is the same concern to support industrial activity, for example in the European Commission's Communication on Industrial Policy (2012) and in Veugelers (2013). In addition to actions to support industrial competitiveness, the communication mentions six priority areas to foster innovation: advanced technology systems for clean production, sustainable construction, key enabling communication and information technologies, sustainable vehicles, bio-based products, and smart grids.

Finally, it is important to note that China has also made rapid progress toward the creation of innovative capacity and the increasing of knowledge-intensive activities, aims that are embodied in the Medium- and Long-Term Plan for the Development of Science and Technology (2006–2020) and in the 12th Five Year Plan (2011–2015) (Lazzonick and Li 2012).

For large developing countries, like Brazil, the current scenario represents a tremendous challenge, since they are facing a competition, led by Chinese production, but involving other Asian producers, who combine labor costs, scale, exchange rate, and strong government incentives that result in manufacturing goods at a very low cost. The competition is also reinforced by the leading global companies from developed countries that leverage their global scope to reinforce proprietary assets such as brands, marketing channels, and technology capabilities that are able to command global value chains with greater flexibility and efficiency. And in the post-crisis context, the strengthening of policies to support industrial and technological activities, both by developed countries and by developing countries, reinforces this context of fierce competition.

3 Theoretical Background

This section aims to show up the theoretical and conceptual framework that will be analyzed to analyze the evolution of the Brazilian productive structure in the post-crisis scenario. Since we are evaluating the recent evolution of the Brazilian industrial structure in face of changes in the world economy, that theoretical background should first validate the importance of the industry for economic development. But it should also provide insights into the conditioning factors for the analysis of industrial development, international insertion, and external competition, especially for developing countries.

From the beginning, it should be noted that the theoretical basis used moves away from orthodox economics. In that approach, the profile of sectoral specialization would not influence economic growth. This view may be associated with traditional neoclassical models, where growth depends on the accumulation of factors and technical progress, which in turn would be exogenously determined, as well as with the more modern models of endogenous growth. In traditional models derived from the work of Solow (1956), and even in its more modern versions that seek to broaden the concept of capital and incorporate human capital stock into production functions, sectoral specialization has no impact on long-term growth. In the new theories of endogenous growth (Romer 1990; Grossman and Helpmann 1991), there is the recognition that R&D activities, due to their partially public good character, can generate positive externalities. In this case, growth would be specific to R&D activity, but not to the sector, i.e., it might make sense to stimulate R&D activities through economic policy, but not necessarily specific manufacturing sectors.

We depart from an alternative view, combining elements of four different heterodox approaches, which have in common the evaluation that the direction of structural change and, in particular, manufacturing development and diversification, are important for long-term economic growth.

The first is the Kaldorian approach of growth and productive specialization. For authors, who follow this approach, industrial growth should be privileged, since it is characterized by involving static and dynamics economies of scale, concentrating technical progress and presenting greater linkage effects on the upstream and downstream sectors (Kaldor 1989). Another important proposition of this approach is that economic growth is demand driven, not resource constrained. Manufacturing products would also have greater income elasticity in the international market, compared with agricultural or mining products, with their growth contributing to avoid restrictions in the Balance of Payment (McCombie and Thirwall 1994).

The second important theoretical influence is the approach which follows the Schumpeterian approach, which emphasizes the importance of industrial activity but focuses on more specific aspects of manufacturing. The authors, who follow this approach, give more importance to the evolution that occurs within the industry and between its different sectors, in particular, the differences in terms technical progress and innovative capacity across sectors. This second group recognizes that there are sectoral patterns of technological change, which in turn depend not only on the technical basis, but also on different forms of learning and different degrees of opportunities, cumulativeness, and appropriability of technological trajectories (Dosi et al. 1988, 1990). These characteristics are translated, in empirical studies, into typologies of classification of economic activity and products, which has guided the evaluation of sectoral patterns of production and foreign trade at a more disaggregated level, opening the industry in different segments and subsectors.[3] Still in the Schumpeterian framework, it also should be emphasized the literature on National Systems of Innovation (NSI), which highlight that the industrial and innovative performance depends not only on the individual performance of companies and sectors, but also on the way in which they interact with each other and with others actors and institutions. They reflect, therefore, historically constructed local cultural and institutional conditions that guide the learning process.[4]

The third theoretical current that underlies the analysis of this chapter is the Latin American Structuralism. One of the hallmarks of structuralist thinking is the recognition of the role of technical progress as the engine of capitalist dynamics, but subject to differentiated global projections.[5] Cassiolato and Lastres (2005) and Guimarães et al. (2007) also point out that the Schumpeterian view is compatible and

---

[3]For example, the taxonomies that seek to describe sectoral patterns of technical change and innovation, such as Pavitt (1984) and Malerba and Orsenigo (1997); also the technological intensity classifications proposed by UNCTAD (2002) and Lall (2000).

[4]The key pioneering references within this approach are the works of Lundvall (1992), Nelson (1993), and Freeman (1995).

[5]Pebrisch's (1949) pioneering work is an obligatory reference, as well as Furtado (1961).

convergent with one of the key aspects of Latin American Structuralism, which is the acknowledgment of the asymmetrical conditions that developing countries face in relation to the central countries. The international economic and technological asymmetries between developed and developing countries could be deepened mainly by the existing asymmetries in relation to access to knowledge and learning. Considering the cumulative character of learning and the construction of capabilities inside the firms and in the System of Innovation, there are barriers that prevent the transmission of knowledge created in the central countries to developing countries.

Finally, the last important theoretical background is the approach that underlines how the domain of knowledge and innovative activity is controlled globally. As emphasized by Chesnais (1996, 2013) and Serfati (2008), the access of developing countries to technological assets and knowledge is largely conditioned by the way that the competition process crosses national borders and is modified by the strategies of Transnational Corporations (TNCs). This aspect is important because the understanding of the limits and possibilities of industrial and technological development in developing countries cannot be complete without an analysis of changes in the global productive and technological structure, and of the ways that the domestic structure interacts with these transformations. It is not, however, a question of denying the importance of internal factors, but rather, as emphasized by Tavares (1985) in her classic study on Brazilian industrialization, to recognize that the strategies of global oligopolies and TNCs do not exogenously determine the dynamics of accumulation of developing countries, but articulate with it and modify it from within.

4 Recent Brazilian Manufacturing Industry Performance

Manufacturing industry was the engine of the Brazilian economic growth in the period 1930–1980, when the country constituted a relatively diversified and integrated industrial structure, driven by the domestic market and by the Import Substitution (IS) strategy.

From 1980, with changes in internal and external constraints and the adoption of successive restrictive economic policies for industrial development, there was a loss of industry dynamism and the interruption of the process of catching-up and convergence of Brazilian productive structure, distancing the country from the advanced economies and even from other developing countries.

The frustration accumulated over the course of the 1980s crisis as a result of low GDP growth, low investment rates, fiscal and financial crisis, high inflation rates, and worsening of social conditions, gave way to a shift in terms of development strategy. In relation to the more protected and autarchic economic structure of the previous period, identified as the major cause of stagnation and production inefficiency, the predominance of a policy of greater trade and financial openness was observed from the 1990s, while the role of the State was reduced.

According to Laplane et al. (2003), Brazil presented important changes in its manufacturing production due to higher international competition. Parts of the manufacturing production chain were not able to compete with cheap foreign products and national production was replaced by imports. Moreover, as Coutinho (2003) points out, the instability in the domestic growth rates, combined with a macroeconomic regime of high interest rates and appreciated currency, induced a 'regressive specialization' in the Brazilian economy. The rate of investment in the business sector was concentrated in industries less exposed to international competition and anchored in natural resources and scale advantages. On the other hand, in the more technology intensive sectors, firms focused more on defensive investment, which aimed at ensuring the local market sales without the greater commitment of resources to capacity expansion, product differentiation, and technological innovation. The result was a decrease in the degree of diversification and integration of the productive system with loss of density in several production chains due to higher imports of components and capital goods and a chronic difficulty to increase the relative share of the sectors most intensive in knowledge and with greater capacity to generate technological spillovers.

It is important to highlight that the process of 'regressive specialization' cannot be dissociated from the loss of capacity of the Brazilian

State to invest directly in the modernization of traditional infrastructure and in science and technology (S&T). In the midst of the fiscal and financial fragility of the 1980s and the more liberal politics of the 1990s, the state lost its ability to induce and coordinate private business investment. In the same way, the use of more active policies of industrial development was left in the background, since an option was made for more horizontal policies, focused basically to improve the 'business environment' without more selective policies based on the recognition of differences in the technological and economic characteristics of different productive sectors or productive chains (Laplane et al. 2003).

In this context, the economy remained stuck in a stop-and-go process, alternating short periods of growth, soon stalled and replaced by periods of stagnation and low growth. In large part, the beginning of the twenty-first century represented a continuity of this movement. Until 2003, the economy was still marked by instability in growth rates and alternating periods of faster and low growth (De Conti 2013).

But from 2003, the economy started to show higher rates of growth. The average rate of GDP growth between 2004 and 2008 was 4.8%, in contrast to that observed since the 1980s (slightly above 2% a year between 1980 and 2003). The higher GDP growth was the result of a combination of factors, both in the external and in the domestic scenario. From the external point of view, as highlighted in the previous section, the synchronized growth of central and developing economies and, especially, China's growing influence on prices and demand for commodities boosted Brazilian exports, contributing to the country expansion (De Conti 2013).

If the external sector pulled the growth in the beginning of the cycle, later the internal market dynamics also became increasingly favorable. Although exports played a key role in the accumulation of reserves and the decrease in external vulnerability,[6] domestic demand fulfilled the decisive role in the growth cycle, which was led by the resumption of consumption, which, in turn, stimulated investment growth. Domestic demand was stirred by the recovery observed in the labor market, with a

[6]For more details regarding the discussion on the Brazilian external vulnerability, see the chapter written by Biancarelli et al. for this book (Chap. "New Features of the Brazilian External Sector since the Great Global Crisis").

very positive evolution associated with the combination of reduction of unemployment rates with an increase in the share of formal workers in the total employment. The upsurge observed in the minimum wage also contributed to a more accentuated recovery of wages among the lowest income strata, leading to a process of inclusion of a large number of people into the consumer market. The expansion of consumer credit in a setting of falling interest rates was also important (Baltar 2013).

The recovery of the labor market, credit, and domestic consumption meant the return of an important mechanism of dynamic feedback for the economy, which sustained the growth of income and consumption, industrial production, and finally, resulted in higher investments. The improvement in the conditions of profitability of the business system, at the beginning of the cycle more concentrated in the commodity sectors, later spread to companies of consumer goods and capital goods, substantially improving the conditions of self-financing of the investment.

In addition to self-financing, the expansion of credit with BNDES (Brazilian Bank of Development) assumed a decisive role (Almeida et al. 2013). It was also important the resumption of investment in infrastructure and the Growth Acceleration Program (PAC), which in addition to the volume of resources, helped to coordinate the expectations needed to encourage private investment.

As it can be seen in Fig. 1, industrial production responded to this new context, showing strong growth from 2003 onwards. Growth continued robust and accelerated from 2006 until the outbreak of the GFC in August 2007. The anti-cyclical policies had the power to stimulate a relatively rapid recovery, but with signs of exhaustion after 2011. Since then, industrial production has not been able to recover the pace and finally entered a process of sharp decline from the end of 2014.

Stagnation in industrial production is directly related to the intensification of international competition observed in the post-crisis period and highlighted in Sect. 1. With the persistence of its effects in central countries, especially in the European Union, and the slowdown in China, the international dispute has become fierce, with aggressive strategies of all exporters of manufactured goods to penetrate markets that have accomplished to maintain some demand growth.

Fig. 1 Brazil: Industrial production index (seasonally adjusted). January 2002 = 100. 2002 a 2016. *Source* IBGE: Pesquisa industrial mensal (Monthly Industrial Survey). Available at http://www.pim-pf.ibge.gov.br/

The synchronized growth of the global economy in the pre-crisis period, while fostering the effects on commodity markets, mitigated the effects of strong competition by Asian producers. After the international crisis erupted, in contrast, the recession or slow growth in several markets exacerbated the competition. In the case of Brazil, the combination of demand maintenance, with the rapid return of appreciation of the Brazilian currency after the devaluation occurred immediately following the outbreak of the crisis up to mid-2011, resulted in a situation of displacement of domestic production (Hiratuka 2015).

To better understand the evolution of the manufacturing industry in Brazil, it is important to evaluate the contribution of the variables of aggregate demand (Fig. 2). In the period from 2002 to the outbreak of the international crisis, there is an increase in domestic and foreign demand, albeit with different intensities. At the beginning of the cycle, the performance of exports was important, supported by a strong increase in exports of agricultural commodities and minerals

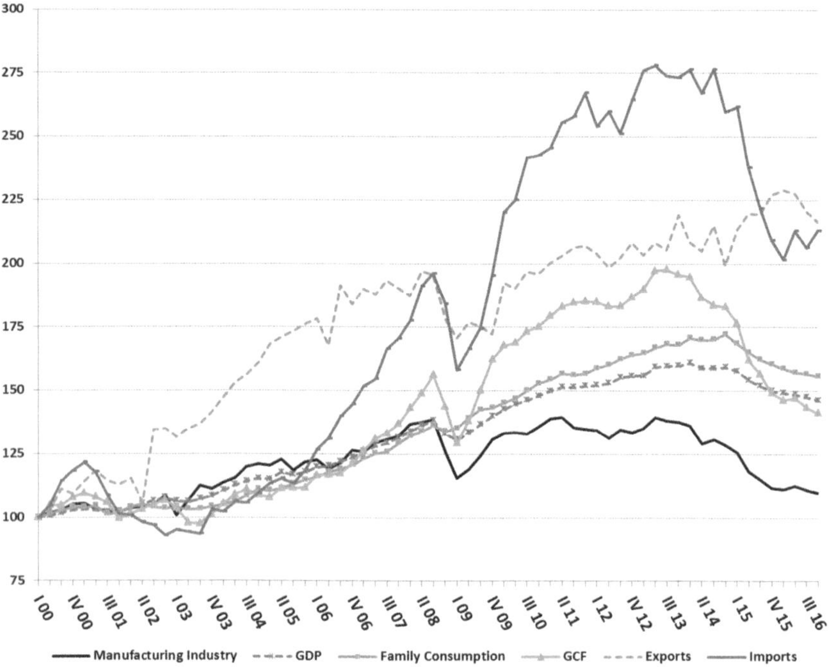

Fig. 2 Volume index of selected GDP components and manufacturing industry GDP. Brazil. Quarterly seasonally adjusted index (1° Quarter 2000 = 100). 2000–2016. *Fonte* IBGE: Contas Nacionais Trimestrais (Quarterly National Accounts). Available at http://www.ibge.gov.br/home/estatistica/indicadores/pib/defaultcnt.shtm

due to vigorous Chinese demand. But it is also possible to observe a brief cycle of strong expansion of gross capital formation in the period 2005–2008, with rates higher than consumption and public spending. The increase in domestic consumption, which will last until the end of 2014, was driven by the already mentioned process of increasing wages, income transfers, and credit expansion. It should be also noted the high dynamism of imports during this period, growing well beyond exports, and the industrial product.

Between mid-2008 and 2009, during which the negative impacts of the GFC were observed in Brazil, there was a strong contraction of investments, exports, and imports. Yet, household consumption and also public expenditure continued to grow as a result of the countercyclical policies adopted. Among these policies, it is worth mentioning the payroll tax reduction for a wide range of sectors, reduction of electricity tariffs, support measures under the Investment Support Program (ISP), aimed at reducing investment costs and local content programs, mainly oil and gas and automobile.

The recovery of exports and capital formation was immediate, reaching the pre-crisis level in 2010. The recovery trajectory remained until mid-2011, when there was a relative stagnation of exports and investments. Investments would still grow again between mid-2012 and mid-2013 and then entered in a strong downward trend until 2016. Family consumption continued to grow until 2014.

The industrial product responded to the stimuli of the aggregate demand in the middle of 2009 and presented expressive rates of growth in 2010. However, from then on there was a deceleration in the rates of growth of the industrial production, followed by a period of stagnation until 2013, which ended in a vertiginous fall until 2016.

The previous analysis raises some important questions. If consumption kept growing until the end of 2014, what factors explain the negative trajectory of the industrial production from the beginning of 2011? Even gross capital formation kept growing until mid-2013. Our explanation is that the exponential growth of imports and the leakage of internal demand largely explained the negative performance of the industrial product. Before the crisis, although imports were increasing at an accelerated pace, industrial production was largely in line with domestic family consumption growth. In the post-crisis period, on the other hand, it is possible to see clearly the drop in industrial production, while imports growth accelerated. The point to be highlighted is that the evolution of the industrial product in the period 2011 to 2014 was not due to insufficient demand, but to its leakage to abroad. The lack of demand will be observed later. From 2015 onwards, for the first time since 2003, the family consumption slowdown, and coupled with the strong decline in investments that started in mid-2013, led to a strong contraction of the industrial production. Not even the reduction of imports and the slight recovery of industrial exports in 2015 changed the trajectory of fall of the industrial product.

Table 1 Quarterly trade volume index—3°. Quarter 2014 over 3°. Quarter 2008. Selected regions and countries

	Exports	Imports
World	**8.7%**	**8.1%**
North America	**13.0%**	**5.9%**
USA	14.4%	3.8%
Canada	2.2%	7.7%
South and Central America	**−0.4%**	**20.8%**
Brazil	1.7%	32.1%
Europe	**1.0%**	**−6.4%**
Total	0.4%	−7.4%
Intra-UE	−6.5%	−7.3%
Extra-UE	14.7%	−7.7%
Asia	**25.5%**	**27.6%**
Japan	−10.4%	7.1%
China	45.2%	59.2%
Korea Rep.	49.5%	17.3%
Others	**−2.1%**	**17.0%**

Source WTO Quarterly merchandise trade volume
Available at https://www.wto.org/english/res_e/statis_e/short_term_stats_e.htm

To explore further that argument, it is worthwhile to observe in a more detailed way the different trade performance observed in different world regions. When considering exports, information on exported and imported volume index, Table 1 shows how Asia, especially China and Korea, maintained a significant rate of trade growth. However, China has maintained import growth above exports, while Korea had clearly adopted a strategy of pursuing external markets at a faster pace than imports as a way of coping with the crisis. The effort of the USA and European countries to raise exports as a way of adjusting its productive sector in the face of the crisis is also evident, with growth rates far above imports. In Europe, despite the contraction of intra-European trade, non-European trade also points to the search for external markets as a reaction to the crisis, combined with a reduction in the absorption of imports from the rest of the world.

South and Central America, on the other hand, made an inverse adjustment, that is, they had the role of absorbing imports from the rest of the world. When the data from Brazil are observed, the information is revealing. While exports were only 1.7% higher in the comparison of

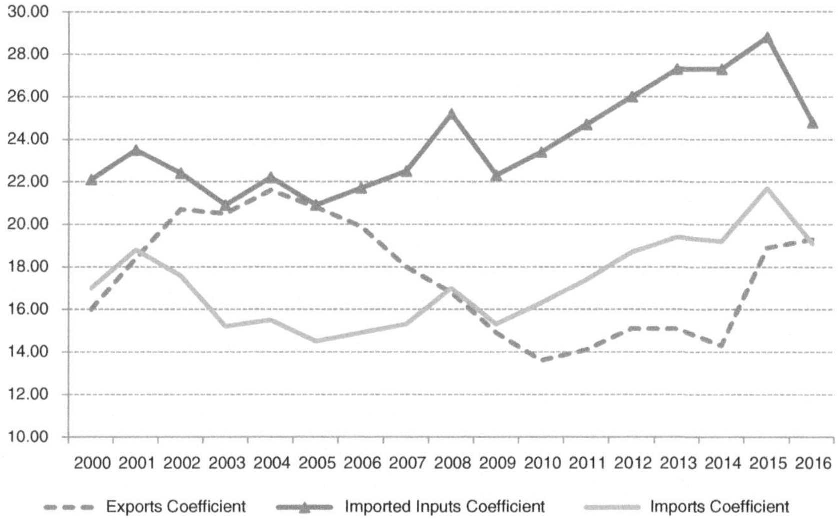

Fig. 3 Manufacturing industry coefficients of imports, imported inputs and exports. Brazil, 1996–2016 (in %). *Source* CNI (Brazilian National Industry Confederation). Available at http://www.portaldaindustria.com.br/estatisticas/coeficientes-de-abertura-comercial/

the two periods, imports were 32% higher. In other words, most of the countries of the world reinforced the search for external markets, consolidating the scenario of fierce competition in the post-crisis period. The Brazilian domestic market has become an important part of this competitive fight.

It is also possible to observe the evolution of some other trade indicators. The import coefficient (IC) of the manufacturing industry, which evaluates the participation of the imports in domestic apparent consumption (domestic production plus export minus imports), increased from 15.3% to 22% between 2009 and 2015. The imported input coefficient (IIC) that measures the share of imported inputs in the total inputs used by the manufacturing sector increased from 22% to 28% in the same period (Fig. 3). The currency appreciation observed since 2003 certainly has had an influence on the increase in coefficients. However, even after the reversal of the appreciation trend, with the real effective exchange rate showing tendency to devaluation from the end of 2011,[7] the coefficients continued to increase until 2015. The Coefficient of Exports, in contrast, fell sharply over the period 2003–2010 and remained relatively stagnant in the post-crisis period from 2010 to 2014, only recovering from 2015 onwards, as the result of the recession.

The evolution of the two indicators related to imports corroborates the argument, especially since 2009, of the increased competition between imported and domestic products and the substitution of imported domestic inputs, reducing the effects of intra-industrial linkages, and with negative impacts on domestic production.

It is also important to emphasize the trade balance of manufacturing goods, classified according to the technological intensity of traded products. As can be seen in Fig. 4, Brazil's positive balance is concentrated in the low-tech sector, while the medium-high and high technological intensity sectors showed a persistent tendency of negative results from 2007 to 2013, remaining at a high level in 2014. In 2015 and 2016, the reduction in the volume of the deficit already reflects the strong decline in the domestic manufacturing production and the recession in the domestic market.

It is worth mentioning again that although the emphasis for the deterioration of the Brazilian industrial production situation is in the post-international crisis period, it reveals important structural problems that have accumulated over many years. These problems become more serious with the changes taking place in the global scenario, as highlighted in Sect. 2 of this chapter. The main difficulty is related to the mobilization of investments by the industrial sector for modernization, an increase of productivity and international competitiveness, especially in productive sectors more intensive in innovation and in the use of technological knowledge (Laplane 2015; Cassiolato et al. 2015).

As Baltar et al. (2016) highlighted, in an important set of Brazilian industrial sectors, especially in the most technologically intensive, competition with imports in the final market, stimulated by an appreciated

[7]Real effective exchange rate calculated by IPEA, based on weighted arithmetic mean of the country's bilateral real exchange rates against 24 selected trading partners.

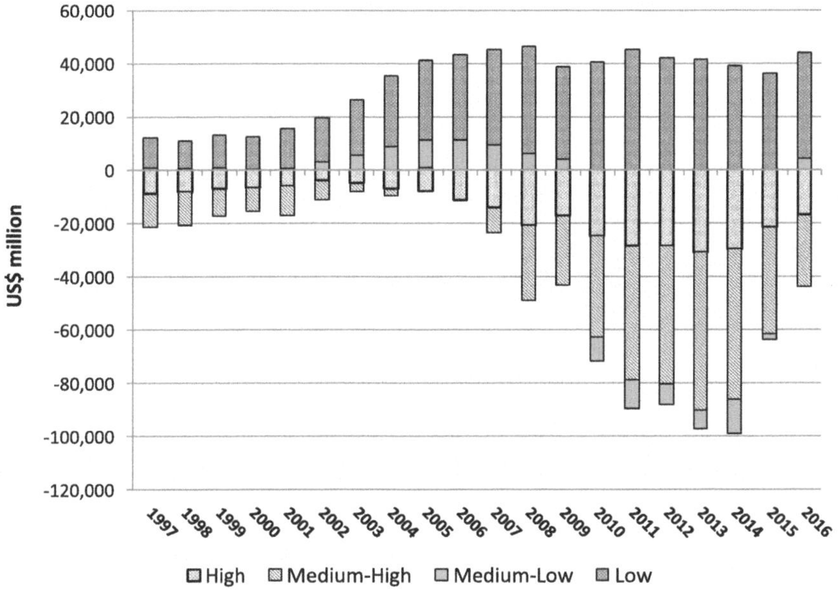

Fig. 4 Trade balance of manufacturing goods, classified according to technological intensity. Brazil, 1997–2016. In US$ millions. *Source* MIDIC (Brazilian Ministry of Industry and Trade). Available at http://www.mdic.gov.br/index.php/comercio-exterior/estatisticas-de-comercio-exterior

currency, seems to have had important impacts on investments. On the other hand, sectors that were able to maintain higher markups, especially in the branches most related to basic inputs and natural resources, were not so affected by this channel.

Thus, the process of 'regressive specialization' of the Brazilian productive structure observed since the 1990s has not been interrupted. The pre-crisis growth cycle, as well as the resumption of more active industrial policies from 2004, was not able to change this situation.

The difficulty in mobilizing resources toward more knowledge-intensive activities can be seen from Fig. 5. The ratio between total expenditures with innovative activities and net sales revenue shows a downward trend. And the ratio of internal R&D activity to net sales revenue is much lower, although it has shown some slight upward trend in 2011 and 2014 compared to the levels of previous years.

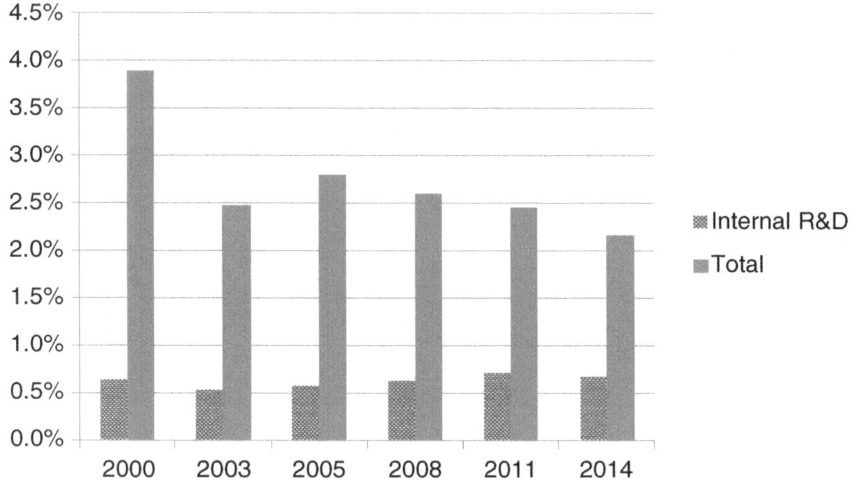

Fig. 5 Expenditures with innovative activities and Internal R&D expenditures as a percentage of Net Sales Revenues. Brazil. In %. *Source* IBGE/PINTEC (Brazilian Innovation Survey). Data Available at http://www.pintec.ibge.gov.br/

The difficulty of facing global competition can also be seen considering the information from the ranking of the companies that invest most in R&D in global terms. As highlighted in Sect. 2, the degree of concentration in the largest companies is quite large. Brazilian's companies share in the top 2,000 corporate investors in R&D in the 2012 ranking was only 0.5% of the total in terms of R&D spending and zero in terms of patents.

At the same time that the Brazilian TNC has a low engagement with innovation activities, the affiliates from abroad operating in Brazil also have a limited contribution to the Brazilian system of innovation. Although the parent companies of a transnational corporation that are in the ranking are located in relatively few countries, they have a highly spread structure of production and trade around the world, as their 500,000 subsidiaries span over 202 countries. Considering the 250 largest companies, Brazil is the seventh country with the largest number of subsidiaries and the first among the developing countries, with a 3% share of the total. Despite having a large number of foreign affiliates among the largest global R&D investors, apparently their impact

Table 2 Triadic patents share of countries. Selected years. In %

Country	1990	2000	2013
Japan, USA, and European Union (28)	94.87	92.13	82.48
China	0.04	0.16	3.51
Korea Rep.	0.20	1.63	5.75
India	0.03	0.12	0.98
Taiwan	0.03	0.09	0.84
Brazil	0.03	0.07	0.19
Russia	0.06	0.15	0.21
Mexico	0.02	0.02	0.04

Source OECD (2016)

on the national economy is still very low and these companies seem to have not contributed much to improving Brazil's insertion in terms of control over technological assets. In the same way, the national companies have not had much prominence in the global scenario (Hiratuka 2010, Cassiolato et al. 2015).

Considering the performance of the country as a whole, and not only of top companies or foreign affiliates, the Brazilian situation does not become more encouraging. Table 2 shows information on triadic patents, but different from Fig. 1, it is possible to see the distribution of patents other than those registered in the USA, European Union, and Japan.

Few countries have achieved an effective increase in participation over the period. It should highlight Korea and China (especially in the 2000s) and, on a somewhat lower level, India and Taiwan. Brazil, Russia, and Mexico performed were much less prominent. It is worth noting that in 1990, Brazilian participation was similar to that observed by China, India, and Taiwan, but the evolution of these countries was much better than Brazil.

The productive and technological fragility of the Brazilian manufacturing industry is particularly worrying given the new challenge that is being drawn globally from the trajectory of some disruptive technologies, which tend to change the standards and competitiveness requirements of today's industrial sectors (internet of things, cloud computing, advanced robotics, autonomous vehicles, genomics, renewable energy, 3D printing, among others). Just as the process of China upsurge has imposed a new level of economies of scale and scope, and thus of competitiveness for a wide range of industrial sectors, this cluster of innovations can the potential to promote another wave of structural changes in competitiveness. The development and diffusion of these technologies in Brazil could be hampered by the fact that the country has not even adequately internalized the capabilities and the technological know-how in the sectors that is the pattern of the current structure of the more advanced industrial countries.

5 Final Remarks

This chapter presented the recent performance of Brazilian manufacturing industry, emphasizing the difficulties encountered in the post-crisis period when the environment of global competition became wilder. The slow growth in world demand since then has made the search for markets and the need to reduce idle capacity a powerful lever to stimulate competition and the mobilization of various instruments for the conquest of market share in the global markets by companies and countries. The lack of prospect of a firm resumption of growth in the main economies suggests that this environment tends to remain for a relatively long period.

At the same time, the theoretical framework presented in the chapter drew attention to the need for developing countries to move toward a diversified production structure, but with an increasing share of manufacturing sectors with a higher degree of incorporation of innovation and technological progress.

Considering this context, it can be said that the challenges posed to Brazilian productive structure to maintain a robust manufacturing sector and, more importantly, to move toward an industry that is able to more effectively incorporate important technological advances and innovative capabilities, contributing to Brazilian economic and social development, are enormous.

The information presented in this chapter indicated that in the Brazilian growth cycle observed before the GFC, the increase in domestic demand was accompanied by the growth in industrial production.

However, with the changes that occurred after the crisis, there was a significant displacement of domestic production by imports, since the growth of the internal demand was decoupled from the industrial production. The increase in trade coefficients did not promote a greater productive and technological development, nor a more virtuous international insertion in the flows of technology, production, and trade. On the contrary, the post-crisis period was marked by unbalanced and asymmetric internationalization, which outsourced the domestic market to imports without promoting a greater trade and productive insertion of the Brazilian industry abroad.

With the difficulty for the manufacturing industry to resume growth, and with the change in the economic policy promoted by the Michel Temer's Government, after the impeachment of Dilma Rousseff, some simplistic solutions based on a fuzzy idea of insertion in global value chains have been presented as a way of recovering dynamism in exports and industrial competitiveness. This evaluation is accompanied by the idea that the path to a virtuous insertion in the global chains would include the expansion of trade liberalization with reduction of tariff and non-tariff barriers and greater emphasis on trade facilitation measures, as well as favorable policies for the protection of TNCs, FDI, and intellectual property rights.

These measures, however, do not automatically guarantee the benefits of better integration into the global chains and have to be articulated with a broader development policy that assures the generation of income and employment in more dynamic segments of productive activity. A more virtuous insertion in regional or global value chains will depend, on the one hand, on the strategy adopted by the subsidiaries of foreign companies present in almost all Brazilian industrial sectors and, on the other hand, on greater investments in productive resources and intangible assets by the fragile national companies. These investments could allow deepening the still timid process of accumulation of capacities and productive and commercial internationalization.

The production growth linked to domestic demand is as important as the external market. The developments in recent years have revealed opportunities and potential expansion fronts for the Brazilian economy that allow us to glimpse important factors to face the challenges highlighted above: A mass consumer goods market that has not yet exhausted its capacity to expand, the huge demand for public goods such as health and education, large investment opportunities in infrastructure in various areas such as energy, telecommunications, transport, and in the chain of natural resources and agribusiness.

In all these sectors, there are potential demands that can stimulate broad industrial and service production chains and foster the quest to incorporate technological capabilities and move toward more innovative processes, products, and services. In addition, it could contribute to the access of the majority of the population to basic services such as health, sanitation, housing, and transport. However, the mobilization of this articulation would require a redoubled effort to coordinate the various instruments already existing around these mobilizing axes. Recent years have seen a search to rebuild an important set of instruments to support productive and technological development demobilized during the 1990s. However, it would be necessary to strengthen these instruments and the capacity for coordination between the public sector and the private sector and among the various institutions responsible for industrial and technological policy, especially in those areas where the capacity to organize the expansion of markets was under public control. Unfortunately, the new government seems to be going in exactly the opposite direction.

References

Aglietta, M., & Riberioux, A. (2005). *Corporate governance a drift: A critique of shareholder value*. London: Edward Elgar.

Almeida, J. C. G., Cintra, M. A. M., Novais, L. F., Jacob, C. A., & Filleti, J. P. (2013). Padrões de Financiamento das Empresas: a Experiência Brasileira. In M. A. Cintra & B. Silva Filho (Eds), *Financiamento das corporações: perspectivas do desenvolvimento brasileiro* (pp. 15–68). Brasília: Ipea.

Baldwin, R. (2011). Trade and industrialisation after globalisation's 2nd unbundling: How building and joining a supply chain are different and why it matters. *NBER Working* Paper, n. W17.716.

Baltar, C. T., Lima, G. T., & Hiratuka, C. (2016). Real exchange rate and investment in the Brazilian manufacturing industry. *Journal of Economic Studies, 43*(2), 288–308.

Baltar, C. T. (2013). *Economic growth and inflation in an open developing economy: The case of Brazil.* PhD Thesis, Department of Land Economy, University of Cambridge.

Berger, S. (2013). *Making in America.* Cambridge, MA: MIT Press.

Cassiolato, J. E., & Lastres, H. (2005). Sistemas de Inovação e Desenvolvimento: as implicações de política. *São Paulo em Perspectiva, 19*(1), 34–45.

Cassiolato, J. E., Szapiro, M., & Lastres, H. (2015). Dilemas e perspectivas da política de inovação. In N. Barbosa, N. Marconi, M. Canêdo Pinheiro & L. Carvalho (Eds), *Indústria e Desenvolvimento Produtivo no Brasil* (pp. 377–416). Rio de Janeiro: Elsevier/FGV.

Chesnais, F. (1996). *A mundialização do Capital.* São Paulo: Xamã.

Chesnais, F. (2013). Present international patterns of foreign direct investment: Underlying causes and some policy implications for Brasil. *Revista de Economia Contemporânea, 17*(3), 376–422.

Coutinho, L. (2003). Macroeconomic regimes and business strategies: An alternative industrial policy for Brazil in the wake of 21st century. In J. E. Cassiolato, H. M. Lastres, & M. L. Maciel (Eds.), *System of innovation and development: Evidence from Brazil* (pp. 311–329). London: Edward Elgar.

De Conti, B. (2013). A crise mundial e os desafios de um novo padrão de desenvolvimento. In CGEE, *As mudanças mundiais em curso e seus impactos sobre as perspectivas de desenvolvimento do Brasil* (pp 13–54). Brasília, DF: Centro de Gestão e Estratégicos.

Dedrick, J., Kraemer, L. K. E., & Linden, G. (2009). Who profits from innovation in global value chains?: A study of the iPod and notebook PCs. *Industrial and Corporate Change, 19*(1), 81–116.

Dernis, H., Dosso, M., Hervás, F., Millot, V., Squicciarini, M., & Vezzani, A (2015). *World corporate top R&D investors: Innovation and IP bundles: A JRC and OECD common report.* Luxembourg: Publications Office of the European Union. Available at http://oe.cd/ipstats.

Dosi, G., Pavitt, K., & Soete, L. (1990). *The Economics of Technical Change and International Trade.* Pisa: LEM Book Series.

Dosi, G., Freeman, C., Nelson, R., Silverberg, G., & Soete, L. (1988). *Technical Change and Economic Theory.* London: Pinter.

European Comission. (2012). Industrial policy communication 2012. *A Stronger European Industry for Growth and Economic Recovery.* Available at http://eur-lex.europa.eu/legal-content/EN/TXT/PDF/?uri=CELEX:52012DC0582&from=EN.

Freeman, C. (1995). The national system of innovation in historical perspective. *Cambridge Journal of Economics, 19*(1), 5–24.

Furtado, C. (1961). *Desenvolvimento e Subdesenvolvimento.* São Paulo: Fundo de Cultura.

Gereffi, G., & Korzeniewicz, M. (1994). *Commodity chains and global capitalism.* Westport: Greenwood Press.

Gereffi, G., Humphrey, J., & Sturgeon, T. (2005). The governance of global value chains. *Review of International Political Economy, 12*(1), 78–104.

Grossman, G. M., & Helpman, E. (1991). *Innovation and growth in the global economy.* Cambridge, MA: MIT Press.

Guimarães, V., Peixoto, F., Cassiolato, J. E., & Lastres, H. (2007). Convergências e complementaridades da corrente neo-schumpetriana com o pensamento estruturalista de Celso Furtado. In J. Sabioa, & F. e Cardim De Carvalho (orgs). *Celso Furtado e o século XXI.* Baureri: Manole e Rio de Janeiro: IE/UFRJ.

Haley, U. C. V., & Haley, G. T. (2013). *Subsidies to Chinese industry: State capitalism, business strategy and trade policy.* New York: Oxford University Press.

Hiratuka, C. (2010). Transnational corporations and the internationalization of research and development activities: The relative importance of affiliates in Asia and Latin America. In A. Dephande (Ed.), *Capital without borders* (pp. 185–203). London: Anthem Press.

Hiratuka, C. (2015). nserção comercial brasileira frente às transformações na economia global: desafios pós-crise. In N. Barbosa, N. Marconi, M. Canêdo Pinheiro & L. Carvalho (Eds.), *Indústria e Desenvolvimento Produtivo no Brasil* (pp. 295–336). Rio de Janeiro: Elsevier/FGV.

Imai, K. (1990). Patterns of innovation and entrepeneurship in Japan. In A. Heertje & M. Perlman (Eds.), *Evolving technology and market structure: Studies in Schumpeterian economics* (pp. 187–202). Ann Arbor: University of Michigan Press.

Jensen, M. (1990). The eclipse of public corporation. *Harvard Business Review, 67,* 60–70.

Kaldor, N. (1989[1981]). The role of increasing returns, technical progress and cumulative causation in the theory of international trade and economic growth. In N. Kaldor (Ed.), *Further Essays on Economic Theory and Policy.* New York: Holmes & Meier.

Lall, S. (2000). The Technological structure and performance of developing country manufactured exports, 1985–98. *Oxford Development Studies, 28*(3), 337–369.

Laplane, M., Coutinho, L., & Hiratuka, C. (2003). *Internacionalização e Desenvolvimento da Indústria no Brasil.* Instituto de Economia da Unicamp, São Paulo, Editora Unesp and Campinas.

Laplane, M. (2015). Inovação e Competitividade no Brasil pós-crise. In N. Barbosa, N. Marconi, M. Canêdo Pinheiro, & L. Carvalho (Eds.), *Indústria e Desenvolvimento Produtivo no Brasil* (pp. 337–358). Rio de Janeiro: Elsevier/FGV.

Lazonick, W., & O'Sullivan, M. (2000). Maximizin shareholder value: A new ideology for corporate governance. *Economy and Society, 29*(1), 13–35.

Lazzonick, W., & LI, Y. (2012). China's path to indigenous innovation. *Sase Conference Paper,* Cambridge.

Lundvall, B. Å. (1992). *National innovation systems: Towards a theory of innovation and interactive learning.* London: Pinter.

Malerba, F., & Orsenigo, L. (1997). Technological regimes and sectoral patterns of innovative activities. *Industrial and Corporate Change, 6*(1), 83–118.

McCombie, J. S. L., & Thirlwall, A. P. (1994). *Economic Growth and the Balance-of-Payments Constraint.* London: Macmillan.

National Economic Council, Council of Economic Advisers, and Office of Science and Technology Policy. (2011). *A strategy for American innovation.* Washington: White House.

OECD, WTO and UNCTAD. (2013). Implications of global value chains for trade, investment, development and job. Paper Prepared for the G-20 Leader Summit. Available at http://www.oecd.org/trade/G20-Global-Value-Chains-2013.pdf.

OECD. (2016). *Science, technology and innovation outlook 2016.* Paris: OECD. Available at http://www.oecd-ilibrary.org/science-and-technology/oecd-science-technology-and-innovation-outlook-2016_sti_in_outlook-2016-en.

Paviit, K. (1984). Sectoral patterns of technical change: Towards a taxonomy and a theory. *Research Policy, 13,* 343–373.

Pisano, G., & Shih, W. (2012). *Producing prosperity: Why America needs a manufacturing renaissance.* Harvard: Havard Business School Press.

Prebisch, R., & Cabanãs, G. M. (1949). El desarrollo económico de la América Latina y algunos de sus principales problemas. *El trimestre económico,* 16, 347–431.

Romer, P. M. (1990). Endogenous technological change. *Journal of Political Economy, 98*(5), 71–102.

Sefarti, C. (2008). Financial dimensions of transnational corporations, global value chain and technological innovation. *Journal of Innovation Economics, 2*(2), 35–61.

Solow, R. M. (1956). A contribution to the theory of economic growth. *Quarterly Journal of Economics, 70*(1), 65–94.

Sperling, G. (2013). The case for a manufacturing renaissance. Available at http://www.whitehouse.gov/sites/default/files/docs/the_case_for_a_manufacturing_renaissance_gene_sperling_7-25-2013_final_p....pdf.

Sturgeon, T. (2002). Modular production networks: A new American model of industrial organization. *Industrial and Corporate Change, 11*(3), 451–496.

Tavares, M. C. (1985). *Acumulação de capital e industrialização no Brasil.* Campinas: Editora da UNICAMP.

UNCTAD. (2013). World investment report. *Global value chains: Investment and trade for development.* New York and Geneva: Nações Unidas.

UNIDO. (2011). Industrial development report 2011. *Industrial energy efficiency for sustainable wealth creation capturing environmental.* Vienna: Economic and Social Dividends.

Veugelers, R. (2013). *Manufacturing Europe's future.* Brussels: Bruegel Blueprint 21.

Financialisation and Investment Behaviour Among Non-Financial Corporations in Brazil Since the Global Crisis

Ricardo Gottschalk and Edgardo Torija-Zane

1 Introduction[1]

Over the past few decades, the world has seen a shift towards finance-driven globalisation. At the corporate level, the shift has been associated with deeper and closer relations of non-financial firms with international financial markets. The rise of institutional investors, the refocusing of firms towards "core business" along with other phenomena such as the fragmentation of productive processes in global value chains gave rise to a "shareholder value" model of corporate governance, which

[1]The views expressed in this chapter are those of the authors and do not necessarily represent the views of the institutions of relevant affiliations.

R. Gottschalk (✉) · E. Torija-Zane
Division on Globalisation and Development Strategies, UNCTAD,
Geneva, Switzerland
e-mail: ricardo.gottschalk@unctad.org

E. Torija-Zane
e-mail: edgardo.torijazane@unctad.org; edgardotz@gmail.com

P. Arestis et al. (eds.), *The Brazilian Economy since the Great Financial Crisis of 2007/2008*, https://doi.org/10.1007/978-3-319-64885-9_7

has become a key feature of the so-called financialisation process. This model rewards financial equity investors through financial payments such as dividend distribution and share buybacks and gives secondary markets—where financial assets are traded and price signals emanate—a predominant role in terms of capital allocation. While in some countries, such as the USA or the UK, financialisation has become the dominant form of intermediation between investment and savings, in Continental Europe and East Asia, but also other parts of the world, the role of financial markets and institutional investors in resource allocation is tempered by the still significant presence of large state-owned corporations, and financial institutions, like development banks, which are not necessarily oriented towards the purpose of profit maximisation or remunerating shareholders (Batsch 2002).

Since the 1980s, finance-driven globalisation and the rise of shareholder power resulted in a decoupling of profits and investment at the firm level and also at a country level. Large profits have not necessarily been reinvested in the own firm's expansion. Instead, earnings are recycled through financial markets and used for other purposes, such as the financing of the activity of other economic units promising higher returns, in the same country or abroad. While many saw this as a source of markets efficiency, others feared that finance, so prone to generate speculative cycles, would end up deterring overall investment and hurting economic growth. Some have even argued that financialisation is an important factor behind the slowdown of accumulation (Stockhammer 2004).

The present chapter examines the behaviour of Brazilian listed corporations and asks to what extent and in which ways financialised practices also have taken hold among Brazil's large corporations. It focuses on the corporate investment patterns observed during the post-2008 crisis period. The main goal is to evaluate to what extent corporate behaviour in Brazil fits in with the financialisation narrative and what indigenous elements in such behaviour might be unveiled. The chapter contributes to the theoretical literature on this subject by bringing to light how macroeconomic factors, specific to developing countries such as Brazil, intertwine with the shareholder model of governance in shaping corporate decisions. Among these factors, it is worth highlighting the economic instability caused by the country's fragile insertion in global financial markets, which creates vulnerabilities and frequent external shocks.

Section 2 of this chapter sets the stage by revising the main changes in corporate strategies, with emphasis on refocusing and financialisation practices at the international level. Section 3 discusses corporate restructuring and behaviour in Brazil since the 1990s, highlighting the roles of privatisation, changes in corporation law and external financial insertion in shaping the current corporate environment. Section 4 explores corporate behaviour among Brazil's non-financial corporations drawing on balance sheet data from non-financial firms listed on Brazil's stock exchange (BM&FBOVESPA). Section 5 then examines corporate indebtedness since the global crisis, from a sectoral perspective. Section 6 summarises and concludes.

2 Corporate Strategies at the International Level: Refocusing and Financialisation

The world economy has undergone significant transformations in the past few decades. The opening of new markets through trade and capital account liberalisation, the increase in cross-border capital flows and mounting levels of private and public debt, as well as the revolution in information and communication technologies (ICTs) have marked a shift towards finance-driven globalisation and financialised investment strategies.

At the corporate level, the changes in the economic environment have been associated with three connected developments: the fragmentation of the productive process in global value chains, the refocusing of the activities of large conglomerates around their "core business" and the financialisation of the performance criteria. The previous dominant corporate model commonly known as "managerial capitalism" that corresponded to the "Golden Years" progressively moved to the "investor capitalist" logic in which the decisions at the level of the financial system have an increasing relevance in the sphere of production (Useem 1996).

The first of these developments was the result of advances in technology, including improvements in transport and logistics, and the deregulation of trade and investment flows, both of which allowed the fragmentation of production into discrete activities. Large corporations built business networks involving intra-group affiliates across multiple locations and independent external suppliers, often based overseas (OECD et al. 2013). Consequently, the global economy became increasingly structured around global value chains, and more deeply integrated and interdependent.

The second and closely related trend has been corporate refocusing. Since the 1980s, the historical trend of vertical integration and diversification of large conglomerates has been reversed (Markides 1992; Milberg 2008). This refocusing of corporate strategies was a response to changing patterns of competition following the growing globalisation of markets for goods and services. Enlarged markets meant more business opportunities, but also stronger competitive pressures to reduce costs. The growing reliance on outsourcing and subcontracting in productive processes was part of the employers' efforts to cut costs. Reducing labour costs was one of the objectives, but not the only one. Many corporations divested entire lines of business or were broken up following hostile takeovers and leveraged buyouts (Liebeskind and Opler 1992). Such internal breakups were motivated by the need to enhance managerial efficiency through cost reductions in response to the growing complexity of intra-firm organisation, and by what came to be considered "excessive" diversification (Weston et al. 1990). Corporate restructuring was thus primarily designed to increase the profitability rate and the market value of a firm (Jensen 1989).[2]

The third shift in the corporate landscape is the growing influence of shareholders in corporate decisions. The greater shareholder influence was the result of the growing activity of professional asset managers as activist intermediary investors in the context of the development of capital markets. Since the 1970s, but even more so in the last twenty years,

[2]Indeed, restructuring also served the purpose of paying out shareholders through stocks repurchases financed with the asset sales (Krier 2005).

institutional investors have owned an increasing proportion of public equity shares.[3] The subsequent decline in the participation of individual shareholders has been noticeable in developed countries. According to UNCTAD (2016a), the predominant shareholders in over half of the top 100 multinational enterprises (MNEs) are financial institutions.

The concentration of shares in the hands of a relatively few professional investors has given them increased power to participate in the decisions of publicly held corporations and therefore the possibility of an activist's stance towards management to enhance corporate profits (Krier 2005). This active role contrasts with the passive behaviour of the atomistic savers that directly owned shares in the period of "managerial capitalism" but had little influence on manager's decisions.

The activism of professional asset managers took place in two ways. Financial investors, therefore, owning a significant part of the equity of a group and having a strategic position, started to ask a high level of information disclosure on the firm's activities and exert their voting rights in the shareholders' meetings. "Market discipline" has been the other mechanism to influence managers. Institutional investors holding shares for "tactical" allocation purposes also provided a channel to influence corporate policy by "voting with their feet"; that is, by selling shares of the firm when they are not satisfied with a company's performance or policy (Bastch 2002). To communicate more efficiently with this type of investor and following requests from regulators, companies started providing quarterly earnings releases rather than annual or semi-annual and heavily invested in their financial communication teams.

Based on the notion that those managing publicly held companies are obligated to maximise shareholder value, the "agency theory" (Jensen and Meckling 1976) called for a proper alignment of interests between shareholders (the principals) and managers (the agents). Incentive practices included compensation packages to top executives with stock options and other benefits linked to the share value of the company.

---

[3]Institutional investors are financial institutions that accept funds from third parties for investment not under their own name but on such parties' behalf. They include pension funds, mutual funds and insurance companies.

Corporate managers have relied on a range of practices to enhance financial returns to meet the expectations of asset managers and other shareholders. Among the most common practices, it has been the growing use of firms' earnings for dividend distribution and stock buybacks. The latter increases stock prices to the benefit of shareholders and top managers. Managers are often offered stock options, for example, as part of compensation packages. More aggressive mechanisms to increase financial returns have become quite common, such as mergers and acquisitions through leveraging, often followed by asset restructuring involving the sale or spin-off of non-core business activities within the corporate portfolio. Thus, strategic refocusing and the rise of shareholder power constitute a major shift in management policies from one of "retain and reinvest" to that of "downsize and distribute" (Lazonick 2015, p. 2).[4]

The globalisation of corporate activity, the refocusing of corporate strategies and greater shareholder power were widely welcomed on the grounds that these would enhance economic efficiency and increase production. It was argued that the fragmentation of the production process into separate activities placed in different locations would facilitate a stronger focus on comparative advantages and a more efficient division of labour than would have been possible prior to the ICT revolution. Moreover, corporate refocusing would improve firms' results by helping reduce "excessive" conglomerate diversification (Ross et al. 1999, p. 775; Brealey and Myers 2000, p. 946). Finally, as mentioned above, the growing role of institutional investors and professional asset managers in corporate decision-making was seen as promoting efficient corporate governance and solving "agency problems" arising from the separation of ownership and control.

A common belief among the supporters of shareholder primacy was that financial intermediaries and capital markets would intermediate efficiently between agents with funding needs and those with funding capacities (Friedman 1970; Brav et al. 2008; Greenwood and Schor 2009).

[4]See also Lazonick (2013), particularly on the practice of stock repurchases by cash-rich companies.

Therefore, payouts by companies to their shareholders would not threaten the availability of resources for investment, since any project expected to be profitable would easily find interested investors in the global capital markets. It was argued that financial globalisation would help organise the productive system around global value chains, with professional financial intermediaries ensuring the smooth reallocation of surpluses from different activities to their most efficient uses.

Against these favourable views on the soundness of the "investor capitalism", many raised concerns that these changes were, in fact, harmful to corporate shareholders, and, more generally, adverse to real investment, innovation and employment generation. These concerns included the following points:

i) Shareholder value behaviour seems to be excessively focused on short-term earnings at the expense of real investment and innovation, both requiring a long-term valorisation horizon (Stout 2012). Pressures to generate financial gains in the stock markets and the threat of hostile takeovers whenever the profitability decreases may dissuade managers to engage in projects that do not produce immediate returns. In addition, their compensation packages, based on stock options, reinforce short-term behaviour.

ii) Shareholder value as the corporate governance ideology may not be in the interest of stakeholders. An example of this has been the maximisation of profits through the adoption of labour reducing policies and wages cost reduction, a further practice that goes in favour of the short-term interests of shareholders and managers, but against other stakeholders of the firms (Palley 2007, p. 4). The "downsize and distribute" model may have strong reverberations at the macroeconomic level, since lower wages and job destruction debilitate household income. The excessive reliance on mortgages and consumer credit to sustain aggregate demand and compensate the fall in income generates macroeconomic fragility and thus uncertainty, which is also deterrent to productive investment.

iii) Corporate globalisation, restructuring and rising shareholder power have increased the role of capital markets in the intermediation between savings and investment. But this intermediation has been prone to short-termism and herding behaviour, and occurs in imperfect markets, unable to create the right signals for productive and profitable investments. Such a system left to its own devices will not be able to allocate resources in ways to generate socially desirable outcomes. Their growing weight in the economy would lead to resource misallocation, creating cycles of bubbles followed by bursts. Empirical work establishing a link between the financialisation of corporate strategies and adverse impacts on fixed capital formation has drawn both on macroeconomic data (Stockhammer 2004; van Treeck 2007) and firm-level data (Tori and Onaran 2015).[5] Indeed, a gradual decoupling between corporate investments and profits has been observed over the years, which may be partly explained by shareholder-driven corporate practices (UNCTAD 2016b).

Meanwhile, and besides the potential negative effects of the financialisation of corporate strategies, it is highly likely that the persistent decline in public investment in the major developed economies and more generally a passive fiscal policy have also deterred more vigorous corporate investment. The fragile recovery in key developed economies after the 2008–2009 global crisis and uncertainty about the future may be playing a role in profit expectations.

In developing countries, shareholder value plays a smaller role, even though it has increased in recent years. This is because, in many such countries, large private shareholders are often wealthy families, and ownership concentration is generally higher than in developed countries (Claessens and Yurtoglu 2013). Moreover, listed companies are often part of larger business groups and conglomerates. In these ownership configurations, management practices are less likely to be dominated by the interests of institutional investors or by executives guided by compensation schemes linked to share value of the firm. The next section discusses the case of Brazil, showing that, while its large corporations have started to move towards shareholder value type of governance, their governance structure and behaviour still share several

[5]Focusing on European Union countries, Tori and Onaran (2015) highlight a number of stylised facts that show a declining investment to profit ratio, a growing ratio of financial assets to total asset, rising financial payments and income, and stagnant investment rates. They suggest that financialisation has hit the manufacturing sector in the UK particularly hard.

characteristics with corporations from other developing economies, such as high levels of ownership concentration and divergence between economic ownership and control (voting rights).

3 Corporate Restructuring and Behaviour in Brazil Since the 1990s

While corporate behaviour in developed countries has evolved markedly because of the three inter-connected forces described in the previous section, in Brazil, the corporate landscape also witnessed significant changes. The privatisation process starting in the mid-1990s and changes in the Brazilian Law of Corporations in 2001,[6] all of them are reforms that, in principle, favoured the shareholder model of governance. However, for historical reasons, the influence of shareholder power among Brazil's corporations has been, in practice, significantly less strong than in developed countries.

In Brazil, company ownership has historically been concentrated in the hands of wealthy families, which gives them management control over the companies (Habbard 2010; Gottschalk 2001). Among listed companies, ownership structure that prevails is the closely held as opposed to the widely held model of corporations. In the closely held model, the main interplay of interests that is often observed is that of dominant shareholders—often families—versus minority shareholders. In this case, the dominant shareholders exert control over both the board and the management of the company. It gives them the power to rule as they wish, which may be in favour of growth-enhancing strategies, but also might involve extraction of rents against the interests of minority shareholders (Bavoso 2016).

This model thus contrasts with the widely held model, in which ownership is dispersed among many shareholders. The issue the literature on shareholder value raises in relation to the widely held model is the

[6]The Brazilian Law of Corporations, or *Lei das Sociedades. Anônimas* in Portuguese, Law No. 6404 of 15 December 1976, was amended by Law No. 10.303 of 31 October 2001.

Table 1 Size of financial system in Brazil

Years	Per cent of GDP
Domestic credit by the financial sector (average values)	
1996–2000	64.1
2011–2014	100.5
Stock market capitalisation (average values)	
1989–1992	3.6
2011–2014	43.3
Stocks traded—total value (average values)	
1992–1995	9.6
2011–2014	30.5
Insurance companies' assets (end of year)	
2000	3.4
2013	10.4
Mutual funds' assets (end of year)	
2000	25.2
2013	49.7

Source authors' estimations based on World Bank, World Development Indicators (2016)

agency problem, namely the possible conflict between management and shareholders. The incentives that have been created to increase alignment of interests between these two constituencies have been a major contributor to financialisation practices, as discussed earlier in this chapter.

In the closely held model, voting rights are concentrated, reflecting concentration of capital ownership. Moreover, in Brazil's capital markets most companies hold a system of dual classes of shares—those with voting and those with non-voting rights—which reinforces the concentration of voting rights. According to Habbard (2010), in 2005, 86% of listed companies on BM&FBOVESPA, Brazil's stock exchange, had such a system of shares. This system allows for a large gap between economic ownership and voting power. For example, in 2002, among BM&FBOVESPA listed companies, the largest shareholders had 46% of economic ownership (measured in terms of cash flow rights) but 71% of all voting rights of the company (Aldrighi et al. 2006, Table 1).

In the second half of the 1990s and early 2000s, Brazil underwent a process of capital market reforms. These included: (i) reform of the

Brazilian Law of Corporations, which was amended in 2001 to, among other changes, reduce the ceiling of non-voting shares as a proportion of total shares from two-thirds to 50%, and allow minority shareholders (both with and without voting rights) to nominate a board member (Habbard 2010); and (ii) the creation by BM&FBOVESPA stock exchange, also in 2001, of the so-called *Novo Mercado*. The latter consisted of new voluntary listings whereby corporations opting for such listings had to meet more stringent corporate governance requirements, designed to mirror those of best international corporate governance practices.[7] Nowadays, BM&FBOVESPA has, in total, 6 listing segments, three of which are part of Novo Mercado. The stated aim was to further develop Brazil's capital market and provide a range of segments that could cater to different corporate profiles and needs. Of course, the specific aim was to attract foreign investors by ensuring their rights and guarantees and reducing their risks.[8]

In the same period, Brazil undertook a process of privatisation of many of its state-owned enterprises, also as part of broader reforms intended to change the corporate ownership structure in Brazil and further boost the country's capital markets as a source of finance for economic growth. This process involved the privatisation of companies from telecommunications, energy, mining and steel and banking thus targeting mainly utilities, natural resource and financial sectors (Habbard 2010).

These reforms were strongly encouraged by international organisations and think tanks such as the World Bank (and its International Finance Corporation arm) and the OECD. Their expectations were that such reforms would help broaden corporate capital ownership,

---

[7]The new listings created were: Level 1, Level 2 and *Novo Mercado*. The following were among the requirements all three listings had to meet: minimum free float of 25% of capital, share dispersion efforts and enhanced disclosure of quarterly financial statements. In addition, Level 2 and Novo Mercado listings included: 20% of independent board directors, two-year term for board members, compliance with IFRS or US GAAP reporting standards, mandatory recourse to private arbitration and six-month lock-up period following an IPO. Finally, Novo Mercado had to follow the one share one vote principle (Habbard 2010, pp. 17–19; Gottschalk 2001, p. 36).

[8]See BM&FBOVESPA, available at http://www.bmfbovespa.com.br/en_us/listing/equities/listing-segments/about-listing-segments/. Accessed 17 November 2016.

increase foreign investor participation and promote the shareholder value ideology. Their ultimate aim was the promotion of private sector development and economic growth through the dissemination of good corporate governance, growth of investment and enhanced capital market efficiency (IFC 2009; OECD 2003).

However, despite all reform efforts including privatisation, assessments that followed these reforms indicate that corporate ownership has become even more concentrated in Brazil. Privatisation led to transfer of ownership to wealthy families, although it also saw increased foreign capital participation in Brazil's equity markets. As a consequence, Brazil's wealthy families enhanced their positions as block-holders and therefore their control over listed corporations. Foreign investors, in turn, became in some instances co-controllers, while in others they acquired full company ownership, in the process de-listing and transforming these companies into TNC subsidiaries (Habbard 2010).

The ownership configuration that has emerged because of such reforms, therefore, still differs considerably from that found in developed countries, with higher ownership concentration than, say, in the UK or the USA (Claessens and Yurtoglu 2013). Still, while ownership structure differs, privatisation, changes in Brazil's corporate law and external investors' penetration in Brazil's stock exchanges did contribute to the growing importance of shareholder value in guiding corporate behaviour. In addition, it should be noted that, during similar period, financial intermediation in Brazil gained prominence, particularly in the past 15 years or so. This can be evidenced by different financial market measures, such as domestic credit provided by the financial sector, the size of assets of insurance companies and mutual funds, and stock market capitalisation (Table 1).[9] This rise contributed to the growth of the influence of shareholder groups in corporate decisions.

The links between the Brazilian economy and the global financial system also witnessed structural changes. Between the early 1990s and

[9]The paradox is that, despite a considerably larger financial system whereby domestic credit expanded from 64% in 1996–2000 to 101% in 2011–2014 and stock market capitalisation grew from below 4% in 1989–1992 to 43% in 2011–2014, real capital accumulation as a proportion of GDP did not pick up as one might have expected.

the 2000s, the Brazilian economy became financially more liberalised. Consequently, ever larger movements of cross-border capital flows have entered and then left the country. Such flows, which were quite large at times, were often driven by policy decisions in developed source economies, although also by political cycles in Brazil. During the upside phase, they generated financial asset bubbles and currency appreciations, mispricing investments and therefore sending the wrong signals for capital allocation. At the corporate level, this made companies more vulnerable to the vicissitudes of international finance. The often sudden reversal of such flows in turn caused massive exchange rate depreciations and inflationary pressures. Most of these capital flows were driven by short-term financial incentives and therefore little ended up financing productive investment. Instead, these flows contributed to an environment characterised by high macroeconomic instability.[10]

In this environment, Brazil's policymakers have become trapped in their efforts to implement "credible" policies and to learn how to play the "confidence game", meaning they have to guess what policies financial markets think are good for addressing macroeconomic instability caused by volatile capital flows (Krugman 1998). Often these policies have taken the form of pro-cyclical monetary and fiscal tightening, therefore reinforcing the immediate recessionary effects of the outflows.[11] Given the close alignment between confidence building and orthodox policies, Brazil has lacked fiscal space for adoption of alternative macroeconomic policies that might be more appropriate to tackle its economic difficulties.[12]

While external financial liberalisation has constrained macroeconomic policy space, an analogous phenomenon can be observed at the corporate level, with growing presence of foreign investors in Brazil's

---

[10]See Chap. "New Features of the Brazilian External Sector Since the Great Global Crisis" in this book. Also, for an early account of country experiences with capital inflows and outflows since the early 1990s, see Gavin et al. (1995); for a more recent analysis, see Akyüz (2013).

[11]On the role of confidence-building policies in explaining macroeconomic outcomes, see Bresser-Pereira (2001).

[12]See Grabel (2000) for an extensive discussion on the relations between policy credibility and confidence building in emerging markets.

equity markets restraining the room for long-term corporate growth strategies. Emerging Global Advisors (EGA), an asset management company, affirms in its investment strategy commentary, targeted at foreign equity investors in the emerging markets, that:

> [D]ividends are a window into the earnings health of a company. The payment of dividends is dependent upon both the ability and the willingness of a company to disburse cash. Corporate strategy and corporate financial structure, therefore, play an important role in establishing dividend policy. (EGA 2015, p. 1)

Still in the same commentary, EGA notes that, since 1987, the MSCI EM, a market capitalisation index for equities of emerging economies, has yielded dividends accounting to over 40% of rolling 10-year returns.[13] And that since 1995, its corporate dollar earnings have increased about 6.5% per annum, while dividends have grown 8%, which shows that, since then, EM companies have increased their dividend payout ratio. Further, EGA states that in Latin America (where Brazil's equity markets account for a sizeable share of the region's total equity markets)[14] dividend payout is above the average for emerging markets, in a context in which, in their own analysis, "[r]elatively high capital expenditure, low free cash flow and depressed margins suggest that capital expenditure should be diverted to higher dividends for shareholders" (EGA 2015, p. 3).

Therefore, pressures for dividend distribution from international asset managers and investors seem to have become a reality, indicating yet again growing importance of shareholder value in emerging economies. However, in addition to financialisation practices associated with shareholder value such as dividend distribution and stock repurchases, in Brazil, macroeconomic instability has encouraged other

---

[13]The MSCI EM is a market capitalisation index created by Morgan Stanley Capital International (MSCI) to measure performance of equity markets. It consists of indices from 23 emerging economies, including Brazil.

[14]According to AGF Investments (2016), Brazil had a weight of 7.4% in the MSCI EM index in September 2016, with a share of 57% within the subgroup of Latin American countries.

practices that have become dominant among Brazil's large corporations. In an unstable and uncertain macroeconomic environment, real interest rates increased at times as a policy response, encouraging agents to seek higher and safer returns in the financial sphere, by investing in short-term financial assets. More critically, though, external financial liberalisation increased the portfolio choices for corporations by providing additional sources of profitability outside the real economy. With liberalisation, firms had easier access to the international financial markets, and were able, among other financial operations, to make arbitrage gains by exploiting interest rate differentials of foreign and domestic markets. The result was that, facing uncertainty about the returns and risks associated with real fixed investments firms often borrowed abroad, not to invest in real assets but in financial assets instead.[15] Some profited from speculative activities, such as carry trade (Caballero et al. 2015), while others invested in productive projects, and many hedged against growing risk by acquiring overseas subsidiaries and financial vehicles to access foreign currency and financial assets.

Thus, while shareholder power became increasingly influential in Brazil's corporate behaviour, the sort of financialisation practices that have come to dominate the country's corporate landscape were those associated with countries inserted in the global financial system at the peripheral level, and less so those practices common to corporations based in the core of the system. The result of this type of international financial insertion was that it was not followed by higher rates of real investment, as expected by policymakers. Stronger growth performance was observed in the 2000s, following the "lost decade" of the 1980s and the mediocre 1990s. Brazil, however, has not managed to revive the levels of investment, dynamism and structural transformation observed in the 1960s or 1970s. The growth cycle of 2003–2012 was excessively based on the expansionary effects of the commodity cycle, lacking the investment levels required in manufacturing for further structural transformation.

---

[15]As Demir (2009) noted, these practices were common among several emerging economies that underwent external financial liberalisation in the 1980s and 1990s.

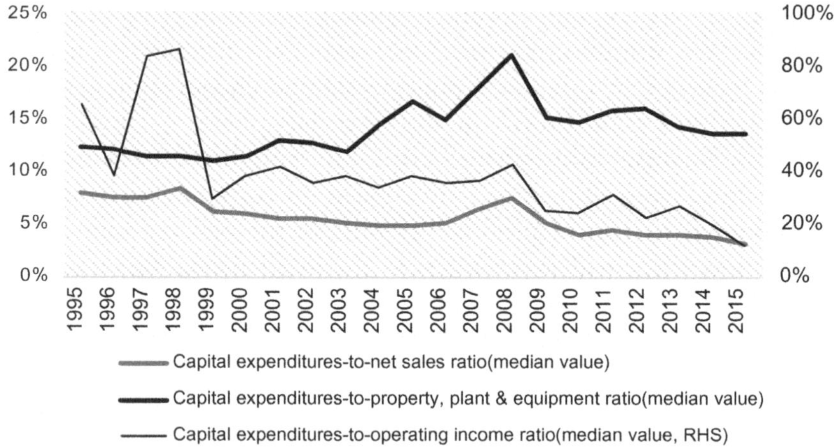

Chart 1 Brazilian nonfinancial corporations: investment rates. *Source* authors' estimations based on data extracted from Thomson Reuters, Worldscope database. Available at Subscription Service (Accessed March 2017)

4 Microeconomic Trends: The Behaviour of Brazil's Non-Financial Corporations

Drawing on balance sheet data and income statements from 255 non-financial firms listed on Brazil's stock exchange BM&FBOVESPA, obtained from Thompson Reuters *Worldscope,*[16] it is possible to identify a number of relevant trends regarding corporate behaviour in Brazil.

First, corporate investment, after peaking in 2008, has slowed down after the global financial crisis, as shown in Chart 1 by the ratio of capital expenditures to capital stock ("property, plant and equipment"). Capital expenditures also declined as a per cent of sales. In the post-crisis period, the median operating income of Brazilian firms kept rising despite the slowdown in investments. Investment weighted 43% of operating income in 2008, but only 12% in 2015 (median values

[16]The Worldscope database provides detailed historical financial statement contents for corporations.

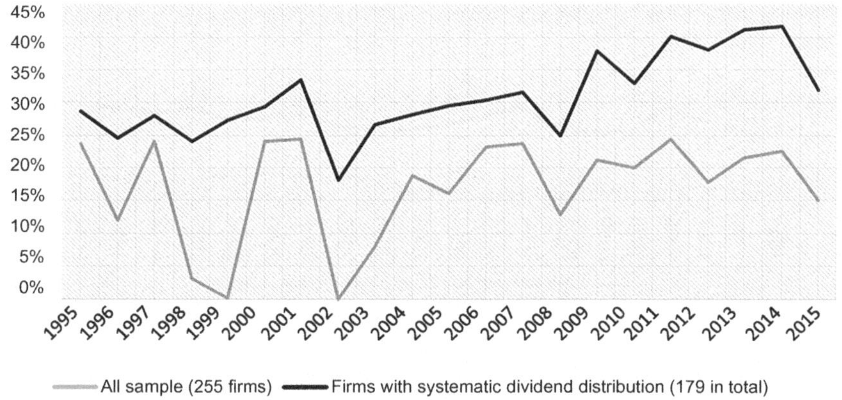

Chart 2 Brazilian non-financial corporations: cash dividends paid as share of net income (after tax)—median values. *Source* authors' estimations based on data extracted from Thomson Reuters, Worldscope database. Available at Subscription Service (Accessed March 2017). Firms distributing dividends systematically are those that have done so in five consecutive years at least once over the period 1995–2015

of non-financial firms). As such, the "profit-investment nexus", the dynamic interaction which arises because "*profits are simultaneously an incentive for investment, a source of investment and an outcome of investment*" (Akyüz and Gore 1996, p. 461), has been weakening in Brazil.

Second, payouts through dividend distribution have remained stable among the whole sample, but have markedly risen in the subgroup of firms that distribute cash dividends in a systematic fashion (Chart 2). It should be also noted that around 30% of the listed firms in Brazil do not regularly distribute dividends.[17] The increase in dividends, as explained in Sect. 2, is a feature of the behaviour of financialised firms.

Third, balance sheet data shows that financial assets held by non-financial firms (cash and short-term assets, which include marketable securities) have steadily increased as a proportion of total assets in the period 2003 to 2009, and have then stabilised remaining at higher levels

[17]Entities considered here as firms distributing dividends systematically are those that have done so in five consecutive years at least once over the period 1995–2015.

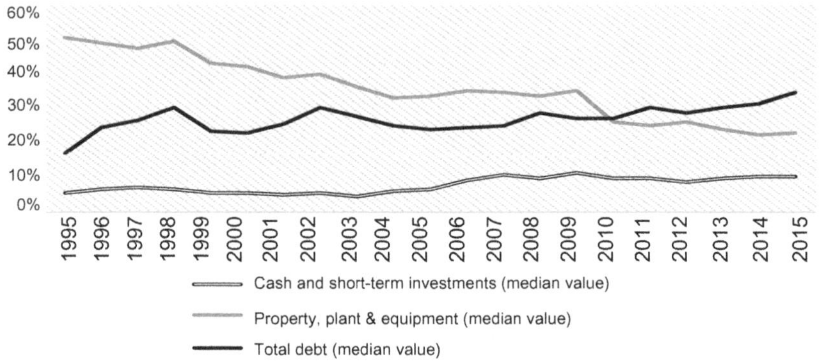

Chart 3 Brazilian nonfinancial corporations: selected balance sheet items (in per cent of total assets). *Source* authors' estimations based on data extracted from Thomson Reuters, Worldscope database. Available at Subscription Service (Accessed March 2017)

than in the 1990s. In contrast, the share of fixed assets in total assets has declined (Chart 3).

Meanwhile, the weight of total debt in firms' balance sheets has increased since 2009. This indicates that the slowdown in investment of large companies was not a consequence of lower availability of funding, but arguably by other factors including the bearish prospects of aggregate demand and lack of appropriate incentives to engage in long-term (risky) projects in the real sector.

One relevant aspect of the concomitant increase in debt and financial assets is the possibility that corporations with access to international markets could use external debt to engage in carry trade activities (Bruno and Shin 2015). In the case of Brazil, the possibility to invest in government debt in local currency yielding high nominal interest rates makes the bet particularly attractive in presence of large capital inflows and expectations of nominal appreciation of the Real. Companies conduct carry trades at times when ample liquidity is available, on the premise that changes in the financial environment will occur gradually, and that the exchange rate will be more stable than interest rate differentials. However, this strategy can become a significant source of risk

Table 2 Leverage ratios among non-financial corporations, 1995–2014 (median values, %)

	1995–2002	2003–2008	2009–2015	2015
Debt-to-total sales	37.6	34.1	48.3	55.1
Debt-to-fixed assets	60.9	70.8	104.1	128.5
Debt-to-equity	52.4	53.5	63.3	75.4
Interest payments-to-total sales	9.3	5.6	3.9	5.9

Source authors' estimations based on data extracted from Thomson Reuters, Worldscope database. Available at: Subscription Service (Accessed: March 2017)

for such companies if there are abrupt changes in the exchange rate.[18] Firms may still enter into carry trade bets when they believe they have an information advantage to predict movements in the foreign exchange market (Geczy 2007) or in case they expect a government bailout in case of important turndown in the value of the currency of risk.[19]

Fourth, and still in connection with the noticeable increase in non-financial corporate debt, all leverage indicators have gone up in the post-crisis period (Table 2). This is not a trend limited to Brazil's large corporations, but generalised across the developing world. According to IMF (2015) estimates, the corporate debt of non-financial corporations in major emerging economies increased from about $4 trillion in 2004 to $11 trillion in 2010, and to well over $18 trillion in 2014. The ratio of corporate debt to GDP also increased in many developing and emerging economies after the global financial crisis. Drawing on data from Brazil's Institute on Capital Markets (IBMEC) and Brazil's Central Bank, Brazil's *Centro de Estudos do Instituto IBMEC* (CEMEC) shows that, between December 2010 and 2015, non-financial corporate debt in Brazil increased from 37 to 60% of the country's GDP (CEMEC 2016, p. 5).[20]

[18]Indeed, Brazilian corporations engaged in derivatives carry trade before and after the global crisis, and incurred large losses when the Real depreciated sharply in the final quarter of 2008 (see Prates 2015, p. 116).

[19]Executives may also make bets with financial assets trying to push up the company's earnings to make some extra profit when they think the opportunity arises and to boost the firm stock price and thus the value of their own stock holdings.

[20]IBMEC stands for *Instituto Brasileiro de Mercado de Capitais*.

Balance sheets from non-financial companies listed on BM&FBOVESPA's stock exchange show that total corporate debt grew 117% in real terms in the years 2010–2015. Measured in dollar terms, such an increase was 32%.[21] Since the Brazilian economy expanded 13.5% over the same period, this implies that corporate debt increased significantly as a proportion of GDP, as indicated earlier by CEMEC drawing on different data sources.

Non-financial corporations have also increasingly relied on bond financing in international financial markets, and on cross-border bank lending. CEMEC (2016) shows that foreign debt as a share of total debt by non-financial corporations in Brazil went up from 20.5 to 25.7% between December 2010 and 2015, reflecting the fact that, in terms of GDP, the former increased from 7.6 to 21.4% over the same period. This growth has taken place under highly favourable financing conditions, including the fast expansion of liquidity driven by the Quantitative Easing (QE) programmes pursued by the central banks of the major advanced economies. A growing concern is that the rise of corporate indebtedness, driven primarily by the greater availability of global liquidity rather than by firms' own profitability, has been reflected in the rise in the ratio of interest expenditures to total sales of firms in the most recent period. The ratio, at 3.5% in 2012, a low value from a historical perspective, went progressively up to 4.6% in 2015. This poses potential risks to these firms, as it has made them more vulnerable to interest rate changes and external shocks. In addition, greater borrowing in foreign currency is also creating currency mismatches for firms engaged in non-tradable activities, thus threatening economic stability (Chui et al. 2016; IMF 2015). Still according to CEMEC, foreign debt of non-financial corporations increased 49.3% in the year 2015 alone, against 6.4% of their domestic debt. Most of the sharp increase in foreign debt is explained by the strong nominal depreciation of the domestic currency in that year (CEMEC 2016, p. 4).

[21] Brazil's CPI-IGP DI was used as a deflator.

5 Debt and Investment in Brazil Since the Global Crisis: A Sectoral Perspective

A critical question is whether the growing indebtedness among Brazil's non-financial corporations has contributed to the expansion of their productive capacities and the diversification of the country's productive structure.

Data from balance sheets of non-financial corporations show the telecommunications sector was in top position, in terms of debt growth between December 2009 and 2015. The sector's debt grew by 300% in real terms, an outcome explained by *Oi*, a leading telecommunications company in Brazil, which drew heavily on debt financing to support extremely rapid growth of its capital stock, a process that ended up with the company filing for bankruptcy protection in June 2016 (Pacheco et al. 2016). Oil and gas came second, recording a debt growth of 261%, but coming first by far as the largest contributor to total corporate debt growth, explaining 44% of its total expansion over the period under analysis.[22] Health care (dominated by health care providers) and chemicals came third and fourth, registering debt growth of 196 and 157%, respectively, while industrial goods and construction and materials came together in fifth position with debt growth of 107%. However, basic resources and utilities were, after oil and gas, the sectors that contributed most to total debt growth explaining 13 and 9.5% of its total expansion, due to their proportionally large debts. Total corporate debt expansion, therefore, came mainly from commodity-related, resource-based industries, as well as utilities (see Table 3).

Large debt acquisition by resource-based corporations is what one might indeed expect in the context of growing role of international financial markets in providing funds to Brazilian companies, to the extent that these corporations are often more engaged in foreign trade

[22]The sectorial breakdown corresponds to the Industry Classification Benchmark (ICB), an industry classification taxonomy. The ICB uses a system of 10 industries, partitioned into 19 supersectors, which are further divided into 41 sectors, which then contain 114 subsectors. This chapter calls "sector" what the ICB refers to as supersectors.

and/or with the capacity to raise resources in the international financial markets.

Taking the corporate sector as a whole, the ratio of investment to capital stock fell in Brazil from 2009 onwards (Chart 1). Looking across different industries, real capital stock growth was strongest in the oil and gas sector at 159% between 2009 and 2015, followed by chemicals, automobiles and parts, health care and retail (see Table 3). Thus, oil and gas, chemicals and health care are the sectors that are ranked among the top five in terms of both real debt and capital stock growth. In contrast, among the remaining industries in the top five in terms of debt growth, telecommunications saw only relatively modest capital stock expansion, while industrial goods and construction both registered deep capital stock contraction.

Two main facts stand out. First, the relationship between debt and capital accumulation is variable across different industries, although oil and gas, chemicals and health care were among the top four both in debt and capital accumulation. Second, the rise in debt was faster than the capital stock in the most relevant sectors, implying a higher ratio of debt to capital stock in 2015 compared to 2009 for all sectors, except automobile and travel. The question then is to what extent debt was channeled towards increasing productive capacities or, instead, alternative uses, such as financial investments.[23]

Despite some heterogeneity in sectoral patterns and range, easy access to cheap finance and debt financing did not support investment in sectors situated close to the technological frontier and that had the greatest potential to contribute to overall productivity growth, such as industrial goods (and services) and technology, both of which exhibited dismal investment growth performance. Instead, leveraging and investment remained overwhelmingly concentrated in natural resource sectors. These sectors are particularly sensitive to changes in global growth and commodity price fluctuations, and are more prone to adding to macroeconomic and financial risks than to supporting structural transformation. The results somehow support the view of Palma (2015), who

[23]Debt growing at faster rates than investment could also reflect a strategic choice in terms of the funding mix for the expansion of the firm or higher requirements in terms of working capital.

Table 3 Growth of debt and capital stock among non-financial corporations between 2009 and 2015 (per cent)

Sector	Contribution to total debt growth	Change in debt at constant R$	Contribution to total growth in the capital stock	Real Capital stock growth	Debt-to-capital stock in 2009	Debt-to-capital stock in 2015	Sector share in total debt in 2015	Sector share in total capital stock in 2015
Automobile and parts	0.2	32.6	0.6	104.9	145.3	94.0	0.4	0.4
Basic resources	13.3	55.6	19.3	17.5	55.9	74.1	16.6	23.2
Chemicals	3.6	157.4	4.1	121.2	104.3	121.4	3.3	2.1
Construction and materials	1.2	107.0	0.1	−20.9	75.1	196.5	1.3	0.7
Food and beverage	9.2	89.6	8.5	58.4	118.9	142.3	9.9	7.2
Health care	0.3	196.2	0.2	96.7	143.7	216.4	0.3	0.1
Industrial goods and services	8.4	107.3	12.3	−23.3	142.0	383.7	8.6	2.3
Oil and gas	43.6	261.2	75.0	159.1	56.1	78.2	36.3	48.0
Personal and household goods	1.3	51.9	0.4	−9.7	109.9	184.8	1.6	0.9
Retail	2.3	105.5	2.0	95.5	161.9	170.1	2.4	1.4
Technology	0.1	52.6	−0.01	−38.5	400.8	994.9	0.1	0.01
Telecommunications	7.1	299.5	5.9	60.3	48.0	119.5	5.8	5.0
Travel and leisure	−0.02	−50.7	0.1	10.6	61.9	27.6	0.03	0.1
Utilities	9.5	37.0	-16.1	−62.9	48.0	177.5	13.4	7.8
Total	100.0	116.5	100.0	34.2	66.8	108.7	100.0	100.0

Source authors' calculations, based on Thomson Reuters, Worldscope database. Available at: Subscription Service (Accessed March 2017). Brazil's CPI-GPI used as deflator argued that the surge of cheap finance in the wake of QE programmes ended up financing activities that do not enhance productive capacities, but rather budget deficits and capital flight.

6 Summary and Conclusions

This chapter has examined in detail the role of shareholder value in shaping corporate decisions both in developed countries and in Brazil. Its main analytical contribution has been to look in detail at the main determinants of corporate behaviour in Brazil, highlighting the relative weight of shareholder value along with other corporate features and macroeconomic factors that are specific to developing countries such as Brazil. In addition, the chapter brings to the discussion new empirical evidence on investment patterns by Brazil's listed corporations since the global financial crisis, and discusses these patterns considering recent financialisation trends in Brazil's corporate sector. By looking at corporate trends, the chapter also aims to bring new elements to the debate surrounding the deteriorating economic landscape in Brazil since 2011.

The chapter shows that the corporate landscape in Brazil has witnessed significant changes in the past 20 years. The privatisation process beginning in the mid-1990s, changes in the Brazilian Law of Corporations and growing penetration of foreign investors in Brazil's stock markets following external financial liberalisation have been the key factors that helped create the space for the shareholder model of governance. The corporate governance that emerges in Brazil from the reforms in the 1990s and early 2000s has ownership concentration generally higher than in developed countries, and family ownership still is prevalent. In this ownership configuration, management practices seem less likely to be dominated by the interests of institutional investors or by executive behaviour seeking to meet short-term expectations of shareholders.

Although institutional investors still play a relatively small role in shaping corporate decisions, Brazil's financial sector grew fast in the past 20–25 years as shown by the increasing weight of the sector in total value added. The growing integration of the country in the global financial markets gave access to broader sources of finance, a trend that was intensified in the post-2008 period, in part due to the expansionary monetary policy in main financial centres. It also increased the incentives for companies to engage in financial bets, in particular in the foreign exchange market.

In examining the behaviour of Brazilian listed firms, the chapter looks at their balance sheets, the use of profits as a source of investment, the main characteristics of the recent indebtedness cycle and recent investment patterns. It shows that firms' dynamics reveal several fragilities of open economies when facing pro-cyclical capital flows. Indeed, the period after the global financial crisis has witnessed a large concentration of debt and investment in a few economic sectors linked to the commodity price cycle—mainly oil and gas—and a greater proportion of holdings of financial assets by non-financial firms.

Establishing a causal relationship between corporate behaviour and overall capital investment is a difficult task. The predominant reasons of the slowdown in corporate investment are to be found in the macroeconomic sphere: the fragile global economic recovery, the end of the commodity cycle, low levels of public investment and the shift towards austerity in the domestic policy orientation which, by reducing aggregate demand, hurts business prospects in Brazil and real investment. The financialisation practices of Brazilian corporations therefore seem to be part of a broader corporate strategy averse to real investment in ans environment characterised by low economic dynamism, high domestic interest rates, shocks and uncertainty.

Brazil's path towards long-term sustainable economic growth depends on a dynamic corporate sector that invests strategically and innovates. Financialisation practices in themselves are not a crucial inhibiting factor for unlocking investment and innovation by Brazilian corporations, although in conjunction with other factors they may become an obstacle as well if they increase financial volatility. The most binding constraints still appear to be the absence of long-term horizon due to pro-cyclical government policies, the insufficient public investment and the economic instability caused by Brazil's fragile insertion in global financial markets, which creates vulnerabilities and frequent shocks.

References

AGF Investments. (2016). MSCI emerging markets index overview, *AGF Investments*, 30 September.

Akyüz, Y. (2013). Waving or drowning: Developing countries after the financial crisis, *Research paper 48*. Geneva: South Centre.

Akyüz, Y., & Gore, C. (1996). The investment–profits nexus in East Asian industrialization. *World Development, 24*(3), 461–470.

Aldrighi, D., & Oliveira, A. (2006). Ownership and control structures and performance of firms in Brazil. In *Anais do XXXIV Econtro Nacional de Economia Proceedings of the 34th Brazilian Economics Meeting*. Salvador: ANPEC.

Bastch, L. (2002). Le Capitalisme Financier. *Coll. Repères*. Paris: éd. La Découverte.

Bavoso, V. (2016). Shareholder value, emerging economies and the need to reconcile the corporate objective with sustainable and inclusive goals. In F. Ngwu, O. Osuji, & F. Stephen (Eds.), *Corporate governance in developing and emerging markets: Debates, models and new institutional economics*. London: Routledge.

Brav, A., Jiang, W., Partnoy, F., & Thomas, R. (2008). Hedge fund activism, corporate governance, and firm performance. *Journal of Finance, 63*(4), 1729–1775.

Brealey, R. A., & Myers, S. C. (2000). *Principles of corporate finance* (6th ed.). New York: McGraw-Hill.

Bresser-Pereira, L. C. (2001). Incompetência e *Confidence Building* Por Trás de 20 Anos de Quase Estagnação da América Latina. *Revista de Economia Política, 21–1*(81), 141–166.

Bruno, V., & Shin, H. S. (2015). Global dollar credit and carry trades: A firm-level analysis, BIS Working Paper No 510, Bank for International Settlements: Basel.

Caballero, J., Panizza, U., & Powell, A. (2015). *The second wave of global liquidity: Why are firms acting like financial intermediaries?* (Working Paper No. HEIDWP21-2015). Geneva: Graduate Institute of International and Development Studies. Available at http://www.nbs.rs/export/sites/default/internet/latinica/90/90_9/UgoPanizza_wp.pdf.

CEMEC. (2016). Dívida das Empresas não Financeiras: Evolução Recente e Impacto da Desvalorização Cambial. *Nota CEMEC 03/2016*, IBMEC, March.

Chui, M., Kuruc, E., & Turner, P. (2016). *A new dimension to currency mismatches in the emerging markets: Non-financial companies* (BIS Working Papers No. 550). Basel: Bank for International Settlements.

Claessens, S., & Yurtoglu, B. B. (2013). Corporate governance in emerging markets: A survey. *Emerging Markets Review, 15,* 1–33.

Demir, F. (2009). Financial liberalization, private investment and portfolio choice: Financialization of real sectors in emerging markets. *Journal of Development Economics, 88*(2), 314–324.

EGA. (2015). The power of dividends. *EGA Investment Strategy Commentary.* Emerging global advisors, 10 January.

Friedman, M. (1970, September 13). The social responsibility of business is to increase its profits. *The New York Times Magazine.*

Gavin, M., Hausmann, R., & Leiderman, L. (1995, April 3). The macroeconomics of capital flows to Latin America: Experience and policy issues. Revised version of a background paper for a seminar on *International Capital Flows: Prospects and Policy Issues,* at the annual meetings of the Inter-American Development Bank in Jerusalem.

Geczy, C. C., Minton, B. A., & Shrand, C. M. (2007). Taking a view: Corporate speculation, governance, and compensation. *The Journal of Finance, 62*(5), 2405–2443.

Gottschalk, R. (2001). A Brazilian perspective on reform of the international financial architecture. *Report commissioned by DFID*, Institute of Development Studies, July. Brighton: University of Sussex.

Grabel, I. (2000). The political economy of 'policy credibility': The new-classical macroeconomics and the remaking of emerging economies. *Cambridge Journal of Economics, 24,* 1–19.

Greenwood, R., & Schor, M. (2009). Investor activism and takeovers. *Journal of Financial Economics, 92*(3), 362–375.

Habbard, P. (2010). Corporate Governance in Brazil—An International Trade Union Perspective. *Hans Bockler Stiftung-Trade Union Advisory Committee,* Paper prepared to the OECD. April. Paris: OECD.

IFC. (2009). *Practical guide to corporate governance. Experiences from the Latin American companies circle.* Washington, DC: IFC, OECD and Global Corporate Governance Forum.

IMF. (2015). Corporate leverage in emerging markets—A concern? *Global Financial Stability Report.* Washington, DC, pp. 81–114.

Jensen, M. C. (1989). Eclipse of the public corporation. *Harvard Business Review* (Sept-Oct. 1989), revised 1997. Available at SSRN: http://ssrn.com/abstract=146149.

Jensen, M. C., & Meckling, W. H. (1976). Theory of the firm: Managerial behavior, agency costs and ownership structure. *Journal of Financial Economics, 3*(4), 305–360.

Krier, D. (2005). *Speculative management: Stock market power and corporate change*. Albany, NY: State University of New York Press.

Krugman, P. (1998). The confidence game: How Washington worsened Asia's crash. Available at http://www.pkarchive.org/crises/krugman1.html. Accessed 01 April 2014.

Lazonick, W. (2013). The financialization of the U.S. corporation: What has been lost, and how it can be regained. *Seattle University Law Review, 36*(2), 857–909.

Lazonick, W. (2015, April). Stock buybacks: From retain–and–reinvest to downsize–and–distribute. Washington, DC: Center for Effective Public Management at Brookings. The Brookings Institution.

Liebeskind, J., & Opler, T. C. (1992). *The causes of corporate refocusing* (Working Paper No. 155). Available at http://digitalrepository.smu.edu/business_workingpapers/155.

Markides, C. (1992). The economic characteristics of de-diversifying firms. *British Journal of Management, 3*(2), 91–100.

Milberg, W. (2008). Shifting resources and uses of profits: Sustaining US financialization with global value chains. *Economy and Society, 37*(3), 420–451.

OECD. (2003). *White paper on corporate governance in Latin America*. Paris: OECD.

OECD, WTO, & UNCTAD. (2013). *Implications of global value chains for trade, investment, development and jobs*. G-20 leaders summit. Saint Petersburg.

Pacheco, F., Moura, F., & Lucchesi, C. (2016). Oi Files for Brazil Record $19 Billion Bankruptcy Protection. Bloomberg, 21 June. Available at https://www.bloomberg.com/news/articles/2016-06-20/oi-files-for-bankruptcy-protection-as-talks-with-creditors-stall.

Palley, T. (2007, December). *Financialization: What it is and why it matters* (Working Paper No. 525). The Levy Economics Institute of Bard College.

Palma, J. G. (2015). *Why corporations in developing countries are likely to be even more susceptible to the vicissitudes of international finance than their counterparts in the developed world: A Tribute to Ajit Singh* (Cambridge Working Paper in Economics (CWPE) 1539). Cambridge: University of Cambridge.

Prates, D. (2015). *O regime de câmbio flutuante no Brasil: 1999–2012: especificidades e dilemas*. Brasília: IPEA.

Ross, S. A., Westerfield, R. W., & Jaffe, J. (1999). *Corporate finance* (5th ed.). Chicago, IL: Irwin.

Stockhammer, E. (2004). Financialisation and the slowdown of accumulation. *Cambridge Journal of Economics, 28*(5), 719–741.

Stout, L. A. (2012). The problem of corporate purpose, *Issues in government studies No. 48*. Washington, DC: Brookings Institution.

Tori, D., & Onaran, O. (2015). The effects of financialization on investment: Evidence from firm-level data for the UK. *Greenwich papers in political economy No GPERC17*. Greenwich Political Economy Research Centre, London: University of Greenwich.

UNCTAD. (2016a). World investment report–investor nationality: Policy challenges. *United Nations publication*. Sales No. E.16.II.D.4. New York and Geneva.

UNCTAD. (2016b). Trade and development report. Structural transformation for inclusive and sustained growth. *United Nations publication*. Sales No. E.16.II.D.5. New York and Geneva.

Useem, M. (1996). *Investor capitalism: how money managers are changing the face of corporate America*. New York: BasicBooks, Perseus Books Group.

van Treeck, T. (2007). *Reconsidering the investment-profit nexus in finance-led economies: An ARDL-based approach* (IMK Working Paper No. 1). Macroeconomic Policy Institute, Düsseldorf: Hans Boeckler Foundation.

Weston, J. F., Chung, K. S., & Hoag, S. E. (1990). *Mergers, restructuring, and corporate control*. Englewood Cliffs, NJ: Prentice-Hall International.

Income Distribution, Productivity and Economic Growth: Empirical Evidence in the Case of Brazil

Philip Arestis and Carolina Troncoso Baltar

1 Introduction

Brazil achieved a period of relatively high economic growth over the period 2004–2008, when the world scenario was favourable for the country's trade balance. During that period, Brazil had successive years of current account surpluses and substantially increasing capital flows. That improvement in the external accounts allowed the reduction of the public foreign debt and the built up of international reserves. The government was, then, able to implement an incomes policy, focused on real increases in the minimum wage along the business cycle, with positive consequences for the country's economic performance. During

P. Arestis (✉)
University of Cambridge, Cambridge, UK
e-mail: pa267@cam.ac.uk

C.T. Baltar
University of Campinas, Campinas, Brazil
e-mail: cbaltar@gmail.com; cbaltar@unicamp.br

P. Arestis et al. (eds.), *The Brazilian Economy since the Great Financial Crisis of 2007/2008*, https://doi.org/10.1007/978-3-319-64885-9_8

that period, inflation decreased due to national currency appreciation, improving the purchasing power of workers (Baltar 2015).

Improved purchasing power of workers together with lower inflation for consecutive years is possible if productivity increases or the terms of foreign trade changes in favour of the country. Improved economic performance and increases in investment occurred especially in 2007–2008, which had positive effects on productivity. On the other hand, the national currency appreciated, decreasing inflation and improving the purchasing power of workers. Therefore, the period between 2004 and 2008 was marked by better economic performance, low inflation and increases in the purchasing power of workers.

The GR that emerged after the GFC of 2007–2008 brought challenges to the Brazilian economic performance, with unpleasant consequences for the country's economic growth, despite the maintenance of the incomes policy adopted before the crisis. The Brazilian government was able to intervene effectively through countercyclical policies, preventing further reduction in GDP. However, consumption, investment and exports decelerated, manufacturing production stagnated and GDP growth slowed down substantially, while imports continued rising considerably, although at lower growth rates (Arestis et al. 2015). During this period, the purchasing power of workers kept increasing, but at lower rates compared to the previous period.

In this setting, the aim of this chapter is to analyse in more detail the changes in the purchasing power of workers in the 2000s and during the GR, verifying whether it is a result of changes in productivity or due to changes in the real exchange rate. The latter is related to changes in the nominal exchange rate, which do not depend only on external trade, namely terms of trade, i.e. the relation between the price of exports and imports in US dollars, but also on the relation between the price of tradable and non-tradable goods. The theoretical background is the Kaleckian literature on income distribution and economic growth that accounts for the effects of wage share on economic growth, including the effects of productivity as well as the Kaldorian literature that emphasises the importance of manufacturing for a country's economic growth. However, when we consider an open developing economy dependent on the international scenario, the analysis of the changes in the purchasing power of workers and its effect on the economic activity is more complicated than what the literature suggests. This chapter advances the analysis by considering specificities of the Brazilian economy. An equation for wage share is suggested, and it is estimated for the Brazilian manufacturing sector.

The chapter is organised as follows. After the introduction, Sect. 2 analyses the performance of the Brazilian economy from 1997 until 2014[1], highlighting the effects of the GR and comparing its performance with that before the GFC. Section 3 reviews the literature, focusing specially on the Kaleckian approach that relates income distribution to economic growth. Section 4 analyses the behaviour of the Brazilian wage share and suggests an equation for it, considering specificities of this economy. Section 5 estimates the suggested equation for the Brazilian manufacturing industry. Section 6 summarises and concludes this contribution.

2 Brazilian Economic Performance in the 2000s

Brazil presented a period of relatively high economic activity from 2004 to 2008, when the world scenario was very favourable for this country. The higher demand and commodity prices increased Brazilian exports, both commodities and manufactured goods, to developing countries (Baltar 2013; Prates et al. 2014). This better scenario for the trade balance together with the new boom of capital flows to Emerging Market Economies (EMEs) improved the balance of payments, enabling the government to reduce its foreign debt and accumulate international reserves. Consequently, the country's external constraint decreased, and its economic performance improved with higher GDP growth and lower inflation (Amico 2013; Baltar 2013).

Table 1 shows the Brazilian balance of payments as well as the real exchange rate index[2] from 1997 to 2014.

---

[1]The period of analysis starts in 1997 to cover the changes that have taken place in the 2000s. The year 2014 is the latest year with available information for the Brazilian manufacturing sector.

[2]Real exchange rate is defined as P_iE/P_d, where P_i is international price, E is the nominal exchange rate, defined as domestic units per foreign currency, and P_d is domestic price.

Table 1 Brazilian balance of payments and the real exchange rate index

	Exports in US$ millions	Export change %	Imports in US$ millions	Imports change %	Trade balance	Current account balance	Financial account balance	Real exchange rate index
1997	52982.7	11.0	49301.6	−14.6	3681.2	−30852.0	34011.6	67.59
1998	51139.9	−3.5	59747.2	12.0	−8607.4	−33892.2	38048.6	70.48
1999	48012.8	−6.1	57763.5	−3.3	−9750.7	−25869.4	25525.4	105.59
2000	55118.9	14.8	55850.7	13.3	−731.7	−24793.5	21995.6	96.98
2001	58286.6	5.7	55601.8	−0.4	2684.8	−23721.4	24181.2	120.06
2002	60438.7	3.7	47242.7	−15.0	13196.0	−8096.8	8157.9	132.67
2003	73203.2	21.1	48325.6	2.3	24877.7	3760.1	−2966.6	137.36
2004	96677.5	32.1	62835.6	30.0	33841.9	11346.8	−9020.0	135.04
2005	118529.2	22.6	73600.4	17.1	44928.8	13547.2	−13040.3	110.32
2006	137807.5	16.3	91350.8	24.1	46456.6	13029.9	−13115.1	98.53
2007	160649.1	16.6	120617.4	32.0	40031.6	408.0	2494.7	91.42
2008	197942.4	23.2	172984.8	43.4	24957.7	−30640.5	28806.3	88.95
2009	152994.7	−22.7	127722.3	−26.2	25272.4	−26261.2	26354.0	88.38
2010	201915.3	32.0	181768.4	42.3	20146.9	−75824.1	76011.8	77.05
2011	256039.6	26.8	226246.8	24.5	29792.8	−77032.1	79242.2	74.97
2012	242578.0	−5.3	223183.5	−1.4	19394.5	−74218.4	73953.8	84.09
2013	242033.6	−0.2	239747.5	7.4	2286.1	−74838.9	72695.6	89.89
2014	225100.9	−7.0	229154.5	−4.4	−4053.6	−104181.3	100598.5	91.18

Source Own calculations based on the Central Bank of Brazil (2017) data. Real exchange rate index: June 1994 = 100

Brazil achieved a pick of trade surplus of 46.5 billion dollars in 2006. After that, exports kept increasing until the global crisis in 2008. However, imports grew faster, decreasing this surplus. The evolution of the Brazilian external trade had a direct correlation with the evolution of the real exchange rate. The national currency was devalued after increases in the nominal exchange rate in 1999, 2001 and 2002. The devalued currency stimulated exports of manufactured goods at the beginning of the commodity boom, mainly to Latin American countries' exporters of commodities. The trade surplus of 2003 was enough to generate surplus in the current account.

The current account improved as a result of increasing trade surplus, enabling higher economic activity after 2004 without a rise in external constraint. Yet, the financial account was negative until 2006 due to the external debt amortization (mainly payments to the IMF) that was higher than direct foreign investment and portfolio investment.[3] Improved balance of payments took place at the same time the nominal exchange rate decreased. The nominal exchange rate increased from 1.16 Real per dollar in 1998 to 3.08 in 2003, and then it decreased, achieving 1.83 in 2008 (Central Bank of Brazil 2017).

The decrease in the nominal exchange rate helped to reduce domestic inflation that was high in 2003 (Table 2). Tradable goods inflation became similar to international inflation. But, non-tradable goods inflation was less affected by the nominal exchange rate, and domestic inflation was still higher than international inflation (Baltar 2015). Since the nominal exchange rate decreased and domestic inflation was higher than international inflation, the national currency appreciated in real terms.

The currency appreciation[4] was strong. The real exchange rate decreased 27% between 2004 and 2006 (the real exchange rate index decreased from 135.04 in 2004 to 98.53 in 2006), as a consequence mainly of the decrease in the nominal exchange rate. Exports of manufactured goods decreased, and imports of these goods increased (Prates et al. 2014). Trade surplus fell, but it was still positive due to higher exports of commodity goods that more than compensated the trade

[3]For detailed information on the Brazilian financial account see Central Bank of Brazil (2017).

[4]In the rest of this chapter, currency appreciation is considered in real terms.

Table 2 Growth rates of Brazilian GDP, components of demand and inflation

	GDP growth	Inflation (INPC)	Exports growth	Imports growth	Consumption growth	Investment growth
1997	3.4	6.0	11.0	14.6	2.6	8.7
1998	0.0	3.8	4.9	−0.1	0.2	−0.3
1999	0.3	4.8	5.7	−15.1	0.7	−8.2
2000	4.4	6.2	12.9	10.8	3.0	5.0
2001	1.4	7.5	10.0	1.5	1.2	0.4
2002	3.1	10.2	7.4	−11.8	2.6	−5.2
2003	1.1	17.0	10.4	−1.6	−0.3	−4.6
2004	5.8	6.3	15.3	13.3	3.9	9.1
2005	3.2	5.8	9.3	8.5	3.9	3.6
2006	4.0	3.3	5.0	18.4	4.5	9.8
2007	6.1	4.1	6.2	19.9	5.8	13.9
2008	5.1	6.6	0.5	15.4	5.0	13.6
2009	−0.1	5.0	−9.1	−7.6	4.1	−6.7
2010	7.5	5.1	11.5	35.8	6.3	21.3
2011	4.0	6.6	4.5	9.7	3.5	4.7
2012	1.9	5.4	0.5	0.2	3.2	−4.0
2013	3.0	6.4	2.5	8.3	2.4	5.2
2014	0.5	6.0				

Source Own calculation based on IPEADATA (2017). The components of demand are in Brazilian Real, and the growth rates are in real terms based on 2000 = 100. INPC stands for Consumers' National Price Index

deficit with manufactured goods from 2007. Trade surplus decreased quickly, and in 2008 it became a deficit. This deficit was intensified by the global crisis. Besides that, the currency appreciation generated high deficits in services and financial income, but international reserves did not decrease due to high capital inflows.

Greater economic activity and higher employment together with lower inflation occurred with increased purchasing power of wages. The level of real wages was very low in 2004 due to poor economic performance and high inflation from 1999 to 2003 (Baltar et al. 2010). Higher employment and higher purchasing power of workers stimulated family consumption through debt, despite the high interest rate (Baltar 2013). This credit demand was met by financial institutions in an optimistic period, featured by high employment and real wages, low inflation and positive performance of public and external accounts;

these factors suggest that families had the opportunity to repay their debts, despite high interest rates.

Consumption growth and induced investment had an important role in the Brazilian GDP growth (Arestis et al. 2015; Carneiro and Matijascic 2011; Calixte et al. 2014; Barbosa and Souza 2010). Consumption growth was reinforced by the government policy that increased the minimum wage in real terms.[5] In Brazil, increases in the minimum wage affect not only low labour income, but also lower retirement benefits and social assistance. The minimum wage increased considerably and, at the same time, labour contracts were formalised due to higher supervision and the better economic performance of the Brazilian economy (Baltar and Leone 2015). Consequently, low-income families were able to increase their consumption.

Those increases in consumption had a crucial role in the Brazilian economic performance between 2004 and 2006, but in 2007 and 2008, when the country achieved its higher growth rates, investment became the component of effective demand with higher growth rate, raising the investment rate of the Brazilian economy (see Table 2). Nevertheless, the national currency appreciation stimulated investment in non-tradable sectors or tradable sectors in which Brazil had comparative advantage (Baltar et al. 2016). Firms could adapt to the overvalued currency in sectors that compete internationally, importing intermediate and capital goods (Sarti and Hiratuka 2016). Firms' adaptation also occurred in the production of capital goods to satisfy the high demand due to increased investment in 2007 and 2008.

Increased consumption and investment stimulated domestic production and generated high imports. The Brazilian trade surplus decreased, and GDP growth was lower than consumption and investment from 2004 to 2013 (Baltar 2013). The GFC in 2008 intensified the problem of transferring abroad the effects of higher consumption and investment. Brazil could react to the GFC with countercyclical policies due to the build-up of international reserves and reduction of the public

[5]The formalization of economic activities and the consequent increase in formal employment, at the same time the minimum wage was raised, incorporated part of the population to the consumption of durable goods because they had access to credit.

external debt from 2004. In 2009, GDP decreased, but it recovered quickly. However, GDP growth decelerated from 2011, despite the government attempts to preserve improvements in the labour market and the consumption growth.

The government intervention only avoided higher deceleration of consumption. The decrease in GDP growth became higher than in consumption growth because of higher decrease in exports and investment growth rates. The lower economic activity of developed economies generated idle capacity in many countries, intensifying the international competition of manufactured goods. This intense competition created problems to the Brazilian economy to redefine its strategy of economic expansion with public and private investment in infrastructure and to increase the country's competitiveness in manufactured goods. The increased international competition and the impact of Chinese economic activity affected the Brazilian external trade. Brazil increased both its exports of primary products to China and its imports of manufacturing goods from China. Besides that, cheaper Chinese exports substituted Brazilian exports of manufactured goods to developing countries, such as the South American countries (Baltar and Prates 2014).

The negative effects of the GR on the Brazilian external trade occurred with lower growth of consumption and investment, and GDP growth decreased considerably. Manufacturing production growth also shrank considerably and increases in consumption took place with higher imports. Consumption increased, although at lower rates, due to government stimulus. However, this stimulus was not enough to sustain healthy GDP growth (Arestis et al. 2015).

An important debate to explain the difficulties of the Brazilian economy to sustain higher economic growth rates focus on the production of manufactured products. According to some authors, Brazil is going through a de-industrialisation process,[6] and the low dynamism of the

[6]The debate on the Brazilian de-industrialization process had started before the GR. The argument was that he liberalising reforms were responsible for the reduction of the role of manufacturing production in the country's GDP (see also, Palma 2005; Nassif 2006; and IEDI 2007).

manufacturing production would explain the lower GDP growth rate. For instance, Bresser-Pereira (2009) stresses that the currency appreciation and favourable prices for production and exports of commodity, together with the already existing Brazilian comparative advantage in these sectors, could start a process of 'regressive specialisation'[7] in the country's production structure. In the same way, IEDI (2012) points out that the increasing globalisation of the manufacturing production along with misalignments in the real exchange rate is likely to cause irreversible losses in the manufacturing structure of countries with an overvalued currency.

According to Sarti and Hiratuka (2016), during the GR, developed and developing countries tried to expand their exports to increase sales with the aim of reducing their idle capacity. The consequence for Brazil was a sharp increase in imports that became detached from the country's economic activity and domestic production. In this sense, even if the Brazilian production increased between 2004 and 2008, when the economy grew faster, during the GR the Brazilian manufacturing industry was not able to sustain its previous performance due to a sharp international competition, the consecutive years of currency appreciation and lower domestic sales and exports. Thus, it is possible to affirm that the 'regressive specialization' of the 1990s continued in the 2000s, but after 2008 and, mainly 2010, Brazil started a process of de-industrialisation.

Therefore, the positive impact of an incomes policy, increasing the purchasing power of workers and consumption, was partially transferred to other countries through imports. The currency appreciation and the sharp competition with imports did not stimulate investment to change the productive structure and to make the country's manufacturing production more competitive. In this sense, the international competition and the currency appreciation reduced the positive impact of consumption on GDP because the impact of increased consumption was

[7]The term 'regressive specialisation' was suggested by Coutinho (1997). Regressive specialisation is understood in the Brazilian economy as a decrease in the degree of diversification and integration of the productive system with loss of density in several production chains due to higher imports of components and capital goods.

partially transferred abroad, and the induced effects of consumption on investment were not so high.

In short, the Brazilian economic growth between 2004 and 2008 was a result of a consumption cycle due to credit expansion and an incomes policy that incorporated low-income families to consumption. In a favourable international scenario, capital inflows appreciated the national currency, and the consumption cycle was not enough to stimulate developments in the manufacturing production structure. The consequence was a consolidation of the country's dependence on imports of intermediate and capital goods.

The Chinese effort to maintain its economic growth, despite the GR, sustained the international demand for commodities. The latter was crucial to sustain the consumption cycle in Brazil. However, the Chinese manufacturing exports to developed countries facing the crisis were transferred to developing economies with higher economic activity. This change affected the Brazilian manufacturing production, both for exports and domestic market.

As Table 3 shows, despite the fact that 'regressive specialization' changed the relationship between the growth rates of GDP and manufacturing production, the latter is still very important for the performance of the Brazilian economy. This is clear in terms of different and relevant sessions over the period 1997 and 2014.

The impact of the South East Asian crisis of 1997 on the Brazilian economic activity took place mainly through the manufacturing production. GDP did not decrease, but manufacturing production reduced considerably in 1998 and 1999. The national currency devaluation stimulated exports and decreased imports, mainly manufactured goods (Baltar 2008).[8] However, it was just in the commodity boom over the period 2003 to mid-2008, when exporters of commodities improved their countries' economic activity that the Brazilian manufacturing production increased. This was a result of higher exports of manufactured goods to countries exporters of commodities, such as South American countries. Nevertheless, higher economic growth in Brazil took place

[8]The analysis starts from the south east Asian crisis to show that the manufacturing industry is very important for the Brazilian economy.

Table 3 Brazilian GDP growth, manufacturing growth, real exchange rate index, investment rate and wage share

	GDP growth	Manufacturing growth		Real exchange rate index	Investment rate	Wage share
		Ref. 2000	Ref. 2010			
1997	3.38	2.49		67.59	17.37	41
1998	0.04	−4.84		70.48	16.97	42
1999	0.25	−1.86		105.59	15.66	41
2000	4.39	5.69		96.98	16.80	41
2001	1.39	0.70	0.71	120.06	17.03	41
2002	3.05	2.44	2.09	132.67	16.39	40
2003	1.14	1.85	2.66	137.36	15.28	40
2004	5.76	8.47	9.08	135.04	16.10	39
2005	3.20	1.25	2.24	110.32	15.94	40
2006	3.96	0.97	1.23	98.53	16.43	41
2007	6.07	5.60	6.14	91.42	17.44	42
2008	5.09	2.97	4.15	88.95	19.11	42
2009	−0.13	−8.73	−9.26	88.38	18.07	44
2010	7.53	10.14	9.19	77.05	19.46	42
2011	3.97	0.13	2.25	74.97	19.29	42
2012	1.92	−2.43	−2.38	84.09	18.16	43
2013	3.00	2.71	3.01	89.89	18.19	43
2014	0.50		−4.69	91.18		44

Source Own calculation based on IPEADATA (2017). Two series of manufacturing GDP growth are presented to have information for all years considered: One based on 2000 prices and another on 2010 prices

at the same time the national currency appreciated and net exports decreased. Consumption and investment increased more than GDP and GDP increased faster than manufacturing production. Just in the years of higher economic growth, such as in 2007 and 2008, manufacturing growth increased at the same rate as GDP. This is a new characteristic associated with the regressive specialisation, because during the industrialisation period from 1950 to 1980, when GDP was growing fast, the rate of increase in the manufacturing production sector was higher than the GDP growth rate. The effects of the GR on the Brazilian economy can be seen through a lower manufacturing production growth compared to GDP, especially after 2010 and despite the national currency devaluation after 2012.

As mentioned above, the Brazilian economic growth between 2004 and 2008 was characterised by a consumption cycle due to credit expansion and an incomes policy in favour of low incomes. The behaviour of wage share followed the behaviour of the purchasing power of wages. After the Asian crisis, wage share reduced with the low-economic activity and the higher inflation, and then it recovered when the economic activity increased in 2004, surpassing the values achieved at the end of the 1990s. The evolution of wage share, investment rate and real exchange rate rate suggest that the increasing purchasing power of wages was important for the Brazilian economic growth. This result is coherent with the wage-led growth approach in which higher purchasing power of wages increases the economic activity and affects productivity. The latter reduces the unfavourable impact of higher purchasing power of wages on net exports, confirming the positive influence of higher purchasing power of wages on GDP growth. In this process, induced investment due to consumption makes possible the domestic production to satisfy the higher demand, highlighting the importance of increases in the investment rate. In the Brazilian case, despite the fact that the investment rate has oscillated during the considered period, decreasing when the economic activity is low and increasing when the economic activity is high, this oscillation was relatively low. When the economic activity increases, there may be a significant positive effect on productivity and especially so in view of the change in relative prices, as a result of changes in the real exchange rate, on the purchasing power of wages.

3 Literature Review

The literature on functional income distribution and economic growth establishes a relationship between wage share and economic growth based on Kalecki's (1954, 1971) contributions. For Kalecki (op. cit.), the determinants of economic growth are capitalist consumption and investment, and income distribution intensifies or reduces the effect of them on GDP. Accordingly, there would always be a direct relationship between wage share and economic growth; this is in the sense that for a given behaviour of capitalist consumption and investment, if wage share is higher, GDP grows faster, and vice versa. This means that an incomes policy that increases wage share necessarily affects positively GDP growth, for a given behaviour of capitalist consumption and investment.

Kalecki (1954, 1971) considers the profit margin and functional income distribution as given when analysing the determinants of economic growth. It is implicit in this analysis the stability of the competitive positions of firms in an oligopolistic market; that is, Kalecki (op. cit.) does not consider changes in the competitive position of oligopolistic firms. Changes in markups and in wage share would be a result of changes in the market competitive structure. It is easier to analyse the implications of effective demand to the economy's dynamic when its structure is stable. The assumption of stable economic structure is very restrictive, but this supposition helps to show the unstable nature of a capitalist economy (Keynes 1936) and the cyclical behaviour of its economic activity (Kalecki 1954, 1971). Even without structural changes, the capitalist economy is unstable and presents cyclical behaviour.

Thus, in a simple analysis of the dynamic implications of effective demand, Kalecki (1954) showed that, for a given consumption and investment, if the competitive structure of the economy generated a higher wage share, the economic activity would be greater. This is because greater workers' consumption intensifies the effect of capitalist consumption and investment on GDP.

A more complete analysis of the relationship between wage share and GDP growth requires a study of the effects of capitalist consumption and investment on the competitive structure of the economy. The study of changes in the economic structure is complex, and there is little agreement on how to undertake it and the general validity of the results. In the simple approach of Kalecki (1954) for the study of the relationship between wage share and GDP growth, it is possible to account for situations of stable competitive structure of the economy, in which case there is a direct relationship between wage share and economic growth.

Blecker (1989) advances the analysis in line with Kalecki (1954, 1971) and considers an open economy. Accordingly, GDP is determined by household consumption and investment, but also by net exports. When considering an open economy, there is the possibility of an inverse relationship between economic growth and wage share. Higher wage share means higher costs and prices at the same time as possible higher consumption. Higher costs and prices can make the economy less competitive, negatively affecting net exports and therefore GDP. On the other hand, higher wage share means higher consumption and therefore higher GDP. In this sense, the effect of higher wage share on economic growth would be positive if the effect of higher wage share on consumption of domestic production were greater than the negative effect on net exports.

In contrast, the models that follow the main characteristic of Kalecki's (1954, 1971) model consider that, in economies with stable competitive structures, the determinants of income distribution are different from the determinants of consumption and investment. In stable competitive structures, wage share does not change, but capitalist consumption and investment can change, affecting GDP. The intensity of the GDP change depends on the wage share that is associated with a stable structure of the competition in the economy. In a closed economy, there is a positive relationship between wage share and economic growth. Nevertheless, there is the possibility of an inverse relationship between wage share and economic growth when considering an open economy, even if there is no change in the competitive structure of the economy, as suggested by Blecker (1989). The literature classifies these models as neo-Kaleckian models.

Bhaduri and Marglin (1990) go beyond Blecker's (1989) considerations of the effect of international competition on income distribution and economic growth. For them, profit share (the complement of wage share) affects the behaviour of investment, reinforcing the possibility of an inverse relationship between wage share and economic growth. Higher wage share affects positively consumption and therefore increases the effect of investment on GDP, but it also affects investment negatively, leaving the net effect of wage share on GDP inconclusive, even in a closed economy.

According to Bhaduri and Marglin (op. cit.), the accumulation rate of capital is a function of current profit rate, and the latter depends on the profit margin and the degree of capacity utilisation. For a given capacity utilisation, lower profit margin means lower profit rate and lower capital accumulation. So, higher wage share (lower profit share) would be related to lower investment. Thus, with a higher wage share, the impact of investment on consumption is higher, but investment is lower. In this sense, an increase in wage share has a positive effect on consumption, and therefore, on GDP. However, at the same time, higher wage share means lower profit share and lower profit margin, which in turn, have a negative effect on investment. So, a policy to increase the wage share can have positive or negative effects on GDP, depending on the impact on investment and consumption (Arestis and Baltar 2016).

The literature classifies the models such as Bhaduri and Marglin (1990) as post-Kaleckian models. These models do not analyse, as in Kalecki's (1954, 1971) model, the effect of changes in investment in an economy with stable competitive structure. In Kalecki's (op. cit.) model, total profit affects investment, showing the impact of increasing risk of higher debt on investment. Profit margin is not modified in an economy with stable competitive structure. In the model of Bhaduri and Marglin (1990), profit margins change and affect investment. The study of the relationship between profit margin and investment requires an analysis of the changes in the competitive structure of the economy, what goes beyond Kalecki's (1954, 1971) model and it is a very complex topic. Apart from that, there is doubt whether this is well captured in the Bhaduri and Marglin (1990) model, where it is only assumed that current profit margin affects investment.

Storm and Naastepad (2014) include in their discussion of the relationship between wage share and economic growth the effect of wages on productivity. Accordingly, increases in wages raise productivity growth because it increases the growth rate of GDP (known as Kaldor-Verdoorn effect) and because it stimulates the rate of labour-saving technological progress. The latter occurs because higher wage growth raises firms' incentives to invest in labour-saving research and development.

If greater GDP growth increases productivity, the positive effect of increases in the purchasing power of wages on GDP growth may not occur with increases in wage share. Therefore, the negative effect on net exports will not take place. If increased purchasing power of wages does not lead to increases in productivity, the negative effect of higher real wage on net exports can be high, increasing the probability of a higher purchasing power of wages leading to lower GDP growth.

High increases in productivity take place when the competitive structure of an economy changes. According to Kaldor (1967), the changes in the manufacturing production were crucial to raise an economy's productivity. Accordingly, the faster the rate of growth of the manufacturing output, the faster the rate of growth of labour productivity in manufacturing due to static and dynamic economies of scale or increasing returns to scale. Moreover, there is high and positive relationship between the manufacturing sector growth rate and the productivity growth outside the manufacturing sector; this is so because the manufacturing sector produces goods that can be used by other sectors, thereby providing the possibility for improving their productivity. Finally, the faster the rate of growth of the manufacturing sector, the faster the rate of growth of GDP would be. Therefore, manufacturing production is crucial for a better performance of an economy through the relationship between GDP growth and productivity increase.

4 Theoretical Background

It is possible to assume that there was no important change in the structure of the Brazilian economy when analysing the country's income distribution, productivity and economic growth over the period of this contribution's investigation. Increases in productivity were low, but there were changes in wage share and in the purchasing power of wages, suggesting a direct relationship between the purchasing power of wages and GDP. Trade and financial relations of the Brazilian economy with other countries were crucial to this relationship, but in a very different way to what Kaleckian models suggest. The particularities of the Brazilian economy should be accounted for in the study of the evolution of the wage share. In this section, some stylised facts are presented for the Brazilian manufacturing sectors. These stylised facts suggest relations that are accounted for the equation for wage share as suggested below in this section.

Table 4 Real wages per worker, inflation, real exchange rate, wage share and investment rate for the Brazilian manufacturing industry (value in thousands Brazilian Real)

	Nominal wages/ Industrial transformation value (%)	Real wage	Inflation (INPC) (%)	Real exchange rate index	Investment/ Industrial transformation value (%)
1997	18.12	1979.24	5.99	67.59	13.36
1998	18.11	1946.31	3.78	70.48	14.76
1999	14.98	1831.47	4.85	105.59	12.96
2000	14.03	1816.63	6.22	96.98	11.20
2001	13.84	1831.68	7.49	120.06	13.38
2002	13.12	1789.75	10.20	132.67	12.69
2003	12.99	1717.78	16.96	137.36	11.86
2004	12.97	1782.88	6.27	135.04	11.17
2005	13.64	1823.24	5.76	110.32	11.69
2006	14.07	1894.62	3.26	98.53	11.78
2007	14.64	1946.71	4.09	91.42	16.38
2008	14.10	1979.58	6.57	88.95	15.29
2009	15.97	2023.75	5.04	88.38	15.82
2010	15.73	2125.86	5.11	77.05	15.29
2011	16.06	2141.57	6.60	74.97	14.88
2012	16.80	2243.23	5.43	84.09	15.02
2013	16.94	2299.00	6.37	89.89	15.80
2014	17.41	2323.08	6.04	91.18	15.11

Source Own calculations based on the Annual Industrial Research / PIA (2017). INPC is the Consumers' National Price Index. Real exchange rate index: June 1994 = 100

Table 4 shows the wage share of workers directly related to the manufacturing production,[9] the average real wage of these workers, inflation according to the Consumers' National Price Index (INPC), the real exchange rate index and investment in relation to industrial transformation value of the manufacturing sector, from 1997 to 2014. Investment rate of the manufacturing sector was relatively low in view of the effects of the Asian crisis on the performance of the Brazilian economy.

[9]Wage share is nominal wages in relation to the industrial transformation value to the workers directly engaged in production. Industrial transformation value is the difference between gross value of industrial production and costs of industrial operations.

Nevertheless, it increased in 2007–2008, when the economy achieved higher growth rates. After 2010, when manufacturing production stagnated, industrial investment slowed down and the investment rate of manufacturing sector kept the level achieved in 2007. This behaviour of the investment rate suggests that increases in productivity in the Brazilian manufacturing sector were low, being higher in 2007–2010.

Wage share decreased significantly between 1997 and 2003, and since then it has increased; however, without achieving the value of 1997. This movement of wage share is symmetric with the behaviour of the purchasing power of wages of workers directly related to the manufacturing production. The average real wage of these workers decreased by 13.2% between 1997 and 2003; it recovered the level of 1997 in 2008 and, in 2014, it is 17.4% superior to that level. This increase in real wage in 17 years means an annual growth rate of around 1%, what is lower than the manufacturing sector productivity, as indicated by the wage share of 2014 lower than in 1997.

The low investment rate suggests that important changes in the manufacturing production structure did not take place. However, there were high oscillations in the purchasing power of wages and in the wage share of the manufacturing sector due to changes in relative prices that took place with intense changes in the value of the national currency. The real exchange rate increased 103.2% in 1997–2003; it decreased 45.4% in 2003–2011, and it increased 21.6% in 2011–2014.

Thus, in 1999, 2001 and 2002, the real exchange rate increased considerably, depreciating the national currency.[10] Inflation increased, reaching almost 17% in 2003. There might have been some increase in manufacturing productivity, but the fact that the purchasing power of wages decreased together with lower wage share seems to be related to the currency devaluation. The latter made tradable goods prices increase more than the price of goods and services purchased by workers. The high increase in the nominal exchange rate raised the price of

---

[10] Increases in the real exchange rate occurred because the nominal exchange rate increased more than the difference between Brazilian inflation and the inflation of the trade partners, thereby making the Brazilian production more competitive internationally.

manufactured inputs more than wages and, at the same time, the price of manufactured goods increased more than the average manufacturing production costs. Due to both reasons, the wage share decreased.

After 2003, the Brazilian economic performance improved. The lower nominal exchange rate helped to decrease domestic inflation, but the latter was still higher than international inflation, appreciating further the national currency. Manufacturing production increased, despite the high imports of manufactured goods, as well as the purchasing power of wages and wage share. Productivity increased, but it did not avoid increases in consumer prices being superior to increases in manufactured goods that were made possible by the higher purchasing power of wages taking place with higher wage share. Lower nominal exchange rate increased the price of manufacturing inputs less than wages (despite the higher commodity prices), and the price of manufactured goods increased less than the manufacturing production average cost.

As already mentioned, after 2010, manufacturing production and investment stagnated, and the national currency depreciated. Real wage and wage share kept increasing, although at a lower rate compared to the 2003–2010 one. The GFC increased the international competition of manufactured goods because of idle capacity and the transfer of Asian exports, especially Chinese, from developed to developing countries. The Brazilian manufacturing production was affected, for both exports and domestic market. The purchasing power of wages kept increasing, despite the rise in inflation. The currency devaluation was not enough to make manufacturing firms to transfer higher costs to prices, maintaining the increase in the wage share. Lower profit margins and higher idle capacity of the Brazilian manufacturing since 2011 reduced the current profitability of the sector. Consequently, entrepreneurs demanded from the government actions to establish their current profitability.

The previous analysis considered the whole manufacturing sector, highlighting the importance of changes in relative prices associated with changes in the real exchange rate to the evolution of the purchasing power of wages and the wage share. Kaleckian models consider that increases in the purchasing power of wages reinforce GDP growth and the latter increase productivity (the Kaldor-Verdoorn effect).

In an open economy, this relation supposes that the real exchange rate is determined by external trade; that is, induced investment maintains the economy's competitiveness because any change in competitiveness affects the exchange rate. The latter, in turn, stimulates investment that reinforces the country's competitiveness.

A particularity of a developing economy opened to finance and trade is that external trade does not determine the evolution of the real exchange rate. The latter is determined mainly by capital movements. In these economies, changes in relative prices, related to changes in the wage share, may be associated with changes in the real exchange rate and not with the effect of investment on productivity. Accounting for this possibility, our contribution proposes to include the real exchange rate and investment rate in the wage share relationship. The relevant relationship is thereby as follows in Eq. (1):

$$\frac{W}{Y} = \alpha_0 + \alpha_1 w + \alpha_2 \mathrm{RER} + \alpha_3 \frac{I}{Y} \tag{1}$$

where W is total wages, and Y is industrial transformation value, so $\frac{W}{Y}$ is the wage share, w is the real wage per worker, RER is the real exchange rate index and I is investment, so $\frac{I}{Y}$ is the investment rate of the manufacturing sector. Accordingly, increases in real wage have a positive and direct effect on the wage share. An increase in the real exchange rate means the currency devalues, which tends to increase domestic inflation and changes relative prices in favour of tradable goods. Since the consumption structure of workers has a high share of non-tradable goods, while manufactured goods are mainly tradable, an increase in the real exchange rate tends to reduce the purchasing power of wages and wage share. Wage share is doubly affected by the increase in the real exchange rate. It increases the price of imported inputs in relation to wages as well as the price of manufactured goods in relation to the production average cost. Finally, the investment rate is related to the manufacturing sector productivity. Therefore, increases in the investment rate raise productivity growth. For a given increase in wages, higher investment rate would have negative effects on the evolution of the wage share.

5 Empirical Investigation

This section analyses the evolution of wage share through a panel data analysis considering the different sectors of the Brazilian manufacturing industry. The data source is the Annual Industrial Research (PIA), provided by the Brazilian Institute of Geography and Statistics (IBGE), which makes available information for different sectors of the Brazilian manufacturing industry. The available relevant annual data series are from 1996 to 2014. The economic activity sectors are classified according to the National Classification for Economic Activity (CNAE).

The estimation method applied is the GMM panel data developed by Arellano and Bond (1991) in order to account for the endogeneity of regressors. This method is efficient within the class of instrumental variable procedures.

Table 5 presents the results for all estimations from 1996 to 2014. Equation (1) includes the real exchange rate and investment rate in the wage share relationship as a way to consider the specificities of developing economies. The hypothesis is that changes in relative prices may be associated with changes in the real exchange rate and not with the effect of investment on productivity. These changes in relative prices affect the wage share. With the aim of identifying the impact of the real exchange rate and investment rate in the wage share relationship, we undertake

Table 5 GMM estimates of a dynamic wage share model for panel data

Dependent variable: W/Y	(1)	(2)	(3)	(4)
Constant	−1.14*	−1.16*	0.50	0.60
$(W/Y)_{-1}$	0.65*	0.61*	0.57*	0.54*
$(W/Y)_{-2}$	−0.09**	−0.07	−0.12*	−0.10*
W	0.35*	0.34*	0.23*	0.23*
RER			−0.15*	−0.14*
I/Y		0.06		0.05*
Wald test	319.30 ($p = 0$)	327.04 ($p = 0$)	388.60 ($p = 0$)	390.01 ($p = 0$)

Sample period: 1996–2014; Number of sectors: 20; Number of observations: 320
Instruments: Two and three period lagged variables
Note *significant at 1%, **significant at 5%

four estimations. Estimation (1) only considers as independent variable real wage per worker. Estimation (2) considers real wage per worker and investment rate. Estimation (3) considers real wage per worker and the real exchange rate index. And, finally, Estimation (4) considers real wage per worker, the real exchange rate index and investment rate. The four estimations allow verifying whether the real exchange rate and investment rate affect the wage share and how both variables affect the impact of real wages on the wage share.

All coefficients are significant at 1%. The inclusion of the real exchange rate index, such as in estimations (3) and (4), makes the constant not significant. Lagged wage shares are included in the equation, and they show the first lag is important, which means that an increase in wage share in the previous year has a positive and high impact on wage share in the current year.

Table 5 reveals the importance to consider the real exchange rate in the analysis of the Brazilian wage share performance of the manufacturing sectors. Real wages is the variable with the highest impact on wage share, as expected. The inclusion of the real exchange rate in the equation reduces the impact of real wages on the wage share. The coefficient for investment rate is very small and the sign is the opposite of what expected. The interesting result is that when investment rate is included in the estimation, the coefficient of other variables is kept almost the same, suggesting that changes in wage share were not a result of changes in the productive structure of the manufacturing sector, through investment. Besides that, the inclusion of the real exchange rate reduces the impact of changes in real wages on the evolution of wage share, confirming the importance of changes in relative prices as a result of changes in the real exchange rate.

Thus, the analysis of the evolution of the wage share of the manufacturing sectors confirms that there was no important structural change in the Brazilian manufacturing sectors able to increase productivity. Apart from that, it confirms that the behaviour of real wages and wage share is a consequence mainly of changes in relative prices associated with changes in the value of the national currency.

6 Summary and Conclusions

This chapter analyses the changes in the purchasing power of workers from 1997 to 2014 to verify whether it was a result of changes in productivity or due to changes in the real exchange rate. The results suggest that changes in the wage share are associated with changes in the real exchange rate and not with the effect of investment on productivity, revealing the importance to consider the real exchange rate in the analysis of the Brazilian wage share performance of the manufacturing sector. The results also show that over the period of our study the investment rate did not affect the impact of real wages on wage share, suggesting there was no important structural change in the Brazilian manufacturing sector that was able to increase productivity. In this sense, the increased purchasing power of wages was highly influenced by changes in relative prices associated with changes in the value of the national currency.

Brazil achieved a relatively high economic growth in the early 2000s, when the world scenario was favourable for the Brazilian trade balance. Under this scenario, an incomes policy, focused on real increases in the minimum wage along the business cycle, was undertaken, with positive consequences for the country's economic performance.

The performance of the Brazilian economy in the early 2000s is similar to a Kaleckian model in which economic growth is led by wages. Increases in the purchasing power of wages reinforced GDP growth. GDP growth was led by consumption, stimulated by credit, and by induced investment, stimulated by consumption and exports. In this model, induced investment increases productivity, which, in turn, allows higher purchasing power of wages. Because of this, the country's competitiveness is not affected.

It is implicit in this relationship between functional income distribution and economic growth that the trade balance determines the nominal exchange rate. Therefore, lower exports growth or increases in imports deteriorate the country's trade balance. This would be a result of changes in the economy's competitiveness, and it would increase the nominal exchange rate. Expected investment profitability in the production of exports or in the production for the domestic market that competes with imports would increase, avoiding a decrease in competitiveness and deteriorating further the trade balance.

The hypothesis of trade balance determining the nominal exchange rate is not confirmed in open developing economies that developed their financial sector attracting capital inflow from developed countries. This is the Brazilian case since the 1990s. In favourable international circumstances for the performance of the economy, such as during the commodity and capital flow booms before the GFC, the national currency appreciated, despite the tendency to increasing current account deficit.

The national currency appreciation in times of improved economic performance highly stimulated imports of manufactured goods, but it did not prevent investment and a greater manufacturing production. Nevertheless, the regressive specialisation was consolidated with high imports of intermediate and capital goods. The purchasing power of wages increased, the price of imported inputs decreased and the relation price/average costs of the manufacturing sector decreased, making the purchasing power of wages increase together with the wage share.

Higher purchasing power of wages reinforced the consumption cycle of the 2000s, but it did not impede its cyclical movement. The increase in the purchasing power of wages helped families to pay their debt. But, the increasing number of indebted families and the high share of debt in families' budget tended to restrict consumption growth, even when families had the opportunity to pay their debt. Lower consumption growth associated with the credit cycle decelerated GDP growth. The Brazilian authorities realised the necessity of an expansion plan and implemented the Growth Acceleration Program (PAC).[11] The Brazilian government tried to encourage public and private investment in infrastructure and to reinforce the manufacturing production

[11]The Growth Acceleration Program (PAC) is an infrastructure program of the Federal government of Brazil. The program was launched in 2007 under President Luiz Inácio Lula da Silva's government with the objective of accelerating economic growth. This program continued in President Dilma Vana Rousseff's administration, being called PAC-2. The planned investments were not fully implemented.

competitiveness, aiming at higher exports and lower imports of manufactured goods.

The GFC of 2007–2008 and the GR brought challenges to this new possibility of economic growth. Increased idle capacity and a stronger international competition of manufactured goods reduced the investment to improve the Brazilian manufacturing sector's competitiveness. Transnational firms that operate in Brazil, for example, decided to use their idle capacity in other countries instead of increasing their production capacity in Brazil.

The new expansion possibility for the Brazilian economy failed despite the initial success of the government policy to decrease interest rates and control capital inflows over 2010–2011, thereby regulating increases in the nominal exchange rate. GDP decelerated, despite the government effort to maintain the improvements in the labour market, avoiding a deeper deceleration of consumption. The main determinants of GDP deceleration were lower exports and investment growth. The purchasing power of wages and the wage share kept increasing, despite the Real depreciation. Greater international competition in manufactured goods impeded the transfer of higher costs to prices, thereby affecting the profitability of this production. Nevertheless, it was not this reduction in the manufacturing sector profitability that explains the low investment in the sector, but the risk and uncertainty of investment in a context of high international competition in the manufactured goods market.

References

Annual Industrial Research / PIA (2017). *Statistics from the Brazilian institute for geography and statistics*. Available at www.ibge.gov.br/home/estatistica/economia/industria/pia.

Amico, F. (2013). Crecimiento, Distribución y Restricción Externa en Argentina. *Circus, Revista Argentina de Economía, 5*, 31–80.

Arellano, M., & Bond, S. R. (1991). Some tests of specification for panel data: Monte Carlo evidence and an application to employment equations. *Review of Economic Studies, 58*, 277–297.

Arestis, P., & Baltar, C. T. (2016), Income distribution and economic growth: A critical approach. Paper presented at the 13th international conference, entitled *Developments in economic theory and policy*, Bilbao, Spain.

Arestis, P., Baltar, C. T., & Prates, D. M. (2015). Brazilian economic performance since the emergence of the Great Recession: The effects of income distribution on consumption. *Panoeconomicus, 63*(1), 156–174.

Baltar, C. (2008). Comércio Exterior Inter e Intra-Industrial: Brasil 2003–2005. *Economia e Sociedade, 17,* 107–135.

Baltar, C. (2013). *Economic growth and inflation in an open developing economy: The case of Brazil.* Ph.D. thesis, University of Cambridge.

Baltar, C. (2015). Inflation and economic growth in an open developing country: The case of Brazil. *Cambridge Journal of Economics, 39,* 1263–1280.

Baltar, C. T., Hiratuka, C., & Lima, G. T. (2016). Real exchange rate and investment in the Brazilian manufacturing industry. *Journal of Economic Studies, 43,* 288–308.

Baltar, C., & Prates, D. (2014), *Brazilian export dynamism and the threat of Chinese Exports from 2008 to 2012, VII Encontro Internacional da Associação Keynesiana Brasileira*, São Paulo, Brazil.

Baltar, P. E. A., & Leone, E. T. (2015). Perspectivas para o mercado de trabalho após o crescimento com inclusão social. *Estudos Avançados, 29*(85), 53–67.

Baltar, P. E. A., Santos, A., Krein, D., Leone, E., Proni, M., Moretto, A., Maia, A. G., & Salas, C. (2010). *Trabalho no Governo Lula: Uma reflexão sobre a recente experiência brasileira* (Working Paper No. 9), Global Labour University.

Barbosa, N., & Souza, J. A. (2010). Inflexão do Governo Lula: Política Econômica, Crescimento e Distribuição de Renda. In E. Sader & M. Garcia (Eds.), *Brasil: Entre o passado e o futuro.* São Paulo: Fundação Perseu Abramo e Editora Boitempo.

Bhaduri, A., & Marglin, S. (1990). Unemployment and the real wage: The economic basis for contesting political ideologies. *Cambridge Journal of Economics, 14,* 375–393.

Blecker, R. A. (1989). International competition, income distribution and economic growth. *Cambridge Journal of Economics, 13,* 395–412.

Bresser-Pereira, L. C. (2009). The tendency to overvaluation of the exchange rate. In L. C. Bresser-Pereira (Ed.), *Globalization and competition.* Cambridge: Cambridge University Press.

Calixte, A., Biancarelli, A., & Cintra, M. (2014). *Presente e Futuro do Desenvolvimento Brasileiro*. Brasilia: IPEA.

Carneiro, R., & Matijascic, M. (2011). *Desafios do Desenvolvimento Brasileiro.* Brasilia: IPEA.

Central Bank of Brazil. (2017). *Database, time series information for economy and finance.* Available at http://www.bcb.gov.br/?TIMESERIESEN.

Coutinho, L. (1997). A Especialização Regressiva: Um Balanço do Desempenho industrial Pós-estabilização. In J. P. R. Velloso (Ed.), *Brasil: Desafios de Um País em Transformação.* José Olympio: Rio de Janeiro.

Farhi, M. (2006). O Impacto dos Ciclos de Liquidez no Brasil: Mercados Financeiros, Taxa de Cambio, Preços e Politica Monetaria. *Politica Economica em Foco, 7,* 152–183.

IEDI. (2007). *Empresa Nacional: A Atratividade da Empresa Brasileira.* Analise IEDI. Available at www.iedi.org.br.

IEDI. (2012). *Comércio e indústria.* Análise IEDI, Novembro. Available at www.iedi.org.br.

IPEADATA. (2017). Available at http://www.ipeadata.gov.br/Default.aspx.

Kaldor, N. (1967). *Strategic factors in economic development.* New York: Ithaca.

Kalecki, M. (1954). *Teoria da Dinâmica Capitalista.* São Paulo: Nova Cultural.

Kalecki, M. (1971). Costs and prices. In *Selected essays on the dynamics of the capitalist economy.* Cambridge: Cambridge University Press.

Keynes, J. M. (1936) *The general theory of employment, interest and money.* CW VII. London: Macmillan.

Nassif, A. (2006). Há Evidências de Desindustrialização No Brasil? *Discussing Papers* BNDES, n. 108, Rio de Janeiro, Brazil.

Palma, G. (2005). Four Sources of 'De-industrialisation' and a New Concept of the 'Dutch Disease. In J. A. Ocampo (Ed.), *Beyond reform: Structural dynamics and macroeconomic vulnerability* (pp. 71–116). Stanford: Stanford University Press.

Prates, D., Baltar, C., & Sequeto, M. (2014). A Inserção Externa do Brasil No Contexto da Crise Global. In L. F. Novais, R. F Cagnin & G. Biasoto Junior (Eds.), *A Economia Brasileira no Contexto da Crise Global* (pp. 79–122). São Paulo: Edições Fundap.

Sarti, F., & Hiratuka, C. (2016). Assimetrias No Processo De Internacionalização Da Economia Brasileira No Século XXI. In H. M. M. Lastres, J. E. Cassiolato, G. Laplane & F. Sarti (Eds.), *O Futuro do Desenvolvimento.* Campinas, SP: UNICAMP, IE.

Storm and Naatepad. (2014). Wage-led or profit-led supply: Wages, productivity and investment. In M. Lavoie & E. Stockhammer (Eds.), *Wage-led growth.* London: Macmillan.

Brazilian Fiscal Policy in Perspective: From Expansion to Austerity

Rodrigo Octávio Orair and Sergio Wulff Gobetti

1 Introduction

Brazil post-GFC presents a compelling case study of the interactions between fiscal policy and business and political cycles in a developing economy. The country is noteworthy for being one of the few that dealt relatively well with the most acutest stage of the GFC, maintaining its dynamism throughout most of the 2007–2010 period, but also for the speed of its economic deterioration during the 2011–2014 slowdown, and the subsequent 2015–2016 recession. The contrast in performance is stark when one observes the decrease in growth of the country's gross domestic product (GDP): from 4.6% per year during

R.O. Orair (✉)
Institute for Applied Economics Research and International Policy Centre for Inclusive Growth, Brasília, Brazil
e-mail: rodrigo.orair@ipea.gov.br

S.W. Gobetti
Institute for Applied Economics Research, Porto Alegre, Brazil
e-mail: swgobetti@gmail.com

P. Arestis et al. (eds.), *The Brazilian Economy since the Great Financial Crisis of 2007/2008*, https://doi.org/10.1007/978-3-319-64885-9_9

2007–2010—which placed Brazil close to the top third of countries with the best global performance—to half, or 2.3% per year during 2011–2014, which placed the country among the bottom third, until an accumulated collapse of −7.2% of GDP during 2015–2016, the worst recession in the country's history.

The explanation of the extraordinary performance of the 2007–2010 periods and its subsequent deterioration is not a simple phenomenon. In order to understand it properly, multiple determinants should be considered, from internal factors such as the domestic consumption and credit boom to the country's political crisis, and even external factors linked to the GFC. The focus of this chapter is restricted to fiscal policy and the central hypothesis is that the inflections in the composition and orientation of fiscal policy are crucial elements for the economic performance.

Therefore, the chapter presents an overview of the Brazilian fiscal policy, highlighting two points of inflection. The first is a shift from a sub-period of fiscal expansion driven mainly by public investment and redistributive transfers, to another sub-period characterised by increased tax cuts and subsidies. The second is the radical shift to a period of austerity, after a decade of fiscal expansion (2005–2014). Sections 2 and 4 detail the basic distinguishing traits of these periods and explore their relationship with the performance of the economy.

Another interesting issue in the post-GFC Brazilian experience is how fast public debt deteriorated. Brazil managed to produce significant and continuous primary budget surpluses for over a decade and to reduce its public debt by nearly half (from 60% of its GDP in 2002 to 31% of GDP in 2013). The level of public debt, five years after the GFC, was low for the country's historical standards and average according to international comparisons, indicating a comfortable financial position. Since then, the situation has changed dramatically. Half of the decrease of the public debt (around 15% of GDP) was reversed over only three years, from 2014 to 2016. Such a fiscal deterioration is explained in Sect. 3, where this question is addressed by evaluating the relationship between the dynamics of public debt and the macroeconomic management of the country. This is crucial to better understand the factors that are responsible for the escalation of public debt since 2014, and which have led to significant pressure for fiscal policy to change towards austerity.

The chapter concludes with some considerations regarding the challenges and socio-economic risks imposed by this recent and radical policy shift.

2 Fiscal Policy in Perspective: The Expansionary Period

To understand the post-GFC fiscal policy in Brazil, we must go back to the first term of President Luis Inácio Lula da Silva, Lula (2003–2006). The turbulent 2002 electoral process coincided with a troublesome time in the financial market and, due to the vulnerability of speculative attacks against the national currency, public debt reached its recent historical peak (over 60% of GDP at the end of 2002). With the purpose of appeasing the market, the then-candidate Lula made a public commitment to honour the financial obligations of the country and seeks the necessary fiscal results. The election of Lula in 2003, after three consecutive losses, occurred after a reorientation of the Worker's Party (PT) political project, from a radical reformist programme (of socialist bias, in some aspects) to a pragmatic, social democratic platform with broad alliances that reached the traditional political forces in the centre-right.

The central aspects of macroeconomic policy during the first years of the Lula's administration were a continuation of the previous administration, Fernando Henrique Cardoso's from the Brazilian social democratic party. The so-called 'macroeconomic tripod', whose pillars are a primary surplus target, an inflation target and a flexible exchange rate (dirty float), was kept intact by President Lula, who nominated a big banker (Henrique Meirelles, then president of the Bank of Boston) to command the country's Central Bank. Regarding fiscal policy, the reins were also given to orthodox economists, and the first two or three years of the Lula's administration were similar to Fernando Henrique's, not only in their goal of fiscal consolidation, but also in the two main instruments used—increased tax burden and cuts in public investments.

Therefore, we will adopt a unique timeline, as in Gobetti and Orair (2015), which defines the years of 1995–2005 as a period of fiscal consolidation. In this period, fiscal targets were progressively increased and primary results went from approximately nil results to a surplus of over 4% of GDP. This fiscal adjustment was based on an increase in tax burden of 6.6 percentage points of GDP and a reduction of 1.3 percentage points of GDP in public investment, which allowed for expenditures in social benefits to increase.

It was only during 2005 that the Lula's administration promoted incremental changes in the fiscal regime, marking a shift to a period of fiscal expansion (2005–2014), which was underway when the GFC broke out. On the revenue side, tax policy was reoriented towards greater tax cuts. That change was relevant, because it interrupted a two-decade rising trend of the tax burden, which increased from 23.4% of GDP in 1988 to 33.6% in 2005. During the 2005–2014 period, the tax burden remained stable, oscillating around 33% of GDP.[1]

Additionally, the fiscal target framework was made more flexible through mechanisms that allowed priority investments to be deducted and exempted state-owned companies (Petrobras and Eletrobras) from contributing to the primary surplus. Moreover, reductions of the surplus target were undertaken. The result was that the primary result required by legislation was lowered from 4.25% of GDP in 2004 to 2.65% in 2010. This, together with the increased tax revenue, resulting from the economic dynamism of the period, opened the fiscal space to larger expenditures, especially public investments, which increased at rates exceeding two digits, which were the highest ones for the 2005–2010 periods (see Tables 1 and 2).

Between 2005 and 2010, the general government's primary surplus fell from 3.7% to 2.6% of GDP; its investment rate increased by a similar amount, 1.1 percentage points of GDP, and the investment rate of federal state-owned companies increased by another 0.9% of GDP. In other words, the rate of public investment went from one of the lowest

[1]Orair (2015) presents a description of these tax cuts and analysis of the paradox of tax burden´s stability under a preponderance of tax cuts.

Table 1 Targets and values of public primary surpluses (2003–2015), as a percentage of GDP

Year	Surplus target (A)	Deduction margin				Surplus floor (C = A − B)	Surplus achieved (D)	Non-recurring measures (E)	Recurring surplus (F = D − E)
		Priority investments	Other priority expenditures	Margin expansion	Total (B)				
2003	4.25					4.25	4.37	0.07	4.30
2004	4.25					4.25	4.58	0.08	4.50
2005	4.25	0.06			0.06	4.19	4.83	0.06	4.77
2006	4.25	0.14	0.01		0.14	4.11	4.37	0.18	4.19
2007	4.25	0.19	0.03		0.23	4.02	4.50	0.02	4.48
2008	3.80	0.26	0.01		0.27	3.53	4.07	−0.03	4.10
2009	2.50	0.43	0.08		0.51	1.99	2.05	1.35	0.70
2010	3.30	0.59	0.07		0.65	2.65	3.01	1.15	1.86
2011	3.30	0.50	0.23		0.74	2.56	3.38	0.42	2.96
2012	3.10	0.59	0.28		0.87	2.23	2.33	0.59	1.73
2013	3.10	0.53	0.36	0.42	1.31	1.79	1.82	1.09	0.73
2014	3.10	0.68	0.39	No limit	No limit	No limit	−0.60	0.69	−1.30
2015	−0.85			1.18	1.18	−2.03	−1.93	−0.54	−1.39
2016	−2.64					−2.64	−2.51	0.62	−3.13
2017	−2.10					−2.10	n/a	n/a	n/a

Note We consider the GDP values in the budget laws that are references for achieving targets, and not the updated GDPs.
Source Authors' elaboration with updated data from Orair (2016) and Gobetti and Orair (2017)

levels in its history (2.6% of GDP in 2005) to 4.6% in 2010, which dates back to levels of the early 1990s.

The upturn in public investment not only does it reflect the flexibilization of the fiscal regime, which temporarily removed budgetary constraints, but also a change in the government's position regarding its role in planning, which materialised in the formulation of strategic programmes and investment projects.

The fact that fiscal space was mainly geared towards public investment during 2005–2010 does not mean that these expenses were the only ones that increased. In fact, they were not even the ones that increased the most, in absolute terms. The main reason that explains the increase in primary expenditures is social spending; and this did not start during Lula's administration—although, existing social policies were deepened.

Table 2 Primary revenues and expenses of the federal government—real rate of growth per year (in %)

	Fiscal consolidation	Fiscal expansion		Fiscal consolidation	
	1999–2004	2005–2010	2011–2014	2015	2016
Revenue	5.4	4.5	1.2	−5.9	−2.1
Primary expense	3.6	6.1	3.5	−2.9	4.6
Personnel	2.2	4.3	−0.7	1.9	−2.7
Social benefits	7.1	5.8	4.1	0.4	7.0
Pensions	6.5	4.6	3.4	2.5	7.5
LOAS/RMV	9.2	11.7	6.0	2.2	6.3
Unemployment insurance	4.2	12.5	6.1	−14.2	8.9
Bolsa Família	n/a	8.4	9.2	−6.3	−3.8
Subsidies	5.0	13.2	23.8	−6.3	−8.5
Current and capital expenses	−0.8	8.2	2.9	−12.5	10.5
Investments	−7.7	21.2	−1.4	−36.7	13.5
Others	0.6	5.2	4.3	−5.6	9.9
Memo: GDP	2.7	4.3	2.3	−3.8	−3.6
Memo: Minimum wage	3.1	4.1	1.2	0.9	3.1
Memo: Instituted tax cuts	n/a	n/a	29.1	−3.6	−22.3

Note Values adjusted by the GDP deflator. *Source* Authors' elaboration with updated data from Gobetti and Orair (2017)

Structural pressures for the consolidation of a social welfare state—either through redistributive transfers or the construction of a social protection network including universal public services in areas such as health and basic education—have been in place since the 1980s. This dates back to the renewal of the social contract by the Constitution of 1988, after the re-democratisation of the country.

Such pressures impose a rigidity on the dynamics of social spending, over which the discretionary power of fiscal authorities is very limited. The amounts of social benefits, as well as the supply of social services, are expanded as the population gains access to rights enshrined in the Constitution; or as a result of factors such as the demographic tendency towards an aging population and the formalisation of the labour market, which expands the potential audience of contributory benefits.

At the federal level, social spending increased from 9.1% of GDP to 13.7% between 1991 and 2015, at an annual growth rate of 4.5 per year. It is evident that there is a scale effect that overestimates the analysis of social spending growth rates, because it stems from repressed demands that were inherited from the military dictatorship years. However, even during recent times, social benefits kept increasing at rates above 4% per year, increasing from 5.9% of GDP in 1998 to 9.2% in 2015.

The increase in social spending, driven by structural pressures, must take centre stage in any analysis of the Brazilian fiscal policy, not only for its remarkable impact on the well-being of the population, but also for being mainly responsible for the increase in primary spending over the last three decades. For instance, Resende et al. (2007), Giambiagi (2008), Barbosa Filho and Pessoa (2014), Appy et al. (2015) and Gobetti and Orair (2015) place special emphasis on social spending in their analysis of the Brazilian fiscal policy.

To acknowledge the structural pressures does not imply the denial of discretionary instruments, which may influence the dynamics of social spending. The main instrument is the readjustment of the minimum wage, since most social benefits are indexed to this value.[2] In 2006, President Lula signed a deal with trade unions, defining a rule for annual readjustments of the value of the minimum wage based on the sum of the rates of inflation and real GDP growth. This mechanism accelerated the policy of valuation of the minimum wage, which began in the mid-1990s, providing real gains to the baseline of social benefits of 4.1% between 2005 and 2010, while there was a better performance in the growth of GDP (see Table 2).

In addition, the President Lula's administration restructured and expanded the conditional cash transfer programmes, unifying them under the internationally recognised *Bolsa Família*. These instruments

[2]In 2014, the minimum wage value (BRL724 per month, or roughly USD268) was paid to nearly 25 million beneficiaries of social benefits.

promoted a marked change in the profile of redistributive transfers in favour of those who tend to benefit the families at the base of income distribution. During the same period, no structural measures were put in place to curb the top income concentration through tax measures. According to Singer (2015), Lula's policy was always to 'appease both sides', promoting a slow process of social inclusion and reforms, which would allow for the redistribution of income without exacerbating class conflict, what he calls a 'weak reformism'.

In short, it is possible to describe Brazil's fiscal policy during 2005–2014 as an expansionary period, during which primary results were gradually reduced and the tax burden was kept stable. However, during the first sub-period of fiscal expansion (2005–2010), tax revenue kept up with the accelerated pace of GDP growth (despite tax cuts), not only absorbing the pressures of social spending but also expanding the degrees of freedom in fiscal policy. This allowed for the fiscal space to be channelled into public investments, at the same time a change in the profiles of redistributive transfers was taking place, favouring those that tend to benefit poorer households.

It was under this scenario that the GFC hit the country. The government opted to maintain an expansionary fiscal policy through public investments, redistributive transfers and an emergency package of tax and credit stimuli, as analysed by Barbosa (2013) and Paula et al. (2015). The Brazilian economy reacted positively to the anti-cyclical measures and, after a brief slip in 2009, it grew 7.5% in 2010, its best performance in 25 years.

There are many factors behind the greater economic dynamism of the 2005–2010 periods, including the international liquidity and commodities boom, and the domestic consumption and credit boom. However, we must not neglect the impact of the fiscal policy on economic performance—it became more open to public investments and redistributive transfers.

Orair et al. (2016) provide evidence in this direction, by showing that fiscal multipliers for the Brazilian economy vary according to the stage of the economic cycle and the type of expenditure. The authors' main findings are that (i) in strong expansions, multipliers are not significant and/or not persistent; and (ii) in recessions (and in normal times), multipliers can be significant, persistent and superior to the unit for specific components of expenditures, as in the case of investments and social benefits, which are above 1.5. The fiscal expansion of 2005–2010 favoured the expenditure categories associated with higher multipliers, which helps to explain the economic performance during the period and the quick recover after the GFC.

2010 can be considered as the zenith of the Lula administration. Its fiscal policy was hailed internationally as successful because it managed to beat the global crisis, foster economic growth and, through redistributive transfers, contributed to reduce poverty rates and income concentration in one of the most unequal countries in the world. Lula reached the end of his second term (2007–2010) with record popularity ratings, managing to promote the election of his successor, Dilma Rousseff, then-Presidential Chief of Staff.

During her first term, President Rousseff kept the expansionary orientation of fiscal policy through tax cuts and credit subsidies and not through public investments. Part of this change was due to an overhaul in government strategy, which heavily hedged its bets on the role of the private sector as the main driver for investment. This is partly due to an understanding that many of the large public investment projects had severe flaws and were subject to excessive delays. However, this shift can also be explained by a pragmatic tactic of favouring fiscal stimuli that did not affect the primary surplus, such as credit subsidies, as discussed in Sect. 3, or the inflation, such as tax cuts.

In early 2011, President Rousseff decided to pressure Brazil's Central Bank (BCB) to lower the interest rate. To that end, there would be due compensation from the fiscal policy, raising the primary result to keep inflation under control. On the one hand, President Rousseff was trying to restrict the BCB's operational autonomy and force a shift in interest rates to a level conforming to international standards, and, on the other hand, she did not dare to drop the orthodox assumption that price levels depend on the size of primary surpluses. That is one of the main reasons why the primary surplus grew in 2011 (Serrano and Summa 2016, provide further details and a critical assessment of the orthodox theoretical assumptions; Singer 2015, deals with the strategy of forcing down interest rates from a political science point of view). However, interest rates only decreased during the second half of that year, when new signs of economic downturn appeared.

In 2012 the government decided to reinforce the anti-cyclical policy, through the expansion of tax cuts and subsidised credit, in addition to a reduction in electricity tariffs and a plan for concessions in infrastructure, preventing a larger presence of the private sector. The basic presupposition of this strategy was that private investments would react more quickly than public investments. The remarkable increase in subsidies was also driven by programmes with high electoral visibility (for instance, student financing for private universities and popular housing), which, even though relevant in their own way, increased exponentially and not very judiciously.

The fiscal cost of these measures was high. Tax cuts went from BRL 43 billion in 2010 to BRL 122 billion in 2014, while subsidies went from BRL 31.3 billion to BRL 73.5 billion. The reaction of the private sector was limited to specific sectors of the economy, and the aggregate rate of private investments did not respond to expectations.

The anti-cyclical policy was not able to prevent the downturn in the economy during 2011–2014. Tax revenue slowed down in tandem with the economic activity and as a result of rising tax benefits. While the rigidities of social spending became explicit and, despite lower minimum wage gains due to low economic growth, social benefits continued to increase at rates higher than 4% per year, slightly lower than in previous periods (see Table 2).

Under this scenario, with lower revenue growth, while a significant portion of expenditures maintained their previous rate of growth (social benefits) or were even extraordinary accelerated (subsidies), fiscal policy came to a crossroad. The fiscal space was brutally reduced, while the government was reluctant to change its fiscal target, kept above 3% of GDP. The solution to this dilemma was a mixture of two paths: (i) stronger budget 'locks' on a small portion of discretionary expenses; and (ii) the use of non-recurring measures to inflate fiscal results (one-offs, creative accounting, fiscal gimmicks as the rollover of payments to public banks—known as 'fiscal pedalling', etc.) and increase the deduction margin of the target.

In 2011, the government prioritised the first path and interrupted the process of renewing public investments. In 2012–2014, the fiscal target was achieved, through successive alterations in legislation, and a mixture of the two paths mentioned above. The non-recurring measures reached vast amounts and the deduction margin, which was initially a select portfolio of investments, was expanded and moved away from public investments, with a flexibilization in their criteria (see Schettini et al. 2011; Orair 2016; and Gobetti and Orair 2017, for a more detailed analysis of the non-recurring measures and of the deduction margin changes).

The use of artificial measures to reach the fiscal target was a questionable instrument to provide greater flexibility to the fiscal regime, but it was not enough to avoid more significant budget constraints. In fact, when comparing the rates of increase in expenditures for the 2005–2010 and 2011–2014 periods in Table 2, we see that nearly all components slowed down, but investments were hit hardest and subsidies were the main exception. Orair (2016) investigates the causes of public investments stagnation, beyond the reorientation of the government's strategy and the stricter budget restrictions. These include institutional bottlenecks and government stalling due to political instability since 2013, and allegations of irregularities.

Therefore, a change in the composition of fiscal policy was consolidated with the shift from a first, expansionary sub-period, where the driving engine was public investment (2006–2010), to a second sub-period of growing subsidies and tax cuts, during which public investments were stagnant (2011–2014). These findings are important, because they provide some perspective to the common critique that the government was irresponsible in its expansionary policy through public expenditure during 2011–2014. On the contrary, the total primary expenses during the second fiscal expansion sub-period (2011–2014) increased at a similar rate to the fiscal consolidation period (1999–2004); and slowed down compared to the first expansionist sub-period (2005–2010), although not enough to compensate for the slowdown in revenue.

A more reasonable criticism can be levied, based on theoretical and empirical foundations, on the inefficiency of this new mix of fiscal policy in regaining economic growth. The empirical estimates of Orair et al. (2016), for example, support this conclusion by indicating that the multipliers for subsidies are not significant or not persistent, unlike the multipliers for public investments, which can be over 1.5 during recessions.

From a theoretical standpoint, Kalecki (1943) introduced the discussion of business cycles in economic theory by showing how during recessions, when opposition to an expenditure policy based on public debt by the 'market interest group' is reduced, arises a perspective that the intervention must preferably occur through stimuli to the private sector. However, this is not the most adequate path to reactivate the economy, compared to an alternative of accelerating public investments and stimulating mass consumption. Additionally, it faces a practical difficulty due to the uncertain reaction of entrepreneurs. If the recession is profound, entrepreneurs can be pessimistic about the future and measures tend to have a small effect on investment.

Analysing the Brazilian experience, it is possible to identify some factors that contributed to the uncertain and pessimistic scenario. The debt crises of the euro area in 2011, as well as the renewed slowdown in China, are just a few events that reinforced a vision that the global economy was facing a long-lasting recession that would not spare emerging economies.

In the Brazilian domestic arena, the year of 2013 served as the backdrop for a series of street protests and a political crisis that culminated in the impeachment of President Rousseff in 2016. The inconsistencies of the strategy in reinforcing anti-cyclical policies also led to widespread doubt, such as when the administration back-tracked its decision to reduce the basic interest rate in 2013. In short, given this uncertain and pessimistic scenario that tends to discourage private investment decisions, one may conclude that the shift in the fiscal policy mix to a greater prevalence of subsidies and tax cuts (during 2011–2014), when public investment remained stagnant, was a poor choice. So too could be considered the cut of 36.7% in public investment during the 2015 recession. However, before tackling this issue, it is important to understand what has influenced the change in fiscal policy during the transition to President Rousseff's second presidential term.

3 Escalation of the Public Debt and the Macroeconomic Management Puzzle

The speed with which indicators of indebtedness escalated after 2014 is an aspect that warrants attention in the post-GFC Brazilian experience. To illustrate it, Fig. 1 features box plot diagrams with fiscal indicators that allow for a comparative analysis of the Brazilian fiscal situation. The following conclusions follow:

1. The trajectory of net debt in Brazil is 'V'-shaped: it decreased substantially since 2004, when it converged to a value close to the global median, reaching 30.5% of GDP in 2013. Then it began a steep upward march, reaching a level close to that of 2007 in three years, and towards the upper quarter of the most indebted economies in the world.
2. The trajectory of gross debt is different in shape and intensity. 2004–2013 was a period characterised by certain stability. What followed was a more accelerated rise, which put the country closer to the top quarter of most indebted countries.
3. Brazil produced primary surpluses that were superior to most countries during 2004–2013 and was often placed below the lower quartile that sets apart the countries with the least primary borrowing requirements. This situation changed with the shift into deficits of upwards of 2% of GDP during the 2015–2016 recession. This was nonetheless not that distant from global standards, given the primary deficits of most countries after the GFC.
4. The situation is different when analysing the nominal interest: Brazil is an outlier with an average close to 6% of GDP.
5. This outlier position is partially explained by the relatively high inflation in the country. The real implicit interest rate, which is simply the average interest rate over the net debt, minus the inflation rate, permits to control this effect and, again, highlights Brazil's position. The rate of 9 per year has changed little over the years and has few parallels worldwide.

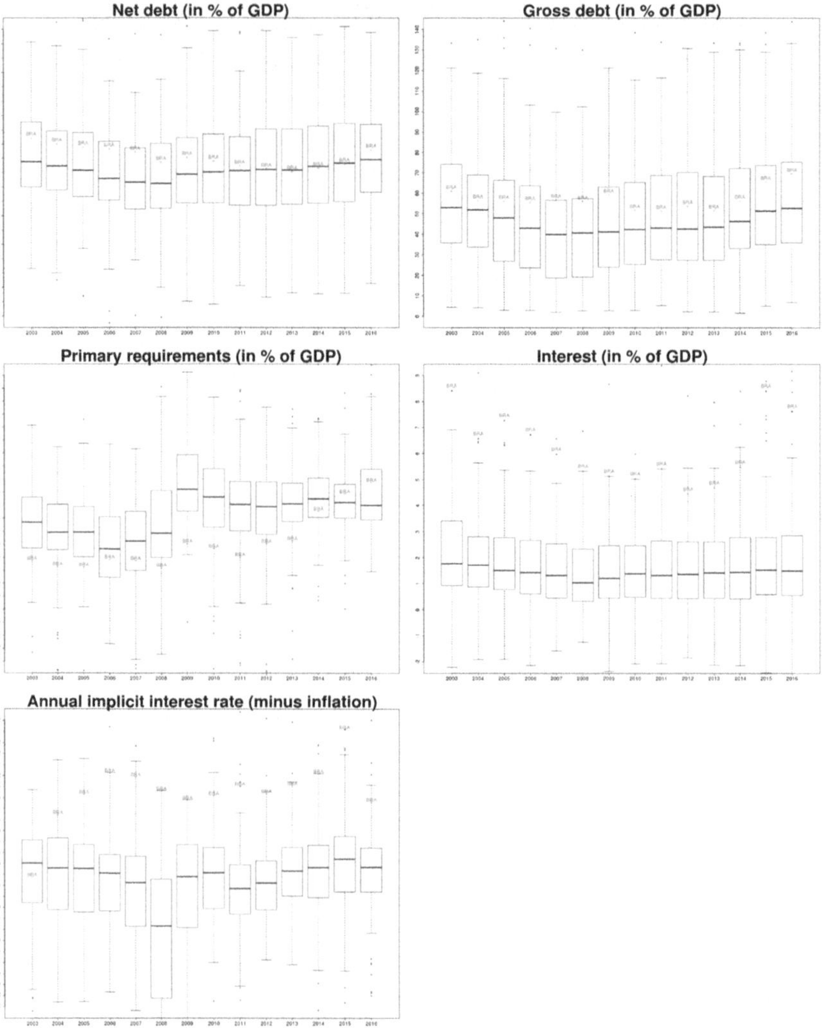

Fig. 1 Box plot diagram featuring indicators of the public sector (2003–2016). *Source* Authors' elaboration based on IMF (2016) data and Central Bank of Brazil. *Note* Sample of 91 countries with all available information

Such findings lead us to question the Brazilian idiosyncrasies: What explains the speed of the recent deterioration of public indebtedness? Why is there such a large difference between gross and net debts? How is it possible to be an outlier when it comes to interest?

These are not simple questions, especially so in terms of the dynamics of public debt answer to the complex interaction among the major macroeconomic policies (monetary, credit, exchange and fiscal policies). Therefore, it will be necessary to present a few concepts and mechanisms regarding these policies.

Gross debt is the total liabilities, mainly bonds issued by the National Treasury (TN). Net debt corresponds to the difference between liabilities and assets—the main ones being international reserves under control of the BCB and TN credits with public banks, such as loans to the Brazilian Development Bank (*Banco Nacional de Desenvolvimento Econômico e Social*—BNDES).

When the government goes to the exchange market and trades national currency for US dollars, which is invested in the international market and incorporated as reserves, or when it lends to the BNDES under subsidised interest rates to finance private investments, it increases the liquidity of the national economy. Therefore, the BCB sells TN bonds in exchange for this additional currency to mop up liquidity, an operation called 'sterilization'. This is because the monetary policy in Brazil is very focused on liquidity control through the repo and reverse repos of short-term bonds by the BCB.

Another alternative would be for the TN to issue longer-term government bonds and finance the purchase of assets and, by keeping ahead, it avoids repo operations. Under both alternatives, the result of the government's decision to expand its international reserves or capitalise public banks yields simultaneous increases in the gross debt. Therein lays the explanation to the paradox: The government, during the 2005–2013 periods, produced successive primary surpluses and substantially reduced its net debt, but simultaneously accumulated assets that resulted in an increased gross debt.

A comparison between the composition of public debt in 2004 and 2014 can clarify this. The net debt reached 50.2% of GDP in 2004 and, due to the inexpressive volume of international reserves and of credit with the BNDES (3.7 and 0.9% of GDP, respectively), it was slightly lower than the gross debt, of 56.2% of GDP.

Taking advantage of a bonanza period in its balance of payments accounts, the government undertook an aggressive strategy of paying off external debts, avoiding issuing foreign exchange-linked bonds and, especially, accumulating international reserves, which reached USD363.3 billion (BRL982 billion), or 17% of GDP in 2014, becoming a net creditor of foreign currency.[3] This public debt-management policy, despite its excesses and high cost, which we will address further, was nonetheless successful in reducing the financial vulnerability of the public sector. It was also central to the post-GFC fiscal policy because it established more favourable conditions for the government to engage in an anti-cyclical policy.

However, the operationalisation this policy was hindered by two structural obstacles of the Brazilian economy: the high interest rates and the weakness of the mechanisms of long-term financing. This second obstacle worsened during the scenario of the GFC, when traditional sources of funding for the BNDES, the main provider of long-term credit, proved insufficient to meet the challenge of occupying the space left behind by the withdrawal of private sources of financing. The solution was to inject funds into the BNDES so that the bank could expand its credit lines with subsidised interest. The TN performed a first capitalisation in 2008 and, with the extension of the anti-cyclical policy, repeated this operation numerous times, which drove its credits with the public banks to total USD180.7 billion (BRL487.9 billion), or 8.4% of GDP in 2014. The country arrived in 2014 with a different composition of its public debt compared to the previous decade: net debt decreased to 32.6% of GDP, while the gross debt of 56.3% of GDP changed very little due to the accumulation of assets.[4]

Therefore, another characteristic of the fiscal expansionary period (2005–2014) was the configuration of an asymmetric profile of public indebtedness, with a large volume of assets and liabilities and a significant differential of rates of return between them; with the macroeconomic management being unable to push domestic interest rates to values more in line with international standards. The non-financial public sector accumulated around 25% of GDP in low return assets, from

[3]Chapter "New Features of the Brazilian External Sector since the Great Global Crisis" of this book provides a deeper discussion and relevant analysis of the external sector.

[4]For a deeper view of the public debt management, see Gobetti and Schettini (2010) and Pellegrini (2011).

BNDES credits that paid the TN at rates close to domestic inflation, to international reserves that did not manage to even cover inflation rates. At the same time, liabilities were kept between 50 and 60% of GDP and were repaying creditors at real rates over 5% per year, with little change over the entire period.

It is difficult to explain the reasons behind the high interest rates and the resistance against their decrease in Brazil. However, for the purpose of this chapter, it is worth pointing out the consequences of this enigma; such as the high burden on public debt and the significant pressure over fiscal policy to produce high primary surpluses.

In short, the public debt management during the fiscal expansion period (2005–2014) had some merit; for instance, the reduction of the external vulnerability of the public sector and the facilitation of financing of investment projects during a time when the financial market was retracting. However, it also created another problem of a dynamic nature, namely the asymmetric profile of public indebtedness, featuring a large volume of financial assets and liabilities, and a high differential rate of return among them. That maintained the need to generate high primary results to contain the rise of public debt whenever the economy did not perform well in terms of GDP growth.

While the differential between the real interest rate and GDP growth was small and the government was producing primary surpluses, it was possible to reduce the net debt. With the persistence of high interest rates in an economy under recession, it was necessary to produce primary surpluses above 4% of GDP during 2015–2016, just to contain the mounting public debt. It was precisely during this period that the primary result indicator deteriorated: the average primary surpluses of 2.8% of GDP during 2005–2013 transformed into a 2.5 GDP deficit in 2016. Here lies the main explanation for the rapid rise of net debt in Brazil, which between 2014 and 2016 increased 13.3 percentage points as a proportion of GDP (from 32.6% to 45.9%), more than triple the primary deficit accumulated.

The current problem with the Brazilian public debt is not so much its amount, but rather its dynamics. The level of indebtedness is still within both international and Brazilian historical standards and has a much less vulnerable structure than in the recent past. However, it would be difficult to contain the rise in public debt over the next few years, so long as high differentials between real interest rates and GDP growth exist—even if the fiscal policy manages to yield primary surpluses.

A second important aspect is that the pressure for fiscal adjustments tends to grow disproportionately during the episodes of escalation of the public debt. This phenomenon goes beyond economic analysis and the purpose of this paper, requiring consideration of political factors and power relations. However, it is helpful to explain the shift in the orientation of fiscal policy soon after the 2014 elections for a new period of fiscal austerity. That phenomenon was similar to what occurred during the 1998–1999 and 2002–2003 currency crises, when pro-cyclical fiscal adjustments were driven by shocks in public indebtedness, but its start was delayed until after the election.

4 Fiscal Policy in Perspective: The Shift Towards Austerity

After 2011, the expansionary fiscal policy of the Workers' Party (PT) administrations, which had previously been considered successful, became a target of fierce criticism, at times focused on its fiscal irresponsibility, and at others on the inefficiency of anti-cyclical policies, such as in Barbosa Filho and Pessoa (2014), Mesquita (2014) and Nóbrega (2016). These criticisms grew, influenced in no small part by the political polarisation of the country, as the economic and fiscal situation deteriorated and the government made extensive use of artificial measures to meet the primary result targets. 2014 was a landmark year: Criticisms reached their peak when the economy became stagnant (with a GDP growth of 0.5%), the primary result saw its first deficit in 16 years and public indebtedness started to rise after more than a decade of almost continuous decrease.

Paradoxically, the downturn of the economy occurred without significant tensions in the labour market. The tax cuts and credit subsidies enabled entrepreneurs to recompose their profit margins and restructure their debts, without having to resort to major lay-offs. At the same time, redistributive transfers continued to provide real gains to the households at the bottom of income distribution. The period of fiscal expansion (2005–2014) was generally characterised by a process of simultaneous decrease in unemployment rates and in indicators of inequality. The income of the poorest population grew more than that of the average strata, which might have deepened the distributive conflict, thereby leading to popular support of the government, as discussed in Singer (2015).[5]

The electoral debate of 2014 accounted for a possible shift in fiscal policy. Soon after the elections of 2014, the re-elected President Rousseff was captured by the 'political power' of the austerity thesis (Sebastian Dellepiane-Avellaneda 2015), according to which fiscal adjustment would be a necessary condition to recover credibility and resume economic growth.[6] The re-elected President, then, announced a change in the government's economic team, which would be led by Joaquim Levy, former Secretary of the Treasury and who by then held a directorship in the largest Brazilian private bank (Bradesco). The goal was for Levy to recover the credibility that had been lost, through stricter fiscal rigour. The government's fiscal strategy for 2015 was then guided by the example of Lula administration in 2003 and materialised in a proposal that combined a fiscal adjustment of 1.7% points of GDP within one year and a realignment of macroeconomic prices (exchange rate and the prices of energy and fuel), as explained in the official document MF (2015).

The result of this fiscal adjustment was far below expectations. First, because most of the legislative measures of raising taxes and revising rules for the concession of social benefits met with resistance in

[5]The indicators of poverty and inequality, based on household surveys, have shown a decreasing tendency over the decade 2005-2014, due to the higher growth of income at the bottom of the income distribution, as demonstrated by Ipea (2015). However, recent studies, such as Medeiros et al. (2015), based on tax data, which captures more accurately the income of the richest in terms of the income distribution, show that top income concentration has changed little since 2006.

[6]During the electoral debate, the opposition defended the austerity thesis and the government defended the country's fiscal situation, the success of its economic policy faced with a dire international scenario and the need for a mere 'fine tuning' of fiscal policy, which would not compromise the legacy of PT administrations. For a deeper analysis of the period, see Levy (2014) that provides a good example of the conventional narrative and Barbosa (2013) for the official one.

Congress, and the government was forced to pay off massive liabilities from previous years. At the same time, it promoted a real contraction of 2.9% in other expenses, with a fall of 36.7% in public investment. Second, because of the country's deep recession that crippled revenue, thereby precluding the achievement of the fiscal targets.

Seeking to mitigate this situation, the Rousseff administration reviewed its strategy in late 2015/early 2016 to a gradual fiscal consolidation, replacing Levy with a heterodox economist (Nelson Barbosa) in the Ministry of Finance, but by then it was too late. In a few months, the country witnessed a worsening of the political crisis. The president lost the support of most allied political parties and an impeachment process in the Congress was launched in May 2016, when the president was temporally removed from her position. That process culminated with her impeachment in August 2016, under controversial allegations of fiscal responsibility crimes during the austere year of 2015.

The Vice-President, Michel Temer, a traditional and conciliatory politician, member of Brazil's largest political party (PMDB), took office after the impeachment. He made an alliance with the opposition and rebuilt a political coalition with a conservative edge. The Temer administration nominated Henrique Meirelles as Ministry of Finance and continued a fiscal policy guided by the hypothesis of expansionist austerity, revamping it; however, towards a position that market confidence and economic growth would be regained with the furthering of an agenda of liberal-oriented structural reforms.

Making use of a new majority in Congress, at the end of 2016, the government approved a Constitutional amendment that instituted what it called 'new fiscal regime', a rule that limits the growth of government primary expenditures to the rate of inflation for two decades. Soon after, President Temer submitted an ambitious proposal of social security reform that is discussed in the Congress in 2017, together with a labour reform.

The emphasis on structural reforms has also allowed to shift the focus from short-term fiscal adjustments and made way for the government to propose lower targets for the primary deficits, above 2% of GDP for 2016 and 2017. Indeed, the outcome of the 2015 fiscal adjustment was counterproductive, in the sense that fiscal indicators kept deteriorating and the country remained plunged into recession. In 2016, for example, the fiscal target accommodated an increase in primary expenditures of 4.5% (see Table 2), even though it was an atypical increase, influenced by the effect of the rule of readjustment of the minimum wage on social benefits, which was driven by 2015s high inflation, and by the payment of rollovers from previous years.

In other words, a large portion of the growth in expenditures in 2016 was due to the lagged adjustment of inflation or the payment of past debts. The case of public investment illustrates that the expenses on accrual basis decreased 3.5% in 2016, while on cash basis increased 13.5% due to the payment of rollovers.

The rate of public investment in Brazil started a downward spiral after reaching its recent historical peak of 4.6% of GDP in 2010 and has already been cut in half, as demonstrated by the 2.3% of GDP recorded for 2016; the lowest rate in the last two decades. It is difficult to accurately determine how much of this decline is due to budgetary constraints, or due to more general determinants, such as the paralysis of the government bodies due to the political crisis. Regardless of its causes, the public investment reduction, one of the expenditures yielding the highest multipliers, is a relevant contributing aspect to the low economic dynamism since 2010.

Finally, it is worth highlighting that the fiscal policy of the President Temer administration, even accommodating more modest fiscal targets in the short-term, continues the strategy of promoting a tight fiscal consolidation in the medium- and long-terms. The Constitutional ceiling for government expenditures implies that it will contract at around 4 percentage points of GDP within the decade if the GDP resumes its growth of around 2.5% per year. It is a very bold target if we consider the history and the rigid structure of public expenditure in Brazil. For that very reason, the government is employing a wide set of legislative and Constitutional reforms that, if not approved by the Congress, will make unlikely the achievement of its targets. In short, the current scenario points towards a long-lasting period of fiscal austerity, and not merely a temporary shift.

5 Final Remarks

The shift towards fiscal austerity is associated with a set of legislative changes that cannot be easily reversed, which implicitly tend to lead to a long-lasting austerity period. The main example is the target of the 'new fiscal regime', instituted in 2016 through a Constitutional amendment to freeze public expenditure ceilings, in real terms, for at least 10 years.

There is no question that the mounting public debt and control over expenditures are real problems that must be faced head-on. However, the concrete manifestation of fiscal austerity defended by the current government might introduce unnecessary economic and social risks. First, because there is great uncertainty towards the capacity of fiscal austerity itself promoting growth, as has been shown by international debate.[7] There are few cases of fiscal consolidations that have led to growth, and none whose starting point was a recession as deep as the Brazilian one (Jayadev and Konczal 2010).[8] In successful experiences, exchange and/or monetary policy helped to compensate the fiscal contraction, enabling an economic growth driven by internal or external demand according to Perotti (2011).[9]

In the Brazilian case, fiscal austerity is being implemented during the worst recession of its history, coinciding with a period of dire political crisis and social polarisation. This scenario is compounded by high credit leveraging by enterprises and consumers, after the credit boom of the previous decade, and the expected prolonged international recession, all of which hinder economic recovery driven by private demand.

Given this situation, it does not seem wise to adopt a fiscal regime that greatly restricts fiscal policy, instead of prioritising mid-term

---

[7]See Jayadev and Konczal (2010), Guajardo et al. (2011) and Perotti (2011) for a criticism of the 'austerity myth'. Recently, Alesina et al. (2017) recognised that fiscal consolidations have recessionary short-term effects, which might be mitigated depending on the profile and persistence of fiscal adjustments.

[8]Ireland in 1987 was the only reported case of a country in a soft recession before fiscal consolidation (−0,5% GDP growth) that has regained growth, driven mainly by exports.

[9]Even though the fact that endogeneity problems, beside difficulties to isolate discretionary efforts, avoid precise estimations of the fiscal multipliers, as shown by Guajardo et al. (2011) and by Perotti (2011).

fiscal consolidation and supporting short-term demand. It is reasonable to permit some real increase in expenditure, periodic reviews of the expenditure legislation (during every administration, for example) and special treatment to public investment or other social expenses. As in the main foreign experiences, such as Union European countries that usually limit the evolution of expenditure by the growth of potential GDP and allow for fiscal target deviation (cyclically adjusted) during recessions (Schaechter et al. 2012; and Gobetti 2014).

Second, the success of the target of freezing public expenditure, in real terms, for at least a decade, depends on the approval of a set of structural reforms, interrupting the trajectory of growth of social expenditure, which implies a series of social risks. The new fiscal regime contains changes in the Constitutional minimum spending in health care and education; and, soon after its approval, a radical project for reforming social security was submitted to Congress. These revisions are not likely to end there, given the target of not allowing any increase in primary expenditure in a country undergoing a rapid demographic transition that imposes pressures on pension benefits. Soon it will be necessary to supplement them with new measures such as the detachment of social benefits from the minimum wage or at least the review of the rule that drives minimum wage readjustment.

Therefore, there is a real risk that these reforms will interrupt the late consolidation of a social welfare state in Brazil. This consolidation has been accomplished through a systematic increase in social spending over three decades; also, and despite a series of inefficiencies and distortions, it has enabled the construction of a wide range of social benefits and services that are enormously influential on the well-being of the population, especially the most vulnerable, in a highly unequal country.[10]

It is no coincidence that Brazil has one of the largest levels of public expenditure among developing countries, with primary expenses at the rate of 34% of GDP, as well as some of the largest levels of coverage of social security and assistance benefits, and of public health and

[10]According to Hanni et al. (2015) the redistributive impact of the fiscal policy in Brazil is the highest among Latin American countries, reducing the Gini coefficient in 7.1 percentage points mainly due to the effect of public transfers.

education services. The structural pressure of social expenditure, as we have seen, is mainly responsible for the inertial and rigid behaviour of Brazilian public expenditures, which increased at an average real rate of 4.2% per year in the federal level alone over the past two decades.

Of course, it is unreasonable to expect that these rates of expansion could be maintained indefinitely, but this does not imply the need to abruptly tether it to the rate of inflation. There are many alternatives for the gradual control of expenditures, while the government gains time to promote wider discussions and evaluations about the budget and its financing structure. The new fiscal regime signals towards a rupture with the social welfare state instead of towards making it financially sustainable.

References

Alesina, A., Barbiero, O., Favero, C., Giavazzi, F., & Paradisi, M. (2017). *The effects of fiscal consolidations: Theory and evidence* (NBER Working Paper No. 23385). Cambridge: NBER.

Appy, B., Lisboa, M., Mendes, M., & Lazzarini, S. (2015). A Rigidez do Gasto Público: Problemas e Soluções. *Interesse Nacional, 8*(31).

Barbosa, N. (2013). Dez anos de política econômica. In E. Sader (Ed.), *10 anos de governos pós-neoliberais no Brasil: Lula e Dilma*. Boitempo: São Paulo.

Barbosa Filho, F. H., & Pessoa, S. P. (2014). Desaceleração recente da economia", In CDPP (Ed.) *Coletânea de capítulos da agenda Sob a Luz do Sol*. São Paulo: Centro de Debates de Políticas Públicas.

Dellepiane-Avellaneda, S. (2015). The political power of economic ideas: The case of 'Expansionary Fiscal Contractions'. *The British Journal of Politics & International Relations, 17*(3), 391–418.

Giambiagi, F. (2008). 18 anos de política fiscal no Brasil: 1991/2008. *Economia aplicada, 12*(4), 535–580.

Gobetti, S. W., & Schettini, B. (2010). Dívida Líquida e Dívida Bruta: uma abordagem integrada para analisar a trajetória eo custo do endividamento brasileiro. *Texto para Discussão, 1514*. Brasília: Ipea.

Gobetti, S. W. (2014). Regras fiscais no Brasil e na Europa: um estudo comparativo e propositivo. *Texto para Discussão, n. 2018*. Rio de Janeiro: Ipea.

Gobetti, S. W., & Orair, R. O. (2015). Política fiscal em perspectiva: o ciclo de 16 anos (1999–2014). *Revista de Economia Contemporânea, 19*(3), 417–447.

Gobetti, S. W., & Orair, R. O. (2017). Resultado Primário e Contabilidade Criativa: reconstruindo as estatísticas fiscais 'acima da linha' do governo geral. *Texto para Discussão, n. 2288*. Brasília: Ipea.

Guajardo, J., Leigh, D., & Pescatori, A. (2011). *Expansionary Austerity: New International Evidence* (IMF Working Paper 11/158). Washington, DC: Interrnational Monetary Fund.

Hanni, R., Martner, M., & Podestá, A. (2015). El potencial redistributivo de la fiscalidad en América Latina. *Revista Cepal, 116*, August, 7–26.

IMF. (2016). *World Economic Outlook Database*, October. Available at https://www.imf.org/external/pubs/ft/weo/2016/02/weodata/index.aspx.

IPEA. (2015). PNAD 2014: Breves análises. *Nota Técnica*, 22. Brasília: Ipea.

Jayadev, A., & Konczal, M. (2010). The boom not the slump: The right time for austerity. University of Massachusetts Boston *Economics Faculty Publication Series*. Paper 26

Kalecki, M. (1943). Political aspects of full employment. *The Political Quarterly, 14*(4), 322–330.

Levy, J. V. F. (2014). Robustez fiscal e qualidade do gasto como ferramentas para o crescimento. In CDPP (Ed.), *Coletânea de capítulos da agenda Sob a Luz do Sol*. São Paulo: Centro de Debates de Políticas Públicas.

Medeiros, M., Souza, P. H., & Castro, F. A. (2015). O Topo da Distribuição de Renda no Brasil: primeiras estimativas com dados tributários e comparação com pesquisas domiciliares (2006–2012). *Dados—Revista de Ciências Sociais, 58*(1), 7–36.

Mesquita, M. (2014). A política econômica do governo Dilma: a volta do experimentalismo, In CDPP (Ed.), *Coletânea de capítulos da agenda Sob a Luz do Sol*. São Paulo: Centro de Debates de Políticas Públicas.

MF. (2015). Reequilíbrio Fiscal e Retomada da Economia. Brasília: Ministério da Fazenda. Brasília: Ministério da Fazenda.

Nóbrega, M. (2016). Construção e Desmonte das Instituições Fiscais. In F. Salto & M. Almeida (Eds.), *Finanças Públicas: da contabilidade criativa ao resgate da credibilidade*. Rio de Janeiro: Record.

Orair, R. O. (2015). Desonerações em alta com rigidez da carga tributária: o que explica o paradoxo do decênio 2005–2014? *Texto para Discussão, n. 2117*. Brasília: Ipea.

Orair, R. O. (2016). Investimento Público no Brasil: trajetória e relações com o regime fiscal. *Texto para Discussão, n. 2215*. Brasília: Ipea.

Orair, R. O., Gobetti, S. W., & Siqueira, F. F. (2016). Política Fiscal e Ciclo Econômico: uma análise baseada em multiplicadores de gasto público. In STN—Secretaria Do Tesouro Nacional. *XXI Prêmio Tesouro Nacional de Monografias*. Brasília: STN.

Paula, L. F., Modenesi, A. M., & Pires, M. C. (2015). The tale of the contagion of two crises and policy responses in Brazil: A case of (Keynesian) policy coordination? *Journal of Post Keynesian Economics, 37*(3), 408–435.

Pellegrini, J. A. (2011). Dívida Bruta e Ativo do Setor Público: o que a queda da dívida líquida não mostra? *Texto para Discussão, n. 95*. Brasília: Núcleo de Estudos e Pesquisas do Senado.

Perotti, R. (2011). *The 'austerity myth': Gain without pain?* (NBER Working Paper 17571). Cambridge: NBER.

Rezende, F., Oliveira, F., & Araújo, E. (2007). *O dilema fiscal: remendar ou reformar?* Rio de Janeiro: FGV Editora.

Schaechter, A., Kinda, T., Budina, N., & Weber, A. (2012). *Fiscal rules in response to the crisis—toward the 'Next Generation' rules: A new dataset* (IFM Working Paper 12/187). Washington, DC: International Monetary Fund.

Schettini, B. P., Gouvea, R. R., Orair, R., & Gobetti, S. W. (2011). Resultado Estrutural e Impulso Fiscal: uma aplicação para as administrações públicas no Brasil—1997–2010. *Pesquisa e Planejamento Econômico, 41*, 233–285.

Serrano, F., & Summa, R. (2016). Aggregate demand and the slowdown of Brazilian economic growth in 2011–2014. *Nova Economia, 25*(special issue), 803–833.

Singer, A. (2015). Cutucando onças com varas curtas O ensaio desenvolvimentista no primeiro mandato de Dilma Rousseff (2011–2014). *Novos Estudos, 102*, 43–71.

Economic and Social Policies Inconsistency, Conventions, and Crisis in the Brazilian Economy, 2011–2016

Marco Flávio da Cunha Resende and Fábio Henrique Bittes Terra

1 Introduction[1]

Keynes (1973, 1980a, b, and 1982) and the Post Keynesians, summarized in Arestis et al. (2016), prescribed economic policies aiming at solving the two main issues of the monetary economies of production, namely unemployment and its unequal income share. To Keynes (op. cit.), the main macroeconomic policies are the monetary, exchange rate, and fiscal policies. Each has its own tools and specific goals and if their operation is coordinated and coherent, the two

[1]Marco F.C. Resende thanks FAPEMIG/CNPq for their financial support.

M.F.C. Resende (✉)
Federal University of Minas Gerais, Belo Horizonte, Brazil
e-mail: resende@cedeplar.ufmg.br

F.H. Bittes Terra
Federal University of ABC, São Bernardo do Campo, Brazil
e-mail: fhbterra@gmail.com

P. Arestis et al. (eds.), *The Brazilian Economy since the Great Financial Crisis of 2007/2008*, https://doi.org/10.1007/978-3-319-64885-9_10

ultimate objectives of economic policy mix are expected to be reached. Besides the State cooperation with the private activity through economic policies, Keynes (1973) claimed for a good institutional environment, that is, a set of speeches, laws, functional bureaucracy, executions of contracts, etc., that allows the best business-making process.

The complementarity between the public and private initiatives comes from the economy's nature: Its dynamic depends on private investment which is, however, undertaken under uncertainty, as it is impossible to know at present, when investment occurs, whether it would be profitable or not. If there is uncertainty, entrepreneurs do not know the results of their decisions so they can only expect some outcome. In what do the entrepreneurs' expectations rely on? In several instances, some more or less known, and some only supposed with more or less confidence. Among this information, there is one special to ground expectations: conventions, i.e., a public shared belief.

Considering this, Keynes (1973, 1980a, b, and 1982) and the Post Keynesians (Arestis et al. 2016) offer theoretical models capable of analysing what has gone wrong with Brazil's economy, which went through two different periods since 2003. From 2003 to 2010, it experienced growth, though it decreased by 0.2% in 2009, due to the Global Financial Crisis. Over 2011–2016 Brazil first showed signs of stagnation up to 2014, and then went into its worst recession ever, 2015–2016. Thus, this chapter aims at analysing, based on the Keynesian notion of conventions, what has gone wrong with the Brazilian economy after 2011. Specifically, we investigate what were the problems of both the economic policies and the overall institutional environment the governments of the period framed, to understand how the Brazilian government brought about conventions grounding expectations that leaded entrepreneurs to hoard instead of investing. This contribution adds to the relevant literature by offering an analysis that focuses on the consequences of the State economic action, but spotlighting the role of conventions on it.

The chapter has four other sections beyond this introduction. Section 2 describes, at its first subsection, the Post-Keynesian notion of convention, whereas the second subsection discusses the role government plays in framing conventions. Section 3 presents, markedly based on Keynes's writings, the Post-Keynesian macroeconomic policy mix, namely exchange rate, monetary and fiscal policies. Then, Sect. 4 analyses what has happened to the Brazilian economy over 2011–2016. Section 5 presents the final remarks.

2 Conventions and the Role of Government in Framing Them

The Notion of Conventions and Post-Keynesian Developments on the Topic

In Keynes's (1973) monetary economy, uncertainty is crucial, since agents' decisions in the present builds the future of the economic system; yet, the information required for the decision-making process is only partly available. So, future cannot be foretold and, consequently, agents can seek protection against losses that may result from their investments, such as liquidity preference outcomes, revealing the agents' conventional behavior to gain protection against uncertainty (Carvalho 2015; Ferrari-Filho and Conceição 2005).

One pillar the agents base their uncertain decision is conventions, whose essence "lies in assuming that the existing state of affairs will continue indefinitely, except in so far as we have specific reasons to expect a change" (Keynes 1973, p. 152). To Dequech (1999), convention can be understood as a collective rule of behavior. Plihon (1995) interpreted convention as a mimetic behavior. To Dow (2010, p. 8), convention relates to expectations, though both are formed interdependently. Davis (2005) saw conventions "as interactive, as is confidence, individual and collective [...] individuals concentrate on change, and so makes the convention itself more likely to be precarious" (p. xiii). Modenesi (2012) and Carvalho (2014) considered convention a belief shared by many individuals.

Thereby, we summarize convention as a public opinion prevailing in some instance. It forms a conventional reasoning, which agents use as an important aspect to form their expectations. As future economic events cannot be calculated, decision-makers guide themselves, based on their *confidence* on their own expectations. Decisions are not just a matter of expectations but also of how one trusts on what is expected. Hence, if conventions partly help forming expectations under uncertainty, the state of confidence of agents also depends on them.

Two further elements in the decision-making process are intuition and animal spirits. Intuition is a mechanism agents use to subjectively mix material and abstract data (like conventions) to reach conclusions. If entrepreneurs' intuition finds a stimulating conclusion, a positive expectation about profiting, they invest. So, they put into action their animal spirits, a spontaneous optimism that leads them to face the risks of investment (Carvalho 2014).

Nevertheless, as a great number of independent decision units coexist, if each decision-maker does not account for the other's expectations, plans may not succeed and expectations would despair. Consequently, there is convergence of expectations, giving room for convention as a belief shared by many individuals and which they consider for their state of confidence upon which they reason prospects (Carvalho 2014).

The Role of Government in Framing Conventions

Convention and conventional behavior are relevant elements within the core assumptions of Keynes's General Theory (GT) (Modenesi et al. 2012).[2] Convention matters for the agents' state of confidence, but their belief may change over time, showing the fragile basis upon which individuals form expectations under uncertainty.[3] Then, which are the forces that guide or influence conventions? Does government play a role in the raise and maintenance of a given convention? Although Keynes has not explicitly formulated the connection between the government

[2]As Davis (2005) pointed out, "the genuinely revolutionary positions found in The General Theory appear to depend on important respects upon the new views Keynes developed there regarding to history and conventions" (p. 149).

[3]As Keynes (1973) states "a conventional valuation [...] is liable to change violently as the result of a sudden fluctuation of opinion due to factors which do not really make much difference to the prospective yield; since there will be no strong roots of conviction to hold it steady" (p. 154).

and conventions in his works, his GT has passages regarding this link. To make it clearer, some quotes are useful, as per below:

> The considerations upon which expectations of prospective yields are based are partly existing facts which we can assume to be known more or less for certain, and partly future events which can only be forecasted with more or less confidence [...] It is reasonable, therefore, to be guided to a considerable degree by the facts about which we feel somewhat confident, even though they may be less decisively relevant to the issue than other facts about which our knowledge is vague and scanty. For this reason the facts of the existing situation enter, in a sense disproportionately, into the formation of our long-term expectations. (Keynes 1973, pp. 147–148)

The knowledge of future is "vague and scanty." So, government's speeches, plans, policies, and even circumstantial measures may be included in the set of "existing facts which we can assume to be known more or less for certain," furnishing to the decision-makers more instances, and consequently confidence, in their expectations. Therefore, the government can frame economic conventions as it plays the following roles: (i) it issues exogenous money and affects the creation of endogenous money; (ii) it stipulates taxes and gathers revenues; (iii) it undertakes a wide scope of public policies; (iv) it establishes laws which builds the society's institutional structure; and (v) it has the legal jurisdiction to reinforce the power of law. Carvalho (1992) enlightens the idea:

> The state has powers to influence or even to determine future paths [...] all these factors allow the state to lead the process of development of a monetary economy [...] it is not a question of replacing private property or the market [...] but of allowing the state to issue the signals that markets are not able to and of pointing out. (p. 205)

Government can provide both the rules of markets' operation and the signals that market fails to offer. If uncertainty is pervasive, in a considerable degree agents ground expectations in the signals issued by governmental speeches, plans, policies, and so forth. Keynes (1973) gave further hints to advance the link between governmental actions and the prevailing conventions, emphasizing the role of fiscal and monetary policies, "the long-term market-rate of interest will depend, not only on the current policy of the monetary authority, but also on market expectations concerning its future policy" (p. 202), and

> The State will have to exercise a guiding influence on the propensity to consume partly through its scheme of taxation, partly by fixing the rate of interest [...] I conceive, therefore, that a somewhat comprehensive socialization of investment will prove the only means of securing an approximation to full employment. (p. 378)

Ferrari-Filho and Conceição (2005) and Arestis et al. (2016) interpreted Keynes' "socialization of investment," concerning the government's role in providing institutional mechanisms to mitigate uncertainty and stimulate investment. Accordingly, Marcuzzo (2010) argues that Keynes' (1980a) suggestions on fiscal policy (FP) account for stabilizing confidence—that is, conventions. This same interpretation is compatible with Minsky's (1986) "Big Government" and "Big Bank" institutions which ensure economic stability and regulate the unstable financial system. As Arestis et al. (2016) argue:

> In this uncertain world [...] economic policy is the main source of solidity that private enterprises have to support their expectations and investment. In this sense, economic policy [...] in a context of coordination and discretion, is capable of facing insufficient effective demand as well as building a good institutional environment, which is essential to keep the entrepreneurs' expectations confident and stimulate their animal spirits. (p. 151)

Successful policies depend on the government persuading the agents not only that its actions are in the right way, but also that people believe it: "a convention is a tool deployed to coordinate expectations that inform each agent what the other ones expect from a given stimulus" (Carvalho 2014, p. 257). Also, the effectiveness of economic policies rests on the strength of the dominant convention, i.e., it depends on how many individuals are confident that the others share the same belief and that the government is reliable enough to allow a common opinion that its intentions are trustworthy. Given that, Carvalho (2014) argued that the agents are more sensible to the government policies when they have a shared belief, which led a great number of agents to give a similar response to a governmental stimulus.

Thus, in the Post-Keynesian approach, government can guide conventions. Further, the success of its policies depends on how proper and pervasive is a convention it stimulated. To sum up, all means of governmental influences on the institutional structure of society should be coherently coordinated to guide conventions. So, what are the goals and operational guidelines of the Post-Keynesian macroeconomic policies?

3 Post-Keynesian Macroeconomic Policy Mix

Arestis et al. (2016) explain the three reasons that make macroeconomic policy crucial for overcoming unemployment and income inequality:

> Firstly, they serve as an anchor to the business sector's expectations, signaling the general tendency the government pursues [...]. Secondly, one of the macroeconomic policies, namely the fiscal one, is able to directly impact effective demand [...] preventing insufficient effective demand. Thirdly, macroeconomic policies, together with the political and juridical stances, build the society's institutional structure. The more prone-to-business, stable, credible and transparent such environment is, the more it would favor good and trustful expectations, stimulating investments. (p. 153)

The State must issue the signals that markets cannot furnish, by creating a stable and safe economic environment that shows the directions it pursues to generate full employment and equitable income share. Thus, a State gains coordination through: (i) institutional reforms to improve the channels that connect agents, leading to better information provision and offsetting income inequalities; (ii) economic planning to coordinate conventions and expectations of the economy's future path;

(iii) a day-to-day concern with the circumstances, to face the failures of the monetary economy (Carvalho 1992; Arestis et al. 2016). The government coordination of agents' expectations is required to manage its daily operation and to lead the agents toward the society's intentions.

In terms of FP, Keynes (1980a) argued that the public spending should be split into two budgets: the ordinary (current) and the capital budget. The latter covers discretionary investment expenditures, mainly those made by no one if the State does not move them, in a long-term investment plan that is a device to smooth economic cycles (Arestis et al. 2016). The State must complement, and not compete with, the private sector, creating a crowding-in effect. The State's long-term plan coordinates the agents' conventions, as it is a long-run commitment to accomplish and sustain an adequate level of aggregate demand, showing the "state's readiness to compensate for reductions in private investments with its own expenditures" (Keynes 1980a, p. 322).

Accordingly, investment in infrastructure is the most adequate for the capital budget. Many studies highlight features of this kind of investment, such as its long-term payback, its huge cost, its relevance for generating gains on productivity, lower production costs, and better profits (Aschauer 1989; Calderón and Sérven 2004), as well as its improvements to the income share and poverty reduction (Rozas and Sánches 2004; Calderón and Sérven 2002). Thus, infrastructure investment has a dual character as it has a long-term payback and high costs to private firms that make them, however it provides several essential elements for improving firms' profits.

There are two further aspects of the Post-Keynesian FP. The current budget embraces the public services the State furnishes and it should be in surplus or in equilibrium all the time so that the public budget reaches intertemporal equilibrium. Moreover, FP is a tool to implement institutional reforms, particularly income ones through taxation and incomes policy, improving the consumption propensity and social stability.

In terms of monetary policy (MP), Keynes (1973) saw it bearing a hard task—to set a financial system yield curve, which is not an opportunity cost to productive investment. That strongly depends on agents' response to the Central Bank (CB) as its interest rate works on the agents' speculative money demand. In financial markets, agents bargain assets to profit through the difference between the actual and future interest rates. They first consider the CB rate, which is the basic rate of return of the economy; depending on what they consider will happen to it, they negotiate debt.

The CB controls its interest rate to impact other variables such as price, exchange rate, and expectations. Yet, this tool is considered by the agents as a fundamental rate of return. Then, CB has, in its operations, an eye at the aspects it oversees and another eye at the agents' expectations. In this sense, conventions are key for a successful MP. Given uncertainty, if conventions are misguided, agents have even less information of what expect of the movements between the current and future interest rates. When the CB changes its interest rate without considering the agents' expectations, it may stop agents from negotiating debt; thereby, in an extreme case, there is the ineffectiveness of the MP, as Keynes (1973) illustrated:

> a monetary policy which strikes public opinion as being experimental in character or easily liable to change may fail in its objective of greatly reducing the long-term rate of interest [...] The same policy, [...] on the other hand, may prove easily successful if it appeals to public opinion as being reasonable and practicable and in the public interest, rooted in strong conviction [...], and promoted by an authority unlikely to be superseded [...] the rate of interest is a highly conventional, rather than a highly psychological, phenomenon (p. 203).

Hence, the financial system yield curve is a conventional phenomenon, set by reciprocal deals between the CB and agents in the financial system. These negotiations first consider the basic rate of interest and if the CB is reliable, there is room for them to occur. Different opinions about the future interest rate make agents speculate. Still, diverse opinions found themselves in the convention that the CB would not stablish its future interest rate based on non-reasonable ideas. If the convention is that the CB has no basis and coherence in setting its interest rate, the shared belief would probably understand that the MP is misleading.

The other MP tool is regulation. It is laws/rules that stipulate what can be done in the financial markets. Like the interest rate, regulation should be stable, because it directly impacts agents' behavior in financial markets. If the CB continuously switches the regulatory framework, it sets an uncertain environment where agents become confused about which business is allowed.

So, MP should be conducted with parsimony, pragmatism, transparency, and a kind of ruled discretion. CB interest rate does not help reaching full employment at any cost, but in accordance with the economic circumstances. Also, if the regulatory framework changes a lot, it constitutes bad conventions. Conventions about the current and future behaviors of MP are fundamental to its own success and, reciprocally, a well conducted MP is essential to build fine conventions.

In terms of the exchange rate policy (ERP), Ferrari-Filho (2006) argues that Keynes suggested a managed exchange rate that could change regarding the circumstances. A stable currency brings at least three benefits: (i) permits better estimations of the production costs of imported inputs; (ii) allows businesspeople, seeking to sell tradable goods to external or internal markets, to improve their revenue calculus; and (iii) stabilizes the real wage in foreign money, enabling finer assessment of the domestic demand. Thus, a managed exchange rate pursues stability and furnishes predictability to entrepreneurs (Arestis et al. 2016).

However, exchange rates are not easily managed. On that, Keynes (1980b) had two concerns: first, the ERP should not kidnap the CB interest rate, what would happen if the exchange rate management uses the interest rate to attract foreign financial capital. If so, the interest rate volatility tends to rise, leading to a higher opportunity cost to productive investment. The second concern deals with the autonomy of the CB interest rate given by capital controls over capital flows. Without capital controls, the management the exchange rate solely relies on the interest rate, elevating its level and making it more volatile.

The exchange rate stability is also a MP's goal, since all external flux changes the liquidity conditions at the money market. Again, this feature stresses the need of coordinated economic policies, which is the key to construct good conventions about the economy's future trail. If the government does not swap its economic policy in a peremptory manner, within this economic policy framework, good conventions are expected.

Having argued about the links between government's actions and conventions, we analyze next the Brazilian economy slump after 2011. Over 2003–2010, Brazilian economy passed through a boom. From 2011, but mainly since 2014 onwards, Brazil has been suffering its worst recession ever. How the economic policies and their influence on conventions help explaining what happened to Brazil is the topic of the next section.

4 The Role of Conventions in the Brazilian Economic Slump: 2011–2016

To understand Brazil's economic downturn over 2011–2016, a brief analysis about the previous period, 2003–2010, is needed. Brazil went through a full economic cycle, being the period 2004–2008 the boom phase, with 4.8% annual average growth. That period came along with a benign external scenario, which improved Brazilian exports by 105%, and the trade terms by 12.5%, chiefly because of the expansion of mining and agriculture commodities' international prices. In the financial sphere, international liquidity grew until 2008, when the great financial crisis (GFC) emerged (BCB 2017).

Two main factors influenced the Brazilian growth from 2004 onward: the external scenario and the strengthening of the domestic market. The latter was due to: (i) the pass-through effect of the positive external context to the internal market; (ii) the minimum wage real appreciation; (iii) the social policy of income transfer; and (iv) the increase in the credit/GDP ratio. These elements fortified households' consumption, which met the installed productive capacity utilized in the manufacturing industry by 79.7% in 2003, whereas in 2008, when the GFC started affecting Brazil, its occupation was around 83% (Ipedata 2017), a level incapable of exerting inflationary pressures on the labor market. Reasons (ii) and (iii) arose as Lula da Silva's government (2003–2010) widened old social and wage policies to enhance the internal market and reduce poverty and income inequality; (iv) occurred as the government implemented credit policies, lifting the credit/GDP ratio from 25% to 40% over 2003–2008 (Ipeadata 2017).

However, Brazil's boom was not investment driven, but export- and consumption-led. Over 2004–2008, the investment rate widened by 11.9%; still, it departed from a low level, 17.3% of the GDP in 2004, reaching 19.4% in 2008; during 2003–2007, the investment/GDP ratio was always below 18.1% (Ipeadata 2017), insufficient to guaranteeing a sustainable growth. So, Brazil grew while there was idle productive capacity to attend exports and consumption.

In 2008, the GFC erupted and affected Brazil, with growth decreasing by 0.2% in 2009, but it increased by 7.5% in 2010 and 3.9% in 2011 (Ipeadata 2017). Brazil's recovery, according to Arestis and Terra (2015), was due to: (i) the heated domestic market in view of increasing wages and income transfers; (ii) exports to developing countries, chiefly to China; and (iii) the economic policy measures in a counter cyclical stance after the end of 2008.[4] These measures boosted the aggregate demand and the investment rate, which reached 20.5% of the GDP in 2010 (Ipeadata 2017). Furthermore, this demand-led recovery was again based on idle industrial installed capacity—in 2009 and 2010 their rates were 80.6% and 83.3%, respectively (Ipeadata 2017). Again, consumption and the external sector drove Brazil's economy without having the investment levels at the rate required for achieving sustainable growth. Having this in mind, we now analyze the causes of the meltdown of the Brazilian economy from 2014 and subsequently.[5]

Exchange Rate Policy and Conventions

Starting with the ERP, the Brazilian currency was kept overvalued in real terms almost over the full period 2011–2016. Regulations on capital flows and foreign exchange derivatives were adopted by the

[4]Arestis and Terra (2015, p. 534) itemized the counter cyclical measures the Brazilian government launched. On the counter cyclical role of public banks, see Chap. "The Brazilian Credit Market During the Great Recession" of this book.

[5]The period 2011–2016 comprehends two Presidents, Dilma Rousseff and Michel Temer. Rousseff was in charge from January 2011 to April 2016, when an impeachment took her off the cabinet. Then, in April 2016, Temer became President. Over this period, Rousseff took most of the economic policy measures; thereby, we focus on the actions she ventured.

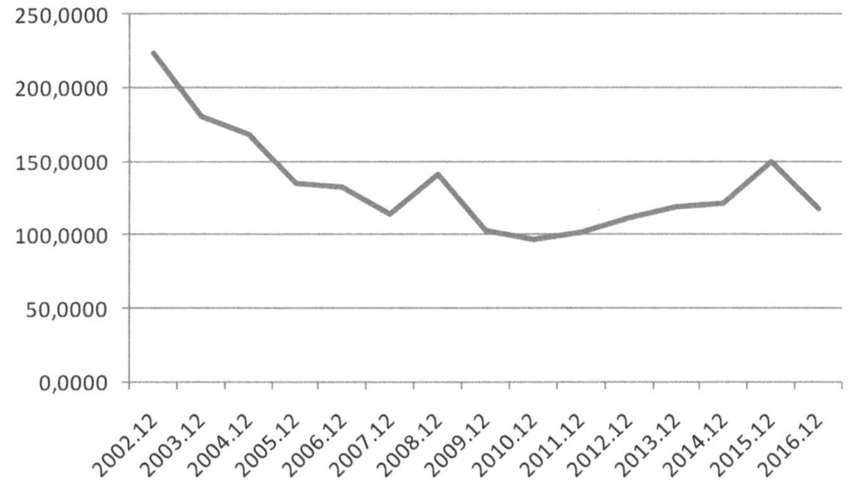

Fig. 1 Brazilian/US$ real effective exchange rate, 2002–2016 (2010 = 100). *Source* Ipeadata (2017) Authors' own elaboration

government (De Paula and Prates 2015), but it was not sufficient to eliminate the great currency appreciation observed during the last years. Figure 1 reports that at the beginning of 2011, the real exchange rate (RER) attained its highest level, with a soft devaluation starting in 2012. This overvalued RER brought the following consequences to Brazil: Smashed profits in the tradeable goods sector, especially so given that there was a ceiling for investments in the manufacturing industry and for productivity gains in the whole economy.[6] This process had a large brunt, going from low investment/GDP ratio to the re-escalation of the primary sector both in the Brazilian GDP and exports (Bresser-Pereira et al 2015; Rossi and Mello 2016).[7] Investment reached 20.9%

[6]There were different sectorial impacts of the overvalued RER. The greater international prices of mining and agriculture commodities reduced the RER in these sectors. However, the manufacturing industry (like the textile, electronics, capital goods industries, etc.) was badly affected.

[7]Rossi and Mello (2016) saw a contradiction at the modernization of the consumption standard for a significant part of the Brazilian population. As a necessary condition to overcome the underdevelopment and the regressive production of the country, the supply that met this new consumption pattern came from imports enabled by the overvalued RER and so the Brazilian industry did not respond to it.

of the GDP in 2013 (Ipeadata 2017), the highest during 2003–2016, and dropped to 16.4% in 2016 (IBGE 2017).

On the one hand, Gala (2008) argues that the manufacturing firms are the most dynamics because of their increasing returns of scale and technology-intensive products, features that enhance their learning-by-doing process and technological progress. On the other hand, an overvalued currency climbs the real wage in foreign money, changing the tradeable/non-tradeable trade terms in disfavor of the first, which greatly concerns the manufacturing industry. So, the overvalued currency implies profit rate reductions, in particular at the industrial sector, since non-tradable goods, salaries included, are cost of production of tradable goods.

Since Rousseff's government kept the credit, social and wage policies introduced by Lula da Silva, her government had an incoherence, that Lula da Silva had already had, between the ERP and the socioeconomic-institutional reforms encompassing the policies of minimum wage real valorization, credit expansion, and income transfers, which changed the consumption patterns in the country. These policies contradictorily enticed the elevation of the domestic consumption concomitantly with the reduction of the profit rate due to the overvalued RER and the real wage appreciation higher than the productivity gains.

The currency appreciation increases real wages in the short run, in accordance with the intentions of social policy. However, it smashes the profit rates in many industrial sectors, discouraging investments which are crucial to expand the supply capacity. So, in the medium and long term, smaller supply levels relate themselves to smaller employment levels. Moreover, since the productivity gains in the industry are bigger than in the other sectors due to both static and dynamic scales economies and industry-related technological progress (Bresser-Pereira et al. 2015), smashed industrial profits lead to lower investments and productivity gains in the whole economy as well as to smaller increases in real wages.

Besides, it is worth noticing that there was an increase in Brazil's average salary accompanying the minimum wage real valorization. Thereby, along with a better income share, a greater demand for labor-intensive services emerged. As Brazil went through a demographic transition in which the economic active population stagnated, the larger demand for services started pressurizing the labor market, culminating to a constant salary expansion (Resende et al. 2013).

This contradictory signaling of economic policies generated optimistic conventions, investment, and productivity only in the sectors attached to primary commodities. The flat profit and investment rates in the manufacturing industry did not trigger a production expansion to satisfy the larger domestic consumption, which was met by imports and fulfilling empty productive capacity. Thus, the economy grew while there was idle capacity, a living on borrowed time economic growth. Even with the progress of the primary exports, Brazil's current account deteriorated from a 2011 deficit equal to 2.95% of the GDP to 4.24% in 2014 (BCB 2017).[8] This scenario pinpointed future elevation of the external fragility, depriving investment because agents' confidence declined as conventions identified a deteriorated future external position of Brazil.

Nonetheless, from October 2010 on, the government broadened its control of capital and foreign exchange derivative measures it introduced in October 2009, to restrain the influx of external capital into the Brazilian economy. After starting her term in January 2011, Rousseff started an ERP that managed the trend of the exchange rate devaluation, hoping to make the Brazilian manufacturing industry reenter the international markets through exchange rate competitiveness.[9] Beyond Rousseff's ERP, the lower Real was due to some other factors, like the reversion of positions of investors fostered by the foreign exchange derivatives regulation, the reduction of the policy rate and the deterioration of the external context because of the euro crisis by mid-2011. Thus, in December 2011, the nominal exchange rate was devalued by 12.6% in relation to its December 2010 value; in 2012, it had an additional 8.9% devaluation. In terms of the effective RER, those

[8]The enhanced current account in 2016 (-1.31% of GDP) due to the recession emerged from 2014 and onward (BCB 2017).

[9]This and other MP and FP's measures were Rousseff's attempt to limber the New Macroeconomic Consensus macroeconomic policy practiced in Brazil. The Brazilian media called that attempt the New Macroeconomic Matrix..

percentages were 5.4% and 9.8%, respectively (Ipeadata 2017). Still, the 23.3% nominal exchange rate devaluation between 2011 and 2013 was insufficient to offset the 2003–2010 56.8% RER valuation (Ipeadata 2017).

The BCB took measures to attain the mild currency devaluation, namely controls on capital flows and on foreign exchange derivatives, foreign reserves accumulation, and hedge contracts through exchange rate swap operations. Capital controls began in 2011, when the government rose taxes on short-term capital influx. However, the government started changing the rule as per the international liquidity. It implemented capital controls, then elevated the levy and briefly afterward retired the rule; all in a very short period between 2011 and 2012. This attitude made clear that its actions were temporary and did not follow any long-term strategy. Following what was happening in the international front, regulation in Brazil changed too much in a short period of time, disturbing what agents expect of the future. In such a case, what should be done to frame good conventions in an unstable context is not changing the measures as fast as the world swings, but making them stable. Otherwise, expectations would switch a lot too, making it harder the occurrence of investments.

Notwithstanding the swinging capital controls, the buffer offered by foreign reserves was inflated over 2011–2014: it augmented from US$288.575 million in 2010 to US$362.551 million in 2014 (BCB 2017). Because of the difference between the Brazilian base rate, named Selic, and the world average interest rate, Brazil pays a higher return to buy foreign money than it receives by investing its American Dollars in bonds worldwide. As over 2011–2014, the fiscal situation in Brazil got worse. The burden of hoarding foreign money ended up being too heavy for a deteriorating FP. Agents knew that and their conventions built disheartened expectations of what to expect from the match between the exchange rate and fiscal policies in Brazil.

Furthermore, the BCB supply of hedge contracts, which had been used in Brazil since 1995, was subsequently used in a larger scale after 2011. These contracts were the main method the ERP controlled the trend of the national currency in Brazil, aiming at mildly devaluating it.[10] The BCB sold short-term contracts hedging the agents against exchange rate losses. Furthermore, with this operation, the BCB eased agents' expectations of variations on the value of the national currency so that it could manage a smoother exchange rate.

Yet, as the intention of the BCB is to protect the agents against currency devaluations, whenever it happens, BCB affords it. As the nominal exchange rate fell 34% over 2011–2014, the BCB had costs with that policy. Still, the fast elevation of the amount of exchange rate swaps contracts was another issue. Arestis and Terra (2015) report that Brazilian government had almost US$100 billion in this sort of liabilities in 2014, nearly one-third of the country's foreign reserves.[11] The bulk of liabilities was raised up to a significant portion of the Brazilian assets, and once again what would be a good figure to agents' confidence started being a misleading and costly to the economic policy.

In short, the credit, social, and wage policies together with exports boosted the Brazilian growth, but the ERP maintained an overvalued currency, whose consequences were smashed profits and the worsening of the current account. Capital controls, foreign reserves accumulation and hedge contract policies offered contradictory signals insofar as they were unstable or negatively influenced the fiscal situation. Likewise, the overvalued currency led to the re-escalation of the primary sector both in the GDP and in the exports, diminishing the productivity gains of the economy. Consequently, agents' confidence declined given the incoherence between these policies: Consumption was fostered by social policies, but investment was inhibited by an overvalued RER (Arestis and Terra 2015). These features consolidated a maximum limit to the investment rate and, consequently, to the dynamics of economic growth.

---

[10]The BCB also issued a so-called reverse exchange rate derivative to curb the currency appreciation. As this tool is commonly used to avoid devaluations of the exchange rate, the one used to restrain valuations was called 'reverse' swaps.

[11]These hedge contracts do not deliver American Dollars to their holders and so they do not let the foreign reserves volatile. The BCB pays in *Real* the amount equivalent to the change in the value of the exchange rate. Nevertheless, the contracts are a liability of the BCB and so they impact the public debt and the FP.

Lastly, 2015 had intense exchange rate depreciation, around 47% (Ipedata 2017). Brazil suffered an overshooting, though the world was not going through any similar problems. It was a Brazilian issue, an outcome of conventions that understood that Rousseff had a misleading macroeconomic policy framework—as it was stressed in the previous sections, coordination and coherence among economic policies are needed to generate good conventions, which are crucial to boost investment in an uncertainty context. Although the economic recession was already there in 2015, conventions disheartened by the political crisis and the judicial operation against corruption and money laundering crimes that took place in Brazil by the end of 2014 onward also contributed to the 47% currency devaluation that happened that year—an overshooting bigger than the one Brazil had during the 2008 international economic crisis.

Conventions and Fiscal Policy Problems

After 2011, Brazilian economy started feeling the path of the world economic policies (Euro Crisis, Quantitative Easing provoking depreciation of the developed countries' currencies, China "New Normal," the higher competition on international markets, etc.) and of its own problems. Even accounting for a currency devaluation, its magnitude was not sufficient to offset the fall in the exports, that was so important to the dynamics of the Brazilian economic growth years before. Without the external drive, FP was due to foster growth.

When Rousseff's cabinet started in 2011, as a counter cyclical measure, it pursued decreasing primary surpluses, which went from 2.89% to 1.74% of GDP between 2011 and 2013 (Ipeadata 2017). Then, some manufacturing sectors (automobile, household appliances, building material, and basic basket goods, etc.) gained tax allowances; similar allowances emerged to the taxes on the wage bill of the economy. The tax allowance started for a few sectors of the manufacturing industry, but it was spread to other sectors in a confused manner, following lobby pressures. The lack of strategy, lobby-guided, and in a confused manner by which the tax allowance policy was implemented, jeopardized optimistic conventions.

Moreover, in 2011 Rousseff launched the second phase of the *Program for Growth Acceleration* (PAC), a four-year plan of public investments mainly in infrastructure (such as public sanitation, housing, transports, energy and hydric resources). The Program had features of a Keynesian investment policy as it was a plan of public investments, previously announced to the public opinion, lasting for the medium term and could be used in a counter cyclical manner. The PAC was expected to flag the government guaranteeing a minimum level of future aggregate demand and improvement of infrastructure. Altogether, it would beckon conventions supporting optimistic expectations that encourage investments, however, economic, and political problems avoided it. Resende et al. (2013) explain:

> the rules of spending public resources, the managerial State capacity, institutional norms and legal framework that set a relatively bureaucratic structure to the Brazilian National State and make it hard the expansion of the public outgoings (in particular, investments), the bidding process and the public-private partnerships. Beyond of not making several of its endeavors, PAC did not imply a substantial increasing in the public investment, which standstill around 2.5% of the GDP. Moreover, given the public sector primary surplus target, there is no available resources for a reasonable enhancement of the State capability of investing. Neither the government presents an organized capital budget, capable of fulfilling the gaps of the private investment and assuring the heightening of the infrastructure, competitiveness of the domestic products, positive expectations of future income and aggregate demand [...] public investment is not made in a planned and transparent mood to coordinate the expectations and strategies of private investments. (pp. 106–107)

Hence, the FP issued contradictory signals. It both pursued primary surpluses instead of effective counter cyclical outgoings and had an ambitious program of investment that, if fully accomplished, would jeopardize the primary surplus, although there was a reduction in primary fiscal surpluses during Rousseff's government; but it was not sufficient to settle an effective counter cyclical FP. Moreover, mainstream policy prescriptions turned Brazil unable to produce a capital budget as big as required by the PAC. Over 2011–2013, Brazilian government made primary surpluses of 2.89% in 2011, and 1.74% of GDP in 2013, whereas its interest payments summed out nearly 4.5–5.5% of the GDP as the restrictive MP practiced in Brazil, a common feature of the Inflation Targeting Regime, which required huge amounts of resources to be affordable.

Such a policy was incoherent with an expansionary FP aimed at financing public investments, with an income sharing policy and with measures seeking to augment the aggregate consumption. Furthermore, the tax allowance damaged both the primary surplus and the level of disposable resources to finance PAC investments. Instead of just giving up on the resources related to the tax allowance, the government should have gathered them to finance PAC expenditures since it directly impacted effective demand as well as it had a greater fiscal multiplier than the one emerging from tax allowances. Since public investment did not increase and private investment did not respond to the tax allowance policy,[12] two demand drivers, exports and investment, slowed down, reducing taxes, and even more so as the economic activity was getting cooler.

The continuity of tax allowances to the manufacturing industry as part of the counter cyclical fiscal measures was also withdrawing resources from the Brazilian Treasury. Brazil's public finance commenced suffering, first a stagnation of levy collection and, from 2014 onward, a strong reduction of public revenues. Nevertheless, public expenditures did not follow the same trend of the tax gathering. Over 2011–2014, they increased and so the fiscal condition of the Brazilian economy deteriorated quickly. BCB (2017) confirms that the Federal government (including the BCB) went from a primary surplus of 1.74% of the GDP in 2013, to a deficit of 0.49% in 2014, 1.77% in 2015, and 2.45% in 2016. As it could not be otherwise, the general government[13]

[12]Aggregate investment had lower quarter variations from 2012 onward, as IBGE (2017) reports: 2011, 7.37% of quarterly average variation, 2012, 2%, 2013, 4.85%—a soft recovery—, 2014, - 1.47% and 2015, -10%.

[13]General government circumscribes counties, provinces and Union. However, Union, i.e., the Federal government, owns the clear majority of debt. In Brazil, more than 95% of the gross debt was a liability of the Union over 2006–2016.

gross public debt swelled from 53.7% of the GDP in December 2012, to 65.5% in December 2015.

In view of that, conventions about the trend of FP in Brazil were pessimistic, even being the actions it afforded that meant to sustain the economic activity. Moreover, contradictory beckons issued by the FP (primary surpluses and tax allowances along with the PAC) also jeopardized conventions. Public opinion wondered whether the FP's intentions were set in the right direction, yet they were too costly and crumbled the fiscal situation, resulting in the upturn of the public debt. Anyhow, not only economic reasons accounted for the bummer conventions hovering over Brazil. A political crisis that emerged in 2013 and lasted until the impeachment of Rousseff, in April 2016, also bolstered the idea that public finance under her government was disordered.

By the end 2014, Rousseff won her second presidential election and started a new term in January 2015. Now that the fiscal situation in Brazil was so downgraded, Rousseff changed the strategy and decided to promote a fiscal consolidation via austerity at the time of an economic deceleration. As Arestis and Terra (2015) argue, these measures had a market-based nature given that the policy actions of Rousseff's first government were interpreted like too interventionist. Still, there were two attempts of reaching fiscal consolidation; the first was a fiscal shock proposed by Minister Joaquim Levy, and the second, a gradual consolidation undertaken by Minister Nelson Barbosa. They were not successful. Both plans buoyed the conventions that Brazil was melting down and that the market-based fiscal consolidation would withdraw public investment. Conventions were already not good; still they have not got anything to back any chance of healing with the fiscal measures the government was executing after 2015.

That was the fiscal input to the Brazilian crisis. The country's economic shrinkage amounted to 0.1% in 2014, -3.8% in 2015, and -3.6% in 2016 of the growth rate. Conventions did not change when the fiscal consolidation policy entered into the scene in 2015 as well as they did not get better after Rousseff's impeachment, as Brazil's economy continued its downward path in 2016. Rather than fiscal consolidation, conventions are looking for demand drivers to promote sustainable growth, a role that public investment is expected to

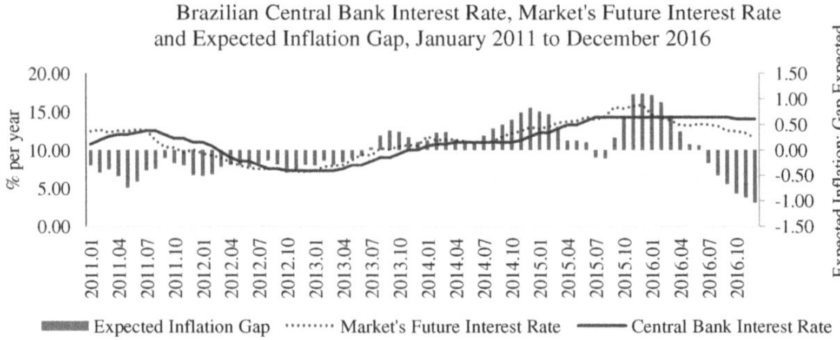

Fig. 2 Brazilian Central Bank Interest Rate, Market's Future Interest Rate and Expected Inflation Gap, January 2011 to December 2016. *Source* Authors' own elaboration based on BCB (2017). *Note* Expected Inflation Gap is the monthly expected Inflation minus the series' average

accomplish; otherwise, an absence of prone-to-invest convention outcomes would occur, given that expectations of future have no upholds. In an uncertain world, backless conventions mean no investment, unemployment, and economic downturn.

An Erratic Monetary Policy

Under Rousseff, the MP was managed in a diverse way in relation to past governments since the Inflation Targeting was initiated in 1999. Although the Regime was still in force, a sort of its mollification was tried by the BCB, which raised its interest rate up to 12.50% per year in 2011, but by the end of 2011 until October 2012, it cut its interest rate to 7.25%, the lowest rate in decades.

Figure 2 shows that the market rate followed BCB's intentions and its future rate (one year ahead) was, then, at Selic's current level. This shows that the MP was successful in building positive conventions about the future of its own policy. However, at the beginning of 2013, the market rate started decoupling from Selic, signaling that conventions were changing because of expected higher inflation, which obliged the BCB to raise the interest rate; so, in the dawn of 2014, conventions of higher future inflation were calmed. Still, by mid-2014, conventions saw higher inflation again and so, and because actual inflation was expanding, the market rate increased. However, perhaps due to the electoral period, the BCB later raised its rate, what culminated on more deteriorated conventions on future inflation. When the BCB finally moved its interest rate up, conventions were so sensible that compelled it to an intense climb. If productive investment was already tender, the higher opportunity cost of the financial system yield curve made it even harder to occur.

What has gone wrong with the BCB MP? Brazil historically has two characteristics in terms of the conduct of MP. First, because of the 1980s hyperinflation period, Brazilian population is too sensitive to variations of inflations rates, what makes price-makers start protecting their yield by moving their prices upwards. This fear of inflation can be seen through the automatic contracted price readjustments overspread throughout the economy, which adjusts actual prices by past inflation (like rents, energy, schools, and the minimum wage). Thus, the ongoing convention in Brazil commonly bears fear of inflation. Second, the financial system in Brazil, chiefly the concentrated banking system, has a strong communication power and easily helps forming conventions. This implies a very-sensible-to-inflation market rate, what makes Selic very responsive to inflation too. This is promoted by the Inflation Targeting Regime, in which the interest rate is the exclusive tool to inflation targeting. So, Selic is very much sensible to inflation, expected inflation and conventions that remarkably fear inflation, making it hard for the BCB to drive a prone-to-investment Selic.

Thus, if the BCB's intention is to reduce the Selic and if it makes it happen on conventions that the lower interest rate would continue in the future, it should take full care of inflation expectations. In Keynesian terms, this would be the construction of the guidance necessary to ground conventions, building an institutional environment keen to productive investments. Though, to accommodate inflation, Rousseff's government started freezing administered prices, mainly oil and its products, as well as changing contracts of energy producers in a unilateral negotiation. It also excluded some products of the inflation index to smooth its trend and transformed the superior range of the inflation target in the pursued target. BCB undertook those actions without accounting for the public's expectations on the economic policy goals. Contrarily, the government insisted that it was seeking the inflation target blank, that the exchange rate was entirely market determined, and that the fiscal situation was fine. Given that, the MP was erratic.

After seeing for a while that the scenario was not as fine as communicated, conventions about Brazil pointed to a hazy future. This explains why Brazil has taken so long to rebuild positive conventions on MP and on the expected future inflation. As Fig. 2 shows, this happened by mid-2016 and just after that convention that enabled the BCB to reduce the Selic, which is still high, paying the price of leading conventions. The fiscal consolidation programs plastered public demand drivers, making Brazilian dive faster into the recession. At the monetary management sphere, Selic's level worked as if the diving air tube was filled with rocks. Investment, in turn, was reduced.

Further Issues: "Lava Jato" Lawsuit and the Political Crisis

In addition to the contradictions within the macroeconomic policies, and between them and the institutional reforms, there were two further non-economic problems reinforcing the Brazilian economic problems. The -3.8% growth rate in 2015 gave room for a political crisis and the impeachment of Rousseff, based on a doubtful crime against fiscal rules. Even after her fall, with President Temer in charge, the political crisis is still enduring.

Moreover, the so-called Lava Jato lawsuit has been the biggest judicial operation against corruption and money laundering crimes in Brazil since when it began in 2014. It investigates criminal relations between political parties, politicians, and big corporations, and has fueled the mentioned political crisis. Furthermore, the lawsuit investigates giant companies, such as Petrobras and Oderbretch, which account for a significant part of investment in the country.

These non-economic facts are fomenting conventions of volatility in Brazilian politics as it is uncertain if the current set of politicians reaches the end of their terms. Consequently, it only generates short-term policies, what means that fiscal consolidation produces reduction of public investment, whereas private investment is reduced by the companies directly influenced by the "Lava-Jato". The fragility of the current government, in view of these two non-economic issues, curbs the economic leadership. Again, conventions fulfill prospects of a bad future, making liquidity preferred to investment, and pushing the economic growth down and the employment rate down.

5 Final Remarks

Brazil has been going through its bitter moment in history. Economic contradictions and more recently a period of economic and political problems have provoked conventions that dishearten the expectations of the country's economic future. The issues rest in contradictions within the macroeconomic policy mix and between them and the institutional reforms, as also debated in Chap. "Brazil at Crossroads: A Critical Assessment of Developmentalist Policies" of this book. Over 2011–2016, noticeably between 2014 and 2016, the political crisis and the impact of "Lava Jato" also heated the controversial atmosphere in the country and casted despaired conventions and expectations.

In contrast to what the government has been doing, conventions of a better future would only emerge if agents saw the economic policy as trustful and aimed at building demand drivers, notably public investment, monetary and exchange rate stability, and good institutional environment. These Keynesian and Post-Keynesian policies were not implemented in Brazil, although some critics argue that the failed experience of Rousseff's macroeconomic policy was Keynesian. As Resende et al. (2013) stated, this was not the case. Thus, the Keynesian economic policies this paper presents are the right choice to foment conventions that would forge expectations of a better future. If policies, such as the orthodox fiscal austerity and the restrictive inflation targeting, are still in place, and diverse from Keynesian economics, we would agree with the conventional view that no great economic possibilities for our grandchild are in place.

References

Arestis, P., & Terra, F. H. B. (2015). Economic policies to improve the current state of the Brazilian economy. *Challenge Magazine, 58*(6), 532–549.

Arestis, P., Ferrari-Filho, F., & Terra, F. H. B. (2016). Post Keynesian macroeconomic regime policy. In F. Ferrari Filho, & F. H. B. Terra (Eds.), *Keynes: Ensaios sobre os 80 Anos da Teoria Geral*. Porto Alegre: Tomo.

Aschauer, D. A. (1989). Is public expenditure productive? *Journal of Monetary Economics, 23*, 177–200.

Banco Central Do Brasil (BCB). (2017). *Séries Temporais do Banco Central do Brasil*. Brasília: BCB. Available at http://www.bcb.gov.br/pt-br/#!/n/SERIESTEMPORAIS.

Bresser-pereira, L. C., Oreiro, J. L., & Marconi, N. (2015). *Developmental macroeconomics*. London: Routledge.

Calderón, C., & Servén, L. (2002). *The output cost of Latin America's infrastructure gap* (Working Paper No. 186). Santiago: Central Bank of Chile.

Calderón, C., & Servén, L. (2004). *The effects of infrastructure development on growth and income distribution* (Working Paper No. 270). Santiago: Central Bank of Chile.

Carvalho, F. J. C. (1992). *Mr Keynes and the post keynesians*. Aldershot: Edward Elgar.

Carvalho, F. J. C. (2014). *Expectativas, Incerteza e convenções*. BNDES-Biblioteca Digital.

Carvalho, F. J. C. (2015). Keynes on expectations, uncertainty and defensive behavior. *Brazilian Keynesian Review, 1*(1), 44–54.

Davis, J. J. (2005). M. Keynes on history and convention. In G. Harcourt & P. Riach (Eds.), *A 'Second Edition' of the General Theory* (Vol. 2, pp. 149–162). London: Routledge.

De Paula, L. F., & Prates, D. (2015). Cuenta de capitales y la regulación de derivados del mercado de divisas: la experiencia reciente de Brasil. *Investigación Económica, LXXIV*(291), 79–115.

Dequech, D. (1999). On some arguments for the rationality of conventional behaviour under uncertainty: concepts, applicability and criticisms. In C. Sardoni & P. Kriesler (Eds.), *Keynes, post-keynesianism and political economy*. London: Routledge.

Dow, S. C. (2010). Keynes on knowledge, expectations and rationality. In *Center of Capitalism and Society Conference on Microfoundations for Modern Macroeconomics*. New York.

Ferrari-Filho, F., & Conceição, O. A. C. (2005). The concept of uncertainty in post Keynesian theory and in institutional economics. *Journal of Economic Issues, XXXIX*(3), 579–594.

Ferrari-Filho, F. (2006). *Política Comercial, Taxa de Câmbio e Moeda Internacional: uma análise a partir de Keynes*. Porto Alegre: UFRGS.

Gala, P. (2008). Real exchange rate levels and economic development: Theoretical analysis and empirical evidence. *Cambridge Journal of Economics, 32*, 273–288.

Instituto Brasileiro de Geografia e Estatística (IBGE). (2017). *Séries Históricas e Estatísticas*. Brasília, Brazil. Available at http://seriesestatisticas.ibge.gov.br/lista_tema.aspx?op=0&de=75&no=12.

Keynes, J. M. (1973). The general theory of employment, interest and money. *The collected writings of John Maynard Keynes* (Vol. 7). London: Macmillan.

Keynes, J. M. (1980a). Activities 1940–1946: Shaping the Post-War world—employment and commodities. *The collected writings of John Maynard Keynes*, (Vol. XXVII). London: Macmillan.

Keynes, J. M. (1980b). Activities 1940–1944: Shaping the Post-War world—The clearing union. *The collected writings of John Maynard Keynes*, (Vol. XXV). London, UK: Macmillan.

Keynes, J. M. (1982). The monetary policy of the Labour Party. *The collected writings of John Maynard Keynes*, (Vol. XXI). London: Macmillan.

IPEADATA. (2017). *Dados Macroeconomia*. Brasília, Brazil: IPEA. Available at http//:www.ipeadata.gov.br.

Marccuzzo, M. C. (2010). Whose welfare state? Beveridge versus Keynes. In R. Backhouse & T. Nishizawa (Eds.), *No wealth but life—Welfare economics and the welfare state in Britain, 1880–1945* (pp. 189–206). Cambridge, UK: Cambridge University Press.

Minsky, H. (1986). *Stabilizing an unstable economy*. New Heaven: Twentieth Century Fund Report.

Modenesi, A. M., Modenesi, R. L., & Martions, N. M. (2012). *Convention, interest rates and monetary policy: A post-Keynesian-French-conventions-school approach*. Rio de Janeiro, Brazil: VII Encontro Internacional da Associação Keynesiana Brasileira.

Plihon, D. (1995). A ascensão das finanças especulativas. *Economia e Sociedade, 5*, 61–78.

Resende, M. F. C., Rocha, I., Camuri, P., & Borghi, R. (2013). Câmbio, Salários, Política Fiscal e Coordenação do Investimento. In IV Dossiê da Associação Keynesiana Brasileira.

Rossi, P., & Mello, G. (2016). Componentes Macroeconômicos e Estruturais da Crise Brasileira: o Subdesenvolvimento Revisitado. *Brazilian Keynesian Review, 2*(2), 252–263.

Rozas, P., & Sánchez, R. (2004). *Desarrollo de infraestructura y crecimiento económico: revisión conceptual.* Santiago: ECLAC.

The Impact of the Global Financial Crisis on the Brazilian Stock Market

Bruno Pontes de Arruda and Michel Ferreira Cardia Haddad

1 Introduction

This chapter examines the impact of the Global Financial Crisis (GFC) of 2007–2008 over the Brazilian stock market and contextualises its developments, encompassing a period of almost ten years after the beginning of the above-mentioned crisis. The chapter has two main goals. Firstly, it analyses important negative movements seen in the Brazilian stock market in the recent period of nearly two decades; secondly, it tests the hypothesis of financial contagion from financial markets in the USA to a number of important Brazilian stock market sectors.

Michel F. C. Haddad would like to thank CAPES (Coordination for the Improvement of Higher Education Personnel) as well as the Cambridge Trust for the financial support to develop this research.

B.P. de Arruda
Bradesco BBI, São Paulo, Brazil
e-mail: bruno.arruda@bradescobbi.com.br

M.F.C. Haddad (✉)
University of Cambridge, England, United Kingdom
e-mail: mfch2@cam.ac.uk

P. Arestis et al. (eds.), *The Brazilian Economy since the Great Financial Crisis of 2007/2008*, https://doi.org/10.1007/978-3-319-64885-9_11

The Brazilian stock market main index increased substantially since the 2000s. However, the GFC suddenly stopped its sustained and pronounced growth since January 2000. Therefore, the econometric analysis employed in the present chapter aims at producing quantitative evidence of financial contagion and volatility transmission to the Brazilian stock market from the US financial markets during the GFC.

In summary, the main contribution of this chapter is to provide evidence that increases in the correlation of various seemingly unrelated stock market sectors in Brazil can be considered as part of a financial contagion episode as a consequence of the GFC relevant negative events, such as the Lehman Brothers bankruptcy. To that end, a number of robust Lagrange Multiplier (LM) tests are performed on the standardised residuals of multivariate-based GARCH (Generalized Autoregressive Conditional Heteroskedasticity) model with DCC (Dynamic Conditional Correlation) estimators.

Following this introduction, the chapter is divided into four sections, and it proceeds as follows. Section 2 details the Brazilian stock market time-series. Section 3 gives a brief account of financial contagion modelling and presents the theoretical framework. The empirical results are shown in Section 4. Finally, Section 5 summarises and concludes.

2 Boom, Bust, and Recovery in the Biggest Stock Market in Latin America

The following subsections offer an overview as well as an analysis of distinct phases (i.e. boom, bust, and recovery) of the Brazilian stock market. Negative return movements as a consequence of turbulent times – from January 2000 to February 2017 – are highlighted as well as analysed.

Brazilian Stock Market Overview

The main Brazilian stock market is located in the city centre of Sao Paulo, and it is managed by BM&F Bovespa,[1] which is the most

[1] "BM&F" refers to the "Brazilian Mercantile and Futures Exchange". Moreover, the word "Bovespa" is an acronym in Portuguese for "Sao Paulo Stock Exchange".

important institution in Brazil for intermediate equity market transactions. Bovespa operates under the supervision of the CVM,[2] which plays an analogous role in the Brazilian capital market to that of the SEC in the USA. There are 349 listed companies at Bovespa, out of which 338 are domestic companies (representing 97% of the total listed companies), totalling 833 billion dollars in market capitalisation.[3]

The Ibovespa (i.e. Bovespa Index) is the main index of the Brazilian stock market, tracking around 50 stocks traded on Bovespa. In terms of liquidity, the stocks that constitute the Ibovespa theoretical stock portfolio represent the vast majority of the trade volume as well as the respective registered financial value. Therefore, the respective index is understood as a representative sample of the Brazilian stock market, aiming at capturing investor behaviour as well as their respective consequences for the Brazilian stock market. However, one of the main limitations of the index refers to its high level of concentration on a relatively small number of stocks (Malacrida and Yamamoto 2006).

Finally, the Brazilian stock market is a significant emerging market and the largest in the Latin American region. It corresponds to nearly 50% of the Latin America as well as 1.2% of the world in terms of total market capitalisation. In January 2017, BM&F Bovespa was placed as the 19th largest stock exchange in the world by total market capitalisation.[4]

The Brazilian Stock Market Bonanza and Crash

In 2007, the overall economic conditions were favourable in Brazil. Until that time, the Brazilian GDP had been experiencing its eighth consecutive annual positive growth (in 2007 alone, the GDP growth was at 6.1%)

[2]CVM is an acronym in Portuguese (i.e. "Comissão de Valores Mobiliários") for the Securities and Exchange Commission of Brazil.

[3]As of February 24, 2017. Source: World Federation of Exchanges (2017).

[4]It worth noting that despite the fact the Brazilian Stock market is almost as large as the sum of remaining Latin American stock markets in terms of market capitalisation, the Latin American stock market region as a whole is still underdeveloped in comparison with other regions. For instance, the total Latin America market capitalisation represents 2.4% of total market capitalisation worldwide (World Federation of Exchanges 2017).

and a stable and lower than two-digit rates of unemployment, at 9.3%.[5] However, the interest rate remained at its historically high level. The Central Bank policy rate was 11.25% at the end of 2007, but the respective average[6] for the period from 2000 to 2007 was 17%, reaching a peak level of 25% at the end of 2002, amid Brazilian elections.

These three macroeconomic conditions combined—which had been the case of the Brazilian economy until 2007—among other microeconomic factors (e.g. leverage level, investment position, and type of ownership) usually contribute to a higher number of companies that start considering the equity market as a more reasonable option to raise funds compared to the debt security market (i.e. funding through bond issuing) or the banking system (i.e. credit through loans). For companies in general, a higher GDP growth can be translated into a possible scenario of a greater demand for their products and services as well as a higher margin to set higher prices. As a consequence, one can expect that a greater number of financial investors would potentially be interested in buying stocks following such positive economic outlook. Therefore, it is reasonable to expect that financial investors visualise attractive future profit levels by investing in listed companies, which can possibly be translated into higher dividends as well as price asset appreciation movements.

On the other hand, a higher level of interest rates is reflected in a more expensive credit, increasing companies financing costs, which acts to reduce the level of expected corporate future profits. Therefore, under such conditions, it is expected that more companies opt to raise funds through stock markets, for instance, issuing an Initial Public Offering (i.e. IPO). From 2004 to 2007, the number of IPOs issued at the Brazilian stock market grew by 814% (from 7 to 64 IPOs), and the respective value skyrocketed from 1.5 billion dollars in 2004 to 29.6 billion dollars in 2007, an increase of 1,856%.[7] However, after the GFC and also due to subsequent internal problems in Brazil, the Brazilian IPO market plummeted and has not recovered until the time of the writing of this chapter.

[5]Source: International Financial Statistics (IFS).

[6]This average was calculated based on the Central Bank policy rate (end of each year).

[7]Source: B3 (2017).

As most stock markets around the globe, the GFC affected sharply the Brazilian stock market, which was growing at a sustained manner since the beginning of the 2000s. In a period of eight years and six months (from January 3, 2000 to May 20, 2008) the index increased 334%.[8] The figure below depicts a sample period of 17 years and two months (Fig. 1).

A number of relevant negative events and subsequent news were circulating around the time that the Brazilian stock market index reached its peak value (i.e. May 20, 2008). On March 14, 2008, the US Federal Reserve (the Fed) agreed to provide a loan of $25 billion dollars to Bear Stearns.[9] At that moment, the Brazilian stock market index still experienced a sustained accumulated increase of 19% until May 20, 2008.

However, despite the effort made by the Fed and only two months after the Bear Stearns bail-out, the market was flooded with a number of highly relevant as well as revealing bad news, including the Lehman Brothers bankruptcy. Based on an avalanche of negative news and as expected, market agents translated that negative news into a lower level of investment confidence. Consequently, in less than six months after it had reached its peak, the Brazilian stock market index suffered severe losses, losing near to two-thirds (depreciation of 60%) of its total index value.

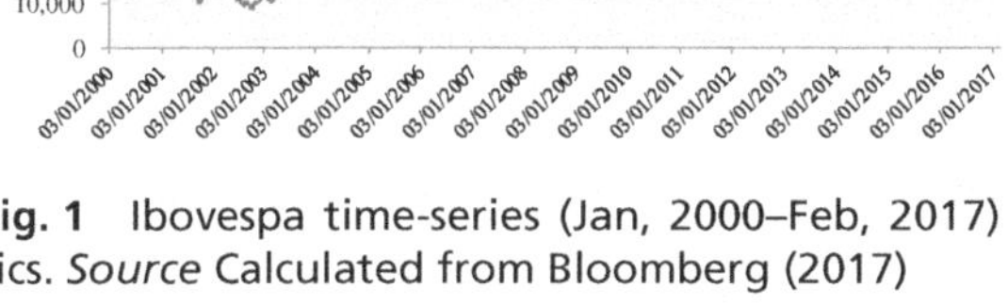

Mean ($\bar{x}$)	41,518
Standard-deviation (s)	19,434
Median (Med)	47,639
Max Value	73,517
Min Value	8,371
Range (Max - Min)	65,146
Skewness	-0.29
Kurtosis	-1.37
Starting date	03/01/2000
Ending date	24/02/2017
Nb. Obs (n)	4,249

Fig. 1 Ibovespa time-series (Jan, 2000–Feb, 2017) and respective sample statistics. *Source* Calculated from Bloomberg (2017)

[8]Source: Bloomberg (2017).

[9]See Rimkus (2016).

The Letters Soup Crisis Lexicon: V-shaped and U-Shaped Busts-Recoveries

Alphabetic letters are usually mentioned in the economic jargon aiming at describing similar shapes observed in the respective time-series, such as the V-shaped bust-recovery. For instance, Hong and Tornell (2005), in their research on how economies recover from currency crisis mention the following:

> (…) currency crises that lead to a so-called V-shaped recovery (an initial drop followed by a sharp pickup in the growth rate) tend to be caused mainly by illiquidity, whereas a U-shaped recovery (an initial drop followed by sluggish recovery) is typically preceded by an investment boom (p. 73).

However, besides the fact that specific periods of some financial time-series seem to have a similar shape to letters of the English alphabet, there is no consensus on the formal definition of what precisely consists a V-shaped or U-shaped bust-recovery, thereby leaving relevant questions without proper answers, such as:

- What are the expected durations of typical V-shaped and U-shaped busts-recoveries?
- How deep a time-series fall and subsequent recovery need to be in order to be labelled as a V-shaped bust-recovery instead of a U-shaped one?

In fact, it is difficult to define a letter-shaped bust-recovery in a precise manner due to the fact that for relevant aspects related to it one needs to make arbitrary assumptions, such as defining what would be a typical duration and intensity of such shaped bust-recovery. On the other hand, labelling certain time-series can be a useful strategy in order to highlight, illustrate, and discuss some patterns as well as relevant negative movements within a specific time-series, as adopted and discussed in the next subsections of this chapter.

The Drops Within Ibovespa V-Shaped Bust-Recovery: Crisis Made in the USA

Analysing the Brazilian stock market time-series, it is possible to see a potential V-shaped bust-recovery[10] being formed, starting at the end of May 2008 and ending at the beginning of January 2010. The figure shown below analyses the whole V-shaped bust-recovery, and the subsequent text focuses only on the negative events that contributed specifically to the bust stage of the V-shaped bust-recovery (Fig. 2).

In January 15, 2008, amid rumours regarding the level of exposure of the fifth-largest bank of the Euro Area (i.e. Societé Générale) after its supposedly rogue trader episode, the index was at 59,907 points. After 59 days (March 14, 2008), the Fed agreed to bail out Bear Stearns. At that date, the index was showing a stable growth, reaching 61,991 points. In the subsequent 67 days (May 20, 2008), despite additional negative news, the index soared to 73,517 points (peak level for the sample). However, at this point, the Ibovespa V-shaped bust-recovery had started.

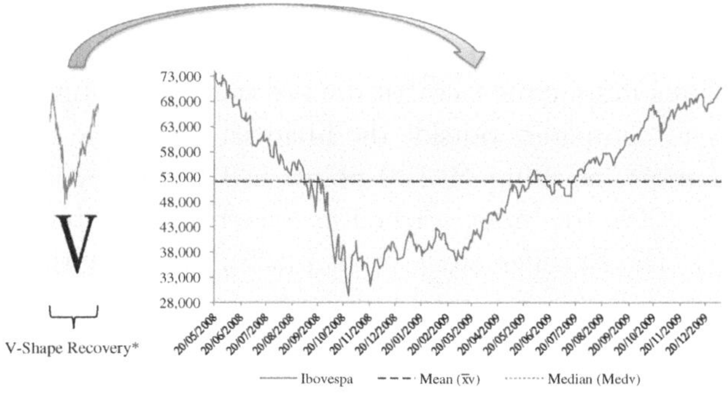

Mean ($\bar{x}_v$)	52,050
Standard-deviation (s_v)	11,057
Median (Med_v)	52,138
Max $Value_v$	73,517
Min $Value_v$	29,435
$Range_v$ (Max_v - Min_v)	44,082
$Skewness_v$	0.01
$Kurtosis_v$	-1.16
Starting $date_v$	20/05/2008
Ending $date_v$	06/01/2010
Nb. Obs (n_v)	405

* Format of the V-Shape within the whole sample.

Fig. 2 Ibovespa V-shaped bust-recovery and respective sample statistics. *Source* Calculated from Bloomberg (2017)

[10]The word "potential" refers to the fact that the V-shaped bust-recovery analysed in this section was performed without using an econometric technique that would test if there was a break in the respective time-series.

In the subsequent 52 days, the index dropped 18% and in July 11, 2008, there was the failure of IndyMac Bank. In September 7, 2008, there was a US federal government takeover of Fannie Mae and Freddie Mac. At this date, the index dropped another 16% compared to the level in July 11, 2008 (i.e. IndyMac Bank failure date). In September 14, 2008, the Bank of America acquired Merrill Lynch and only one day after that (i.e. September 15, 2008), Lehman Brothers went bankrupt. The Lehman Brothers bankruptcy is understood as the most symbolic financial crisis event since the Great Depression of the 1930s.

In September 17, 2008, the American International Group (AIG) was bailed out by the US government, through lending of $85 billion dollars provided by the Fed. At that time, the index was at 45,909 points, which represented a devaluation of 5% after only two days of the bankruptcy of Lehman Brothers. Nearly a week after the bail-out of AIG, Washington Mutual banking assets were sold to JPMorgan Chase, with the intervention of the Federal Deposit Insurance Corporation. In September 25, 2008, the index was at 51,828 points, which refers to a positive growth rate of 13% compared to around a week earlier. In October 6, 2008, the Fed announced short-term loans to banks, totalling $900 billion dollars.

However, the Brazilian stock market index was devalued by 19% in the 11 days that followed the Washington Mutual acquisition by JPMorgan Chase. Only one day after, despite the fact that the Fed started lending $1.3 trillion dollars directly to companies outside the financial sector, the index dropped by 5% once more, reaching 40,140 points in October 7, 2008. Finally, in October 27, 2008, the index reached its lowest value within the V-shaped bust-recovery. The Brazilian stock market index lost more than a quarter (i.e. devaluation of 27%) of its total index value in a period of only 20 days, reaching 29,435 index points before starting its recovery process (i.e. the second part of the V-shaped time-series).[11]

Based on the high frequency of relevant negative and revealing news as detailed above, the level of financial investment confidence was negatively affected, as one could expect. The increasing uncertainties on what else could happen next and how serious and deep the financial

[11]This subsection describes a mere summary of relevant news released by the media at the time of the GFC. Therefore, the events described in this subsection are not exhaustive and more news can be added to that list. For more details on such events, see Zingales (2008), Arestis and Karakitsos (2013), and Rimkus (2016).

and economic problems were at that time, were translated into an increased level of market volatility, which in its turn was translated into an Ibovespa total depreciation of 60% in a period of five months (from May 20, 2008 until October 27, 2008).

The Ibovespa U-Shaped Bust-Recovery: Commodities Shock and Political Unrest

The subsequent Brazilian stock market letter-shaped bust-recovery consists of a potential[12] U-shaped bust-recovery,[13] spanning from November 4, 2010 until February 24, 2017.[14] It refers to a period of nearly six and a half years, covering a turbulent period in the Brazilian recent history as well as a sluggish recovery in commodity prices after the GFC, as shown below.

After its beginning, the U-shaped bust-recovery started its declining trajectory towards its persistent lower band level. It started with 72,996 index points and ended with 66,662 index points, after reaching a minimum value of 37,497 index points in January 26, 2016. However, between its beginning and ending, one can realise some pronounced falls on the time-series, as shown in Fig. 3.

Besides the recent political problems faced by Brazil, which affected the economy as a whole and impaired investor confidence, there was a commodity negative price shock. Negative movements in commodities international prices are relevant due to the fact a number of important (in terms of market capitalisation) listed companies in the Brazilian stock market are producers and exporters of soft commodities (e.g. agricultural goods), hard commodities (e.g. mining industry), and energy commodities (e.g. oil industry).

---

[12]Once more the word "potential" is used. For more details, see footnote 10 above.

[13]One can argue that the Ibovespa U-shaped period would be more similar to a number of "W-shaped" instead of a "U" one, due to some of its spikes within it. However, the core concern is on analysing relevant falls in the time-series (which can potentially be translated into wealth destruction) rather than showing the ideal format as well as appearance of a specific letter-shaped bust-recovery.

[14]The date of February 24, 2017 also refers to the end of the sample period analysed in the present subsection.

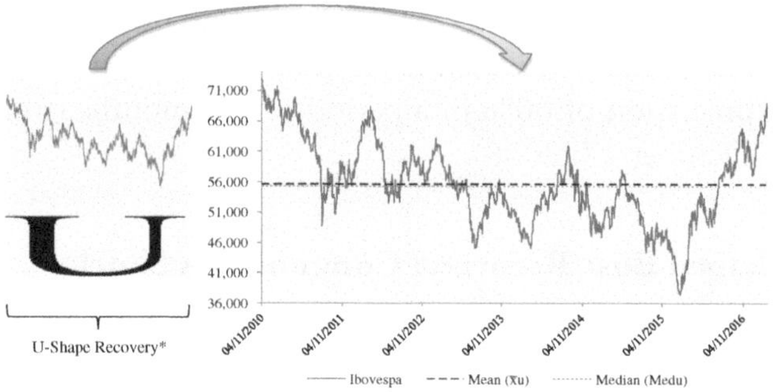

Mean ($\bar{x}_u$)	55,647
Standard-deviation (s_u)	6,711
Median (Med_u)	55,249
Max $Value_u$	72,996
Min $Value_u$	37,497
$Range_u$ (Max_u - Min_u)	35,498
$Skewness_u$	0.14
$Kurtosis_u$	-0.29
Starting $date_u$	04/11/2010
Ending $date_u$	24/02/2017
Nb. Obs (n_u)	1,564

* Format of the U-Shape within the whole sample.

Fig. 3 Ibovespa U-shaped bust-recovery and respective sample statistics. *Source* Calculated from Bloomberg (2017)

By analysing the progress of important type of commodities for the Brazilian stock market, from November 2010 to February 2017[15] one can verify that the energy commodities dropped by 34%; moreover, metals and minerals as well as agricultural commodities decreased by 29% and 19%, respectively, for the same period of time.[16]

Regarding the Brazilian listed companies whose revenues heavily depend on the foreign market (more specifically, commodities exporters), in an opposite direction of the plummeting commodities prices, there was a relevant overall depreciation of the Brazilian currency (i.e. “Brazilian Reais”) during the same period. The Brazilian currency depreciation was 85%, from 1.68 Brazilian Reais/US Dollars (in November 4, 2010) to 3.11 Brazilian Reais/US Dollars (in February 24, 2017).[17]

Complementing the negative global commodity pricing shock, there were a number of internal facts and problems involving politics that potentially affected the Brazilian stock market performance,[18]

[15]Months in which the U-shaped bust-recovery started and ended, respectively.

[16]It refers to monthly indices based on nominal US dollars (World Bank, 2017).

[17]Brazil/US foreign exchange rate, Brazilian Reais to one US Dollar, daily, not seasonally adjusted (St. Louis Fed 2017).

[18]It is worth noting that it is difficult to precisely measure the impact of a problem released by the media. Table 1 lists events which potentially affected the performance of the Brazilian stock market. Due to the fact that this subsection focuses mainly on internal problems that Brazil was facing during the U-shaped bust-recovery; this subsection does not list important news regarding external economically relevant countries, such as US, Europe, or Asia.

Table 1 Summarised list of important events during the Ibovespa U-shaped bust-recovery

Date	Ibovespa Index Points	Δ% Ibov. within Intra Period	Days from Previous Event	Event Description
Oct 31, 2010[a]	71,561	n/a	n/a	Dilma Rousseff was elected as the President of Brazil.
Nov 4, 2010	72,996	2%	4	Starting date of the U-Shaped Ibovespa, at 72,996 index points.
Jun 7, 2011	63,218	-13%	215	President Rousseff's chief of staff resigns amid corruption allegations.
Jun 20, 2013	48,214	-24%	744	Protests and riots in several Brazilian cities, in which is considered as the biggest public demonstrations of civil unrest in the Brazil's recent history.
Oct 26, 2014[a]	50,504	5%	493	Dilma Rousseff was re-elected as the President of Brazil.
Mar 17, 2015	50,285	-0.4%	142	Progress on the Petrobras corruption scandals.
Dec 2, 2015	44,915	-11%	260	Congress agrees to launch impeachment proceedings against the President of Brazil.
May 6, 2016	51,718	15%	156	Brazilian Senate votes in favour presidential impeachment trial.
Aug 5, 2016	57,661	11%	91	Starting date of the Olympic Games held in Rio de Janeiro.
Aug 31, 2016	57,901	0.4%	26	Brazilian Senate approves the removal of President Dilma Rousseff from office. Subsequently, Michel Temer is sworn in as the Predisent of Brazil.
Dec 13, 2016	59,281	2%	104	Brazilian Senate approves 20 years period of government austerity reforms.
Feb 24, 2017	66,662	12%	73	Ending date of the U-Shaped Ibovespa, at 66,662 index points.

[a]As on the 31st of October, 2010 and 26th of October, 2014 were Sundays, the Ibovespa index points refer to the next working days (i.e. Mondays): 1st of September, 2010 and 27th of October, 2014, respectively
Source BBC (2017) and author's own construction

contributing to the pre-announced index falls within the U-shaped bust-recovery period, as summarised in the above table.

As detailed in Table 1 above, the first sustained negative movement within the U-shaped bust-recovery was between November 2010 and June 2011, resulting in a 13% of negative return. The second sustained negative movement occurred from June 2011 until June 2013 (an additional 24% in negative return). Finally, the third and last sustained negative movement within the U-shaped bust-recovery was from March 2015 until December 2015, totalling 11% of negative return.

3 Crisis Transmission to the Brazilian Stock Market

This section offers the conceptual definition of financial contagion adopted in the present study; the theoretical framework used aiming at testing the crisis transmission hypothesis to the Brazilian stock market during the GFC; and finally, it is provided a brief discussion on potential vectors of contagion.

Conceptual Definition of Financial Contagion

Financial contagion analysis is a part of a broader field of interest, namely that interested in characterising the propagation of financial negative shocks through different markets or economies. On the one hand, there are analyses focused on the spread of perverse crisis effects through real economic variables from developed markets to emerging ones or those spilling over from emerging markets to some of their counterparts, denominated "monsoonal effects" and "spillovers", respectively (Masson 1998). On the other hand, "financial contagion" itself focuses on the propagation of shocks through less evident contagion vectors. Those definitions will be described below.

- ***Monsoonal Effect***. Consists of shifts in developed countries' economic policies—in general to mitigate the effects of negative economic momentums, triggering financial crisis in emerging markets. Examples of this effect could be the rise of Fed fund rates, and its impacts on other countries' balance of payments or the appreciation of the US dollar, resulting from a hike in Fed funds rate, ceteris paribus. The latter example affects countries with high level of exposure to US dollars-denominated debt and relatively low foreign reserves as well as companies with high level of debt in foreign currency with high ratio level of revenues and/or assets in domestic currency (Masson and Mussa 1995; Masson 1998).

- ***Spillover***. The definition of spillover has to do with the explicit interdependence of two or more emerging markets related to macroeconomic fundamentals. For instance, the devaluation of emerging markets' currency may cause other emerging markets' real exchange rate to appreciate, affecting in different directions their trade balances (Masson 1998).
- ***Financial Contagion***. This phenomenon is related to the propagation of financial crisis through latent factors. In general, the theory which supports events of such nature relates to the existence of multiple equilibria in a given economy. The equilibrium in which such economy lies on is not stable and, consequently, may be shifted at any given moment provided shifts in investors' expectations. In effect, financial contagion is, in general, a consequence of self-fulfilling panic, which is followed by an investor's herd behaviour (Masson 1998).

Sachs et al. (1996) discuss this effect in the light of the Mexican peso devaluation of 1994–1995. The authors conclude that a necessary condition for the Mexican crisis to occur was the overvalued currency in the preceding months. However, the propagation of such crisis to Argentina in March–April 1995 was due to self-fulfilling panic. King and Wadhwani (1990) built a model in which contagion emerges as the outcome of agents' rational attempt to use imperfect information about events relevant to equity values to price their assets. The authors test their model in the context of 1987s Wall Street Crash and conclude that financial contagion may indeed occur in the face of a failure in some market's mechanisms. Furthermore, the authors provide evidence that correlations between markets tend to shift upwards in face of such events and that, to some extent, volatility may be consequently self-sustaining.

Perhaps the most prominent criticism to the financial contagion analysis is that comprised by Forbes and Rigobon (2002). According to the authors, the (unconditional) correlation factor of the markets being tested is biased upwards due to the increase in each market's volatility. An adjustment factor to account for such bias is then proposed and, finally, the authors conclude that there was no financial contagion in the tested series over the 1987s Wall Street Crash and over the 1994 Mexico crisis.

Theoretical Framework of Financial Contagion Modelling

The present analysis aims at providing evidence of financial contagion over the Brazilian stock market from US specific triggers during the GFC. Therefore, due to the great relevance as well as global influence of the US financial markets and as a consequence of highly negative events from the GFC, there was a significant increase in the correlation levels of distinct Brazilian stock market sector indices (y_t, which represents the log return of the sector indexes)—which are seemingly unrelated under the light of exogenous events originated in the US financial markets—and which significant higher level of correlation can be translated into the contamination of the Brazilian stock market as a consequence of the GFC.

The hypothesis presented in this chapter is detailed as follows: provided that no macroeconomic fundamental variables have significantly changed in the course of one week or a month in Brazil—even because such variables accounting and measurements, such as GDP, are usually fairly delayed compared to the frequency of stock markets data availability; it is, actually, suspected that a common latent factor to stock prices has been drastically affected by the four relevant negative events considered in the present study (Sect. "Key Negative Exogenous Events as Indicators"), as indicators of structural breaks in the time-series[19] (Dungey and Martin 2001).

It should sound quite questionable to throw a quest for arbitrary events, which potentially cause structural breaks in financial time-series. However, such argument is potentially refuted due to the fact that the present analysis deals with two utterly different economies, going through very much distinct economic development processes.

[19]Further discussion of the different forms of financial contagion and volatility spillovers can be found in Billio and Caporin (2005).

For instance, expected cuts in the Fed rates and international commerce factors could strengthen the relationship between financial markets through real economic variables (e.g. by boosting consumers demand and investment and/or raising imports/exports, factors which directly affect GDP level).[20]

An improved methodology for testing the hypothesis of financial contagion arose from Engle and Sheppard's (2001) dynamic conditional correlation (DCC) model, which accounts for each series' volatility, overcoming the aforementioned upwards bias issue. The structural breaks in the time-series refer to a significantly higher correlation level between pairs of the Brazilian stock market sector indices as a consequence of exogenous factors. To this end, a series of robust Lagrange Multiplier tests on the standardised residuals of multivariate-based GARCH-DCC models will be performed. A major advantage of this model is the detection of possible changes in conditional correlations during the GFC, which can be translated into a measure of investor behaviour in response to negative events as well as media news and, most importantly, the direct impact on the Brazilian stock market indices (Celık 2012).

Therefore, in order to test our hypothesis of financial contagion to the Brazilian stock market, we shall perform the following three subsequent steps[21]: (i) fit a multivariate (BEKK) GARCH model to the Bovespa market sector indices time-series; (ii) estimating DCC time-series for Bovespa market sector indices; and (iii) applying a robust-LM test to verify the presence of financial contagion involving the market sectors in the Brazilian stock market.[22]

Firstly, in order to fit a multivariate (BEKK) GARCH model to the Bovespa market sector indices time-series, we let y_t be an $N \times 1$

[20]The relation between real economic variables and the contagion phenomenon is discussed in Baur (2011).

[21]Other studies which apply the same approach—however, with slight variations—are Billio and Caporin (2005), Cappiello et al. (2006), and Frank et al. (2008).

[22]Notice that for the sake of simplicity we will refer to theoretical parameters and estimates in order to provide a brief estimation context to the reader. All centred-page formulae refer to theoretical parameters unless explicitly stated otherwise.

stochastic vector, and θ be a finite vector of parameters, considering the following representation of y_t

$$y_t = \mu_t(\theta) + \varepsilon_t$$

where y_t represents a vector of log returns of each of the four Bovespa sector index analysed in this chapter. The term $\mu_t(\theta)$ corresponds to the conditional mean of y at instant t, and ε_t refers to an error term that satisfies

$$\varepsilon_t = H_t^{1/2}(\theta) y_t$$

where $H_t^{1/2}(\theta)$ is a positive definite matrix, and y is a stochastic with first moments given by $E(y_t) = 0$ and $E(y_t y_t') = I_N$, where I_N is the identity matrix of order N.

Let $\Im_t$ be the information set $\left\{y_0^{(k)}, \cdots, y_t^{(k)}\right\}$. Assume that $y_0^{(k)} \sim \left(\mu_y, \sigma_y^2\right)$ and take an arbitrary realisation of k. In particular let $\Im_{t-1}$ be the σ-field generated by the set $\{y_0, \ldots, y_{t-1}\}$. Finally, let $\tilde{y} := y_t - \mu_t(\theta)$, where, in our exercise, $\tilde{y}$ represents the sector indexes once they have been controlled for their conditional mean structure. In practice, the sample analogue of $\tilde{y} := y_t - \mu_t(\theta)$ would be the residuals of a VAR(1) model, which would play the role of $\overline{\mu_t}(\bar{\theta})$. Then, the conditional variance of the process is given by

$$(\tilde{y}|\Im_{t-1}) = \left(\varepsilon_t \varepsilon_t' | \Im_{t-1}\right) = H_t$$

Therefore, provided that all the conditional mean structure of y_t has been accounted for (and removed by means of considering the residuals of the VAR(1) model mentioned above), we have that H_t is the conditional covariance matrix of y_t.

Since we are ultimately interested in checking whether the conditional correlations of the indices remain unchanged in the face of a series of exogenous factors, the approach will be to model such correlation, purge it from the series and test whether all the correlation has indeed been removed during the period in which we suspect there is a structural break in the series. If, after removing our estimated conditional correlation from the series, there is still correlation left in such period, we may conclude that the modelled structure has changed, provided our model has not been able to remove all the structure based on the first fitted model. To do so, the second step is to estimate (and fit to our data) the DCC model as proposed by Engle (2002), which is given by the following decomposition of the conditional covariance matrix

$$H_t \equiv D_t R_t D_t'$$

in which

$$D_t = \operatorname{diag}\left\{ h_{11,t}^{1/2}, \ldots, h_{NN,t}^{1/2} \right\}$$

with $h_{11,t}$ following any X-ARCH process, in particular a GARCH process in the present chapter,

$$R_t = \operatorname{diag}\left\{ h_{11,t}^{-1/2}, \ldots h_{NN,t}^{-1/2} \right\} \cdot H_t \cdot \operatorname{diag}\left\{ h_{11,t}^{-1/2}, \ldots h_{NN,t}^{-1/2} \right\}$$

and with the $N \times N$ positive definite matrix $R_t = \left(r_{ij,t}\right)$ given by

$$R_t = \left(1 - \sum\nolimits_{p=1}^{P} \alpha_p - \sum\nolimits_{q=1}^{Q} \beta_q\right)\bar{R} + \sum\nolimits_{p=1}^{P} \alpha_p \left(\varepsilon_{t-p}\varepsilon_{t-p}'\right) + \sum\nolimits_{q=1}^{Q} \beta_q R_{t-q}$$

with ε_t being the standardised innovations of ε_t, $\bar{R}$ being the unconditional covariance matrix of ε_t and α_i, $\beta_i \geq 0$, $\forall i$ such that $\Sigma_p \alpha_p + \Sigma_q \beta_q \leq 1$.

The log-likelihood function is given by

$$\widetilde{l_1}(\phi|\Im_t) = -\frac{1}{2}\sum_{t=1}^{T}\left(N \ln(2\pi) + 2\ln|D_t| + \ln|I_N| + \tilde{y}_t' D_t^{-1} I_N^{-1} D_t^{-1} \tilde{y}_t\right)$$
$$= -\frac{1}{2}\sum_{i=1}^{N}\left(T \ln(2\pi) + \sum_{t=1}^{T}\left(\ln\left(h_{it}\right) + \frac{\tilde{y}_{it}^2}{h_{it}}\right)\right)$$

Notice that this function is identical to the sum of the univariate quasi-likelihood (of the univariate X-ARCH models). Then, by correcting the specification of the correlation matrix, one obtains the following conditional quasi-likelihood function for the second stage

$$\widetilde{l}_2\left(\psi \middle| \hat{\phi}_{ML}, \Im_t\right) \propto -\frac{1}{2}\sum_{t=1}^{T}(\ln|R_t|) + \varepsilon_t' R_t^{-1}\varepsilon_t$$

where $\{\varepsilon_t\}_{t\in T}$ is a series of standardised residuals from the first stage estimation.

It is worth noting that both the consistency and asymptotic normality of the DCC parameters estimators do not depend on the hypothesis of normality of returns. Therefore, even under the assumption of heavy-tailed returns, the estimators still present the desirable properties. Moreover, the relative loss of efficiency due to the Limited Information Maximum Likelihood (LIML) estimation has been accounted for by applying the Newton-Raphson algorithm to the second stage score-functions.[23]

As mentioned previously, our estimation method is performed in three steps. The first step consists of estimating the variance matrix H_t whilst keeping the correlations matrix R_t fixed (and equal to the identity matrix). Such matrix is estimated by fitting a BEKK Multivariate GARCH model. In particular, each diagonal term of such matrix corresponds to a univariate GARCH(1,1) model (i.e. corresponding to the square root of the conditional variance of the series). In other words, we are simply estimating the matrix analogue of the following well-known equation:

$$Corr(A, B) = \frac{Covar(A,\ B)}{\sqrt[2]{Var(A)}\sqrt[2]{Var(B)}}$$

[23]For all theorems and proofs, we refer the reader to Newey and McFadden (1994) for consistency and asymptotic normality of the estimators, Engle and Sheppard (2001) for the specification of first-stage score functions and, finally, to Pagan (1986) for the efficiency of two-stage estimators under iterative estimation procedures.

The next step consists in plugging the estimated covariance values in and estimating the correlations matrix. The discussion about efficiency arises from the fact that we are estimating parameters based on a matrix of estimates (the covariance matrix). As a consequence, unless the first step estimates are 100% accurate, which is not the case, the variance of the second step should increase (due to the interaction of "old" errors with "new" errors). Nevertheless, the procedure described above—namely applying an iteration of the Newton-Raphson algorithm (or other Taylor expansion-based algorithm)—has been proven to solve the issue.

Finally, the null hypothesis of no financial contagion will be tested through a Lagrange Multiplier robust test to the standardised residuals of the models described above, fitted to the log returns of the sectors indexes taken together.[24] It is assumed the same structure previously considered to the endogenous variable. Therefore, let $y_t|\Im_{t-1} \sim \mathrm{N}(0, \mathrm{H}_t)$. Then we may define the series $u_{it} = y_{it}^2 - h_{it}$ and test whether an arbitrary series $k_{g,t-1}$ is capable of predicting the behaviour of the generalised residuals of the sector index series squared (u_{it}). Notice that we have modelled the conditional variance of the indices (h_{it}). Provided they have zero-mean, the squared residuals are a sample estimate of their (instant) variance. The test statistic is given by

$$C = \left[T^{-1}\sum_{t=1}^{T} u_{ij,t}\lambda_{g,t-1}\right]^2 \left[T^{-1}\sum_{t=1}^{T} u_{ij,t}^2\lambda_{g,t-1}^2\right]^{-1}$$

where C is the test statistic based on the Lagrange Multiplier test and where $\lambda_{g,t-1}$ is the residual of the regression of the test conditions $\{k_{g,t-1}\}$ on the score functions. The test statistic distribution is as follows: $C \xrightarrow{\ell} \chi^2_{(1)}$.

The idea behind the Lagrange multiplier test is to impose a constraint to the score function (which is related to the sample analogue of a conditional distribution series, the likelihood function evaluated at its

[24]Other studies which apply the same methodology to test for the absence of financial contagion are Cappiello et al. (2003) and Hesse et al. (2008).

maximum point) and test whether the restriction binds, if the Lagrange multipliers are different from zero. Provided we have stated that there is no structure left in the treated series (which is the residual of all models we have fit to deal with both conditional mean and variance structure so far), we claim that no additional information added as a constraint to the score function should be able to add predictive power to the fitted model. In effect, under such hypothesis, we expect the Lagrange multiplier to equal zero. This explains the null hypothesis of no contagion: no particular series add predictive power to the model or, in other words, the correlation structure of the multivariate model has been accounted for and purged out of the series. If, in face of new information (e.g. a dummy indicating a particular period) the LM statistic falls outside the null hypothesis "acceptance" region of the test distribution, we conclude that the Lagrange multiplier is different from zero and, therefore, that there is additional dependency structure not accounted for a structural break and, therefore, financial contagion.

In order to test the null hypothesis of no financial contagion over the Brazilian stock market, it is necessary to adjust the generalised residuals. Instead of adjusting the residuals by the conditional variance, one should adjust it by the conditional correlation of the series. In effect, we have: $u_{ij,t} = y_{i,t}y_{j,t} - \hat{\rho}_{ij,t}$. Where $u_{ij,t}$ is the difference between the instant covariance and the estimated correlation between the indices (notice that the conditional variance has already been accounted for). As described above, we expect the series $\left\{u_{ij,t}\right\}$ to present evidence of structural breaks, which is an evidence of financial contagion.

In addition to evidencing financial contagion to the Brazilian stock market as above detailed, it is also important to understand and justify which potential vectors—other than macroeconomic fundamentals—that could have caused assets to abandon their specific drivers to plunge in tandem, causing conditional correlations to soar.

Potential Vectors of Contagion

Provided that companies' capital structure has not changed over the course of events, valuation in general can be negatively affected by a hike in the companies' cost of debt and capital. This point will be further developed in Sect. "Vectors of Contagion". We would like to emphasise, however, the two following aspects:

- A surge in country risk level, which directly affects the cost of equity as calculated by the so-called international CAPM (Capital Asset Pricing Model) model as well as impacting the cost of any foreign-denominated debt issued by a domestic company (Sharpe 1964).
- A potential surge in local interest rates in an attempt to offset capital outflow movements. It is worth noting that the cost of equity and the cost of debt are affected in the WACC (Weighted Average Cost of Capital) as well as the debt-to-equity balance is potentially affected whilst companies are trying to adapt themselves to such a new economic reality (Merton 1974).[25]

4 Empirical Discussion and Results

The present study aims at investigating the presence of financial contagion and volatility spillovers to relevant Bovespa sector indexes by using the methodology discussed in the previous section, which are briefly discussed in what follows.

A Brief Discussion of the Adopted Indices

When considering emerging economies, the growing importance of the Brazilian stock market should be recognised. The first aspect to point out is the average growth in both capitalisation and liquidity of the Brazilian stock market. When the GFC struck markets worldwide, the total market capitalisation of Bovespa was approximately around $750 billion dollars. The average daily turnover was roughly $1.1 billion dollars (considering the last 12 months average). The average market capitalisation of 2016 was roughly $670 billion dollars and a daily turnover

[25]We refer the reader to Merton (1974)'s seminal discussion on the matter.

of \$1.7 billion dollars; i.e. an increase of 55% in turnover paired with a decrease of 11% in market capitalisation (Bloomberg 2017).

The second relevant point to highlight refers to the concentration of the Ibovespa index. Brazil is known to be a relevant commodities exporter. Furthermore, a handful of massive commodity companies accounts for a great percentage of the Brazilian Ibovespa composition. Despite the fact that in March 2017 the financial services sector of Brazil accounted for 35% of Ibovespa, commodities-related sectors were highly relevant for the Brazilian stock market index. For instance, basic materials and energy sectors concentrated 15% and 12% of the index, respectively, as in March 2017.

Data

Due to the relative importance of the composition of Ibovespa index as well as lack of enough available historic data for some time-series sectorial indexes for the selected sample period, financial contagion was tested using the following sector indexes: financial services (IFNC), basic material (IMAT), consumer goods (CONS), and heavy industry (INDX). The selected period ranges from January 3, 2007, to February 23, 2012. The "turbulence period" was set from October 14, 2007 until December 30, 2010.

As detailed in the first part of this chapter, the sample period chosen to analyse the crisis transmission to the Brazilian stock market corresponds to a highly turbulent time within the whole sample period, at the epicentre of the GFC.

Key Negative Exogenous Events as Indicators

In this subsection, the series of indicators used to test for financial contagion are briefly described. Four dates are considered (i.e. the "w" series), representing dummies indicating that the period is comprised of some pre-defined arbitrarily chosen series of highly relevant events. In mathematical terms, $w_t^{(\tau)} := I(t \in \tau)$, with $I(\cdot)$ the indicator function. They relate to four series of events ($\tau = 1, 2, 3, 4$) starting at four particular dates and remaining there for the two trading months to follow:

- *26 February 2007* ($\tau = 1$): it corresponds to the day in which Alan Greenspan (Chairman of the US Fed at that time) publicly alerted markets of an imminent recession, resulting from what he classified as the end of an economic expansion cycle. (Greenspan 2007)
- *21 May 2007* ($\tau = 2$): UBS announced the discontinuation of its high-risk loans division's activities. In addition, one week earlier, General Motors financial division announced roughly $300 million dollars in financial losses. Moreover and most importantly, this date was chosen because it was when the National Association of Business Economists cut by impressive 500 bp its US GDP growth forecast. According to the report published by the association, this cut was directly linked to the upward-trending interest rates revisions, which were carried out by the Fed that caused the high-yield subprime mortgage default risk to surge.
- *14 October 2007* ($\tau = 3$): one week earlier (October 5, 2007) Merrill Lynch subscribed $5.5 billion losses in ABS (Asset-Backed Securities), which were translated into a negative direct impact of $0.50 dollar per share. This caused market stress to surge. Indeed, after plunging 12% in two days, the implicit volatility of the Chicago Board Options Exchange (CBOE) rebounded 3%, indicating that chaos was about to hit Wall Street's trading desks. On the date of interest (i.e. October 14, 2007), a fund was put together by Citigroup, BofA, JPMorgan Chase and $80 billion dollars estimated funds were provided by the US Treasury. The objective was to act as a stabilisation agent, avoiding major assets fire sale, which would unquestionably aggravate investor confidence. However, one day latter, Nomura bank announced $600 million dollars losses and the closing of its ABS-related activities in the USA. Moreover, Citigroup announced the write-off of roughly $6 billion dollars' worth of assets related to the subprime market. Still within the period of interest, the real estate confidence was announced to be on its lows being the eighth plunge running that was at the back of the then unseen default ratios and melting real estate property prices. Following those relevant events, the then Chairman of the Fed (Ben Bernanke) delivered a realistic speech in New York; a relevant quote is as follows:

> The further contraction in housing is likely to be a significant drag on growth in the current quarter and through next year. […] A full recovery of market functioning is likely to take time and we may well see some set-backs. (Bernanke 2007)

That was, indeed, a remarkably realistic forecast.

- *7 September 2008* ($\tau = 4$): it refers to the day of Fannie Mae and Freddie Mac's bail-outs. The US government committed up to \$200 billion dollars to save the government sponsored enterprises (GSEs) from utter collapse. Since the GSEs were the two largest lenders to the subprime mortgage market, by bailing out those institutions, the US government acquired around \$5 trillion in potentially bad debt. Few days later, Lehman Brothers announced \$4 billion losses, put its whole operation for sale and filled to Chapter 11,[26] in the largest such filling in the US history: \$639 billion dollars. Moreover, Bank of America acquired Merrill Lynch for \$50 billion dollars. The following days were considered as the darkest throughout the recent history of capital markets, not only in the US stock market, but in all markets around the globe.

Empirical Evidence of Contagion in the Brazilian Stock Market

After applying the LM-robust specification tests, which in this case is translated into financial contagion tests, it is concluded that for one particular date, namely October 14, 2007, the null hypothesis of "no contagion" was refuted at the 5% significance level for all combinations of sector indexes, as shown below in Panel A of Fig. 4. The date corresponds to the speech of Ben Bernanke quoted above, which for most of the risk-averse market players sounded almost exactly as the official kick-off of the GFC.

Given the series of events, any breathing stock market player would be fairly risk averse and attentive by that time.[27] Apparently, the bail-outs

[26] It refers to Chapter 11 protection in the US Bankruptcy Court in New York.

[27] Complementary GARCH-DCC estimation can be found in Arruda (2012).

Panel A: Contagion test results for chosen dates and respective key events

	$w_{t-1}^{(1)}$ (26/02/07)		$w_{t-1}^{(2)}$ (21/05/07)		$w_{t-1}^{(3)}$ (14/10/07)		$w_{t-1}^{(4)}$ (07/09/08)	
k,s	LM	Prob	LM	Prob	LM	Prob	LM	Prob
ICON vs. IFNC	**8.64***	0.00	1.60	0.21	**11.23***	0.00	1.21	0.27
ICON vs. IMAT	1.63	0.20	**2.87**	0.09	**4.25***	0.04	2.10	0.15
ICON vs. INDX	2.62	0.11	1.24	0.26	**7.33***	0.01	1.23	0.27
IFNC vs. IMAT	2.37	0.12	**12.60***	0.00	**11.77***	0.00	**7.79***	0.00
IFNC vs. INDX	**22.30***	0.00	**13.64***	0.00	**22.07***	0.00	1.89	0.17
IMAT vs. INDX	**7.57***	0.01	**5.95***	0.01	**13.03***	0.00	1.26	0.26

* indicates values significant to 5% and bold values are significant to 10%

Panel B: Conditional correlation series involving financial services (IFNC), basic materials (IMAT), and heavy industry (INDX) sectors

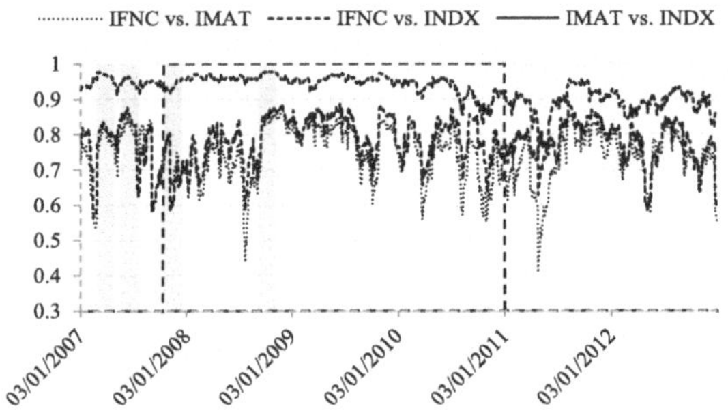

Panel C: Conditional correlation series involving consumer goods (ICON), financial services (IFNC), basic materials (IMAT), and heavy industry (INDX) sectors

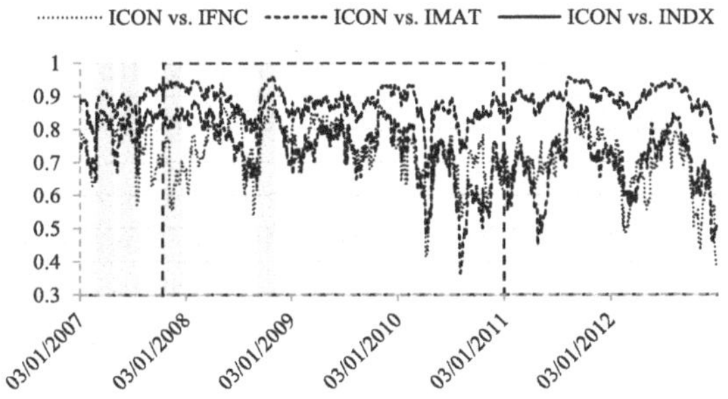

Fig. 4 Contagion test results and conditional correlation series. *Source* Bloomberg (2017) and author's estimates (2017)

of Fannie Mae and Freddie Mac did not cause correlations to suffer any structural break, as the null hypothesis of no contagion was not refuted even at the 10% significance for 5 of the 6 pairs of the series. Panels B and C of Fig. 4 above show the conditional correlation series, depicted along with the dashed area representing what was labelled as "turbulence period" for the present analysis, from October 14, 2007 to December 30, 2010; also depicted are the four grey shaded areas, which indicate the four events described above and the two respective subsequent months.

Despite the graphic inspection that shows abrupt shifts in correlations in nearly all events, from an econometric perspective, only the third event showed massive structural breaks across all indexes. Interestingly enough, it seems like over the period of such event, conditional correlations suffered a downward shift. Nevertheless, it still characterises a structural break in dynamic conditional correlations, and therefore, it was verified the financial contagion hypothesis.

Vectors of Contagion

In this subsection, the vectors of contagion are highlighted and explored, which potentially helped spreading the effects of the GFC over the Brazilian stock market. Differently from the US market, where the banking sector—and to a lesser degree, the financial services sector—took the blow and spread the crisis horizontally to sectors such as Telecommunications and Utilities, in Brazil the stock market was influenced by latent variables, which were indirectly affected by the US market shock, as depicted below in Fig. 5 and subsequently analysed.

- Liquidity *Plunge (Flight to Quality and Cash Shortage)*: it is reasonable to assume that the GFC triggered a well-known phenomenon called "flight-to-quality", or perhaps in this case a "flight to safety" of investments from emerging markets. Indeed, as investors believe that emerging markets' fundamentals are rather weak—regardless of the fact that sometimes this is not the case—and fear that crisis effects could be deepened by such fragilities, capital moves from emerging markets to developed ones (Fratzscher 2012).

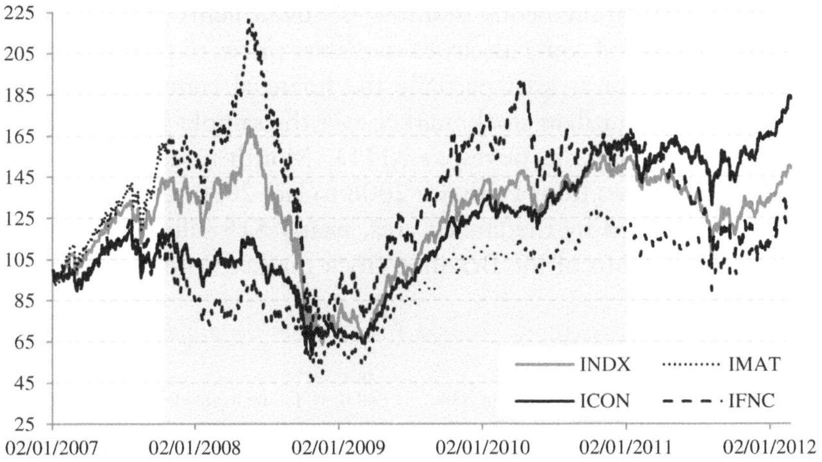

Fig. 5 Ibovespa sectorial indexes time-series (Jan, 2007–Feb, 2012). *Source* Bloomberg (2017) and author's own elaboration

A side effect of it refers to the appreciation of value reserves, such as gold or the US dollar. The fact that the US currency was gaining value in face of the GFC—whose epicentre was precisely the US economy—may sound somewhat surprising.[28] Panel A in the Fig. 6 below, presents the DXY index (US Dollar Currency Index), which measures the value of the US dollar relative to a basket of foreign currencies—in the light of the GFC.

In addition, hedge funds had cash flow issues to cover short-put positions to deal with consequent outflows and margin calls, a fact that further added to the sudden capital outflow in emerging markets, in particular in the Brazilian market. That said, it is noted that a large deal of assets traded in the Brazilian market is not exactly liquid. Indeed, a sudden assets sale in a market such as the Brazilian one could trigger a massive overhang (Boyson et al. 2014).

[28]Provided that the crisis developed around the US banking system, one would expect that the impact in real countercyclical assets, such as gold or other currencies, would be more relevant. However, the movement described above occurred only because the currency in question is the US dollar (i.e. the key-currency in the international monetary and financial system).

In effect, the simultaneous draining of investments combined with the small liquidity of some assets, caused asset prices to plunge together, what would explain at least partially the financial contagion phenomenon within the Brazilian stock market over the sample period. Panel B, Fig. 6 below, depicts the Bovespa's MTD (Month-to-date) investment inflows and outflows from February 2008 to late 2010. Over a period of 5 months, indicated by the circled area, nearly $15 billion dollars were suddenly drained out of the Brazilian stock market (foreign capital outflow from Bovespa).

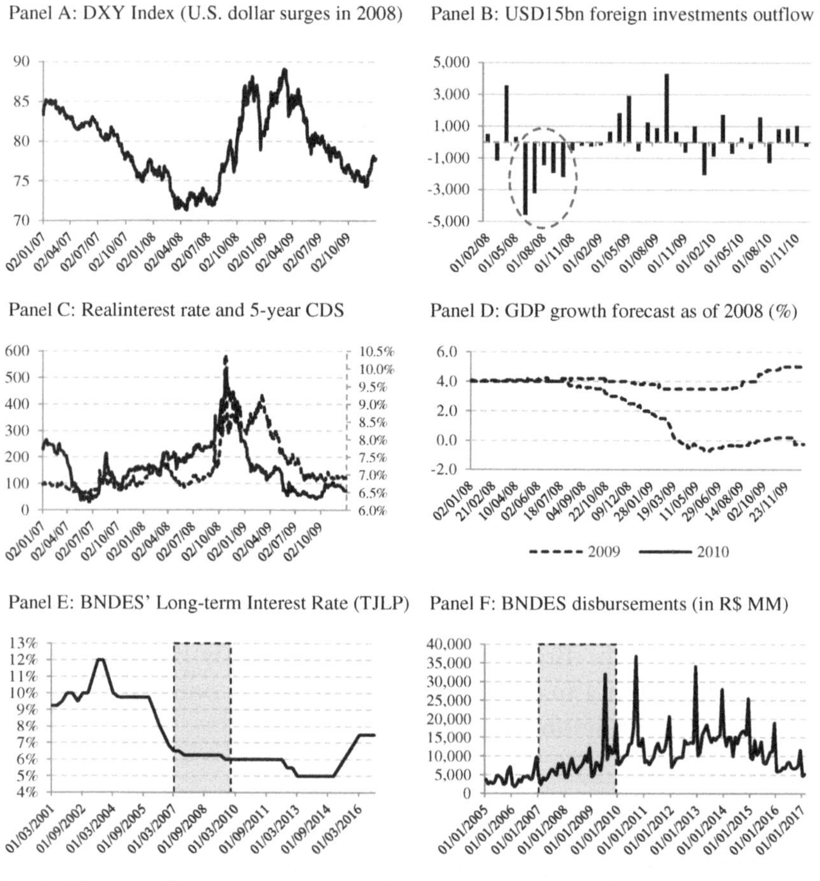

Fig. 6 The Brazilian economy at a glance. *Sources* Calculated from Bloomberg (2017) and author's own elaboration

- Real Discount Rate and Valuation *(WACC and Growth at Perpetuity)*: How does investors' risk perception would be influenced by a potentially systemic global crisis? Starting with the country risk component, the assets sell-off described above was largely correlated with a surge in Brazil's country risk. Indeed, Panel C in Fig. 6 depicts Brazil's 5-year CDS (Credit Default Swap) spread. After wondering around with 100 bp for nearly two years, the spread suddenly skyrocketed to nearly 600 bp by October 2008. As a consequence, the Brazilian real cost of equity employed to discount companies' cash flow (to equity) has surged.

Likewise, it is possible to observe a relevant spike in real interest rates aiming at compensating the US dollar appreciation and capital outflow, which caused the cost of marginally acquired debt to surge. When these two factors are combined, they pulled the WACC upwards throughout all assets within the Brazilian economy. Regarding the short-term growth outlook, which to some extent affects long-term growth in discounted cash flow perpetuity and actually drives nearly all revenue projections to domestic companies, it started to dip in two or three months before the "D-day" (October 14, 2007) and eventually plummeted once the GFC caused global markets to collapse. Panel D in Fig. 6 below, depicts the projections of GDP growth for 2009 and 2010 as of a particular date in 2008 (as depicted by the Brazilian Central Bank).

It is instructive to stretch the sample beyond the end of 2009 to emphasise one point: the stimulus policy started in 2006 has been, in fact, perpetuated until the recent Michel Temer administration took office in mid-2016. Panels E and F of Fig. 6 depict the BNDES disbursements as well as (nominal) interest rates charged in most credit operations carried out by the development bank,[29] which can be compared with the respective market rates (real), as depicted in Panel C of Fig. 6.

[29]In Panel E, the so-called TJLP, acronym for "long-term interest rate", is highlighted, which is calculated based on the centre of the inflation target plus a risk spread.

5 Summary and Conclusions

Based on the analysis and tests presented in this chapter, it is possible to conclude that once the GFC became evident, it contaminated the Brazilian stock market. As a consequence of key negative events (i.e. the four ones described in Sect. "Key Negative Exogenous Events as Indicators"), the dynamic conditional correlations suffered a sudden structural break. This break is an evidence of crisis transmission (i.e. financial contagion) from negative events originated in the US financial markets to Brazilian stock market sectors.

The most interesting and puzzling effect of financial contagion analysis, which was discussed and verified in this study, is that a singular cluster of negative events—such as a series of highly unexpected billionaire write-offs and loss subscriptions by US financial institutions, caused market capitalisation of listed companies form distinct sectors in Brazil to melt down as a perverse side effect.

Even in the absence of nearly any direct real economic variables linking the sectors analysed to the epicentre of the GFC, markets worldwide plunged in tandem with the US banking and real estate sectors. The implications of such conclusion refer to the fact that cross-market diversification may serve investors poorly when it is needed the most, as correlations do not sit still in the face of nearly systemic risks.

References

Arestis, P., & Karakitsos, E. (2013). *Financial stability in the aftermath of the great recession*. London: Springer.

Arruda, B. P. (2012). Análise da estrutura de dependência da volatilidade durante a crise do subprime. Unpublished manuscript, *EESP-FGV*. Available at http://bibliotecadigital.fgv.br/dspace/handle/10438/9811.

B3 (2017). *Profile and history*. Available at http://ir.bmfbovespa.com.br/static/enu/perfil-historico.asp?idioma=enu.

Baur, D. G. (2011). Contagion and the real economy during the global financial crisis. In R. W. Kolb, John Wiley & Sons, (Ed.), *Financial contagion: The viral threat to the wealth of nations* Inc., Hoboken: NJ, USA. doi:10.1002/9781118267646.ch24.

BBC. (2017). Brazil profile—Timeline. *BBC News*. Available at http://www.bbc.co.uk/news/world-latin-america-19359111.

Bernanke, B. (2007). Bernanke: Housing woes to slow growth. The Associated Press. Available at http://www.washingtonpost.com/wp-dyn/content/article/2007/10/15/AR2007101501281.html. Accessed March, 8, 2017.

Billio, M., & Caporin, M. (2005). Multivariate Markov switching dynamic conditional correlation GARCH representations for contagion analysis. *Statistical Methods and Applications, 14*(2), 145–161.

Bloomberg. (2017). *Bloomberg professional*. [Online]. Available at Subscription service. Accessed March, 17, 2017.

Board of Governors of the Federal Reserve System (US). (2017). Brazil/ U.S. Foreign Exchange Rate [DEXBZUS]. Retrieved from FRED, Federal Reserve Bank of St. Louis https://fred.stlouisfed.org/series/DEXBZUS. March, 27, 2017.

Boyson, N., Helwege, J., & Jindra, J. (2014). Crises, liquidity shocks, and fire sales at commercial banks. *Financial Management, 43*(4), 857–884.

Cappiello, L., Engle, R. F., & Sheppard, K. (2006). Asymmetric dynamics in the correlations of global equity and bond returns. *Journal of Financial Econometrics, 4*(4), 537–572.

Celık, S. (2012). The more contagion effect on emerging markets: The evidence of DCC-GARCH model. *Economic Modelling, 29*(5), 1946–1959.

Dungey, M., & Martin, V. L. (2001). Contagion across financial markets: An empirical assessment. In *New York Stock Exchange Conference Paper,* (pp. 16–17). *Hawaii.*

Engle, R. (2002). Dynamic conditional correlation: A simple class of multivariate generalized autoregressive conditional heteroskedasticity models. *Journal of Business and Economic Statistics, 20*(3), 339–350.

Engle, R. F., & Sheppard, K. (2001). Theoretical and empirical properties of dynamic conditional correlation multivariate GARCH. *National Bureau of Economic Research,* No. w8554.

Forbes, K. J., & Rigobon, R. (2002). No contagion, only interdependence: Measuring stock market comovements. *The Journal of Finance, 57*(5), 2223–2261.

Frank, N., Gonzalez-Hermosillo, B., & Hesse, H. (2008). *Transmission of liquidity shocks: Evidence from the 2007 subprime crisis*. International Monetary Fund: Washington, DC, US.

Fratzscher, M. (2012). Capital flows, push versus pull factors and the global financial crisis. *Journal of International Economics, 88*(2), 341–356.

Greenspan, A. (2007). Greenspan fears recession—report, *CNN*. Available at http://money.cnn.com/2007/02/26/news/economy/greenspan/index.htm?section=money_latest. Accessed March, 8, 2017.

Hesse, H., Frank, N., & González-Hermosillo, M. B. (2008). Transmission of liquidity shocks: Evidence from the 2007 subprime crisis. *IMF Working Paper*, No. 8–200. International Monetary Fund: Washington, DC, US.

Hong, K., & Tornell, A. (2005). Recovery from a currency crisis: Some stylized facts. *Journal of Development Economics, 76*(1), 71–96.

King, M., & Wadhwani, S. (1990). Transmission of volatility between stock markets. *Review of Financial Studies, 3*(1), 5–33.

Malacrida, M. J. C., & Yamamoto, M. M. (2006). Governança corporativa: nível de evidenciação das informações e sua relação com a volatilidade das ações do Ibovespa. *Revista contabilidade e finanças, 17,* 65–79.

Masson, P. (1998). Contagion: Monsoonal effects, spillovers and the emerging market crises. *IMF Working Paper* 98/164, Washington, DC, US.

Masson, P., & Mussa, M. (1995). Long-term tendencies in budget deficits and debt. *Proceedings, Federal Reserve Bank of Kansas City*, pp. 5–55.

Merton, R. C. (1974). On the pricing of corporate debt: The risk structure of interest rates. *The Journal of Finance, 29*(2), 449–470.

Newey, W. K., & McFadden, D. (1994). Large sample estimation and hypothesis testing. *Handbook of Econometrics, 4,* 2111–2245.

Pagan, A. (1986). Two stage and related estimators and their applications. *The Review of Economic Studies, 53*(4), 517–538.

Rimkus, R. (2016). The financial crisis of 2008. Date: 2008/ Region: Global. *CFA Institute*. Available at https://www.econcrises.org/2016/08/17/the-financial-crisis-of-2008/.

Sachs, J., Tornell, A., & Velasco, A. (1996). Financial crises in emerging markets: The lessons from 1995. *National Bureau of Economic Research,* No. w5576.

Sharpe, W. F. (1964). Capital asset prices: A theory of market equilibrium under conditions of risk. *The journal of finance, 19*(3), 425–442.

Zingales, L. (2008). Causes and effects of the Lehman Brothers bankruptcy. In*Committee on oversight and government reform.* Washington, DC, US: House of Representatives.

Foreign Exchange Derivatives and Financial Fragility in Brazil

Maryse Farhi

1 Introduction[1]

Profit-seeking agents, banks and other financial institutions actively react to regulatory, institutional and macroeconomic changes. As Minsky (1986) stressed, this happens mostly through the introduction of financial innovations. However, the introduction of new instruments, new practices, new strategies, new markets, and even new institutions varies according to the macroeconomic specificities.

The Global Financial Crisis (GFC), which began in 2007 in the US (USA) subprime mortgage market, had a profound impact across emerging markets. One of its main transmission channels was financial innovations that have spread since the 1990s, when developing

[1]This chapter is partly based on Prates and Farhi (2015).

M. Farhi (✉)
Institute of Economics, State University of Campinas, Campinas, SP, Brazil
e-mail: maryse.farhi@gmail.com

P. Arestis et al. (eds.), *The Brazilian Economy since the Great Financial Crisis of 2007/2008*, https://doi.org/10.1007/978-3-319-64885-9_12

countries joined the process of financial globalization, becoming emerging market economies (EMEs); although, that process was uneven, yielding different results. While in Asia securitization emerged at a rapid pace, it was quite the opposite in Latin America, which still trails on, unable to develop a liquid secondary market. Despite their differences, financial derivative markets have grown in all those countries and present an important common aspect: the importance of Foreign Exchange (FX) rate derivatives.

This does not necessarily mean that FX derivative operations have higher volume than those linked to interest rates or stock indexes. The peculiarity of emerging economies stems from the position of their national currencies at the lower end of the international hierarchy of currencies.[2] FX rates have always been at the core of all emerging countries' crisis. Thus, FX derivatives have the potential either to allow hedging risks, to mitigate the crisis or to exacerbate its depth due to leveraged bets that turn sour.

Not only does its paramount importance assert itself in times of crisis, but all along the cross-border finance cycles.[3] In FX derivatives markets, the carry trade expresses itself as a bet in a short position in the funding currency and a long position in the target currency (Gagnon and Chaboud 2007), reproducing in a synthetic and highly leveraged way the canonical carry trade (Burnside et al. 2006; Gagnon and Chaboud 2007; Kaltenbrunner 2010). Regarding Latin America countries, BIS (2015) states that "capital inflows and reversals pose a number of challenges for monetary authorities in EMEs. Among the various types of capital flow, currency carry trades raise particular concerns because they may be destabilizing and contribute to extended periods of currency appreciation, moving and keeping the real exchange rate away from its fundamental equilibrium, and thus eroding competitiveness. Currency carry trades may also be associated with currency crash risks because, in their typical form, they are funded mostly by debt" (p. 2).

---

[2]See Fritz et al. (2014) and Cohen (2009).

[3]Cross-border finance encompasses both capital flows—portfolio investment and bank loans that result in spot currency markets' operations—and operations with FX derivatives.

Brazil stands out among the EMEs in terms of the FX derivatives market because the greater liquidity and depth (i.e., higher number of trades and turnover) of its organized segment (BMF and Bovespa[4]) in comparison with both the FX spot market and the FX over-the-counter market (OTC).[5] Thus, in times of heightened risk aversion, international agents frequently use Brazilian FX derivatives market as a proxy to the entire group of EMEs.

Many studies have already shown that, due to its higher liquidity and its accessibility to all sorts of agents, the first dollar future contract (30 days between each settlement date) has become the locus of formation of the BRL/USD exchange rate (Kaltenbrunner 2010; Ventura and Garcia 2012; Chamon and Garcia 2013; Fritz and Prates 2014; Prates 2015; Rossi 2012). Yet, unlike these authors, our focus is not the central role of the FX derivatives market in the Brazilian exchange rate dynamic, but the relationship between this market, banking competition, and financial fragility in Brazil at the time of the GFC and its aftermath. Our aim is to analyze the aforementioned factors after the 2007/2008 GFC although a brief retrospective analysis is necessary for the understanding of the crucial role of FX derivatives in Brazil.

Be it as an instrument to market's agents or to the monetary authority, the FX derivative markets in Brazil have an overwhelming importance in the determination of FX rate, with all its macroeconomic consequences. The particular Brazilian institutional and regulatory framework of the exchange rate markets provide some important explanatory element to this excessive role. Another element is the existence of a liquid offshore market that entices arbitrage operations between the two venues by the banks and nonresident investors. It shows that complete financial openness is not a precondition for the existence of liquid derivative markets in an emerging economy. The Brazilian case underlines the key influence of FX derivatives along with capital flows in the exchange rate that is

[4]The BM and F merged with Bovespa, the main Brazilian stock exchange on March 25, 2008.

[5]According to Avdjiev et al. (2010), the BRL was the second most traded currency worldwide in the organized derivatives markets in 2010, while the financial volume of FX derivatives traded onshore OTC markets were lower (USD18 billion in April 2010) than in other emerging markets, such as Korea.

still missing in the theoretical models of the determination of nominal exchange rates in the era post Bretton Woods (Prates 2015).

Besides this introduction and the final remarks, the arguments are organized chronologically in three sections, as follows. Section 2 brings the specific features of Brazil's FX derivative markets and a short historical review of its evolution: new macroeconomic regime, enhanced financial openness and the first cross-border finance cycle. Sections 2 and 3 analysis the contagion effect of the GFC and its aftermath (the new cross-border finance cycle and the regulatory response). Section 4 assesses the Brazilian political and economic crisis, followed by the final remarks.

2 Brief Historical Review

The dynamics of Brazil's FX derivative markets are associated with a set of regulatory, institutional and macroeconomic factors, which have reinforced each other since the mid of the 1990s. Four of these features attract special attention:

1. The institutional framework of the Brazilian currency market wherein FX accounts (bank deposits) is prohibited, with only a few exceptions. Consequently, nonbank residents and nonresidents cannot hold FX spot positions. Only banks authorized by the BCB to have FX portfolios can hold these positions.[6] This same institutional feature underlies the non-deliverable character of the FX derivative markets, namely, profits or losses in this market settle exclusively in domestic currency (BRL). Because of this, any agent can hold positions in the FX futures market as long as they fulfill minimum standards required by the Brazilian exchange. Besides, it allows all market's agents—for instance, the monetary authority—to assume short positions irrespective of the existence of foreign reserves.

[6]There are few exceptions. Multilateral institutions and insurance companies that deal with foreign trade area allowed FX bank accounts. However, their use is very limited (Rossi 2012).

2. Institutional traits of the Brazilian financial system have also contributed to the growth of the FX derivatives market, among which the increase in banking internationalization in Brazil since the mid-1990s. After the banking crisis in 1995, the government fostered the entry of new foreign banks, with expertise in derivatives trading. These banks contributed to the growth of the secondary government bond markets, shares (stock exchanges), and especially derivatives, acting as brokers (on behalf of clients) and for their own account. Yet, despite their "*savoir faire*," their entry did not lead to a deepening of the domestic capital market as a source of business financing, be it securities or equities, unlike the trend observed in several Asian emerging countries according to BIS (2003a and 2003b).
3. The unrestricted access of foreign investors to the FX futures market since January 2000. The adoption of a floating exchange rate regime in 1999 increased the demand for FX hedge and the opportunities to earn speculative and arbitrage profits through FX derivatives. This specific feature of the FX derivatives in Brazil increased its liquidity and reinforced its dual role (hedge and speculation) in distinct occasions, as in 1999, when the macroeconomic impact of the adoption of a floating exchange rate was smoothened as relevant agents hedged their FX risks with the BCB acting as their counterpart. Or, on the other hand, in 2008, these markets enhanced the effect of the GFC as a high number of agents held a leveraged position that resulted in heavy losses.
4. The obligation to register all derivative operations carried out in the onshore market, including the OTC markets. This specificity of the Brazilian derivatives market has reduced the opacity of OTC operations, thus contributing to the policy response to the crisis.

In line with the dominant trend among emerging economies, the Brazilian government responded to its (1999) currency crisis by the adoption of a new set of economic policies based on an inflation targeting policy, a (dirty) floating exchange rate regime and a target for primary budget surplus.[7] Known as the New Macroeconomics Consensus,

[7]For a detailed analysis of the similarities and specificities of emerging economies currency crises in the 1990s, see Kregel (1998a, 1998b, 1999, 2000).

this set of policies was implemented during Fernando Henrique Cardoso's (FHC) second term. The adoption of a floating exchange rate regime increased the demand for FX hedge and the opportunities to earn arbitrage and speculative profits through FX derivatives. Even more so as, despite the new macroeconomic regime, the interest rate differential remained high.

The increase of Brazil's banking internationalization in the mid-1990s, as referred to earlier, opened the way to a much higher internationalization of the Brazilian banking system as more foreign banks entered the country through acquisitions or mergers with national banks. At the same time, despite the high cost of the public programs for the restructuring and strengthening of the financial system and the reduction of the state public sector in banking activity (estimated at 9.7% of GDP), public and private banks programs reduced financial fragility and potential systemic risks. Its benefits became clear in 1999, when a FX crisis did not trigger a banking crisis, thus reducing its macroeconomic effects. Among the emerging countries that faced financial crisis in the 1990s, only Brazil did not have a "twin crisis" (FX and banking crisis).[8] A deepening of the process of financial openness in January 2000 accompanied the new macroeconomic regime. All former regulations were removed and a new resolution (Resolution CMN n. 2689) allowed the unrestricted access of nonresident (i.e., foreign) investors to all segments of the domestic financial market, including the derivatives market and guaranteed equal treatment to domestic and international investors. These factors interplayed with banking competition fostered by foreign banks' strategies in the first term of Luis Inácio Lula da Silva (hereafter Lula), who took office on January 2003 and kept a very similar macroeconomic policy framework.

Contrary to the high-risk aversion and shortage of external capital flows[9] during 1999–2002, from 2003 to the threshold of the financial

[8]In the first year after the adoption of floating exchange rate policy, South Korea, Thailand, and Mexico respectively suffered a contraction of their GDP of 5, 8, and 6.2% respectively; while Brazilian GDP grew by 0.7%.

[9]See Akyuz (2010).

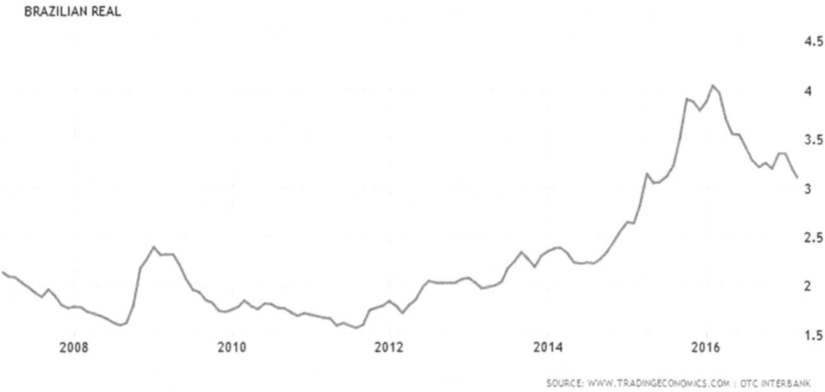

Fig. 1 Evolution of Brazil's spot FX rate 2007–2017

crisis of 2008, the enforcement of the new macroeconomic regime took place in an exceptionally favorable international setting, with rising commodity prices and a boom of capital flows to emerging countries (Prates 2015; Ocampo 2007; Akyüz 2010).[10] The incoming wave of foreign capital and their synthetic expression via the derivative markets were overwhelming, and Brazilian Real surged (Fig. 1). The BCB faced a dilemma: In the short run, a FX appreciation was essential to fight inflation, but, in the long run, it severely undermined the competitiveness of Brazilian economy.

Its option was to allow the FX appreciation, without reducing the very high interest rate that attracted foreign flows. Nevertheless, at the same time, it started to buy foreign currency to redeem external public debt and constitute foreign reserves that would reduce the country's external vulnerability. In December 2008, these reserves amounted to US$207 billion, or around 12% of GDP. Brazil became a net external creditor, that is, despite the federal government debt denominated in foreign currency, it held more foreign currency assets than it owed in foreign currency debt.

[10]For an overview of this context, see Ocampo (2007).

Issuance of public bonds used in repo operations sterilized the monetary emission needed to those purchases, inflating gross public debt. Hence, the growing analytical importance of the distinction between gross public debt that encompasses the totality of debts from the federal, state, and municipal governments (with the exception of state-owned companies and the BCB) and net public debt that portraits the balance of assets (mostly, international reserves) and liabilities of the non-financial public sector (except Petrobras) and the BCB.[11] We discuss, ahead, the impact of this kind of monetary sterilization.

The Brazilian economy became fully open to capital inflows and outflows in 2005, with the liberalization of residents' capital outflows. For the first time, domestic entities were able to buy unlimited foreign currency directly from the banks and invest them abroad. Nevertheless, despite this broad liberalization, one key institutional feature of the Brazilian currency market, pointed out in the Introduction, remained untouched, namely the prohibition of FX accounts by residents and nonresidents established by the International Exchange and Capital Market Regulation (RMCCI).[12] Another important measure, adopted on February 2006, exempted foreign investment in public bonds and venture capital funds from income taxes.

As mentioned above, the "other side of the coin" of the ban of FX currency accounts is the obligation to settle all transactions in the domestic currency (the BRL). Consequently, the Brazilian FX derivatives (futures and OTC) market is non-deliverable, i.e., profits or losses in these operations settle in BRL. Precisely for this reason, they are outside the scope of the FX market regulation (the aforementioned RMCCI). There are no limits to market positions in the FX derivatives market of banks and, especially, other agents' whose access to the spot market is bared, as long as they fulfill the minimum standards required by the Brazilian exchange (BM & F/Bovespa) (Kaltenbrunner 2010).

---

[11]For more details on this distinction, see: http://www3.tesouro.gov.br/english/public_debt/downloads/Debt_Report_Fiscal_Indicators.pdf.

[12]See: http://www.bcb.gov.br/?RMCCI.

In the case of FX futures market, the main agents have been resident banks (whether Brazilian or foreign-owned), resident institutional investors, non-financial resident companies and nonresident investors. The wide range of participants has ensured greater trade volume, liquidity and depth of this market and contributed to its preeminent role in the setting of the spot market exchange rate.

As Kaltenbrunner (2010) and Rossi (2010) pointed out, between 2003 and mid-2008, foreign institutional investors, primarily hedge funds, were the most important investor group in the Brazilian FX futures market, fostering a currency appreciation trend. The huge differential between the internal and external interest rates associated with a falling country risk, under the very favorable international context, led foreign investors to bet heavily on the appreciation of the Brazilian currency. That took place in the FX futures market, which resulted in a devaluation of the USD price (Prates 2015) along with bets on the reduction of long-term interest rate.

Those are kinds of derivatives carry trade that differ from the canonical carry trade through spot market operations, that is, borrowing low-interest-rate currencies and lending high-interest-rate currencies. In FX derivatives markets, the carry trade expresses itself as a short position in the funding currency and a long position in the target currency (Burnside et al. 2006; Gagnon and Chaboud 2007, BIS 2015). Also very popular among foreign investors, was a combination in the futures markets of a long position in the target currency combined with a long position in interest rates.

The derivatives carry trade is even more attractive in Brazil due to the non-deliverable feature of the FX derivatives market. Foreign and domestic agents could engage in it without disbursing one single USD, until October 2010 as they could meet their margin requirements via domestic borrowed securities or guarantees from local banks (see Sect. 3). As BIS (2015) points out: "An important advantage of non-deliverables is that there is no need to deliver the notional amount, so that returns can be obtained with a far smaller investment" (pg. 7). In other words, non-deliverables derivatives have a higher leverage than deliverable ones.

Table 1 Volume traded—Brazilian FX market

	Daily averages (USD milhões)				Change (%)	
	2001	2004	2007	2010	2007/2004	2010/2007
Spot[1]	3461	2568	4754	5508	185.1	115.9
Primary	1665	1845	3390	3906	183.8	115.2
Interbank	1796	723	1364	1602	188.6	117.5
Derivatives	2463	2670	8844	23,286	331.2	263.3
Local[2]	1916	1674	3390	7313	202.5	215.7
Cross-Border[3]	547	996	5454	15,973	547.6	292.9

Source BIS. *Triennal central bank survey of foreign exchange and derivatives market activity*, 2010 e 2013. URL: www.bis.org.
Notes
1. The sum of the daily averages overestimates the value traded due to double counting
2. Future and OTC contracts
3. Non-Deliverable Forwards (NDF)

The outstanding performance of the BRL futures market has contributed to boosting the trading of the Brazilian currency on foreign OTC markets through non-deliverable forward (NDF) contracts.[13] This market is not transparent and it is nearly impossible to obtain accurate information about it.

Consequently, the macroeconomic setting has reinforced the liquidity and depth of the Brazilian FX futures market (see Table 1). According to Johnson (2007), in the first quarter of 2007, "BM&Fs U.S. Dollar contract led the sector (i.e., the foreign currency sector) for the second year in a row with a 51.4% increase to 10.97 million contracts. It was followed by CMEs Euro FX contract which rose 22% to 6.73 million contracts."

The existence of a deep futures market has made it possible for banks that have an account with the local exchange to sell BRL in the offshore OTC market (meeting the demand of international investors who were betting on the BRL appreciation) and simultaneously hedge their exposure in the onshore future market. Although Brazilian banks with foreign branches have also participated in this kind of operation, foreign

[13]On the NDF market of emerging economy currencies, see Ma et al. (2004).

banks have been the most active, standing out as foreign investors' counterparts (Kaltenbrunner 2010). The growth of the NDF market for the BRL, in turn, has enhanced even more the liquidity and depth of the Brazilian futures market, as arbitrage of the prices in the both markets reached considerable amounts. In this setting, many international investors began to use the BRL futures contracts as a proxy for derivatives of other EMEs' currencies, which have been highly correlated with the Brazilian Real (such as the Turkish lira and the South African rand). However, they do not have deep and liquid derivatives markets, which further increased the trading of BRL futures contracts (Prates 2015).

3 The Contagion Effect of the Global Financial Crisis

In mid-2007, the financial crisis in the USA led to an accrued appreciation of the currencies of EMEs' commodity exporters whose main export products' prices rose significantly. In the case of Brazil, the FX appreciation gained further momentum when the country obtained the investment grade from the rating agencies in the first half of 2008. Then, in the second half of 2008, when the subprime crisis turned out to be a global financial crisis, a huge and sudden depreciation of those currencies occurred. Directly hit by a new sudden stop of capital flows and the collapse of commodities' prices, their assets and the exchange rates became important targets of the global deleveraging and "flight to quality."

In this context, enormous financial losses of important non-financial companies of EMEs with heavy short positions in the FX derivatives markets surfaced. In the first semester of 2008, they decided to bet in the continued appreciation of their currencies against the dollar, as the dollar intense depreciation had contributed to the strong increase in commodities international prices. Many of them did so by means of exotic offshore derivatives proposed by international banks. The deepening of the crisis generated a burst in commodity prices and a new trend of dollar appreciation, resulting in huge losses in such derivatives bets (Farhi and Borghi 2009).

Dodd (2009) estimates that "the direct cost to non-financial firms of these derivatives losses, based on the sum of national estimates, is $530 billion. Possibly 50,000 firms in at least 12 economies have suffered derivatives losses" (p. 3). Many of those companies were exporters, who suffer more intensely the impact of an appreciation of their national currency. From a microeconomic point of view, it was understandable that those companies searched to hedge against FX appreciation.[14] However, the volume of their operations, a double digit multiple of their annual exports, revealed that they had also assumed a speculative posture. Dodd (2009), although emphasizing the use of financial derivatives for hedging purposes, also points out its speculative use by Brazilian[15] and Mexican companies along with others from China, South Korea, India, and Hong Kong.

In Brazil, foreign investment banks, rapidly mimicked by private national banks, also began to offer low rate loans tied to FX derivatives. For the banks, these operations provided an insurance against exchange rate depreciation (which historically led to macroeconomic instability, with negative effects on the borrowing cost and the debtors ability to pay), perceived as increasingly likely due to the worsening of the international crisis. However, the debtor would have to pay the accorded rate plus the variation of the FX rate in case of a depreciation. The downward trend of the BRL/USD exchange rate since 2003 had led agents to underestimate the risk of these operations (Fig. 1). Several other medium size companies—in the industrial, construction and commerce sectors along with medium size banks—with a primary focus on the domestic market also engaged in it due to their lower interest rates, although at smaller volumes. As Kregel (2011) points out, the expectation of a sustained appreciation of the Brazilian currency had fostered

[14]"One important way firms may have cut the exposure to currency risk has been the growing reliance on financial derivatives to hedge currency risk" (IMF 2008, p. 55).

[15]In Brazil, Sadia, Aracruz, and Votorantim were the first companies whose losses with FX derivatives were made public. Sadia had a short position of USD8.4 billion and recorded, in the third quarter of 2008, a loss of USD370 million; Aracruz recorded losses of USD2.13 billion and the Votorantim Group's of USD1 billion. In late October 2008, the director of Cetip, Jorge Sant'Anna, informed that there were over five hundred companies involved in the FX derivatives (Chiarini 2008).

investment banks to sell OTC market derivatives to export firms who were interested not only in hedging the estimated exports but also in obtaining speculative profits in order to offset the impact of the currency appreciation.

In the case of the larger Brazilian exporting companies, a higher number of the derivative contracts took place in the offshore OTC market, making it impossible to evaluate their size and extension. The FX derivatives contracts performed in the Brazilian market were mostly OTC operations, registered at Cetip (Custody and Settlement Chamber). Data from BM&F/Bovespa show that the non-financial companies' participation in the organized market was quite small in that period. In turn, the Cetip´s information shows USD94.7 billion in non-deliverable forward contracts between banks and their non-financial counterparts in October 29, 2008. They also underline two periods of remarkable increase of the volume of these contracts: The first in late 2005 and 2006; the second began in late 2007 and intensified from August to September 2008.

Prior to the worsening of the crisis, the selling pressure of dollars by Brazilian non-financial companies in the OTC derivatives markets was conveyed through arbitrage to the spot exchange rate, causing further currency appreciation. At its height, the public disclosure of their losses had a dramatic effect. The size of the shock was proportional to the companies' exposure to short derivative bets in dollars. Since these are "out of balance sheet" operations, they are rather opaque. Even in the cases of publicly traded companies, the disclosure of such operations was not mandatory to non-financial companies. In a newspaper article, Lessa (2008) pointed out the urgent need to reform their regulation and supervision, "We cannot go to sleep one night thinking that Sadia, Aracruz, Votorantim and Vicunha are in a good situation, only to find out, the next morning, that they themselves do not know the extent of their losses" (p. A11).

Until the disclosure of the companies' losses, the reduction in foreign capital inflows, higher outflows and the deterioration of the trade balance were the main transmission channels of the international crisis to emerging economies. Uncertainty about the solvency of large industrial enterprises due to losses with FX derivatives played a crucial role to the emergence of a confidence crisis almost similar to that prevailing in developed economies, putting additional pressure on the exchange rate.

On their side, banks were involved, be it as direct counterparts in FX OTC derivatives, be it as credit operations linked to FX derivatives, be it as creditors in regular loans. In those three cases, they faced a significant credit risk. Unaware of the degree of exposure of other banks to the risk of losses in these OTC operations,[16] banks withdrew credit not only to companies and individuals but also to each other in the interbank market (Prates and Cintra 2010). In other words, banks set in motion a movement of absolute risk aversion and liquidity preference.

Therefore, financial innovations represented by FX derivatives amplified the contagion effect of the crisis in Brazil, increasing its financial fragility. As detailed above, institutional and macroeconomic features have reinforced the already key role of this class of derivatives in EMEs, whose currencies stand at the bottom of the currency hierarchy. Hence, unlike the USA and other developed economies, credit derivatives (i.e., Credit Default Swaps—CDS) were not important in Brazil. The relevant market was, and still is, very thin and illiquid mainly because even though banks demanded protection against credit risks, very few agents were willing to sell this protection for a premium much lower than the interest rate paid by public bonds with a much lower risk.

4 The Aftermath of the Global Financial Crisis

The revealed financial fragility did not evolve to a financial crisis because of the countercyclical measures launched by the Brazilian government,[17] among which stands out the actions taken by the three major federal

[16]Unibanco, one of the major national private banks, incurred large losses in FX derivatives operations and was acquired by Itaú in November 2008.

[17]On the Brazilian government response to the contagion effect of the global financial crisis, see Cunha et al. (2011); WTO (2010); and BCB (2010).

public banks that extended more credit to firms and families as private banks reduced their offer. It is worth mentioning the Provisionary Measure n. 443 of October 21, which authorized two of them to acquire participation in private financial institutions based in Brazil, thus avoiding their bankruptcy. Moreover, the government increased the capital of Banco Nacional de Desenvolvimento Econômico e Social (BNDES), boosting its capacity to grant loans to avoid a sharp reduction of credit operations and, consequently, of the economic activity in a context of high liquidity preference of private banks (Rezende 2015). Finally, BNDES performed a coordination role in the process of debt restructuring and/or rolling over of companies that incurred huge losses from FX derivatives (Prates 2010). Thus, they transformed the margin calls due by the companies in long-term credit.

As Minsky (1993) points out, the fragility of an economy is also determined by the institutions in place and by their ability to increase liquidity when needed. In this particular case, the worst was avoided, but at a very high price. Transforming derivatives' margin calls in credit at the height of a speculative bubble took its toll in a longer run. The companies saw their leverage skyrocket and the banks' balance sheet swelled. Later on, the increase in over-indebtedness played an important role in the deepening of the recession discussed in Sect. 4. The contagion effect of the global financial crisis also disclosed shortcomings in the FX derivatives regulation. These losses could not have been previously assessed by their shareholders and banks faced credit risks because the lack of transparency due to the non-consolidation of each agent's derivative positions.

At the end of 2008, the CVM adopted measures to make disclosure of derivatives more transparent and facilitate the analysis of firms' accounting exchange rate's exposure.[18] Among them, are new accounting rules for financial instruments extending from the exotic derivatives to any receivables (Valenti 2009). Under the new rule, issued in December 2008, the disclosure of the table of sensitivity analysis

[18]For more information on these changes, see Rossi Júnior (2011).

in three different scenarios became mandatory (Valenti and Fregoni 2009).[19] Moreover, in November 2009, the BCB established mandatory registration of financial derivatives linked to foreign loans (Circular 3.474). According to the director of relationships with participants of Cetip, Jorge Sant'Anna, the objective of the derivatives center is to disclose information about the companies' deals with derivatives, in such a way that the participants of the market could evaluate their consolidated risks (Pavini and Carvalho 2009).

The authorities and the banks took other measures to improve FX derivatives regulation after the containment of the contagion effect and the surge of a new boom of capital flows to emerging economies arose. The first measure was a private initiative. In December 2010, the Brazilian Bank Association (Febraban) established the Centre for Exposure in Derivatives (CED in the Portuguese acronym), which was the most important step to address the problem of consolidating clients' exposure in the domestic derivatives market.

The others were part of a set of policy measures launched between 2009 and 2011 aimed at curbing the renewed appreciation pressures on the Brazilian currency caused by the resumption of canonical and derivatives carry trade operations over the aforementioned new boom of capital flows. As during the optimistic wave that took place before the global crisis, the FX derivatives market played a central role in the trajectory of the Brazilian currency during this boom. However, at the opposite of its policy in the pre-crisis boom, the Brazilian government, in tandem with many other EMEs, chose not to adopt a hands-off approach to capital inflows. In September 2010, the finance minister, Guido Mantega, declared that an international currency war had broken out, adding: "this threatens us because it takes away our competitiveness."[20] Besides massively intervening in the spot market,

[19]Instruction CVM n 475/2008 disposes that public traded companies must address financial instruments in their periodic balances and makes the disclosure of the risk sensitivity analysis mandatory. That analysis includes the definition of a scenario considered probable by the administration, one with a deterioration of at least 25% (twenty-five percent) in the risk variable considered and another with a deterioration of at least 50%.

[20]Available at https://economia.uol.com.br/ultimas-noticias/reuters/2010/09/27/mantega-ve-guerra-cambial-reitera-arsenal-dogoverno.jhtm.

causing foreign reserves to pile up, the government imposed controls on capital inflows (but not on the outflows) and changed the FX derivatives institutional framework by adopting new regulations with a cyclical or macroeconomic aim (hinder the FX appreciation), as detailed next.

The post GFC scenario combined with domestic factors (mainly the resumption of economic growth, the depth and liquidity of capital and derivatives markets and still high interest rates by international standards) resulted in large capital inflows and strong FX appreciation pressures between 2009 and the third quarter of 2011. Indeed, Brazil became the main destination for capital flows in Latin America in this period (IMF 2010; Fritz and Prates 2014).

The institutional specificities of the Brazilian FX market pose greater challenges to policy makers than those faced in other economies with similarly large derivative markets, such as South Korea. Brazilian authorities had to address the low efficiency of capital controls in dealing with FX derivatives operations (due to their high degree of leverage as it only requires a margin) and the insufficiency of prudential financial regulation that encompassed only financial institutions, not applying to other important agents as foreign investors and corporations. While, in Korea, for instance, prudential regulation was sufficient to curb FX derivatives operations concentrated in the OTC market, where banks are the counterpart of corporations in the FX contracts and where profits or losses settle in US dollars.[21]

In this setting, FX regulations were adopted along with the tightening of capital controls (see Table 1), in successive moves in a trial and error process until they succeeded in curbing the FX appreciation pressures. The increase of an already existing financial tax (IOF in the Portuguese acronym) on foreign fixed income portfolio investments and equity fund[22] had a low efficiency due to the regulatory arbitrage set in

[21]For a detail analysis of the Korean and Brazilian response to the post-crisis optimistic wave and the new approach of the IMF concerning capital controls, see Fritz and Prates (2014).

[22]As already mentioned, since 2006, nonresident investors are exempted from the tax on revenue on their Brazilian financial assets, while national investors are subjected to a tax of 15%.

motion by banks and nonresident investors to circumvent the tougher capital control. Foreign public reserves piled up again.

The higher IOF on capital inflows encouraged the derivatives to carry trade (build-up of long BRL/short USD positions in the FX derivatives market) by nonresidents. This was only possible because the resident dealers' banks assumed the opposite position of nonresident investors in the derivatives market (short BRL/long USD); and, simultaneously, increased their short positions in the spot market. It is worth remembering that banks need to fulfill prudential financial regulation requirement and are the sole institutions able to carry USD positions in the Brazilian spot market.

To close this loophole, the BCB imposed a non-interest reserve requirement, a prudential financial regulation tool, on bank short positions in the spot market in January 2010 (see Table 2). Nevertheless, by switching to short-term foreign borrowing, companies and, mainly, banks were able to find another channel for regulatory arbitrage. On October 2010, the prohibition of meeting margin requirements in BRL via domestic borrowed securities or guarantees from local banks targeted for the first time, the FX derivatives. In March 2011, the government imposed the IOF on short-term foreign borrowing. However, as these private agents were able to make longer-term loans in a context of ample liquidity searching for yield in the international financial market, the government subsequently (in April 2011) extended the IOF to these loans, encompassing even intercompany loans.

As the measures taken had only curbed the pace of currency appreciation, the Brazilian government launched a broader set of FX derivatives regulation at the end of July 2011. The government imposed a financial tax of 1% on excessively long positions on BRL in the FX derivatives market; at the same time, it adopted new rules to improve the market's transparency (see Table 2). It was only then that the speculation over the Brazilian currency was contained and a small depreciation took place. The process of trial and error constitutes the biggest proof of the prominent role of the FX derivatives market in the determination of the exchange rate.

The optimistic period hid growing macroeconomic imbalances in Brazil. Those lingering problems started to assert themselves in May

Table 2 Capital controls, prudential regulation and FX derivative

Date	Number and kind	Tighten or loosen	Measure
Oct/2009	1⁰ CC	Tighten	Implementation of a 2% financial transaction tax (IOF in the Portuguese acronym) on non-resident equity and fixed income portfolio inflows
Oct/2010	2⁰ and 3⁰ CC	Tighten	(i) IOF increased from 2 to 4% for fixed income portfolio investments and equity funds (ii) IOF increased to 6% for fixed income investments
Oct/2010	1⁰ and 2⁰ FXDR	Tighten	(i) IOF on margin requirements on FX derivatives transactions increased from 0.38 to 6% (ii) Loopholes for IOF on margin requirements closed
Jan/2011	1⁰ PR	Tighten	Non-interest reserve requirement equivalent to 60% of bank's short dollar positions in the FX spot market that exceed USD3 billion or their capital base
March/2011	4⁰ CC	Tighten	Increased to 6% the IOF on new foreign loans with maturities of up a year
April/2011	5⁰ CC	Tighten	(i) 6% IOF extended for the renewal of foreign loans with maturities of up a year (ii) 6% IOF extended for both new and renewed foreign loans with maturities of up to 2 years

(continued)

Table 2 (continued)

Date	Number and kind	Tighten or loosen	Measure
July/2011	2^0 PR	Tighten	Non-interest reserve requirement mandatory for amounts over USD1 billion or capital base (whichever is smaller)
July/2011	3^0 FXDR	Tighten	(i) Appointment of the Monetary Council of the Brazilian Central Bank (CMN) as the agency responsible for regulating the derivatives market (ii) Requirement that all FX must be priced according to the same method (iii) Requirement that all FX derivatives must be registered in clearing houses (iv) Requirement that FX exposure of all agents must be consolidated (liquid position) (v) Implementation of a 1% financial tax on all agents' excessively long positions on BRL. This tax can be increased to 25%
Dec/2011	6^0 CC	Loosen	IOF on equity and fixed income (linked with infrastructure projects) portfolio inflows reduced to 0%
March/2012	7^0 CC	Tighten	(i) 6% IOF extended for both new and renewed foreign loans with maturities of up to 3 and then to 5 years (ii) Export advanced payment transactions with maturities of more than a year prohibited

(continued)

Table 2 (continued)

Date	Number and kind	Tighten or loosen	Measure
March/2012	4⁰ FXDR	Loosen	Exporters hedge operations exempted from the IOF
June/2012	8⁰ CC	Loosen	6% IOF only for new and renewed foreign loans with maturities of up to 2 years
Dec/2012	9⁰ CC	Loosen	(i) 6% IOF for foreign loans with maturities of up to 1 year (ii)Export advanced payment transactions maturity extended from 1 for 5 years
June/2013	10⁰ CC	Loosen	IOF on fixed income portfolio inflows reduced to 0%
June/2013	5⁰ FXDR	Loosen	IOF of 1% on excessive long net positions of FX derivatives of all agents reduced to 0%
July/2013	3⁰ PR	Loosen	Non-interest reserve requirement on bank´s short dollar positions in the FX spot market reduced from 60% to 0%

Source Prates and Farhi (2015) based on Central Bank's and Minister of Finance's websites.
Note 1. FX = Foreign exchange; CC = Capital Control; PR = Prudential Regulation; FXDR = Foreign Exchange Derivatives Regulation

2013, after the announcement of Ben Bernanke, president of the Federal Reserve (Fed) that the quantitative easing program would be progressively reduced till it ended (the so-called tapering). The effects of the expected change in the Fed monetary policy resonated around the world, but more acutely in EMEs. Among them, Brazil experienced the sharpest currency devaluation.

Fearing capital flight, in June 2013, Brazilian government suspended all the measures destined to reduce the inflow of foreign capital and curb the FX derivatives carry trade. However, reversing the FX derivatives regulations launched over the optimistic wave was ineffective to stem the currency depreciation when the cross-border finance cycle unwound in a setting of flight to quality (i.e., to US Treasury bonds) and high-risk aversion. The removal of the regulatory toolkit, which only penalized bets in favor of the BRL, was virtually powerless to bring down the depreciation of the BRL/USD exchange rate.

As during the boom, in the bust phase, the changes in investors' positions in the FX future markets were the main determinant of the BRL trend. Indeed, the withdrawal of the financial tax on long positions in June 2013 made it easier for the portfolio adjustment to derivative bets on the BRL depreciation. Only a symmetrical financial tax on both excessive short and long positions (i.e., a FX derivatives regulation that penalizes bets on the BRL depreciation/appreciation) could restrain the volatility generated in the different phases of cross-border finance process.

Furthermore, the BCB did not resort to any kind of spot market interventions to ensure smoother variations of the exchange rate, despite having USD376 billion FX reserves (15.28% of GDP) available. It had already started a tightening in monetary policy and opted to implement credit lines in USD and a new program of currency swap contracts, which trade the FX variation for the cumulative domestic interest rate (Kohlscheen and Andrade 2013). In this class of derivatives, BCB can either buy or sell dollars according to its evaluation of the agents' demand. At that time, it sold dollars to the banks. This program was successful in stemming the currency depreciation for more than a year. In other words, this was a period in which banks that were buying these swaps from the monetary authority registered losses and the BCB had profits.

5 Brazil's Political and Economic Upheaval

Shortly before the presidential election of October 2014, market's participants risk aversion worsened for domestic political and economic reasons combined with the repercussions of the commodities' falling prices and decreasing capital flows to EMEs. The BRL plunged. At year-end, the BCB registered losses of US$7 billion on its position in currency derivatives.

A heated discussion started among economists. Some underlined that those losses resulted in new fiscal expenses; while others pointed out that the notional value of the swap operations represented 25% of the FX reserves and it provided hedge to the economic agents. Each side depicted the swaps operations either as a public intervention in the free market or as an important tool to minimize the extent of the devaluation. While some estimated that these instruments reduced the amount of FX reserves and the protection they offered, others pointed out that as the swaps were non-deliverable (as all FX derivatives in Brazil) they had no impact on these reserves and remembered that the monetary authority used them in the past, irrespective of the availability of foreign reserves. That was, specifically the case at the time of the launch of FX swaps in 2001 (Farhi 2006).

Kawall (2016) stresses another particularity of Brazil. BCB sterilized its purchase of FX using repos operations, instead of banking deposits or bond issued by the monetary authority, inflating the public debt. Thus, the emission of Treasury bonds covers BCB losses with FX swaps and reserves. However, the profits registered in its balance sheet and transferred to Treasury do not abate pubic debt. As Kawall (op. cit.) suggests, "in the Brazilian case, the sterilization mechanism (repos operations) ended up generating a huge expansion of the public debt" (p. 10).

In 2015, the economic policy of the reelected government underwent major changes, taking a more orthodox approach with fiscal austerity accompanied by a significant hike in public services prices that fueled inflation. An aim of minimizing interventions through swaps was also included in order to restore an almost pure floating exchange rate regime in midst of the beginning of an internal political turmoil that prompted a renewed devaluation. Between the first half of 2014 (average price of R $2.30/US$) and the first five months of 2016 (average price of R $3.70/US$), the BRL depreciated by more than 60%. In 2015 alone, it lost almost 33% of its value. This resulted in additional pressures on inflation but had positive impacts on foreign balance as it softened the negative impact of falling commodities "prices and enhanced competitiveness."

After attempting to reduce its intervention, the BCB returned to the FX Market forced by the unusual volatility of the exchange rate due to political uncertainties, economic recession and credit rating downgrade besides adverse international factors. The swap operations incurred in a loss of more than US$23 billion, while the profits on the foreign reserves totaled around US$68 billion. Although the net result was positive, the losses served as an additional argument to those that advocated the end of the use of swaps as policy tool.

In March 2015, at a hearing at the Senate, the president of the BCB, Alexandre Tombini, declared that he believed that "the total amount of USD114 billion of swaps is sufficient to allow the private sector to survive and not going bankrupt because of the exchange rate." He justified that the use of swaps pursued financial stability and that "without it, the system could have suffered a breakdown" (Ribeiro and Marques 2015).[23] In fact, over the post-crisis boom of cross-border finance neither banks nor corporations engaged in high-risk operations linked to FX derivatives, as it happened in the pre-crisis one. Their exposure was mainly due to foreign loans assumed in good times. Hence, the 2015 trend reversal of the exchange rate showed that the enhancement of the FX derivatives regulation framework after the GFC proved to be efficient in curbing the rise in the economy financial fragility.

Until the first quarter of 2016, devaluation pressures continued, fueled by economic recession and accrued political uncertainty that, ultimately, led to the impeachment of President Dilma Roussef. The vice-president, whose policies are considered more "market friendly," replaced her. At that time, the exchange rate reverted its course due to decreasing political uncertainty and a recovery in commodity prices. The BRL ended the first half of the year with a gain of 19.6% over the USD on the spot market. The Brazilian currency led the global ranking of appreciation. For the whole year of 2016, it not only erased the losses incurred at the beginning of the year but also strengthened 21.5% over 2015, snapping a five-year losing streak.

[23]Available at http://www2.valor.com.br/financas/3972766/tombini-estoque-de-swap-cambial-e-suficiente-para-impedir-quebradeira.

Paramount to the strength of the BRL exchange rate is the high level of interest rates. Even though BCB started reducing that rate at the end of 2016, actually monetary policy is even more contractionary than before as inflation is falling at a much quicker pace. While inflation rate fell from 10.67% in 2015 to 6.29% in 2016, interest rate was only reduced from 14.25% in December 2015 to 13.75% at the end of the year of 2016.

As usual, that sharp trend reversal took essentially place in the organized derivatives market. A flurry of activities occurred in it, with all kind of agents rushing to cover their long positions in dollars and place new bets on the Brazilian currency.

In the midst of the worst recession of its history, the BRL appreciation was a mixed blessing: It reduced inflationary pressures but it also harmed exports, the only dynamic economic activity. The expansion of industry's exports lost strength throughout 2016, as the currency appreciated and public mechanisms to encourage foreign trade were virtually extinct.

During this period, BCB resumed currency intervention in an attempt to smooth the appreciation of the currency. This time it used reverse swap by which the monetary authority bought USD against the BRL in exchange for the basic interest rate. However, the FX appreciation did not occur straightforwardly, mostly because the changes in US monetary policy and the result of presidential elections. As a result, the BCB alternated its interventions sometimes using reverse swaps and, in other instances, traditional swaps. As those two kinds of swaps are exactly opposite to each other (meaning that one settles the other before "delivery" date), the net stock of swaps fell from USD106 billion at the end of 2015 to USD29 billion in December 2016.

6 Final Remarks

The influence of derivative markets on the formation of exchange rates has a worldwide reach, even though it is still widely unaccounted for in the theory either by mainstream economists or by post Keynesians. The Brazilian case with all its particularities, namely a foreign exchange market financially integrated and a segment of liquid and deep derivative markets takes that influence to the limit and makes it an excellent empirical evidence and object of analysis.

This chapter shows that the existence of liquid derivative markets in Brazil results mainly from its institutional and regulatory features, despite its incomplete financial openness. The FX derivatives market in Brazil is not only the *locus* of the formation of the spot market rate but also the most important stage of the interaction between private economic agents and monetary authorities in a dirty floating exchange rate regime. As those two groups have opposite objectives in the FX market, the first one seeking maximization of its financial returns while the second one acts in a countercyclical manner to reduce volatility, this interaction frequently turns into a confrontation. The existence of a liquid offshore FX derivatives market, linked by arbitrage to the domestic one, tends to strengthen the position of private agents.

As the 2009/2013 use of capital control and regulatory measures demonstrated, policy makers only succeeded in curbing the FX rate excessive appreciation when they targeted decisively the derivatives market, after many failed attempts to restrain capital inflows and reduce the attractiveness of domestic assets to foreign investors. Other episodes discussed in this chapter show that the key role of FX derivatives asserts itself all along the cross-border finance cycles, sometimes smoothening its impact (as in 1999), other times amplifying its consequences (as in 2008).

References

Avdjiev, S., Upper, & Von Kleist, U. V. (2010). Highlights of international banking and financial market activity. *BIS Quarterly Review*, December.

Bank for International Settlements (BIS). (2003a). *Quarterly Review*, June. Available at http://www.bis.org/publ/qtrpdf/r_qt0306.pdf.

Bank for International Settlements (BIS). (2003b). *Quarterly Review*, December. Available at http://www.bis.org/publ/qtrpdf/r_qt0312.pdf.

Brazilian Senate. (1999). Final report of the inquiry commission. Brasilia. Available at http://www2.senado.leg.br/bdsf/bitstream/handle/id/82020/CPI_Bancos_.pdf?sequence=7.

Burnside, C., Eichenbaum, M., Kleshchelski, I., & Rebelo, S. (2006). The returns of currency speculation. National Bureau of Economic Research Working Paper 12489.

Chamon, M., & Garcia, M. (2013, March 12). Capital controls in Brazil: Effective? *Discussion Paper*, PUC/RJ.

Chiarini, A. (2008, October 29). Exposição a derivativos cai à metade: US$20 bi. Agência Estado, São Paulo.

Committee on the global financial system. (1999). A review of financial markets in Autumn 1998, October, Basle.

Dodd, R. (2009, July). Exotic derivatives losses in emerging markets: Questions of suitability, concerns for stability. *IMF Working Paper*, WP/09.

Farhi, M. (2006). A supremacia dos mercados e a política econômica do governo Lula. Política Econômica em Foco. Centro de Estudos de Conjuntura e Política Econômica do Instituto de Economia da Unicamp (CECON) n° 7 - section V.

Farhi, M., & Borghi, R. (2009). Operations with financial derivatives of corporations from emerging economies. *Estudos Avançados 23*(66). Available at http://www.scielo.br/pdf/ea/v23n66/en_a13v2366.pdf.

Fritz, B., Prates, D. M., & Paula, L. F. R. de. (2014). Keynes at the periphery: Currency hierarchy and challenges for economic policy in emerging economies. In *FMM Conference Inequality and the Future of Capitalism*, Berlin.

Fritz, B., & Prates, D. M. (2014). The new IMF approach to capital account management and its blind spots: Lessons from Brazil and South Korea. *International Review of Applied Economics (Online), 28,* 210–239.

Gagnon, J. E., & Chaboud, A. P. (2007, July). What can the data tell us about carry trades in Japanese yen? *International Finance Discussion Papers*, Board of Governors of the Federal Reserve System, n. 899.

International Monetary Fund (IMF). (2008, October). Regional Economic Outlook: Western Hemisphere. Washington, DC: *World Economic and Financial Surveys*. Available at http://www.imf.org/external/pubs/ft/reo/2008/WHD/ENG/wreo1008.pdf.

Johnson, C. (2007). Trading volume strong start to 2007 in most Markets. *Futures Industry Magazine*, May-June [Google Scholar].

Kaltenbrunner, A. (2010). International financialization and depreciation: The Brazilian real in the international financial crisis, competition and change *14*(3–4), 294–321.

Kawal, L. F. C. (2016). A dinâmica da dívida bruta e a relação Tesouro-Banco Central. Instituto de Estudos de Política Econômica. Available at http://iep-ecdg.com.br/wp-content/uploads/2016/03/160307CapKawallfinal-1.pdf.

Kohlscheen, E., & Andrade, S. (2013, July). Official interventions through derivatives: Affecting the demand for foreign exchange. BCB, Brasilia. Available at http://www.bcb.gov.br/pec/wps/ingl/wps317.pdf.
Kregel, J. (2000). The Brazilian crisis: From inertial inflation to fiscal fragility, levy institute, *Working Paper*, no. 294. Available at http://www.levyinstitute.org/pubs/wp294.pdf.
Kregel, J. (2011). Structured derivatives contracts, hedging exchange appreciation and financial instability: Brail, China and Korea, *Brazilian Journal of Political Economy, 31*(5, 125), pp. 853–857, Special edition.
Lessa, C. (2008, November 19). A economia financeira e a lógica do cassino. *Valor Econômico*, São Paulo. Opinião, p. A11.
Ma, G., Ho, C., & McCauley, R. N. (2004, June). The markets for non-deliverable forwards in Asian currencies, *BIS Quarterly Review*. Available at http://www.bis.org/publ/qtrpdf/r_qt0406g.pdf.
Minsky, H. P. (1986). Stabilizing an unstable economy. McGraw Hill Professional.
Minsky, H. P. (1993). On the non-neutrality of money. *Federal Reserve Bank of New York Quarterly Review, 18*(1), 77–82.
Monetary and economic department. (2015, April). Currency carry trades in Latin America. *BIS papers* 81. Available at http://www.bis.org/publ/bppdf/bispap81.pdf.
Ocampo, J. A. (2007). La macroeconomia de la bonanza económica latinoamericana, *Revista de la Cepal*, n. 93, December.
Pavini, A., & Carvalho, M. C. (2009). Mercado monta central de risco de derivativos. *Valor Econômico*, São Paulo, March 17, p. C8.
Prates, D. M. (2010). Bancos e ciclo de crédito: da estabilização à crise financeira. In L. C. Marcolino & R. deM.Carneiro (Eds.), *Sistema Financeiro e desenvolvimento no Brasil do Plano Real à crise financeira* (pp. 129–159). São Paulo: Publisher Brasil e Editora Gráfica Atitude Ltda.
Prates, D. M. (2014). How to evaluate financial regulation of Brazil. In L. C. Bresser Pereira, J. Kregel, & L. Burlamaqui (Eds.), *Financial stability and growth - Perspectives on financial regulation and new developmentalism* (pp. 237–260). London and New York: Routledge, 1.
Prates, D. M., & Cintra, M. A. M. (2010). The emerging-market economies in the face of the global financial crisis. In S. Dullien, D. J. Kotte, A. Márquez, J. Priewe (orgs.) The Financial and economic crisis of 2008–2009 and developing countries (pp. 53–71). Geneve: United Nations.

Prates, D. M, & Farhi. M. (2015). Foreign exchange derivatives, banking competition and financial fragility in Brazil. *Discussion Paper* n. 3, Multidisciplinary Institute for Development and strategies (MINDS).

Prates, D. M. (2015). O regime de câmbio flutuante no Brasil: 1999–2012: especificidades e dilemas. Brasília: IPEA, 182.

Rezende, F. (2015, March). Why does Brazil's banking sector need public banks? What should BNDES do? *Levy Institute of Economics, Working Paper* 825.

Ribeiro, A., & Marques, F. (2015, March 24). Tombini: estoque de swap cambial é suficiente para impedir a quebradeira. *Valor Econômico.* Available at http://www2.valor.com.br/financas/3972766/tombini-estoque-de-swap-cambial-e-suficiente-para-impedir-quebradeira.

Rossi, P. (2010). O mercado internacional de moedas, o carry trade e as taxas de câmbio. *Observatório da Economia Global,* no. 5, October 2010.

Rossi, P. (2012). Taxa de câmbio no Brasil: dinâmicas da especulação e da arbitragem. *Instituto de Economia*, Universidade de Campinas (Ph.D. thesis).

Rossi Júnior, J. L. (2011). Hedge or speculation? Evidence of the use of derivatives by Brazilian firms during the financial crisis. *Insper Working Paper* 243. Sao Paulo: Insper Institute of Education and Research.

Valenti, G. (2009, January 19). Balanço de 2008 traz desafio às empresas. *Valor Econômico*, São Paulo, *19*(188), p. D5.

Valenti, G., & Fregoni, S. (2009). Onze empresas terão de corrigir balanço. *Valor Econômico*, São Paulo, 23 January, p. D1.

Ventura, A., & Garcia, M. (2012). Mercados futuro e à vista de câmbio no Brasil: o rabo abana o cachorro. *Revista Brasileira de Economia, 66*(1).

The Brazilian Credit Market During the Great Recession

André Moreira Cunha, Marcos Tadeu Caputi Lélis, Andrés Ernesto Ferrari Haines and Pedro Perfeito da Silva

1 Introduction

The debate concerning the role of the State in a market economy is part of *Economics* since its origins. This broad matter holds particular attention when it refers to financial intermediation. It is basically accepted that monetary authorities should have a monopoly of monetary emission and regulate financial markets (Arestis and Sawyer 2007; World Bank 2012; Davidson 2015; Unctad 2016). The specific level of

A.M. Cunha (✉) · A.E.F. Haines · P.P. da Silva
Universidade Federal do Rio Grande do Sul, Porto Alegre, Brazil
e-mail: andre.cunha@ufrgs.br

A.E.F. Haines
e-mail: afhaines@hotmail.com

P.P. da Silva
e-mail: pperfeitodasilva@gmail.com

M.T.C. Lélis
Universidade do Vale do Rio dos Sinos, São Leopoldo, Brazil
e-mail: mcaputi@uol.com.br

P. Arestis et al. (eds.), *The Brazilian Economy since the Great Financial Crisis of 2007/2008*, https://doi.org/10.1007/978-3-319-64885-9_13

regulation and financial supervision may vary in time and space, and it is contingent to the evolution of financial markets themselves. New mechanisms and private strategies, especially when they result in financial crises, induce the update of State intervention parameters (Minsky 1986; Goodhart 2013). Thus, regulatory activism can vary between high and low, be it in the domestic or in the international sphere. More controversial is the question of credit supply through controlled institutions by the State, namely, State-owned banks (SOB).[1]

From a historical perspective, the dissemination of regulatory practices restraining the full freedom of private finance was established after the 1929 crisis. In the following decades, this trend was augmented by the creation or expansion of financial intermediaries controlled by the local or national governments,[2] responsible for direct credit supply (Jayme Jr. and Crocco 2010; Luna-Martínez e Vicente 2012; World Bank 2012, 2015; Ollioqui 2011; Unctad 2016). This process was so intense that when several advanced and emerging and developing countries tried to revert it, through an intense phase of financial deregulation and bank privatizations, especially in the 1980s and 1990s, they were not able to give up some of their SOB. In 2002, in more than 40 emerging countries, including Brazil, Russia, India, and China, assets from these banks constituted more than 25% of the total banking system assets (Hanson 2004). More recent estimates suggest that the SOB assets in the total financial system assets is 22% for emerging countries—proportion that, in the case of advanced economies, would reach 10% (World Bank 2012).

The concern with the role of State financial institutions was renewed in the aftermath of the GFC, triggered in 2007–2008 by the liquidity and solvency problems in the American mortgage market. What seemed as

[1]For the purposes of this article, we will deal with SOB in general, without the worry of specifying whether they are institutions specializing in long-term credit supply, such as development banks. Thus, SOB are public financial institutions whose controlling interest belongs to the State (central government or local governments). For more conceptual details see, among others, Jayme Jr. and Crocco (2010), World Bank (2012), and Unctad (2016).

[2]In addition, of course, of multilateral and regional banks, controlled by several countries. Examples in this regard are: The World Bank, regional development banks in Asia, Latin America, Africa etc.

just a localized problem, soon revealed itself to be a systemic rupture that affected every financial market sector in the world with additional negative effects on the real economy. After such a grave episode, which rapidly came to be called as "The Great Recession" (Arestis et al. 2011; Cynamon et al. 2013), a restored concern about the desirable degree of State activism in financial intermediation was reestablished. Emerging and advanced countries used their SOB to minimize the shortage of private credit. Even the World Bank (World Bank 2012) recognized the positive results this action had on their economies. Thus, the countercyclical role of SOB contrasted with the typical pro-cyclical private sector behavior (Borio et al. 2001; Borio 2012; BIS 2014, 2015, and 2016). As argued by the World Bank (2012), "… the global financial crisis underscored the potential countercyclical role of State-owned banks in offsetting the contraction of credit from private banks, leading to arguments that this is an important function that can perhaps better justify their existence" (p. 11).[3]

In this context, the goal of this chapter is to evaluate the hypothesis that SOB can play a positive role in stabilizing aggregate credit in a downturn. In other words, we have verified the countercyclical characteristics SOB's credit, confirming the views, among others, of Micco and Panizza (2006), Bertay et al. (2012), Thibaut (2012), Cull and Martínez Pería (2012), World Bank (2012), Mazzucato and Penna (2015), and Unctad (2016). We contribute to this literature by using new evidence arising from the recent Brazilian experience. Previous studies relied on descriptive analysis of credit aggregates and suggest that there is evidence that Brazilian SOB would have acted countercyclically in response to GFG (Correa et al. 2010; Unctad 2016).

Our contribution lies in applying MS-DR (Markov-Switching Dynamic Regression) and VEC (Vector Error Correction) models to verify credit behavior (total, private banks' credit, state-owned banks' credit) in Brazil during the 2000s. The evidence we reach confirms that SOB's credit acted in a countercyclical way during the crisis period, while pro-cyclical behavior predominated in the private banks' credit.

[3]The same study states that: "The Brazilian government actively used its state infrastructure bank to engineer the rapid countercyclical response to mitigate the contagion effects from the global financial crisis" (World Bank 2012, p. 106).

This chapter continues as follows: Section 2 presents a short review of the literature on the matter and our theoretical framework, inspired mainly in the Post-Keynesian tradition; Sect. 3 describes credit market in Brazil, the methodology and the results of our study; Sect. 4 summarizes and concludes.

2 State and Financial Intermediation: Literature Review

Post-Keynesian theory sustains that the State should have the responsibility to manage the economy in order to avoid falling into depression and large unemployment. Keynesian *economic policy*, be it fiscal, monetary, financial, or any other is a powerful theoretical contribution in assisting governments to maintain levels of effective demand and mitigate involuntary unemployment, particularly during recessions.[4] It is because markets, if left to work completely by themselves—that is, in an uncoordinated manner—enlarge the main problems of monetary production economies, which Keynes affirmed that the State should use its power to steer the economic system.[5] The importance of countercyclical credit policy according to Keynes is that by sustaining business confidence, it helps to avoid a fall in the investment level (Arestis and Sawyer 2007; Lavoie 2014; Davidson 2015). Here we focus, in particular, on analyzing the extent to which credit policies and SOB were used countercyclically to mitigate the negative effects of the GR on the Brazilian economy.

[4]Keynesian macroeconomic policy coordination would focus mainly on (i) designing fiscal policies with the aim of expanding effective demand; (ii) making monetary policy more flexible aiming at stimulating consumption and investment; and (iii) coordinating and regulating financial and foreign-exchange markets in order to stabilize capital flows and exchange rates. In short, taking up also how Minsky (1986) stated this problem, a modern capitalist monetary economy needs a Big Government and a Big Bank that intervene and regulate through their economic policies and assure that they evolve smoothly over time.

[5]In the General Theory, Keynes (1936, 1962) proposed some economic policies, such as fiscal, monetary, and income policies, in order to address the fact that "[t]he outstanding faults of the economic society in which we live are its failure to provide for full employment and its arbitrary and inequitable distribution of wealth and incomes" (p. 372). See also Arestis and Sawyer (2007).

Conventional literature suggests that there are mainly two reasons[6] that would justify the presence of State's institutions in the direct role of supplying credit: to mitigate market failures and/or to promote economic development (World Bank 2012, 2015; Unctad 2016). The existence of market failures or imperfections, such as incomplete information, externalities, information asymmetry, and imperfect competition, obstructs and may prevent many activities and sectors to access to resources available in the market (Čihák et al. 2012; Anginer et al. 2012; Demirgüç-Kunt et al. 2012). SOB may provide these necessary resources to enable long-term maturation projects. They can also grant credit to entrepreneurs that operate with higher levels of risk that the private sector prefers to avoid. In this conventional perspective, some authors are concerned with SOB efficiency, reasoning that, despite of its development intentions, the use of political criteria in credit allocation would generate distortions that are socially not desirable (Kornai 1979; Shleifer and Vishny 1998; World Bank 2012; Unctad 2016).

Theoretical traditions that diverge from the mainstream view and are inspired, among others, in the seminal works of Schumpeter (1911), Keynes (1936), Gerschenkron (1962), and Minsky (1986), acknowledge the centrality of credit in modern market economies (Arestis and Sawyer 2007; Davidson 2015). Beyond the correction of "market imperfections," it is assumed that the advancement of purchase power by financial institutions, particularly commercial banks (or universal banks with a commercial branch), is key to enable investment

[6] These are split into four visions (i) the social view suggests that SOB should be used to offset market failures, as long as the benefits of its existence outweigh the costs arising from those imperfections; (ii) the "development vision" suggests that the low degree of sophistication and depth of financial markets, which characterize the very condition of "delay," would force the state to act in the credit supply to compensate for the lack of funds from private sector; thus the State would take the economic development promoter function; (iii) in direct opposition to such a perspective there is the "political vision" to which SOB are channeling sources of income by those in power to their political allies; with this, the state credit would not only distort markets as would be systemic inefficiency and corruption; and (iv) the "vision of the agency" shares the social/developmental perspective that the state can complete markets and resolve flaws, but simultaneously points to the risks arising from state action. For more details see the following studies: Jayme Jr. and Crocco (2010), Gutiérrez et al. (2011), World Bank (2012), Luna-Martinez and Vicente (2012), and Ollioqui (2011).

decisions that produce strong economies. These decisions, however, are taken under uncertainty conditions. Thus, for economic agents liquid assets, including State money, become an attractive alternative to store wealth. This attraction grows as the State of confidence deteriorates. When entrepreneurs are optimistic about their investment's returns, they expand their liabilities, so that they can enlarge their assets. On the other hand, when pessimism prevails, they search to reduce their debts, avoiding new investments in illiquid assets. As argued by Mazzucato and Penna (2015), SOB, particularly the development banks, should play a structural role[7] by shaping markets and by "… promoting strategic investments for economic development" (p. 16).

Financial intermediaries, on their part, are also capitalist agents that seek profits and establish strategies of accumulation. Thus, their behavior can sanction or not the non-financial sector's credit demand. Even more, if they fall into a more pessimistic state, they could revise their plans and restrict their credit offer. Therefore, if the banks' optimism drives and reassures the general optimism, their pessimism may represent the interruption of an ascendant phase of a dynamic cycle. In view of this cyclical pattern, non-mainstream authors tend to suggest that it should be up to the State, as monetary authority and through SOB, to stabilize the money supply, mostly the credit, and fulfill the structural role mentioned above. This role should not be just an occasional, but a permanent feature of the modern financial system (Paula 2011; Ocampo et al. 2007; Lavoie 2014; Davidson 2015; Mazzucato and Penna 2015; Unctad 2016).

The GFC represented an important watershed in this debate. Up to the early 2000s, the conventional wisdom considered that direct State intervention in providing financial services should be avoided, because it was thought to generate inefficiencies. Thus, it fell to the State only

[7]Focusing on development banks, Unctad (2016) suggests that: "…development banks are needed to bridge finance from end-savers to development projects. Such bridging should be done by development banks at all levels—national, regional and international—in order to provide the financing needed in the developing world. Development banks can thus be key players for development by providing long-term financing directly from their own funding sources, by tapping into new sources and by leveraging additional resources, including private, through the co-financing of projects with other partners" (p. 6).

to act as a market-friendly regulator. This changed after 2008. Different views emerged, such as: (i) State regulation of financial markets must be reinforced, especially its macro-prudential dimension; and (ii) the countercyclical behavior of SOB began to be perceived as essential to reactivate the credit channels and to increase the effectiveness of monetary policy.

Contemporary research supports these views. For instance, Gutiérrez et al. (2011) argue that SOB, particularly development banks, are essential to mitigate problems arising from the behavior of private banks: In times of crisis, private banks individually have incentives to restrict credit, but, in this way, they hinder the recovery of the economy as a whole. Consequently, borrowers' liquidity might deteriorate, and lead to solvency problems. Such market failure could be mitigated by loans coming from SOB. Additionally, their credit boosts countercyclical monetary policy.[8] Bertay et al. (2012), Cull and Martínez Pería (2012), Čihák and Demirgüç-Kunt (2013), Morck et al. (2013), Mazzucato and Penna (2015), Coleman and Feler (2015), and Unctad (2016) offer similar results and conclusions.

It should be noted that this stabilizing role through credit supply is now offered as a source of justification for maintaining SOB. Based on the studies by the Conference Board of Canada, Gutiérrez et al. (2011) suggest, in an analogy to the existence of armed forces to provide national security, that development banks should be kept continuously in operation, even in "peacetime," that is, when the market is not under stress. Therefore, they would keep tuned-in their organizational skills when mobilized in times of crises, where the role of countercyclical credit supply proves to be essential. Čihák and Demirgüç-Kunt (2013) also point out evidence showing that credit provided by SOB is less pro-cyclical or, even better, it

[8] "The economic literature points to another source of market failure that justifies direct state intervention in the credit market in a countercyclical fashion (...) private banks have limited incentives to lend during periods of economic downturns and low interest rates and do not internalize the fact that, by increasing lending, they would push the economy out of recession. Such coordination failure provides justification for DBs—to ensure continued provision of needed credit to the economy in the face of private sector cutbacks. In these circumstances, state intervention could solve a coordination problem and make monetary policy more effective..." (Gutiérrez et al. 2011, p. 8).

is countercyclical. Concerning the Brazilian experience, Oliveira (2010), Lundberg (2011), Araújo (2012), Mendonça and Sachsida (2013), among others, assess the conditions of credit supply and demand in Brazil, obtaining inconclusive results in relation to the role SOB and the pro-cyclical nature (or not) of the private and SOB credit. Hermann (2010), Oliveira (2010), Araújo et al. (2011a, b), Araújo and Cintra (2011), Lundberg (2011), Araújo (2012), Rezende (2015), Costa (2015), Unctad (2016), among others, are examples of studies that seek to identify: (i) the profile of the Brazilian SOB's credit supply; and (ii) their ability to promote development.

In the next section, we present our main contribution, as we think it has not been undertaken before, which is to apply MS-DR and VEC models to investigate if private banks and SOB were able to stabilize the credit supply in Brazil during the GR. In this sense, we would be following Keynesian theory by assessing if the policy of augmenting SOB's loans managed to keep up the general level of credit in the Brazilian economy during the GR.

3 Credit Behavior in the Brazilian in the 2000s

Stylized Facts, Methodology, and Data

State-owned banks (SOB) have always played a pivotal role in the Brazilian Financial Sector (BFS), responding for most of the long-term funds directed to strategic economic sectors, from agriculture to infrastructure, and granting access to financial services to sectors, regions and segments of the society under-serviced by private banks, due to their higher risks and lower profitability prospects (Jayme Jr. and Crocco 2010; Paula 2011; Rezende 2015; Unctad 2016). Consequently, and despite the privatization process of the 1990s and early 2000s, which reduced its share in the BFS, SOB still represent today half of the financial sector's credit, assets, and deposits.

It is possible to argue that Brazilian SOB represent a complex and heterogeneous system, which includes commercial banks, development banks, and other financial institutions.[9] Some of them belong to the central (or federal) government, in part or totally, while others are controlled by the States that constitute the Brazilian Federation. For instance, large federal banks such as *Banco do Brasil* (*BB*) and *Caixa Econômica Federal* (*CEF*) lead most segments of the BFS alongside with large private banks like *Itaú*, *Unibanco*, and *Bradesco*. In addition, BNDES (the national development bank), other federal banks (like Banco do Nordeste and BASA) and State banks perform an important role in credit markets, filling the gap left by private banks that are unwilling to act vigorously because they prefer short-term operations. SOB are responsible for most of the credit supplied to sectors and regions characterized by higher risks and lower returns' prospects, such as: (i) poorer regions in Brazil—Northeast and North; (ii) microenterprises; and (iii) sectors that depend on long-term finance—Infrastructure, Housing, and Rural. BNDES, the national development bank, also funds, directly (first floor) or indirectly (second floor), most of the long-term finance to investment projects, in the non-financial private sector[10] (World Bank 2015; Unctad 2016).

The evolution of the Brazilian credit supply in the recent years gives the impression that private financial institutions and SOB followed markedly different paths in the aftermath of the GFC.[11] As it can be seen from Fig. 1, while private banks' credit flow waned, SOB sustained the trend of total loans supply. Thus, the relative shares of private credit and SOB in the total credit supply changed. It is the case that in 2003,

---

[9]At the end of June 2016, there were 28 SOBs in Brazil.

[10]The Word Bank (2015) states that "Brazil's development bank BNDES has historically played a major role in providing long-term finance through directed lending … (it) has provided extensive financing for large-scale investments in physical and social infrastructure whose social returns may not be fully internalized by private investors" (p. 36). There is more relevant evidence, and discussion, in Rezende (2015) and Unctad (2016).

[11]"While private sector banks in Brazil and elsewhere contracted lending and loan maturities in the aftermath of the financial crisis, Brazil used its government banks, including BNDES, to play a countercyclical role. The share of credit extended by Brazil's government banks rose from 13 to 18% of gross domestic product between September 2008 and 2009. Thanks to a generous capital injection by the government (R$100 billion in 2009), BNDES was able to extend special credit facilities with maturities of more than one year at substantially discounted interest rates and increased lending, from R$160 billion (at 2005prices) in Q4 2008 to R$277 billion in Q4 2009.The reference interest rate for long-term loans was set at 6%, which was 7.5 percentage points below the market rate" (World Bank 2015, p. 36).

62% of total loans was originated in private institutions (domestic and foreign); however, in 2016, this share fell to 45%. Consequently, and still, by the end of this period, the SOB credit had become predominant. It should be noted that this recovery occurred in a period of strong credit expansion: In 2003, the credit/GDP ratio was 21.4%; in 2015, it reached its peak, 54.0%; later to drop to 50.0% in 2016.

Recent studies (Micco and Panizza 2006; Demirgüç-Kunt and Huizinga 2012; Thibaut 2012; Cull and Martínez Pería 2012; World Bank 2012; Ollioqui 2013; Unctad 2016) point out that although employing different empirical methodologies, the SOB's credit has the potential to act countercyclically, enhancing the monetary policy by the Central Bank. Oliveira (2010, 2014), Correa et al. (2010), Araújo (2012), World Bank (2012), Lawrence (2013), Bonomo et al. (2015), Coleman and Feler (2015), and Rezende (2015) have studied the stabilizing role of SOB in Brazil. Usually, this literature[12] employs descriptive statistics, as expressed in Fig. 1, to compare variations in credit supply (SOB and private) and activity level. Therefore, further research to seek additional evidence, exploring different econometric methodologies, as in this chapter, can be of significant help.

Evidence from the Markovian-Switching Dynamic Regression

To test the hypothesis that the SOB's credit can, indeed, act countercyclically and, thereby, mitigate the recessionary impact of a financial crisis, we apply MS-DR (Markovian-Switching Dynamic Regression) and VEC (Vector Error Correction) models. The first one focuses on the endogenous structural breaks suffered by time series in their average and variance, being useful to deal with parameters' non-linearity, identifying breakpoints and

[12]Exceptions in this regard are Oliveira (2010, 2014) and Bonomo et al. (2014). These studies apply different econometric techniques to assess the impact of SOB's credit in non-financial firms' investment decisions. The countercyclical role and the comparison between the private banks' and SOB's credit do not represent their main research goal. On the other hand, Coleman and Feler (2015) found econometric evidence that SOB acted countercyclically. They suggested that SOB's credit created inefficiencies in the economy. More recently, Krznar and Matheson (2017) analyze the nexus between the financial cycle and business cycle in Brazil. In doing so, they found that dynamics "… of public and private cycles are somewhat different, reflecting the countercyclical use of public banks over 2008–2013" (p. 8).

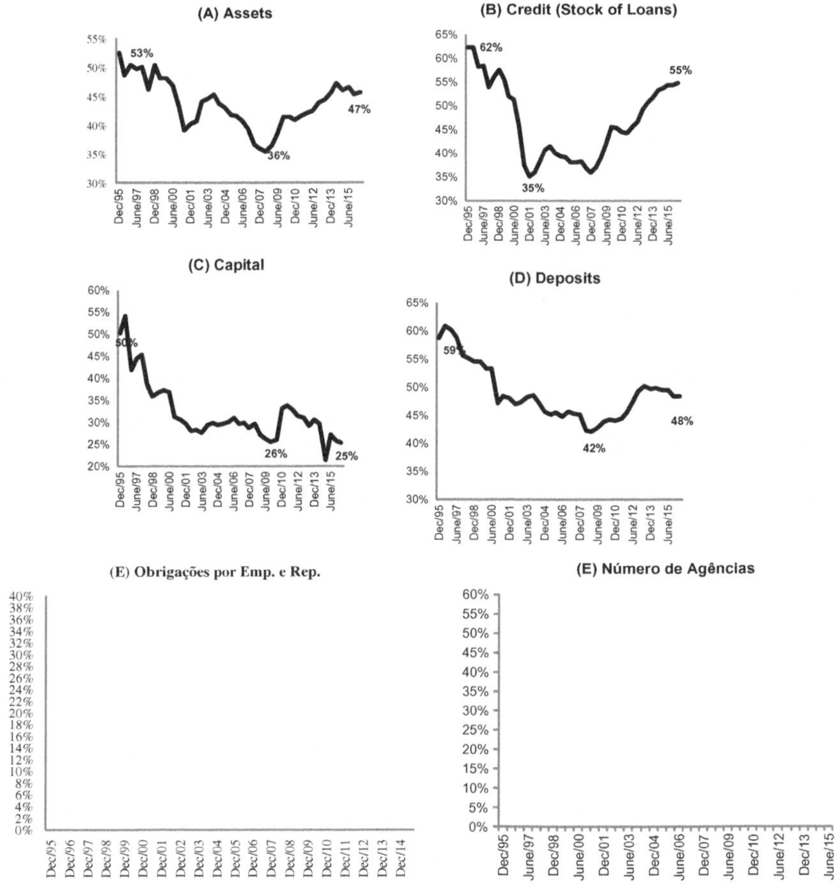

Fig. 1 SOB in the Brazilian Financial System, 1995–2016 (% of total). *Source* prepared by authors, based on data from Central bank of Brazil and IBGE. Accessed on March 10, 2017

regime switching as well as permanence period and transition probability (Quandt 1972; Goldfeld and Quandt 1973; Doornik 2013).

We have also estimated a Vector Error Correction (VEC) model, which is able to evaluate the interactions of co-integrated variables, keeping all of them endogenous and without imposing a priori definitions about causality order. On the one hand, the conclusions of the VEC model show a more structural character than the MS-DR. On the other hand, there is an opportunity cost: The information about regimes is lost.

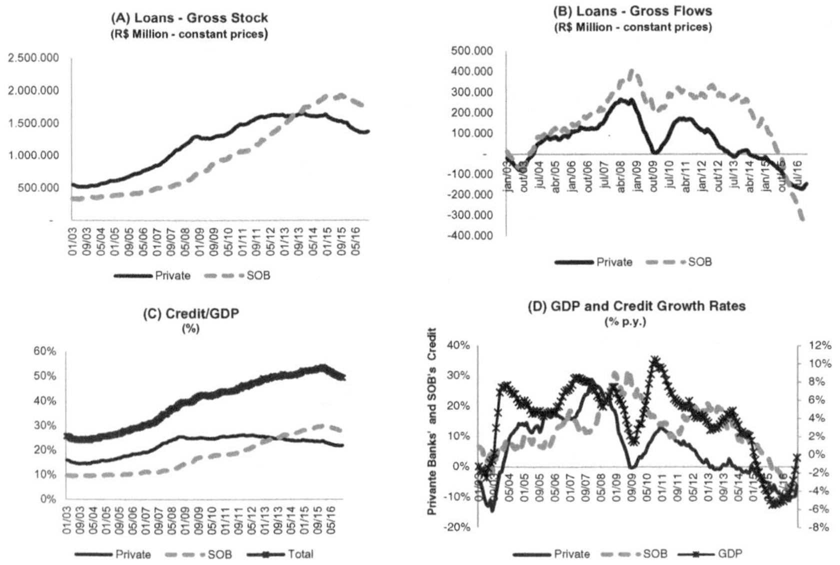

Fig. 2 Credit Market and GDP in Brazil, 2003–2016 (%). *Source* prepared by authors, based on data from Central Bank of Brazil and IBGE, Accessd on March 10, 2017.

According to Doornik (2013), the number of regimes in each model is arbitrary, nevertheless, any simple switching regime model should have:

$$y_t = \mu(0) + \rho y_{t-1} + \varepsilon_t \tag{1}$$

$$y_t = \mu(1) + \rho y_{t-1} + \varepsilon_t \tag{2}$$

Where: $\varepsilon_t \sim N\left[0,\, \sigma^2\right]$, being (1) Regime 0 and (2) Regime 1. Hamilton (1994) specifies the MS-DR model follows:

$$y_t = \mu_{st} + \varepsilon_t, \qquad \varepsilon_t \sim IID\left(0;\, \sigma^2\right) \tag{3}$$

Equation (3) demonstrates that the data generating process of the MS-DR model is influenced by the intercept μ, which changes due to the regime. The model allows an endogenous estimation of the transition probabilities between the "S" non-observed regimes that follow a Markov chain. The probability of reaching regime S_t depends only of the past regime, i.e., S_{t-1} (Doornik 2013).

In terms of our first exercise, we estimate MS-DR models for the accumulated variation in a 12-month period for the credit, supplied by the private and by State-owned banks. Following Doornik (2013), we opt to work with this class of MS models due to the volatile character of the series and because of our rather large ample size. Following Hamilton's (1990) suggestion to choose the number of regimes by visually observing the movement of a variable, we consider it best to employ three regimes. We also estimated a MS-DR model for the Volatility Index (VIX) as it is the most common proxy variable for the global financial cycle (Nier et al. 2014; Rey 2013; IMF 2017; Coimbra and Rey 2017).

In our exercise, the MS-DR estimation performs a similar role to descriptive statistics by showing the co-movement between private and State-owned banks' credit flows and the relationship of each one with the global financial cycle—using a monthly sample from 2004 to 2015.[13] In Table 1, we expose the description of the three variables.

Table 1 Description of the variables

Variable	Name	Description
Global Financial Cycle	VIX	Volatility Index—Monthly average
Private Credit Supply* (flows)	PRIV	Twelve months accumulated variation from credit operations to private sector by private banks
State-owned banks Credit* Supply (flows)	SOB	Twelve months accumulated variation from credit operations to private sector by State-owned banks

Source Central bank of Brazil (BCB); Chicago Board Options Exchange Market (CBOE). Accessed on January 15, 2017. (*) Fig. 2 depicts the evolution of the original time series: stock of loans from private and SOB (panel A); while panel B is the twelve months accumulated flows of loans, being this calculated from the monthly variation of the stock of loans

[13]The selection of the time sample is explained by the needs of the VEC model estimation, exposed in the next section. The beginning of the sample was chosen because of the availability of the Economic Activity Index of the Central Bank of Brazil (IBC-Br). We did not employ the data from 2016 because the unstable behavior of Brazilian economy generates residuals that do not fit conditions such as homoscedasticity, normality, and absence of autocorrelation.

We estimate MS-DR models for each variable. We adopt the non-rejection of the null hypothesis of normality, homoscedastic, and autocorrelation criteria, as well as to minimize information criteria. Every estimation presented well-behaved residuals, considering at least 1% of significance. The estimation of the global financial cycle and of state-owned banks' credit supply shows all parameters with 5% of significance as well as the rejection of the null hypothesis of parameters' non-linearity. On the other hand, the private credit supply presented non-significant parameters and did not reject the null hypothesis of linearity. Because of this result, we decided to complement the MS-DR model by estimating the VEC model in the next section.

Table 2 below presents the transition matrices for each estimated model. We show, in the first place, that each estimated regime is persistent. Secondly, VIX's higher volatility implies its regimes are less persistent than those of SOB and PRIV.

Table 2 Transition matrices of the MS(3)-DR—VIX, SOB and PRIV—2004–2015

VIX	Regime 0, t	Regime 1, t	Regime 2, t
Regime 0, t+1 (Medium)	76.72%	9.71%	28.21%
Regime 1, t+1 (High)	15.98%	90.28%	0.00%
Regime 2, t+1 (Low)	7.30%	0.00%	71.79%
SOB	Regime 0, t	Regime 1, t	Regime 2, t
Regime 0, t+1 (Medium)	95.30%	1.78%	7.43%
Regime 1, t+1 (Low)	1.80%	98.22%	0.00%
Regime 2, t+1 (High)	2.90%	0.00%	92.57%
PRIV	Regime 0, t	Regime 1, t	Regime 2, t
Regime 0, t+1 (Medium)	96.96%	2.36%	0.00%
Regime 1, t+1 (Low)	0.00%	97.64%	10.77%
Regime 2, t+1 (High)	3.4%	0.00%	89.23%

Source Own construction

Table 2 thus shows that the credit supply in Brazil presents more persistence in the low regime, while the global financial cycle is more persistent in the high regime. We interpret this outcome as a result of the strong resistance in Brazil, particularly from private banks, to offer credit, even in a period of larger global liquidity. Additionally, the credit supply data shows a difference between the State-owned Banks' and the private sector in how they move out of a high regime. Thus, while the latter tends to change rapidly from high to low regime, the first does it in minor way to medium regime.

Regarding the regimes' composition, it is important to note the difference between Brazil and the world in terms of acceleration of the credit market. In the rest of the world, on the one hand, the global financial cycle is in the high regime during most of the period. In Brazil, on the other hand, the medium regime covers most of the period for State-owned banks' and private credit supply. Also, for both of them the low regime is longer than the low regime in the global financial cycle. If, on one side, it could be argued that this means that Brazil had little exposition to the negative consequences of the 2007/2008 GFC; on the other side, in turn, it can be said that it implies that the domestic financial system resists offering credit even when there is great global liquidity. In addition, the greater participation of low regime in the State-owned banks' credit turns down the argument of those who criticize its excessive activism. Nevertheless, the growth of State-owned banks credit during that crisis, as the regime switch in 2008 shows, provides evidence that it still managed to act countercyclically. Figure 3 shows the regimes for each variable.

We can see that the countercyclical behavior of State-owned banks' credit emerged twice: (i) after 2008, following the deterioration of the global financial cycle up to the beginning of the private credit low regime in 2009; (ii) between 2012 and 2014, when the State-owned banks kept medium or high[14] regime as the private credit supply fell. Also, the

[14]In Brazil, the 2012/14 high SOB's regime is usually seen from two opposing perspectives. One praises it as a countercyclical action against the fall of the private credit supply; the other criticizes it as excessive activism aimed at sustaining artificially the pace of growth achieved in 2010 and 2011. In between, there is a third view that considers the greater amount of public credit offered as a result of a market dispute between federal commercial banks (such as Banco do Brasil and Caixa Federal) in a context of credit rationing by private banks, which were resisting the reduction of the central bank's interest rate.

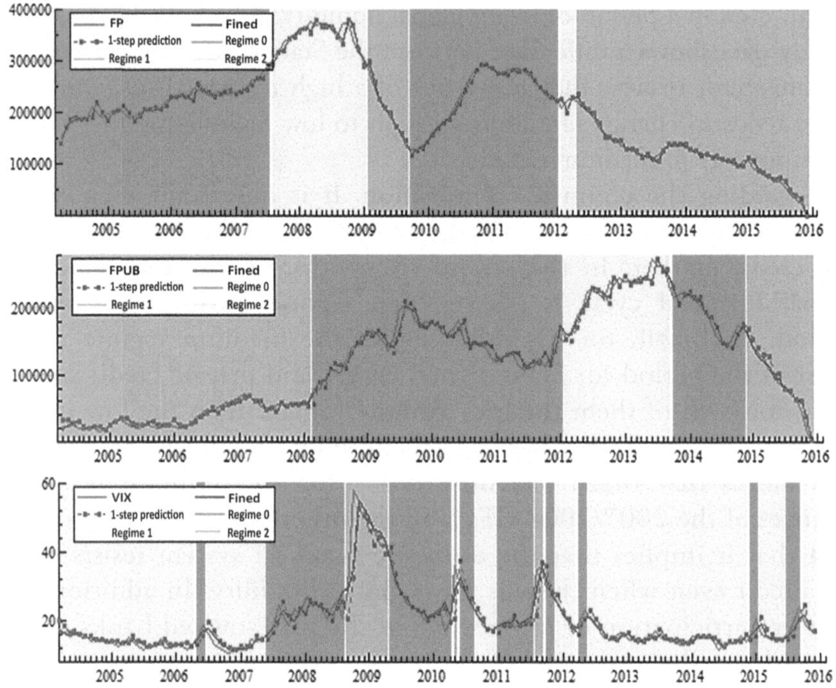

Fig. 3 Adjustment of MS(3)-DR model to regimes—VIX, SOB and PRIV—2004–2015. *Source* Authors' construction

influence of the global financial cycle over the Brazilian credit supply can also be observed twice: (i) the private credit behavior before the GFC; and, particularly, (ii) in 2012, when the return of the global cycle to high regime generated a strong response by private and State-owned banks' credit. Nevertheless, this attitude did not last long due to the deterioration of the Brazilian economy and the tapper tantrum of FED.

Further Evidence from the VEC Model

In this section, we complement our previous exercise by estimating a vector error correction (VEC) model, which is able to evaluate the interactions of co-integrated variables, keeping all the variables as endogenous and without imposing a priori definitions about causality order. Considering the VEC model with more than two variables, it is presented the VEC general formulation for "*n*" variables:

$$\Delta y_t = \beta_0 + \sum_{t=1}^{n} \beta_i \Delta y_{t-1} + \alpha\theta^1 y_t + u_t \tag{4}$$

Where y_t is the variables vector, β_0 the intercept vector, β_i the parameters vectors associated with the models' variables, α the error correction vector, $\theta^1 y_t$ the co-integration vector, and u_t the residuals vector. In this sense, the equation above combines short- (autoregressive vectors) and long-term (co-integration vector) relationships. The stability of the model can be observed through the inverse roots of the autoregressive polynomial. The model is considered stable when it does not present roots out of the unitary circle.

Here, we employed the same data sample from last section, but with some changes: The Economic Activity Index of the Central Bank of Brazil (IBC-Br) and the benchmark interest rate (Selic)[15] are added; monotonic transformation by natural logarithm and seasonal adjustment are applied, and each series' cycle is extracted through the Hodrick-Prescott filter (HP).[16] The selected period is based on the level breakpoints of the global financial cycle's proxy variable (VIX), estimated by the STAMP structural model, which presented one level break in September 2008.

As we mentioned in the Introduction, we are interested in the behavior of private banks' and SOB's credit supply in relation to domestic economic activity and to the global financial cycle, being the benchmark interest rate included as control variable. Our estimations are presented in two ways, using, respectively, the private banks' and the SOB's credit supply as dependent variable. A positive sign from domestic economic activity means that the type of credit is behaving pro-cyclically,

[15]These series were extracted from the Time Series Database of the Central Bank of Brazil (BCB). Accessed on March 10, 2017.

[16]The extraction of the cycle presented only exception, namely the series referring to the benchmark interest rate; for this reason, it only received treatment for seasonality.

while a negative sign implies a countercyclical behavior. Since the high level of the VIX is a proxy to the declining period of the global financial cycle, its sign in relation to the credit supply has the inverse meaning that is: positive means countercyclical behavior, and negative a pro-cyclical one.

The identification of the VEC model begins with the unit root tests for our five variables. Using EViews and Stata, ADF (Augmented Dickey-Fuller), KPSS (Kwiatkowski–Phillips–Schmidt–Shin), PP (Phillips-Perron) tests, as well as other centered on breakpoints tests such as ADF (breakpoint version) and ZA (Zivot-Andrews) are utilised. Most of the series have unit roots in at least one test, considering 95% degree of confidence. Thus, this allows us to model the variables in an econometric structure based on a VEC model (Johansen and Juselius 1990). Nevertheless, even having any stationary series, according to Campbell and Perron (1991), when a co-integrated process between two non-stationary series is attained, adding a stationary series in the VEC model does not lead to significant changes in the robustness of the regression.[17]

Next, we determine the appropriate lag structure, i.e., the number of lags required to capture the dynamic interrelations in the VEC model. Here attention is given to the information criteria of Akaike (AIC) and Schwarz (SBC), as well as to the behavior of residues. We started from a minimum number of lags equal to 2, since it is the minimum quantity to reach complex roots in this system of equations.

Our results show, first, that regarding the information criteria, the SBC and the AIC present the estimation structure with, respectively, two and three lags, as being most adequate. However, the estimation based on two lags has autocorrelation and residual heteroscedasticity, considering a degree of confidence at 95%. To correct this, we estimate

[17]Campbell and Perron (1991) discuss the concept of co-integrated vector and sustain that: "Second, definition 1 does not require that each of the individual series be integrated of order one; some or all series can be trend-stationary. In this respect definition 1 differs from the definition given in Engle and Granger (1987)" (p. 165). In addition, according to Johansen (1988), a vector X_t with k elements is considered as I(1) if this vector X_t is non-stationary and ΔX_t is stationary. Thus, if the linear combination $\beta' X_t$ is stationary, the system is co-integrated. This definition contains the co-integration concept of Engle-Granger, but establishes the possibility of some elements of X_t being defined as I(0).

a VEC (3), which presents white noise residuals, considering a degree of confidence at 95%. The Johansen test is estimated to delimitate the existence and the number of co-integrated equations.

VEC (3) model presents at least one co-integration equation by the trace and maximum-eigenvalue criteria, considering a confidence level at 95%. According to Dickey Jansen and Thornton (2007), if there are relations of co-integration between the variables, the system of equations becomes more stable; therefore, the estimated system is stationary in a set of possible directions. From this conclusion, we decide to estimate a VEC (3) with one co-integration vector. Based on the estimated co-integration vector, it is possible to write the long-run equilibrium equation and interpret each of the parameters X_i from the following tables:

In this case, we can see, first, that, except for the global financial cycle, all the variables are statistically significant, considering a 95% degree of confidence. The State-owned banks' credit supply, as expected, shows a countercyclical behavior in face of the activity level, which presents a negative sign in Table 3. The same countercyclical movement is observed in relation to global financial cycle. Thus, the positive sign of international financial volatility implies that the SOBs' credit supply reacts positively to the financial cycle reversion.

Table 3 Co-integrated vector—Reparameterized equation—2009–2015

Dependent variable: State-owned banks' credit supply (SOB)			
Variable	Coefficient	Standard deviation	T-statistics
IBCBR*	−46.60829	7.39277	6.30457
SELIC*	−1.217857	0.64391	1.89135
PRIV*	0.614129	0.26831	−2.28890
VIX	0.386656	0.74292	−0.52045
C	0.371593		

Source Authors' estimation. * Statistically significant at 5% level

In the case of the private credit supply, the signs of the activity level and of the global financial cycle are opposed to the State-owned banks' credit, presenting a pro-cyclical behavior (Table 4). Additionally, both kinds of credit supply present a mutually positive sign, which could be implied as meaning that the increase of the State-owned banks' supply tends to boost greater credit offer from the private sector.

Table 4 Co-integrated vector—Reparameterized equation—2009–2015

Dependent variable: Private credit supply (PRIV)			
Variable	Coefficient	Standard deviation	T-statistics
IBCBR*	75.89333	12.5164	−6.06352
SELIC*	1.983065	1.12496	−1.76278
SOB*	1.628323	0.48753	−3.33993
VIX	−0.629601	1.19870	0.52524
C	−0.605074		

Source Authors' estimation. * Statistically significant at 5% level

This result, on the other hand, confirms what was advanced by Correa et al. (2010), World Bank (2012), Costa (2015), Rezende (2015), and Unctad (2016). These studies, using descriptive statistics, already signaled the countercyclical behavior of the credit provided by the Brazilian SOB in the recent past. Thus, it is possible to stress that SOB's credit was less sensitive to business cycles (Thibaut 2012). Furthermore, as it is possible to verify, as in Table 3, the SOB's credit supply behaves countercyclically in the period after the GFC. An outcome pushed forward conscientiously by the central government (World Bank 2012; Ministério da Fazenda 2014; Ferrari Filho et al. 2014; Banco Central do Brasil 2014). Thus, it can be stressed rather firmly that SOB's credit was used as an instrument to stabilize the business cycle, since it helped to smooth the volatility of the economy.

Literature not only focused on the Brazilian case, for instance, Micco and Panizza (2006), Bertay et al. (2012), Thibaut (2012), and Cull and Martínez Pería (2012), but also reached similar conclusions to ours, mainly that private banks and SOB followed different paths during financial crises. Particularly, along the GR, when while private banks in Brazil were trying to reduce their risk exposure, becoming more selective when granting credit, SOB adopted less safe positions. In this way, they ended up sustaining the growth of total credit. In other words, SOB's credit in Brazil did not fall with the outburst of the crisis of 2008, as was the case with private credit (Micco and Panizza 2006).

4 Summary and Conclusions

This chapter has the main objective of evaluating if SOB acted with the focus of stabilizing credit supply in Brazil during the GR. According to the literature reviewed, private banks act in a pro-cyclical manner. This kind of behavior intensifies real and financial euphoria, but it can also aggravate a fall in the level of output and employment. Furthermore, it can abruptly pass from one to the other. This is why non-mainstream views, particularly post-Keynesians, affirm that the State should have the responsibility to act countercyclically through its fiscal, monetary, financial, and other tools (Minsky 1986; Arestis and Sawyer 2007; Lavoie 2014; Davidson 2015).

Regarding SOB, the subject of this chapter, non-orthodox views make particular emphasis that the financial sector should not be left to itself, especially amid a financial crisis. Some mainstream researchers have recently also acknowledged this conception (Borio 2012; BIS 2014, 2015, 2016). Their work suggests that SOB, besides resolving market failure setbacks, should also act in a countercyclical manner. This is because SOB credit has the capacity of boosting countercyclical monetary policies. In this way, they can compensate a fall in private banks' credit supply (Micco and Panizza 2006; Bertay et al. 2012; Thibaut 2012; Cull and Martínez Pería 2012; World Bank 2012; Ollioqui 2011; Unctad 2016; Krznar and Matheson 2017).

In the Brazilian case, Correa et al. (2010), Araújo (2012), World Bank (2012), Lourenço (2013), Rezende (2015), among others, evaluated SOB's capacity to stabilize credit supply, paying particular attention to the experience after 2008. In general, these authors employ descriptive statistics, which consists of comparisons of the variation rate in credit supply (both SOB and private banks' credit) in relation to the level of economic activity. In our contribution, we apply MS-DR and VEC models to investigate, using monthly data, the behavior of private banks' credit and SOB's credit. We produce evidence that, in fact, SOBs' credit behaved in a countercyclical manner during the crisis, whereas private banks' credit predominantly behaved in line with the cycle.

In order to reach our conclusion, we have developed two groups of exercises. In the first one, we have estimated MS-DR models for each one of three variables: state-owned banks' credit supply (SOB); private credit supply (PRIV); and global financial cycle (VIX). We find that State-owned and private banks had opposing behaviors in terms of regime transition, composition, and adjustment. The SOB's credit supply entered into high regime when both the Brazilian and the global economy deteriorated, for example, in the aftermath of the GFC. In addition to this countercyclical behavior, the SOB's credit moved softly, without abruptly passing straightforwardly from a high to a low regime.

To reach more robust conclusions, we have performed a final exercise by estimating a VEC model for the period between 2009 and 2015. In this case, results converge to the MS-DR model. More specifically, we have found that: (i) SOB's credit supply acts countercyclically; and (ii) private credit supply shows a pro-cyclical behavior. Additionally, we have found a positive relationship between SOB's and private banks' credit supply, which suggests that State-owned banks can perform an important role in stimulating private disposition to lend. Our conclusions converge with those presented in recent literature on this topic.

The study of the impact of SOB credit on the economy is a broad, complex, and controversial subject. There are still many areas to be researched, particularly those regarding its capacity to promote development and financial stability. Additionally, it also includes the discussion of other crucial issues such as the efficiency of State intervention.[18] In this chapter, we have just focused on the recent experience of SOB's

[18]Regarding the debate and evidence that emphasize the Brazilian case, see, among others, Hermann (2010), Modenesi et al. (2012), Oliveira (2014), Bonomo et al. (2014), Rezende (2015), World Bank (2012, 2015), Coleman and Feler (2015), and Unctad (2016). Krznar and Matheson (2017), in a recent paper about financial and business cycles in Brazil, concluded that the "… active countercyclical role of public banks during the global financial crisis mitigated systemic risk, but also raised questions about the longer-term impact of public banks on the financial system as they are difficult to unwind; the evidence presented here suggests that reducing the size of public banks would entail a negative impact on output over time. Moreover, the rapid expansion of public banks since 2008 contributed to a deteriorating fiscal position and raising doubts about the credibility of the policy framework. Focusing public banks' activities on missing markets, such as providing guarantees for concessions, would improve the allocation of limited financing (…) and the effectiveness of monetary policy" (p.16).

credit in Brazil during the GFC. We hope to have contributed to the understanding of this important matter.

References

Anginer, D., Demirgüç-Kunt, A., & Zhu, M. (2012). How does bank competition affect systemic stability? *Policy Research Working Paper* 5981. Washington, DC: World Bank.

Araújo, V. L. (2012). *Preferência Pela liquidez dos Bancos Públicos no ciclo de expansão do crédito no Brasil: 2003–2010, Texto para Discussão 1717.* Brasília, IPEA: Janeiro.

Araújo, V. L., & Cintra, M. A. M. (2011). *O papel dos bancos públicos federais na economia brasileira, Texto para Discussão 1604.* Brasília, IPEA: Abril.

Araújo, V. L., Pires, M. J. S., Silva, M. F., & Castro, D. A. (2011a). O estado atual das instituições financeiras públicas para o desenvolvimento na América Latina: uma análise exploratória. *Texto para Discussão 1616*, Maio: Brasília, IPEA.

Araújo, V. L., Pires, M. J. S., Silva, M. F., & Castro, D. A. (2011b). O sistema brasileiro de instituições financeiras subnacionais para o desenvolvimento: um panorama. *Texto Para Discussão 1626*, Junho: Brasília, IPEA.

Arestis, P., & Sawyer, M. C. (2007). *Handbook of Alternative Monetary Economics.* Cheltenham: Edward Elgar.

Arestis, P., Sobreira, R., & Oreiro, J. L. (2011). *An assessment of the global impact of the financial crisis.* Houndmills, Basingstoke: Palgrave Macmillan.

Banco Central do Brasil. (2014). *Bulletin—Annual report (several years).* Brasília: Banco Central do Brasil.

Bertay, A. C., Demirgüç-Kunt, A., & Huizinga, H. (2012). Bank ownership and credit over the business cycle: Is lending by state banks less procyclical? *Policy Research Working Paper* 6110, June. Washington, DC: World Bank.

BIS. (2014). *84th Annual report.* Basle: Bank for International Settlements.

BIS. (2015). *85th Annual report.* Basle: Bank for International Settlements.

BIS. (2016). *Economic resilience: A financial perspective.* Basle: Bank for International Settlements.

Bonomo, M., Brito, R., & Martins, B. (2014). Macroeconomic and financial consequences of the after crisis government-driven credit expansion in Brazil. *The Banco Central do Brasil Working Papers 378, December.* Brasília: Banco Central do Brasil.

Borio, C. (2012). The financial cycle and macroeconomics: What have we learnt? *BIS Working Papers* n. 395, December. Basle: Bank for International Settlements.

Borio, C., FURFINE, C., & Lowe. P. (2001). Procyclicality of the financial system and financial stability: Issues and policy options, *BIS Papers* n. 1, March. Basle: Bank for International Settlements.

Campbell, J. Y., & Perron, P. (1991). *Pitfalls and opportunities: What macroeconomists should know about unit roots and co-integration*. Cambridge: MIT Press.

Čihák, M., Demirgüç-Kunt, A., Feyen, E., & Levine, R. (2012). Benchmarking financial development around the world. *Policy Research Working Paper* 6175, August. Washington, DC: World Bank.

Čihák, M., & Demirgüç-Kunt, A. (2013). Rethinking the state's role in finance. *Policy Research Working Paper* 6400, April. Washington, DC: World Bank.

Coimbra, N., & Rey, H. (2017). Financial cycles with heterogeneous intermediaries. *NBER Working Paper No. 23245*, March. Cambridge: National Bureau of Economic Research.

Coleman, N., & Feler, L. (2015). Bank ownership, lending, and local economic performance during the 2008–2009 financial crisis. *Journal of Monetary Economics, 71*(2), 50–66.

Correa, P. R. R. et al. (2010). A estrutura do setor bancário brasileiro e o ciclo recente de expansão do crédito: o papel dos bancos públicos. In *38° Encontro Nacional de Economi—ANPEC*, Dezembro. Salvador: ANPEC.

Costa, F. N. (2015). Atuação anticíclica dos bancos públicos brasileiros. *Texto para a Discussão 258*, Setembro. Campinas, SP: Instituto de Economia/Unicamp.

Cull, R., & Martínez Pería, M. S. (2012). Bank ownership and lending patterns during the 2008–2009. Financial crisis: Evidence from Eastern Europe and Latin America. *Policy Research Working Paper* 6195, September. Washington, DC: World Bank.

Cynamon, B. Z., Fazzari, S., & Setterfield, M. (2013). *After the great recession: The struggle for economic recovery and growth*. Cambridge: Cambridge University Press.

Davidson, P. (2015). *Post keynesian theory and policy: A realistic analysis of the market oriented capitalist economy*. Cheltenham: Edward Elgar.

Dickey, D., Jansen, D., Thornton, D. (2007). A primer on cointegration with an application to money and income. In: B. Rao (Ed.), *Cointegration for the applied economist*. (2nd ed.). New York City: Palgrave Macmillan.

De Luna-Martínez, J., & Vicente, C. L. (2012). Global survey of development banks. *Policy Research Working Paper 5969*, February. Washington, DC: World Bank.

Demirgüç-Kunt, A., Feyen, E., & Levine, R. (2012). The Evolving importance of banks and securities markets. *World Bank Economic Review, 27*(3), 1–15.

Doornik, J. A. (2013). *Econometric analysis with Markov-switching models: PcGive 14*. London: Timberlake Consultants Ltd.

Engle, R. F., & Granger, W. J. (1987). Co-integration and error correction: Representation, estimation and testing. *Econometrica, 55*(2), 251–276.

Ferrari Filho, F., et al. (2014). Brazilian countercyclical economic policies as a response to the great recession: A critical analysis and an alternative proposal to ensure macroeconomic stability. *Journal of Post Keynesian Economics, 36,* 513–539.

Gerschenkron, A. (1962). *Economic backwardness in historical perspective*. Cambridge: Harvard University Press.

Goldfeld, S. M., & Quandt, R. E. (1973). A Markov model for switching regressions. *Journal of Econometrics, 1,* 3–16.

Goodhart, C. A. E. (2013). Powers and scope of the macro-prudential authority. In J. R. La Brosse, R. Olivares-Caminal, & D. Singh (Eds.), *Financial crisis containment and government guarantees* (pp. 29–42). Cheltenham: Edward Elgar.

Gutiérrez, E., Rudolph, H. P., Homa, T., & Beneit, E. B. (2011). Development banks: Role and mechanisms to increase their efficiency. *Policy Research Working Paper* 5729, July. Washington, DC: World Bank.

Hamilton, J. D. (1990). Analysis of time series subject to changes in regime. *Journal of Econometrics, 45*(1–2), 39–70.

Hamilton, J. D. (1994). *Time series analysis*. Princeton: Princeton University Press.

Hanson, J. A. (2004). Public sector banks and their transformation. *6th Annual Financial Markets and Development Conference*, Washington, DC.

Hermann, J. (2010). *O papel dos bancos públicos, Textos para Discussão CEPAL-IPEA 15*. Janeiro. Brasília, DF: CEPAL.

IMF. (2017). *Global Financial Stability Report: Getting the Policy Mix Right*, April. Washington, DC: International Monetary Fund.

Jayme, F., Jr., & Crocco, M. (2010). *Bancos públicos e Desenvolvimento*. Rio de Janeiro: IPEA.

Johansen, S. (1988). Statistical analysis of co-integration vectors. *Journal of Economic Dynamics and Control, 12*(2–3), 231–254.

Johansen, S., & Juselius, K. (1990). Maximum likelihood estimation and inference on co-integration with applications to demand for money. *Oxford Bulletin of Economics Statistics, 52*(2), 169–210.

Keynes, J. M. (1936). *The General Theory of Employment, Interest and Money.* New York: HBJ Book.

Kornai, J. (1979). Resource-Constrained Versus Demand-Constrained Systems. *Econometrica, 47*(4), July. pp. 801–819.

Krznar, I., & Matheson, T. D. (2017). Financial and business cycles in Brazil, *IMF Working Paper 17/12, January.* Washington, DC: International Monetary Fund.

Lavoie, M. (2014). *Post-Keynesian Economics.* New Foundations: Edward Elgar.

Luna-Martínez, J., & Vicente, C. L. (2012). Global survey of development banks, *Policy Research Working Paper* 5969, February. Washington, DC: World Bank.

Lundberg, E. L. (2011). *Bancos Oficiais e Crédito Direcionado—que diferencia o mercado de crédito brasileiro?, Trabalho para Discussão 258.* Novembro. Brasília: Banco Central do Brasil.

Mazzucato, M., & Penna, C. (2015). Beyond market failures: The market creating and shaping roles of State investment banks, *Levy Institute Working Paper* 831, January. Annandale-on-Hudson: Levy Institute.

Mendonça, M. J., & Sachsida, A. (2013). Identificando a demanda e a oferta de crédito bancário no Brasil. *Texto para Discussão IPEA* 1837, Junho. Rio de Janeiro: IPEA.

Micco, A., & Panizza, U. (2006). Bank ownership and lending behavior. *Economics Letters, 93*(2), 248–254.

Ministério da Fazenda. (2014). *Economia Brasileira em Perspectiva.* Brasília: Ministério da Fazenda do Brasil.

Minsky, H. P. (1986). *Stabilizing an unstable economy.* New Haven: Yale University Press.

Modenesi, A. M. et al. (2012). Sistema Financeiro e Política Econômica em uma Era de Instabilidade: tendências mundiais e perspectivas para a economia brasileira. (1st ed.). Rio de Janeiro: Campus/Elsevier.

Morck, R., Yavuz, M. D., & Yeung, B. (2013). State-controlled banks and the effectiveness of monetary policy. *NBER Working Paper* 19004, April. Washington, DC: NBER.

Nier, E., Sedik, T. S., & Mondino, T. (2014). Gross private capital flows to emerging markets: Can the global financial cycle be tamed? *IMF Working Paper* 196, October. Washington, DC: International Monetary Fund.

Ocampo, J. A., Kregel, J., & Griffith-Jones, S. (2007). *International finance and development*. London: Zed Books.

Ollioqui, F. (2011). Public development banks: Toward a new paradigm? Washington, DC: Inter-American Development Bank.

Oliveira, F. N. (2010). Canal de empréstimo bancário no Brasil: evidência a partir dos empréstimos de empresas públicas e privadas. *Pesquisa e Planejamento Econômico, Brasília, 40*(2), 187–212.

Oliveira, F. N. (2014). Investment of firms in Brazil: Do financial restrictions, unexpected monetary shocks and BNDES play important roles? *Banco Central do Brasil Working Paper Series* 366, October. Brasília: Banco Central do Brasil.

Paula, L. F. R. (2011). *Financial liberalization and economic performance: Brazil at the crossroads*. London: Routledge.

Quandt, R. E. (1972). A new approach to estimating switching regressions. *Journal of the American Statistical Association, 67*(338), pp. 306–310.

Rey, H. (2013). *Dilemma not Trilemma: The global financial cycle and monetary policy independence. Jackson Hole Symposium 25*. Kansas City: FED.

Rezende, F. (2015). Why does Brazil's banking sector need public banks? What should bndes do? *Levy Institute Working Paper* 825, January. New York: Levy Institute.

Schumpeter, J. A. (1911). *The theory of economic development: An inquiry into profits, capital, credit, interest, and the business Cycle*. New Brunswick: Transaction Publishers.

Shleifer, A., & Vishny, R. (1998). *The grabbing hand: Government pathologies and their cures*. Cambridge: Harvard University Press.

Thibaut, D. (2012). *Bank ownership and credit cycle: The lower sensitivity of public bank lending to the business cycle*. Paris: Paris School of Economics and Bank of France.

UNCTAD. (2016). *The role of development banks in promoting growth and sustainable development in the South*, Geneva: United Nations Conference on Trade and Development.

World Bank. (2012). *Global financial development report 2013: Rethinking the role of government in finance*. Washington, DC: World Bank.

World Bank. (2015). *Global financial development report 2015/2016: Long-term finance*. Washington, DC: World Bank.

Index

P. Arestis et al. (eds.), *The Brazilian Economy since the Great Financial Crisis of 2007/2008*, https://doi.org/10.1007/978-3-319-64885-9

C

The manufacturer's authorised representative in the EU is Springer Nature Customer Service Centre GmbH, Europaplatz 3, 69115 Heidelberg, Germany. If you have any concerns regarding our products, please contact ProductSafety@springernature.com

Printed and bound by CPI Group (UK) Ltd, Croydon, CR0 4YY
30/09/2026
02225656-0020